Suffering for Territory

DUKE UNIVERSITY PRESS · *Durham & London* · 2005

SUFFERING FOR TERRITORY

· · · *Race, Place, and Power in Zimbabwe*

· · · Donald S. Moore

2nd printing, 2006

Printed in the United States of America on acid-free

Designed by CH Westmoreland

Typeset in Minion by Keystone Typesetting, Inc.

LIBRARY OF CONGRESS CATALOGING-IN-PUBLICAT
Moore, Donald S.
Suffering for territory : race, place, and power in Zimbabw
Donald S. Moore.
p. cm.
Includes bibliographical references and index.
ISBN 0-8223-3582-4 (cloth : acid-free paper)
ISBN 0-8223-3570-0 (pbk. : acid-free paper)
1. Land use—Government policy—Zimbabwe. 2. Land settlement
Zimbabwe. 3. Land settlement—Government policy—Zimbab
4. Land tenure—Zimbabwe. 5. Zimbabwe—Race
relations. I. Title.
HD992.Z63M665 2005
333.3′16891—dc22   2005004618

For Ginger and for Chiratidzo's family

Contents

Preface

A specter is haunting Zimbabwe—the specter of racialized dispossession. In 1890, white settlers, recruited by Cecil Rhodes and promised gold claims and 3,000 acres each, ran up the Union Jack on Salisbury's Harare Hill claiming "possession" of Mashonaland in the name of Queen Victoria.[1] One hundred and ten years later, speaking in the capital Harare, Robert Mugabe marked the twentieth anniversary of Zimbabwe's independence. He decried the "nominal sovereignty" of flags, anthems, and a black president. Mugabe blasted Britain for engineering the Lancaster House Constitution that enshrined legal protection for private property at independence.[2] "Naturally," Mugabe told the national television audience, legacies of imperial rule led to "the current spate of farm occupations by the war veterans." Criticizing Britain's defacto defense of white property and its failure to honor commitments to bankroll resettlement, Mugabe deemed land reform "the last colonial question heavily qualifying our sovereignty."[3] Postcolonial Zimbabwe remained haunted by entanglements of race, rule, and land rights.

In 2000, the Zimbabwe African National Union–Patriotic Front (ZANU-PF) ruling party provided military muscle, police protection, and executive endorsement to enable the occupation of hundreds of white-owned farms by "war veterans." Youth militias joined former guerrilla fighters from the 1970s, spilling onto private property. Amid the economic hardship of massive unemployment and spiraling inflation, many yoked their rights claims to those of actual war veterans. Cell-phone squatters, political opportunists, and violent thugs also took part. The ZANU-PF Web site provided sober rationalization for the "land occupations," while the Movement for Democratic Change (MDC), the major opposition party, decried "land invasions" on a link next to "violence" on its Internet homepage. Amid freedom fighters' claims to land seized by colonial conquest, unfreedoms also emerged. Widespread human rights abuses—including torture, beatings, rape, and detention—have entangled land struggles with orchestrated campaigns of violence targeting oppositional movements, especially the MDC.[4] Among the hardest hit were displaced farmworkers, many of whom were non-citizens excluded from state social services and basic rights.[5] More than 1,000 reported cases of torture in 2002 belie the brutal beatings in multiples much greater inflicted by ZANU-PF youth brigades.

Political, military, and fiscal complexities intertwined to produce what many conceive as an epochal crisis. Already overextended by sending troops to the Democratic Republic of Congo, the ruling party paid compensation to 55,000 veterans of the national liberation war.[6] The political payoff on "Black Friday" in November 1998 broke the bank. Rampant unemployment compounded hyper-inflation that would hit *three* digits, rocketing to over 600 percent in late 2003. Economic devastation fueled political turmoil. The ZANU-PF suffered its first major postindependence defeat in 2000 by losing a national referendum propos-ing amendments to the constitution. In its wake, Mugabe extended executive control and added provisions for the compulsory acquisition of land for re-settlement. Flexing the statutory instrument appropriately entitled "presidential powers," Mugabe asserted sovereignty by amending the constitution by decree.

The 2000 Land Acquisition Act effectively removed Lancaster's "willing-seller-willing-buyer" provisions. No longer constrained by market-mediated land re-form, so-called fast-track resettlement would enable the cash-strapped govern-ment to designate and seize private property, paying only for infrastructural improvements but not the land itself. The targeted large-scale commercial farm sector, almost exclusively white-owned properties, occupied more than a third of the country's arable land. In contrast to the crowded Communal Areas culti-vated by black smallholders, white farms were situated predominately in the *highveld* (plateau) benefiting from higher rainfall and richer soil. This prime terrain, seized through white conquest, became legally designated "European" through Rhodesian policies that produced an uneven geography of agrarian injustice. Colonial rule converted land seizure into legal protection for white property. Racialized dispossession *made* land rights white. By reclaiming the "lost lands" expropriated by colonial conquest, blacks who have occupied white-owned farms since 2000 have resurrected a rallying cry of national liberation voiced during the guerrilla war of the 1970s. Ruling party elites have also de-ployed this populist discourse to advance their own claims to commercial farms designated by the Land Acquisition Act.

By April 2003, more than a quarter of Zimbabwe's territory had been seized, while only about 600 white owners of the formerly more than 4,000 remained.[7] By some estimates, only 400 farms remained unaffected by occupations.[8] The Minister of Agriculture claimed the "successful" resettlement of 300,000 families on 5,000 former white-owned farms.[9] Critics cited on-the-ground figures of less than half that total. But by any estimate, and compared to the 70,000 families resettled in the first two decades after independence, Zimbabwe's new-millennium agrarian politics radically remapped race, rights, and national territory.[10]

Discursively, "war veterans" occupying white farms condensed postcolonial rights claims on sites of colonial dispossession. Many invoking the political identity were born *after* independence, asserting entitlements to a war they never witnessed. These articulations underscore the political construction—rather than fixity—of interests and identities. The younger urban unemployed joined landless former guerrillas, mixing abject poverty with more privileged politicos. Mugabe eventually pulled in the reins on party heavyweights who took possession of multiple properties. Socioeconomically mixed but predominantly poor, so-called war veterans constituted both the wretched of the earth and the liberators of the land.

In 2000, Andy Mhlanga, an ex-combatant and head of the War Veteran's Association, reiterated the liberation struggle's unfulfilled project of fighting for "land and freedom," asking, "Where was the 'rule of law' when white settlers forcibly seized African land?" Denied the right to farm freely at independence, freedom fighters would liberate the land forcibly, beyond the bounds of liberal laws and white mythologies. They conjured the spectral traces of *Chimurenga*, literally, "uprising" or "rebellion," the term for both the 1896 armed resistance against invading British settlers and the liberation war of the 1970s. "The land is ours," Mugabe announced, endorsing the occupation of "white" farms in 2002: "We went to war for it. We are prepared to die for it."[11] Unresolved anticolonial struggles to liberate national territory continue to foment violence in a postcolonial state.

Suffering for Territory provides a critical genealogy of modes of power that produced landscapes of dispossession still haunting Zimbabwe. Focusing on a particular locality, my ethnography illuminates the micropractices of government, sovereignty, and spatial discipline in Kaerezi Resettlement Scheme in Zimbabwe's Eastern Highlands. I privilege ethnographic moments midway between independence and the 2000 land occupations, relying heavily on more than two years of fieldwork spanning 1990–92. I emphasize the geographies of violence historically *sedimented* in landscapes of racialized dispossession. Recognizing

Rekayi Tangwena T-shirt
from African Uni-Tees,
Harare. *Photo by the
author.*

their crucial role in configuring Zimbabwe's ongoing land politics, however, does
not absolve members of Mugabe's dictatorial regime, nor the violence his supporters unleash or the opportunistic accumulation of his cronies. As the country's contingent future unfolds, I foreground how race, rights, and territory
became entangled in the hope that they might be more justly remapped.

My invocations of spatial politics are more than metaphorical. Grounded
geographies matter greatly in *Suffering for Territory*. In 1975, Mugabe escaped
Rhodesian forces through Kaerezi to Mozambique, entangling locality in a liberation war spanning countries. In the 1960s and 1970s, Kaerezi's anticolonial
nationalist chief, Rekayi Tangwena, defied Rhodesian rule by refusing to leave
ancestral lands usurped through white conquest. Evicted after prominent skirmishes in courts, media, and on a chiefdom claimed as private property by a
white owner, Rekayi and his followers shepherded Mugabe to safety, also becoming war refugees in Mozambique. At independence, they returned triumphantly
to Tangwena territory. A national television audience witnessed Rekayi's 1984
burial in Harare's Heroes' Acre, his body claimed as postcolonial state senator as
well as anticolonial chief.

One hazy Harare day in 1991, I crossed Rekayi Tangwena Avenue in a bus spewing diesel fumes. Downtown, African Unity Square celebrated independence, yet few pedestrians realized that the park's pathways followed the design of the Union Jack etched on the landscape by colonial planners. Near the square, I spotted a placard and booth for the silk-screening concession "African Uni-Tees" in a crowded supermarket. Images of Bob Marley—whose Harare concert kicked off Zimbabwe's 1980 independence celebrations—abounded. A decade later, critics of Mugabe's spectacles of power dubbed his heavily armed motorcade and its screaming sirens "Bob and the Wailers." Rastafari also reverberated through the shop's T-shirt designs that linked Ethiopia and an African diaspora.

My surprised eyes fixed on a print that superimposed Rekayi Tangwena's iconic chiefly image—cowry shells sewn to a pointed cap crowning a look of bearded determination—over an outline of Zimbabwe's national territory. The artist-owner, a dreadlocked African American, explained that he did not speak Shona and kindly introduced me to the woman who did the lettering. He had moved to Zimbabwe from his native Oakland in the early 1980s, drawn by the promises of a newly independent black nation. Atop the design, the words read: "MUSAKAN-GANWE ZVATAKARWIRA." Beneath, the translation was in much smaller print: "DON'T FORGET WHAT WE FOUGHT FOR." The "we" remained ambivalent, signaling at once the Tangwena people and the nation of Zimbabwe. So, too, wavered the phrase "what we fought for," at once designating a chiefdom and nation-state—entangled territories conjured by a single Shona term, *nyika*. The lettering proclaimed Tangwena an *ishe* while Kaerezians called him a *mambo*—both terms translated as "chief"—underscoring the graphic designer's unfamiliarity with localized legacies in the Eastern Highlands. Like that T-shirt's representations, this book explores how sovereignty and territory remain fiercely contested in Zimbabwe, how racialized dispossession shapes the contours of postcolonial power, and how the politics of place is always already translocal.

Acknowledgments

I am grateful for the generous support that individuals, institutions, and communities gave to this project. A Fulbright Fellowship, the Social Science Research Council, and the Institute for Intercultural Studies funded twenty-six months of fieldwork in 1990-92. A Ciriacy-Wantrup Fellowship from the University of California at Berkeley enabled field research in 1996. In Harare, I was fortunate to encounter Ben Cousins, Marshall Murphree, and James Murombedzi at the University of Zimbabwe's Centre for Applied Social Sciences; all three of them inspired through their grounded research and engaged politics. John Dzingapeta, Bill Kinsey, Sam Moyo, Bud Payne, Terence Ranger, Blair Rutherford, Heike Schmidt, and Eric Worby generously shared their knowledge of agrarian politics in Zimbabwe. Staff at the Zimbabwe National Archives and National Records Office excavated crucial files for me. Officials in the Ministry of Local Government and its allied branches helped secure my research permission and provided critical assistance. In Nyanga, M. Mandisodza, E. Ngwarai, G. Ngorima and their staff at the District Administrator's office greatly facilitated my research, kindly making time despite over-burdened work responsibilities. N. Marumahoko did that and more in Kaerezi, and deserves my special thanks, as does Caroline Ngorima and her family who graciously shared their home during visits to the town of Nyanga.

I also wish to express my gratitude to the IUCN Regional Office for Southern Africa for sponsoring the Zimbabwean edition of this book.

My greatest debt is to Kaerezi residents whose warm hospitality, ethics of care, and critical insights animated my ethnographic work. Their cultivating practices nurtured enduring friendships, shaping the contours of my own landscapes of affect. While I give pseudonyms to those who feature in the pages to follow, I wish to thank *vanoera Shumba*, *Mwoyo we Mombe*, *Gwai*, *Njiwa*, *Hanga*, *Nhewa*, and members of the Mandondo, Maoko, Mabvudza, Muomba, Nyamuona, and Nya-pokoto families. *Vabereki vaChiratidzo* gave generously of their hearts and hearth in ways at once endearing and enabling. Elijah Nyahuruwa, Chief Magwendere Tangwena, and Kaerezi headmen kindly permitted my research. Bernard Maoko and Alois Mandondo shared with me their Tangwena knowledge, political savvy, and enduring affinities, as well as related research projects. *Ndatenda zvikuru.*

At UC Berkeley, I received crucial write-up support from a Ciriacy-Wantrup Fellowship and as a fellow at the Townsend Humanities Center. Successive chairs of the Department of Anthropology enabled me to take leave from teaching and to spend a year as a visiting fellow in the Program in Agrarian Studies at Yale University. In New Haven, I benefited from the spirit and formidable intellect of that program's director, Jim Scott, as well as from agile interlocutors Kamari Clarke, Shubhra Gururani, Ousmane Kane, and Eric Worby. Vron Ware and Paul Gilroy made their home a welcoming place as did Arun Agrawal and Rebecca Hardin, all offering critical conviviality. In Berkeley, I am fortunate to have schol-ars in anthropology, geography, and kindred fields whose research has shaped my own work. I also owe a great debt to the medical skills of Jeffrey Saal, Brendan Morley, and especially Ellen Bier.

Friends and colleagues offered constructive critique, ethical support, and en-souled practices along the way. Ken Wissoker's editorial input has been a font of productive power. I thank him, Kate Lothman, and Duke University Press's careful reviewers for their substantive and constructive engagements. Don Don-ham, Mariane Ferme, Louise Fortmann, David Theo Goldberg, Akhil Gupta, Nancy Peluso, Lisa Rofel, and Sylvia Yanagisako generously provided critical comments on sections of the manuscript. Conversations and correspondence with Ann Anagnost, James Ferguson, Paul Gilroy, Derek Gregory, Charlie Hale, Donna Haraway, Barnor Hesse, Allen Isaacman, Lisa Lowe, Alois Mandondo, Doreen Massey, Thomas McClendon, William Muomba, Diane Nelson, Charles Piot, Alan Pred, and Leti Volpp also offered enabling insights at critical con-junctures. Iván Arenas, Dace Dzenovska, Jake Kosek, Anand Pandian, Elana Ripps, and Vron Ware shared the inspiration of their emergent research projects. Retort and the Bay Area Marxist Feminist Collective kept me politically sane amid the Madness of King George. Iain Boal, Lawrence Cohen, Amanda Ham-mar, Gillian Hart, Percy Hintzen, Jim Lance, Wendy Lynch, Achille Mbembe, James Murombedzi, AbdouMalig Simone and Rebecca Stein blended com-radely critique and affective solidarities. Charles Hirschkind and Saba Mahmood added analytical insight to formative friendship, keeping the faith while piously transgressing.

This text also bears the traces of friends whose detailed comments on the entire manuscript substantively shaped its final form; my heartfelt thanks go to Amita Baviskar, Jocelyne Guilbault, Tania Murray Li, and Hugh Raffles. Their incisive critique, ethical encouragement, and enduring solidarity animated my work while kindling resources of hope. Orin Starn and Michael Watts took time away from their own research on many occasions, offering enabling critique and advice; for more than a decade, their *apoyo* has entangled my research and writing in transformative ways. I also benefited immeasurably from the wit, wisdom, and support of Arun Agrawal and Daniel Bosch. Ginger and Bill Doll and Doug and Rob Moore elevated my spirit while keeping my feet firmly on the ground, literally helping me walk again after surgical interventions in the wake of a debilitating car accident. My brothers also shared their cartographic expertise, caring beyond the bounds of kinship in ways that complement the many mappings engendered by courageous Kaerezians who are still suffering for territory— *vari kutambudzikira nyika ikoko.*

Abbreviations

AGRITEX	Agricultural Technical and Extension Services
ARDA	Agricultural and Rural Development Authority
BBC	British Broadcasting Company
BSAC	British South Africa Company
CIO	Central Intelligence Organization
CNC	Chief Native Commissioner
CONEX	Department of Conservation and Extension
DA	District Administrator
DC	District Commissioner
DERUDE	Department of Rural Development
DNPWLM	Department of National Parks and Wildlife Management
EZLN	Zapatista National Liberation Army
FRELIMO	Front for the Liberation of Mozambique
IA	Internal Affairs
MDC	Movement for Democratic Change
MNR	Mozambique National Resistance (also known as RENAMO)
NC	Native Commissioner
PC	Provincial Commissioner
NADA	*Southern Rhodesia Native Affairs Development Annual*
NLHA	Native Land Husbandry Act
NDP	National Democratic Party
PA	Provincial Administrator
PF	Patriotic Front
POZ	Parliament of Zimbabwe

PV	Protected Village
RF	Rhodesia Front Party
RSO	Resettlement Officer
SAPES	Southern African Political Economic Series
SRANC	Southern Rhodesian African National Congress
TTL	Tribal Trust Lands
UDI	Unilateral Declaration of Independence
UNESCO	United Nations Educational, Scientific, and Cultural Organization
VIDCO	Village Development Committee
ZANLA	Zimbabwe African National Liberation Army
ZANU-PF	Zimbabwe African National Union–Patriotic Front
ZAPU	Zimbabwe African People's Union
ZNA	Zimbabwe National Archives, Harare
ZNRO	Zimbabwe National Records Office, Harare

Suffering for Territory

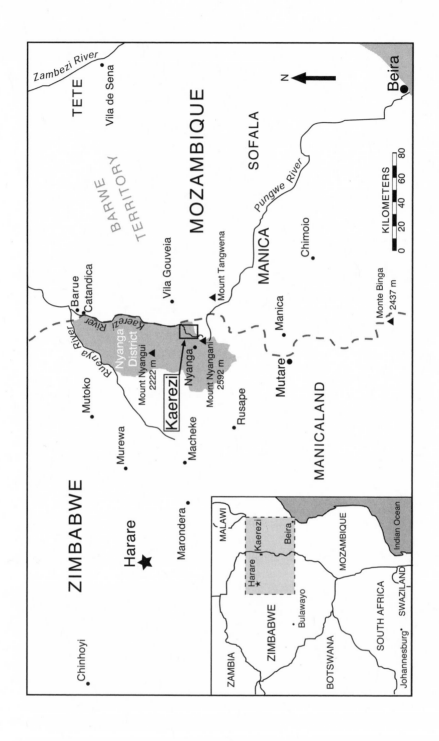

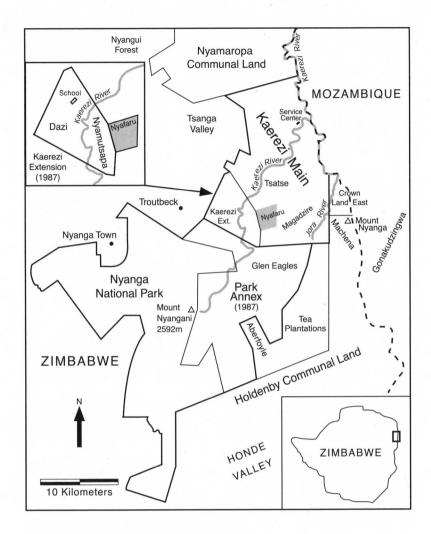

(left) Map 1. Nyanga District, Zimbabwe in regional context.

(above) Map 2. Kaerezi, Zimbabwe, and surrounding areas.

Both maps copyright Robert Moore and Donald Moore, 2004.

SaGumbo plunged a rusty steel rod into packed soil, loosening earth we would soon work with hoes to carve an irrigation channel. In 1991, his toil transformed landscape, tapping a mountain stream's flow to his garden. MaiNyasha, his wife, and their teenage daughter Celia weeded furrows in budding maize fields that fanned out from the homestead's heart: a thatched, round mud-and-wattle cook hut and three smaller, square sleeping huts. A stone's throw from the raised granary, Tsitsi, their youngest daughter drew drinking water from a clear spring. When wild pigs from the neighboring Nyanga National Park marauded crops, SaGumbo emerged from his hut to drive them away by nightfall. Penned in a kraal carefully tucked downstream from their garden, six cattle provided manure, a stout team of oxen offering draft power for subsistence production. After milking a cow, MaiNyasha or Celia could easily heft a heavy pail the short distance to the cook hut. Gathering emplaced acts and environmental resources, their homestead assembled livelihoods. From an administrative optic, however, these agrarian micropractices defied governing grids of rule.[1]

State administrators branded SaGumbo's family and his neighbors "squatters" whose scattered homesteads defied spatial regulations. They lived *inside* Kaerezi Resettlement Scheme but *outside* planned settlement sites. Officials called these planned residential rows straddling a dirt road "villages," as if the pegged yet uninhabited spaces conjured vibrant sociality. Kaerezians called them *maline*, "the lines," the same term used for imposed colonial settlements. Pairing the pluralizing Shona prefix *ma* with the English *line*, the inadvertent double entendre, pronounced "malign," aptly captured popular sentiment.

Those refusing to occupy the lines, the District Administrator warned in a letter to squatters and in charged Kaerezi meetings, risked eviction from the scheme. Months earlier, police had torched squatters' huts in a nearby state forest, plumes of smoke tracing tangible threats. The destitute and displaced soon huddled beneath Red Cross tents placed along the main road and thus visible from rural buses. Despite the recent evictions, Kaerezi's postcolonial chief, a salaried civil servant, commanded his subjects to refuse the resettlement lines. Anyone building huts in the governmental grids, he announced at public meetings, defied his rule. Those adhering to state spatial discipline, he threatened, were subject to chiefly eviction. "If you enter the lines," he told several gatherings, "I will chase [*kudzinga*] you away."

"It's tough," SaGumbo lamented while straddling a ditch; "we're between a hard place and a steel rod."[2] His Shona phrasing further complicated his position, located between *nzvimbo yakaoma*—a place that has become hard, dry, and difficult—and a *simbi*, a steel rod. Place, he implied, has a history of becoming. Place bears traces of historically sedimented processes—the drying and hardening of soil—as well as situated struggles. A single vowel switches *simbi*, steel rod, into *simba*, power. Materializing his metaphor, SaGumbo plunged steel to soil, enacting his predicament. In a place where a chiefdom *entangled* a resettlement scheme, who exercised sovereignty, governed subjects, and ruled postcolonial territory?

Suffering for Territory provides a critical genealogy of modes of power, subjection, and territory in Kaerezi. In this book, I argue for a spatial sensitivity to cultural politics. I insist that *micropractices matter*, that the outcome of cultural struggles remains crucially dependent on the diverse ways land comes to be inhabited, labored on, idiomatically expressed, and suffered for in specific moments and milieus. I conceive Kaerezi's landscape as historically sedimented with environmental resources, human livelihood practices, and power relations. In this perspective, I show how subjects who are not self-sovereign nonetheless exercise agency through "suffering for territory"—my rendering in English of the ChiManyika expressions *kutambudzikira nyika* and *kushingirira nyika*.

Ethnography orients my analysis. Focusing on a particular locality, this study illuminates the micropractices of government, sovereignty, and spatial discipline in Nyanga District's Kaerezi Resettlement Scheme in Zimbabwe's Eastern Highlands. It highlights how, in the 1990s, Kaerezians invoked memories of suffering for territory during colonial rule to stake claims to postcolonial land rights.[3] In doing so, they fused notions of *kushingirira* (to persevere, to struggle valiantly) and *kutambudzikira* (to endure hardship, to suffer) to territory (*nyika*). Shaped by their practices, *nyika* is at once local and national, spanning the semantic terrain of chiefdom, country, and nation. It specifies no single sovereign or mode of subjection. As a contested terrain of landscape, *nyika* is simultaneously symbolic and material.

What governing practices targeted this postcolonial landscape? At independence in 1980, the state purchased Gaeresi Ranch, a white-owned property, to resettle Africans deemed squatters under Rhodesian rule and evicted from the area. Many of those displaced had fled to Mozambique during the war, returning after independence to their ancestral lands. The novel administrative area established for these smallholders, Kaerezi Resettlement Scheme, overlay a chiefdom and rainmaking territory where several sovereigns asserted rule. Thus Kaerezians found themselves subject to both state legal and administrative dictates, as well as to Rekayi Tangwena, a nationalist chief who defied Ian Smith's racial land and labor laws. State officials, a postcolonial chief, his headman, and a rainmaker all sought to influence resettlement. These competing practices of spatial discipline, sovereignty, and subjection all coexisted at the same time in a postcolonial place. Kaerezi's multiple and simultaneous spatialities conjured heterogeneous histories. Some Kaerezians wove colonial rule into the fabric of "traditional authority" that they insisted was precolonial, intertwining temporalities in a postcolonial resettlement scheme. Kaerezi's landscape of rule was not the result of a serial succession of new rationalities and administrative designations *occluding* previous power relations. Rather, previous sedimentations remained consequential even as they became reworked.[4]

Such Kaerezian predicaments of place orient my ethnographic analysis of power, race, and spatiality—a term emphasizing the production of space, its discursive and material practices, as well as its cultural understandings. Focusing on the multiple modes of power in Kaerezi, *Suffering for Territory* combines history and ethnography to offer an anthropological elaboration of governmentality—power relations that enlist subjects in the project of their own rule, guiding conduct and encouraging self-discipline.[5] I deploy this critical analytic to examine grounded practices of sovereignty enacted by colonial and postcolonial state administrations, Tangwena chiefs, and ruling rainmakers. To appreciate the workings of postcolonial power, I argue, analysts need attend to what I later term "selective sovereignties," which compete with state assertions of absolute authority. Subjects of power are active agents yet not self-sovereign authors of their own conscious will.

Both colonial and postcolonial governmentality in Kaerezi, I argue, are intertwined with the legacies of conquest through which Rhodesian rule produced spaces of *racialized dispossession*. *Race* became discursively deployed to legitimate the expropriation of African lands in the name of imperial and later national improvement. Indirect rule incorporated salaried chiefs and headmen into projects of government, procuring taxes and labor while providing conduits of information and administration. I give historical and ethnographic texture to these political technologies, demonstrating their role in racialized rule, tribal territories, and forms of subjection. In Kaerezi, rural subjects and rainmakers also asserted entitlements that challenged chiefly sovereignty and spanned colonial rule. While racialized technologies of rule governed spaces of dispossession, I show how they did not occlude alternative spatialities grounded in Kaerezian cultural practices and understandings.

Accordingly, my ethnographic attention to grounded geographies counters the often uncritical use of spatial metaphors in contemporary cultural theory. I use the term *situated* spatially, culturally, and politically, emphasizing the salience of contingent constellations of practice, milieu, and materiality. In so doing, I also advance an analytic of *ethnographic emergence* wherein Kaerezian spatial struggles informed my emplaced acts of fieldwork. In turn, my understanding of Kaerezi's territorial struggles as constitutive of cultural identity—woven into the fabric of community, politics, and rights—oriented my subsequent analytical engagements with power, spatiality, and racialized dispossession. Ethnographic representation thus emerged across multiple moments and sites through recursive relations among my practices, those of Kaerezians, and analytics—producing sediments and traces contingently assembled in text.

Kaerezi's situated struggles produced an *entangled landscape* in which multiple spatialities, temporalities, and power relations combine: rainmaking and chiefly rule; colonial ranch and postcolonial resettlement scheme; site-specific land claims and discourses of national liberation; ancestral inheritance and racialized dispossession. Entanglement suggests knots, gnarls, and adhesions rather than smooth surfaces; an inextricable interweave that ensnares; a compromising relationship that challenges while making withdrawal difficult if not impossible. Attempts to pull apart such formations may unwittingly tighten them. Guided by this understanding, I show how, spatially and discursively, Kaerezi's cultural politics of sovereignty and territory also entangled locality and liberation, chiefdom and nation-state. Localized land rights became articulated through relational histories of nation, regional anticolonial movements, the legacies of imperial projects in southern Africa, and globalized discourses of development, human rights, and social justice. I link precise locations of huts and fields to urban migrant labor, legacies of an American-trained colonial agriculturalist, and Rhodesian evictions. My historical and ethnographic elaborations, I hope, illuminate Kaerezians' predicaments of power and place. To achieve this goal, however, I first turn sequentially to my three themes of governmentality, racialized rule, and spatiality, clarifying the analytical and political stakes each one foregrounds.

Provincializing Governmentality

Over the past three decades, the concept of governmentality has emerged as a generative approach to power in anthropology and cultural studies. While debates in the 1970s and 1980s pivoted greatly on questions of "structure and agency," the "subject and power"—crucial to the conception of governmentality—became salient keywords orienting analyses in the 1990s and beyond.[6] As part of this shift, academics explored liberalism's legacies and neoliberal rationalities, especially in the global North, probing their "powers of freedom."[7] Rather than dominating through force, these studies asked, how did political technologies guide, encourage, and orchestrate actions among subjects whose agency became deployed—rather than destroyed—by government? What kinds of strategies, knowledges, and techniques targeted the management and improvement of abstract entities such as "population," "economy," and "society"? Privileging institutional sociologies and histories, such innovative studies of *rationalities of rule* rarely took up the prism of ethnography.[8] I counter this trend, grounding governmentality ethnographically in Kaerezi's micropolitics.[9]

In Michel Foucault's formulation, " 'Government' did not refer only to political structures or to the management of states; rather it designated the way in which the conduct of individuals or of groups might be directed. . . . To govern, in this sense, is to structure the possible field of action of others."[10] In contrast to perspectives that conceive conscious intentions to script social action, Foucault called for the study of "effective practices" of power: "Its target, its field of application, or, in other words, the places where it implants itself and produces its real effects."[11] I draw on these insights to pry apart government and the state, conceiving of power relations as articulating subjects and space by shaping milieu through positioned practices. I thus link the material and discursive production of landscapes and livelihoods to those of subjects, sovereignty, and discipline.

Because power relations shape possible *fields of action*, spatial struggles are crucial. "Is not social space always, and simultaneously," Henri Lefebvre asked, "both a *field of action* (offering its extension to the deployment of projects and practical intentions) and a *basis of action* (a set of places whence energies derive and whither energies are directed)?"[12] In my view, governmental projects work, in part, through the production and regulation of landscapes of rule. In sites like Kaerezi, formations of power become grounded through historically and spatially sedimented practices. Geographies and histories of the present pivot on how past struggles gain traction, shape material and discursive fields of action, and enable emergent conditions of possibility. Power relations influence how possible pasts, presents, and futures become linked.[13] Too often analysts conceive contingent connections as necessary, determined trajectories.

By displacing power from the structural dictates of state and capital, governmentality offers a useful means to explore how Kaerezian subjects participate in the projects of their own rule. The state becomes one among other provinces of power rather than its sovereign director.[14] In Zimbabwe, government includes state practices, but it is neither limited to nor isomorphic with them.[15] Tax collection, censuses, and what colonial administrators termed "ethnographical maps" all became instruments of racialized rule. Yet as I later elaborate, tribal subjects in Kaerezi were also tenants subjected to capitalist labor discipline by white ranch owners. At times, white administrators and owners pursued contradictory projects that attempted to orchestrate African actions.

Governmentality works through the agency of subjects, encouraging conduct and forms of self-discipline that target improvements in welfare and security. Subjects' conduct both sustains and challenges regimes of rule. In Kaerezi, subjection became cultivated along with furrowed fields. Colonial labor tenants negotiated with a white rancher and his foreman, propitiated ancestral spirits, and honored both rainmaker and chief. Squatters defied edicts of landowners and state. Postcolonial resettlement administration targeted spatial assemblages of livelihood practices, seeking to enlist scheme residents in the promotion of "development," at once improving their own welfare and that of nation-state. As postcolonial governing technologies situate Kaerezians in an enabling milieu, encouraging self-improvement, such power relations produce *subjection to government*, as well as subjects of action.[16]

Foucault's reflections on governmentality focused on transformations in European regimes of rule, charting the emergence of the economy as an explicit field of intervention in the eighteenth century, of the sciences of state that conceived the population as having its own regularities, and of the forms of surveillance, calculation, and control exercised over the welfare of that population. This emergent constellation of calculating practices, procedures, and institutions—government—he argued, did not target territory, but, rather, the *imbrication* of "men and things." Foucault elaborated:

> Government does not bear on the territory but rather on the complex unit constituted by men and things. Consequently the things which the government is to be concerned about are men, but men in their relations, their links, their *imbrication* with those other things which are wealth, resources, means of subsistence, the territory with its specific qualities, climate, irrigation, fertility, etc.; men in their relation to that other kind of things which are customs, habits, ways of doing and thinking, etc.; lastly men in their relation to that other kind of things again which are accidents and misfortunes such as famine, epidemics, death, etc.[17]

As a project, government thus consists of ruling *relations* in several senses, for it targets relations rather than things, entangling subjects, space, and resources. Yet as Bruce Braun underscored, Foucault's government confronts a territory conceived as already having inherent natural properties. Less appreciated is how political technologies themselves produce territory, including its presumed "natural" features.[18] In this book, I adopt a focus indebted to Foucault, yet depart from his analysis by showing how racialized political technologies produced multiple territories in a single colony: African reserves, tribal chiefdoms, white farms, national parks, and other areas—all imbued with contending practices of space and subjection. In turn, I elaborate several modes of sovereignty entangled in the single site yet multiple spatialities of Kaerezi.

In Foucault's account, sovereign power in Europe targeted two objects since the Middle Ages, the territory and its inhabitants.[19] In this vision, while sovereignty historically preceded governmentality as a European ruling principle, no serial sequence pushes power from sovereignty to discipline and then to government. Rather, Foucault's analytic of governmentality proposed a "triangle: sovereignty-discipline-government, which has as its primary target the population and as its essential mechanism apparatuses of security."[20] I take Foucault's triangle of *sovereignty-discipline-government* as key to highlighting how these contingent configurations of power work in historically, culturally, and geographically specific contexts in Zimbabwe. However, I argue, this triangle does not make for a stable tripod, but rather constitutes a *triad in motion*. As a result, I stress shifting alignments and contingent constellations of power rather than a single ruling rationality.

In the past decade, scholars have traced the imperial circuits obscured in

Foucault's Eurocentric story of modern power.[21] Timothy Mitchell has asserted that colonizing processes entailed "the spread of a political order that inscribes in the social world a new conception of space, new forms of personhood, and a new means of manufacturing the experience of the real."[22] Despite their considerable insights, such analyses of colonial and postcolonial governmentality have tended to emphasize an underlying "grammar of modern power," a coherent "regime of intelligibility," or a unified "political rationality."[23] At times, a Weberian specter of bureaucratic rationality haunts these formations. Assertions of a unitary "logic" purge heterogeneous practices, struggles, and alternatives from analytical recognition. Michael Hardt and Antonio Negri confidently proclaimed that globalization has produced a "single logic of rule," which they term sovereignty.[24] Such blanket pronouncements elide attention to the microtechniques through which power relations work in historically and geographically specific contexts.[25]

This tendency is rendered all the more pronounced by a methodological overreliance on the texts, taxonomies, and forms of knowledge produced by the state—archives of expertise; economic calculations, plans, and censuses; laws, policies, and codified regulations—and a presumption of a corresponding unitary institutional logic. While anthropology has for decades critiqued the Geertzian metaphor of culture as a text to interpret and decode,[26] the discipline's engagement with governmentality ironically emphasizes textual archives at the expense of situated practices. Methodologically, an archival document is often read as a metonym expressive of a signifying system's logic, or as scripted by an underlying structural principle. This tendency entrenches the assumption that the heterogeneity of practices can be "read off" from a single, univocal logic.

Discourse, in many accounts, binds a systemic order of things, while classificatory and taxonomic archives become evidence for government's successful implementation of a ruling logic. A sort of poststructural functionalism renders governmentality a systemic order with discursive desires, logical requirements, and ruling principles.[27] In contrast, I conceive political technologies as an assemblage of practices, apparatuses, and techniques, rather than reducing any regime of rule to a singular "logic," "grammar," or "rationality."[28]

A conceptual pairing of textualism and a unitary logic or singular rationality contributes to assumptions of a new regime of rule erasing, eclipsing, or occluding previous power relations, rather than *articulating* with prior formations. Colonial modernity, in David Scott's influential formulation, then entails a "political rationality through which [an] old footing was systematically displaced by a new one."[29] By *grounding governmentality* in Kaerezian struggles, I emphasize how emergent projects of colonial and postcolonial rule articulate with shifting sedimentations of subjection and spatiality. In this contentious territory, dominion emerges as a product of contest among commoners and several sovereigns—chiefs, rainmakers, property owners, and state administrators. Crucial to projects of governmentality are configurations of "the *imagined territory* upon which these strategies should act," extending to the "*specification of the subjects* of government."[30] Rhodesian administrators designated tribal territories, collected taxes, and administered projects of rule through chiefs and headmen. Yet such political technologies encountered subjects and territories already embedded in ruling relations. For this reason, I elaborate entanglements, with their gnarly knots that defy orderly undoing and the contingent constellations that pull in different directions.

In Kaerezi, attempts to orchestrate *conduct* proved crucial to power and rule. Foucault's elaboration of this keyword fused verb and noun, glossing conduct in its sense of leading others, including "mechanisms of coercion," and as a "way of behaving within a field of more or less open field of possibilities."[31] Conduct both orchestrates and enacts agency, emphasizing how power relations imbue actions, including those "freely" performed. While governing is invariably linked to historical forms of violence, relative freedom—a submission to government—keeps alive the possibility of "refusal or revolt."[32] Ruling regimes in southern Africa employed draconian force and legal instruments, projects of coercion, and persuasion to exclude Africans from rights, spaces, and conduct cultivated by Europeans. A dangerous duet of illiberal and liberal rule wove violent conquest and discourses of imperial improvement into colonies.

To understand legacies of violence in relation to projects of rule, I draw from Antonio Gramsci's reflections on hegemony as a crucial complement to governmentality.[33] I develop three Gramscian insights critical for understanding Kaerezi's contentious landscape: the violence of political economic relations, the discursive construction of interests as crucial to ruling relations, and an emphasis on culture as a critical terrain of political struggle. In turn, I develop these themes to encourage analytical and ethnographic attention to the *spatiality* of power relations and the politics of positioning.

Gramsci explicitly counterposed *dirigere*, to "direct, lead, rule," with *dominare*, to dominate, much as Foucault famously contrasted power and force.[34] Writing from Mussolini's fascist prison, Gramsci elaborated fragments of an analytic of power that educates consent, cultivates conduct, and orchestrates as it compels, fusing force and power. As a Marxist, Gramsci conceived class, an outcome of capitalist social relations of production, as crucial to political inequalities. Though "hegemony is ethical-political," he asserted, "it must also be economic," related to the "decisive nucleus of economic activity."[35] In contrast to Foucault, Gramsci's couplet of civil society and state linked class power, political economic relations, and ruling historical blocs. Governing projects may target self-discipline, but coercion also acts on agents, guiding and encouraging through threats such as evictions, dispossession, and brutal bodily violence.

I take Gramsci's insistence on the violence of political economic relations to supplement governmentality. "Political equality cannot," Gramsci demanded, "exist without economic equality."[36] Gramsci's insights help excavate colonial rule's constitutive violence, linking foundational moments of conquest to legacies of coercion and attempts to manufacture consent through technologies such as so-called labor agreements that bound African tenants to white farms. Rhetorical invocations of "democracy" and "equal rights" prove empty palliatives and disingenuous discourse if the material deprivations of productive inequalities remain. "That the objective possibilities exist for people not to die of hunger and that people do die of hunger," Gramsci wrote from prison, "has its importance," adding wryly, "or so one would have thought."[37] In 2002, Mugabe's ruling party, ZANU-PF, rewarded drought relief to rural constituencies that gave it electoral support. Opposition voters experienced imposed starvation, as well as torture and brutal beatings inflicted by police and ZANU-PF youth brigades. While in 2003 US consumers debated the Atkins diet, as many as 6 million people risked starvation in Zimbabwe. Such global inequalities also imbue Kaerezi's micropractices of power.

An appreciation of political economic injustices, however, is distinct from reducing politics to economics. For Gramsci, hegemony countered the antinomies of economism and voluntarism, offering a powerful "complement to the theory of the state-as-force," while illuminating the "front of cultural struggle."[38] He recognized the power of culture in several senses—its productivity of subjects, identities, and interests; its mobilization of struggle and legitimation of subordination; and its role as medium and ground for contesting social and political inequalities. Hegemonic processes can fetishize culture, using it to discipline consent, impose norms, discriminate, and exclude. When Gramsci suggested that the proletariat "needs to acquire the art of governing," he envisioned such transformations as projects of *cultural politics*. "Just as it has thought to organize itself politically and economically," Gramsci reflected on the working class, "it must also think about organizing itself culturally."[39]

In Stuart Hall's Gramscian vision, power relations make "the field of culture a sort of constant battlefield."[40] Under Rhodesian rule, "custom" became both an instrument of administration and an object of contentious debate. In turn, racialized rule relied on assertions of fundamental cultural differences between Europeans and Africans to legitimate imperial projects of civilizing improvements. Hegemonic formations of rule both orchestrate and compel by shaping the terrain of cultural practices, educating the consent of subjects whose conduct contributes to the conditions of their own subordination. Yet precisely because hegemony is processual, contingent, and contested, it can never be total or complete.[41] Far from natural, even when depicted as such, hegemony requires constant struggle.

For Gramsci, such politics also required "compromise," making "sacrifices of an economic-corporate kind," while taking account of the "interests" of those recruited.[42] Early twentieth-century administrators in the fledgling colony of Rhodesia earnestly advocated for African tenants, opposing white capitalist real estate speculators whose rents were seen to rile unruly natives. Rather than inhering in objective structural locations or cultural essences, interests emerge through social struggle: white colonial administrators and farm owners clashed in moments while aligning in others; some chiefs were deemed loyalists and others rebels; and Zimbabweans born after independence yoked their identities and interests to "war veterans," occupying thousands of white-owned farms while claiming common cause against legacies of racialized injustice.

Hegemony hinges on discursive production, leading subjects to consent by identifying their particular interests with a general, more universalizing one.[43] Gramsci's notion of "contradictory consciousness" stressed processes that fracture identities, interests, and political affinities.[44] Models of "false consciousness" locate objective interests in singular structures. Gramsci appreciated power relations that recruited subjects not by duping them, but by producing emergent interests through compromises, consent, and coercion. In Kaerezi, both chief and state administrators threatened force, allied themselves with populism, and made concessions to rural cultivators maneuvering amid fields of power and practice, crops and soil, ancestral spirits and promises of postcolonial development.

Three crucial moves emerge from my engagements with governmentality and hegemony. First, I argue that capitalist labor discipline needs to be conceived *within* governmentality, not outside it. I echo Frederick Cooper and Ann Stoler's concern with the "muting of political economy" and the "sharp discursive turn away from class analysis" in recent colonial studies.[45] Yet I also oppose economism. Productive inequalities infuse but do not determine cultural politics. Second, I foreground micropractices through which relations of rule work. This *locates* power not at a fixed center, or within a systemic logic, but in relational processes that are translocal yet have highly localized effects. Third, in contrast to metaphors of occlusion, I stress historical sedimentations, at once discursive and material, that entangle subjects and territory.

Conjuring a spatial sensibility, I encourage a more enlivened geography for governmentality and postcolonial studies. My metaphor of provincializing governmentality borrows from Dipesh Chakrabarty's postcolonial critique of Europe's assumed isomorphism with Universal History and Reason.[46] The term *provincializing* suggests a spatial mode of analysis—an emphasis on the production of scale, of a politics of location, of power geometries and geographical imaginaries. Political technologies—of exploration, colonial rule, and the human sciences—have produced the non-West as a terrain of radical alterity. Cultural difference, in Chakrabarty's vision, is a *relational process* rather than ontological essence.[47] By elaborating the heterotemporality and discrepant histories of modern power, he challenged a Universal History with a capital *H*. Left unsettled, however, remains Space with a capital *S*, far too frequently troped yet rarely probed by postcolonial theory.

Scholarly invocations of an omnipotent "imperial gaze" at times suggest the movement of a panopticon whose lens is ground in Europe—an occular export—to the colonies. This hegemony of vision hinges on spatial metaphors radically inattentive to the spatiality of power. Against this grain, I argue, micropractices matter in grounded geographies. Where cultural practices *take place* matters because they are among the critical assemblages that *produce place*. A critically conceived spatiality challenges anthropologists to conceive of identity, territory, and power in more relational terms.

Racialized Rule

An analytical advantage of governmentality is to help illuminate the racialization of power and sovereignty, concepts far too often conceived of as universal features of a color-blind modernity.[48] In Zimbabwe, these processes have been radically territorialized. Rhodesian interventions in the name of improving the welfare of population and nation *racialized space and spatialized race*.[49] Violent dispossession of African property and personhood became the condition of possibility for white land rights, for the laws enshrining them, and for ruling power relations.

Imperial projects of improvement targeted cultural characteristics presumed to inhere in an African alterity anchored in ontological differences of "race."[50] Architects of British colonial rule such as Lord Frederick Lugard proclaimed that imperial states had the "grave responsibility of . . . 'bringing forth' to a higher plane . . . the backward races." Europeans were responsible for developing "the bounties with which nature has so abundantly endowed the tropics" precisely because subject races were "so pathetically dependent on their guidance."[51] Lugard's famous Dual Mandate did double duty: the white man's burden of colonial rule required administration of both nature and natives in the tropics; both were resources to be managed, improved, and developed for the benefit of metropole and colony.

Europeans saw the dwellers of the "Dark Continent" as living in what Fabian terms an allochronic time, a time before the modern.[52] Lugard's "duty" meant guiding Africans forward in Universal History, deploying both physical force and persuasive power. This evolutionary passage required spatial as well as temporal progress. Bringing Africans forward into modernity also incorporated them into a European-inflected spatiality. Administrators argued that distinctively modern orientations toward territory would enable political stability, capitalist wage labor, and national development. Self-improving Africans and crops for the market would be simultaneously cultivated.

By grounding racialized rule in spatial practices, I argue for a more geographically robust vision of governmentality. While Foucault's germinal formulation nodded to the "boomerang effect colonial practice can have on the juridico-political structures of the West," he largely ignored imperial geographies.[53] Similarly, Gramsci focused on Europe, although he lambasted the dictatorship of the Italian ruling class for having "regarded the working people as though they were an inferior race, to be governed without too much standing on ceremony, like an African colony."[54] In Europe as well as in African colonies, the project of producing governable subjects emerged out of legacies of conquest, dispossession, and radical inequalities of rights. Governmental technologies both constructed and sought to regulate differences of "culture" and "race"—within Europe, beyond it, and in relations connecting metropole and colonies.

Inside Europe, Foucault suggested that a discourse of "race struggle" infused formations of political rule with a "counterhistory" that challenged conventional notions of "sovereignty." Long before race became biopoliticized—through practices that suffused sciences examining bodies, populations, and medicine—a "discourse about races, about a confrontation between races, about the race struggle that goes on within nations and within laws" emerged in Europe.[55] Rather than debating Foucault's characterization of modes of power exercised in Europe, however, I build on his *analytic*, linking the crucial triad of sovereignty-discipline-government to racialized rule and territorialities entangled in Africa.[56] Governmentality linked race, space, and power. Similar to apartheid, the Rhodesian project of governing subjects relied on an *ethnic spatial fix*, administering Africans in mutually exclusive, ethnically discrete spaces. Mamdani views this ethnic incarceration as a feature of British indirect rule throughout Africa. In his vision, ethnicity—organized through the template of tribalism—"came to be simultaneously the form of colonial control over natives and the form of revolt against it," a prism through which power and resistance flowed.[57] As both a conceptual and administrative entity, tribes discursively perpetuated what Liisa Malkki terms a "sedentarist metaphysics," rooting people to place.[58] Tribes, as notion and political technology, fused cultural custom, ethnic identity, and administrative territory. Yet affixing identities in tribal territories, I argue, was a *project* of colonial rule rather than a secure accomplishment.[59]

Across Rhodesia's southern border, racialized rule in South Africa enshrined "separate development" in policies of "betterment" and apartheid. In the late 1950s, Nelson Mandela deemed the Nationalist government's policy for administration of the so-called Bantustans a form of "tribalism." "Behind the 'self-government' talks," Mandela concluded, "lies a grim programme of mass evictions, political persecution, and police terror."[60] Opposition on many cultural fronts targeted apartheid's racialized spaces that subjected semicitizens, fomented forced removals, and denied rights to Africans.[61]

Following Mandela's critique of global generalizations, this book excavates constructions of custom, culture, and ethnicity deployed by regimes of rule. It stresses how government works through constitutive exclusions, often when citizens are told that democracy reigns.[62] It focuses on the cultural politics of ethnicity and territory that animate contemporary struggles over belonging and rights. Gilroy asserted that the "raciology of statecraft" and an entrenched "ethnic absolutism" have produced modernity's distinctive "ecology of belonging."[63] Building on such insights from race critical theory, I also argue that race and racisms are "formative features of modernity," not its "aberrant offshoots."[64] Anticolonial struggles inherited the governmental practices of colonial racism, yet they also articulated emergent formations of race, rights, and freedoms.[65] In Zimbabwe, racialized dispossession haunts a postcolony because it was the lifeblood of colonial rule.

My analytic of racialized governmentality counters understandings of race and ethnicity as ontological essence yoked to a reified notion of culture. Racism and culture, Fanon famously asserted, work in "reciprocal action."[66] Political technologies produced the discursive formations of "race" and "culture," constructions with profound material consequences made all the more powerful by imperial insistence that they were "natural" ontological differences located in the "facts" of geography.[67] As Durban's 2001 UN World Conference against Racism reminded many, racialized dispossession remains, to invoke Wole Soyinka's memorable phrase, the "open sore of a continent."[68] More than a half century before, Césaire's "special geography" of Negritude oriented racialized identity by "the *compass of suffering*."[69] In Zimbabwe's Eastern Highlands, idioms of suffering also mapped memories of return to a native land.

SaGumbo remembered the steel rod of Rhodesian rule when Kaerezi was then Gaeresi Ranch. Born there in 1933, he came of age herding cattle and planting wattle as a tenant for the white owner. Men did stints as seasonal migrant laborers, while mothers and wives tended small Kaerezi plots, cultivating gendered geographies as well as family fields. In the 1960s, the rancher expanded plantations, increasing labor demands in an era of rigidly racialized rule. Ian Smith's Rhodesian Front party won white elections in 1962, defiantly proclaiming its Unilateral Declaration of Independence (UDI) from Britain. An international sanctions campaign protested against Rhodesia's regime that excluded Africans from rights, representation, and citizenship. On land legally designated "European," African tenants who defied owners' discipline became squatters subject to forcible removal. Grounded struggles over labor, land, and rights on a single ranch entangled racialized rule in multiple scales, spatialities, and temporalities.

White "ownership" required African dispossession as colonial conquest in the 1890s bequeathed property rights enshrined in racial land laws. State-sanctioned violence propped up protective legislation that effectively mapped exclusionary white claims to private estates. Skirmishes on the ranch in the 1960s and 1970s conjured violent histories of dispossession, fomenting contestations over sovereignty, political subjection, and rights. Since the white ranch overlapped a colonial chiefdom, Gaeresi's labor tenants were also tribal subjects. Officials installed the first government-appointed chief, Dzeka Tangwena, in 1902. Deaths of chiefs produced colonial successions of salaried rulers: Mudima's 1928 inauguration was followed by Kinga's in 1938. Kinga died in 1965 as labor struggles escalated. Tenants rallied behind Dzeka's son, Rekayi Tangwena, selecting him as their new sovereign.

The Rhodesian regime refused official recognition to the rebel chief. By evicting black tenants from Kaerezi, administrators would perform double duty: disbanding the Tangwena chiefdom while purging white property of unruly Africans. Years of skirmishes on the ranch and in courts attracted national headlines and BBC broadcast, news of the Tangwena plight traversing transnational mediascapes. Police bulldozed and torched huts, beat squatters, and unleashed dogs on protesters. In 1991, SaGumbo remembered the precise number and color of cattle seized, and the image of his wife—a baby bouncing on her back, another terrified child clutching her arm—running from police twenty years earlier. MaiNyasha showed me her escape route, vividly recalling the ranch raid.

Those evicted hid in surrounding mountain forests, building lean-tos pelted by heavy rains and sneaking back at night to repair huts and cultivate fields. In response, orderlies plowed under crops and seized cattle. Tangwena squatters found crucial allies at Nyafaru Cooperative, a multiracial experiment encircled by both ranch and chiefdom. Progressive whites purchased property in a "European" area in the late 1950s, defying apartheid-like labor and land laws by having blacks and whites comanage the estate. In the 1960s and 1970s, Nyafaru provided critical support for Tangwena squatters: food, blankets, shelter for children, conduits to national and international media, and legal advice. A 1972 police raid herded squatters' children, left at Nyafaru's school for safekeeping, into a truck bound for the capital. Farmed out to mission schools amid a guerrilla war, children lived apart from their families. SaGumbo's son was among more than one hundred such children. For many, it would be years before they would again see their parents, some reuniting in Mozambique as war refugees. Spatially and politically, Nyafaru linked white ranch, Tangwena territory, African nationalisms in two southern African states, and transnational alliances stretching to Europe and the United States.

Countering Nyafaru's multiracialism, Ian Smith's Rhodesian Front banned African nationalist parties in 1964 and imprisoned their leaders. Two years later, Robert Mugabe grieved in prison for the death of his son, Nhamodzenyika, whose ambivalent name translates as "Problems of Territory and Nation." Born during Mugabe's political exile in Tanzania, Nhamodzenyika died in Ghana where Mugabe once taught school and met his wife.[70] Few recall that it was in Ghana where Mugabe claimed to have "accepted the general principles of Marxism,"[71] or that during his eight years in Salisbury prison, he earned correspondence degrees in law and economics from London University.[72]

Yet in the 1990s, many Zimbabwean schoolchildren could recall dramatic details of Mugabe's 1975 overland escape to Mozambique. A white nun and black nationalists hid Mugabe, briefly released from prison, in a car speeding from the capital to Kaerezi.[73] Nationalists at the cooperative joined displaced squatters, including Chief Rekayi Tangwena, to shepherd Mugabe through Tangwena territory to liberated zones in the newly independent Mozambique. In the hyperbolic words of historian Henry Moyana: "That escape, in a way, guaranteed our independence, it was to give Zimbabwe a dynamic leadership in whom the whole of Africa and indeed the entire third world is very proud."[74] Exaggerations aside, from exile Mugabe helped orchestrate one of Zimbabwe's liberation armies, launching incursions from guerrilla bases located in territory secured by Samora Machel's Front for the Liberation of Mozambique (FRELIMO) forces. Spanning state borders, among African nationalist's strongest populist rallying cry was the promise to reclaim "lost lands" seized by whites through colonial conquest.

Amid the violence of a guerrilla war, Tangwena territory became part of a network of sites stretching from Tanzania, London, and Salisbury to FRELIMO zones, spanning national borders while enabling nationalist politics. When Mugabe's ZANU-PF party swept to victory at Zimbabwe's 1980 independence, electing him prime minister, SaGumbo's chief became a national senator, and two members of the multiracial cooperative headed ministries.[75] Rhodesian evictions, Mugabe's escape, and political opposition to racialized rule entangled Kaerezians' suffering for Tangwena territory with struggles of national liberation.

In the wake of independence, these war refugees returned from exile to reclaim land in Kaerezi. The postcolonial state soon purchased the white ranch, converting the homeland of a prominent anticolonial chief into Kaerezi Resettlement Scheme. Rekayi Tangwena's 1984 televised burial in Harare's Heroes' Acre claimed his body for the nation-state. Yet the body politic entangled with Tangwena's chiefdom linked local, national, and transnational processes. Grounded livelihood struggles—building huts, cultivating crops, herding cattle—articulated with legacies of a nationalist liberation war that promised postcolonial freedom. In 1986, state officials appointed Magwendere, a lineage-mate of Rekayi, as acting Chief Tangwena amid popular objections. Five years later, acting as a chief, Magwendere opposed the lines of state spatial discipline. SaGumbo cultivated his hard place, subject to no single *simba*, no unitary regime of rule.

Spatiality and Power

Cultural practices, social relations, and political economic processes meld with the materiality of milieu, producing place. During the 1950s, male migrant laborers returned home seasonally to work as labor tenants on a white ranch where their wives and mothers farmed family fields. Rainmaking, ancestral appeasement, smallholding agriculture, and political violence spanning vast distances had long shaped Kaerezi, also becoming part of place. So also did capitalist labor relations, colonial administration, and experiences of exile in Mozambique. Postcolonial Kaerezi, in turn, emerged from the specificity of Rekayi's anticolonial prominence, memories of squatters defying white rule, and of administrators in a newly independent nation-state eager to establish examples of African liberation. Such contingent and relational histories produced place.[76]

"Connecting history to a place," de Certeau proposed, "is the condition of possibility for any social analysis."[77] Even the most localized of struggles that link cultural identity and ancestral rights to place in Kaerezi, I argue, are translocally routed, not essentially rooted.[78] Accordingly, I trace practices from farmers' fields and huts to urban migrant labor, African nationalist politics, and experiences of wartime exile in Mozambique. Classical anthropological accounts often mapped a singular spatiality, rooting culture to place. Yet countercurrents simultaneously circulated, appreciating the translocal, transcultural relations in ethnographic sites. Malinowski's 1922 classic, *Argonauts of the Western Pacific*, was a *multisited* ethnography, tracing circuits of travel and exchange. In the 1930s, Ortiz's formulation of transculturation stressed the global histories shaping regionally distinctive cultural formations, while Kenyatta critiqued racialized dispossession of African lands in Kenya.[79]

More than a half century later, amid a mood of disciplinary self-reflection, anthropologists pondered the production of locality. How, Arjun Appadurai and others asked, have anthropological representations "incarcerated" so-called natives in place?[80] Ethnographies were deemed disciplinary in several senses, positioning subjects in spaces of confinement. Countering this "assumed isomorphism between space, place and culture," analysts stressed the *production* of cultural difference through processes of translocal linkage. Essential "cultures" did not dwell in spatially isolated enclaves; rather, cultural difference *emerges* through the very processes that span localities, producing senses of culture and identity that become rooted in particular places.[81] Yet ethnographic work attending to translocal practices that articulate place remains rare despite the mantra of "multi-sited ethnography," the "global-in-the-local," and the "multi-local social spaces" inhabited by mobile subjects.[82]

To foreground Kaerezi as a site of multiple spatialities, I stress grounded entanglements in situ that are linked to southern Africa's regional political economy, Zimbabwe's two major cities, and governing projects of spatial discipline. These complex entanglements also form part of place. To understand micropractices grounded in Kaerezi, I often had to attend elsewhere, focusing on its linkages to faraway sites: Nyanga District Center; Harare offices; archives located in separate district, provincial, and national repositories; and multiracial cooperatives in colonial Rhodesia connected to European shareholders. This research required travel, but, more crucially, an appreciation for Kaerezi as a place entangled with multiple sites, and hence a site of multiplicities.

Much of anthropology's "sense of place" literature relies on a humanist subject that makes places by assigning cultural meanings, thus inaugurating lived place out of dead space.[83] By defining place as "space made meaningful by cultural actors," this literature installs intentionality in place's origin story. Two kinds of assumptions often dwell in *humanist* place: the self-sovereign *subject* whose meanings "make" place, transforming space; and *place*, a locally bounded conception whose history is self-contained.[84] As a result, only "local" cultural processes are seen as rendering places meaningful; translocal flows, actors, and connections tend to get bracketed out of a place's enduring "sense." In Keith Basso's eloquent ethnography of the Western Apache, place became the site where wisdom sits, cordoned off from translocal knowledge, experience, and the multiple spatialities that shape the landscapes of the US Southwest.[85] Places are meaningful, but so, too, are spaces, including abstract and dehumanizing ones. Insofar as places are deemed to have a single sense, culture becomes a shared system of meanings devoid of situated struggles. Place, in this vision, becomes far too *settled* in several senses.

Despite a differently conceived subject, poststructuralists have also romanticized place as the site of authentic, insurrectionary resistance to globalization and capitalism. In so doing, they have helped discursively produce a locally incarcerated horizon of cultural politics. On the one hand, uncritical celebrations of localism assume that cultural identities mapped onto place are necessarily politically progressive. Mandela's blistering critique of apartheid's attempt to engineer place-bound cultural identities through the tribal template warns against such blanket assertions of localism as a *necessarily* progressive basis for cultural politics. By conceiving of place as globalization's Other, and suggesting that territorial struggles and social movements aspire to "defend place" against the encroachments of an "outside," such perspectives occlude the heterogeneous translocal articulations that participants within locally grounded struggles actively forge.[86] Indigenous rights and anti-dam movements have powerfully deployed essentializing assertions that link place and culture while mobilizing through translocal, spatially and culturally hybrid networks.[87]

Yet when analysts imply that resistance is located outside power, they reproduce a notion of globalization impacting localities, viewing place as the reactive site of external forces.[88] Kaerezians' suffering for territory, in contrast, does not seek to defend the local against all outside influences, but rather to shape relations that link Kaerezi to other sites. White capitalist ranching and Rhodesian rule racially dispossessed squatters who, during the late 1960s and early 1970s, defied waves of evictions. Yet national and global media, international human rights supporters, and transnational capital *all* provided crucial support for labor tenants displaced from ancestral land. Place emerges as a distinctive mixture, not an enduring essence, a nodal point where these translocal influences intermesh with practices and meanings previously sedimented in the local landscape.

And what of space, often portrayed as place's Other? I echo Foucault's insistence that "space is fundamental in any exercise of power."[89] I also agree with Lefebvre that capitalism fetishized space, occluding its own historical formation through social relations of production.[90] Abstract, empty, and exchangeable space is a historical product, not an essence. It only *appears* inert, fixed, and dead. Colonial and postcolonial planners in Zimbabwe often promoted this fiction as technocrats charted blocks of abstract space to discipline settlements where landscapes were already alive with grounded livelihoods and spatial meanings. Planning documents are among those representational practices occluding space's production, at times promoting an "overestimation of texts . . . to the point of assigning to these a monopoly on intelligibility."[91] Countering tendencies toward textualism that link academic inquiry and bureaucratic rationality, I foreground spatiality: the production, practice, and power relations of space. In Lefebvre's terms, "Space as locus of production, as itself product and production, is both the weapon and the sign of . . . struggle."[92] While some have invoked Lefebvre to insist that the dynamics of capital, state, and class *determine* the production of space, I build on his critique of "precisely oriented determinism" and his emphasis on "*conjunctures*, which are not reducible to *structures*."[93] I thus counter economistic analyses that have posited capitalism's functional needs as structurally determining a "spatial fix."[94] Accordingly, I stress how Kaerezian conjunctures reveal the production of distinct spaces imbricated in cultural politics and governmental projects, shaped by historical contingency rather than structural determination.

Many scholars take as self-evident the isomorphism among state, force, and territory. In so doing, they implicitly endorse Weber's germinal definition of the modern state as the institutional bureaucracy that "claims the *monopoly of the legitimate use of physical force within a given territory*."[95] Bureaucratic rationalities, in this view, are seen to spread across a sovereign state space, imposing legible order. While I draw insights from James C. Scott's masterful analysis of state schemes, planning, and projects of improvement, I depart from his summation that "the legibility of a society provides the capacity for large-scale social engineering, high-modernist ideology provides the desire, the authoritarian state provides the determination to act on that desire, and an incapacitated civil society provides the leveled social terrain on which to build."[96] Such a vision locates power both spatially and institutionally inside a unitary entity—the state—with functional desires, while relegating resistance to "nonstate" spaces. In contrast, my analysis demonstrates that in Kaerezi, despite orderly grids of villagization, power relations and spatialities were multiple, entangled, and not monopolized by a sovereign state rationality.

Distinct political technologies produced Kaerezi as a distinct and bounded body politic, a "geo-body."[97] While most map this term exclusively to national territory, I rescale it to a chiefdom, rainmaking territory, and even areas claimed by headmen. This move helps unhinge state and sovereignty as well, demonstrating how localized struggles over territorialized power grounded alternative articulations of rule. At the same time, I focus on the production of space in the disciplining of land, labor, and rural livelihoods. Capitalist political economic relations and state development projects were crucial to these processes, but so also were reworked sediments of precolonial migration, conquest, and traditions of authority. Conceiving places as *relational*, including within them links to spaces beyond locality, shifts their conceptual ground.[98]

In Kaerezi, rainmaking, chiefly rule, white ranching, and postcolonial resettlement administration interweave with migrant labor, political violence, and flows of capital and knowledge in ways that link locality to distant sites. Just as multiple spatialities coexist in a single moment within place, so also are experiences of place differentiated across diverse subject positions. Axes of inequality, differences of identity, and power relations make places subject to multiple experiences, not a unitary, evenly shared "sense." Within any one place, social actors become *subjected* to multiple matrices of power.[99] In Kaerezi, gendered geographies emerged through migrant labor and agrarian livelihoods. In turn, patrilineal land holdings and chiefly sovereignty positioned women and men differently in relation to place and territorial suffering.

Entangled Landscapes

Kaerezi's landscape does not comprise a series of successive historical strata, one layered over its predecessor, historical depth transposed into archaeological form.[100] Instead of layered strata, space is striated.[101] Kaerezi is a fractal landscape in which a postcolonial resettlement scheme, chiefdom, and rainmaking territory interweave with smallholder agriculture, ancestral propitiation, and memories of dispossession. In this entangled landscape, multiple spatialities mingle. Neither serial nor successive, they are copresent, sometimes as hauntings, other times as explicit invocations, shaping a plural terrain where no single space prevails. Some attempts to extricate cultural fabrics inadvertently tighten stubborn knots—further binding postcolonial resettlement politics to territories of precolonial and colonial conquest. These tangles pull in different directions at once. Struggles in the 1990s built on, invoked, and reworked prior practices of place spanning colonial rule and drawing from distant sites, from Oakland, California, to Iraq. The cultural politics of place pivot on provisional assemblages, emerging from historical sedimentations yet not dictated by them. Places are without guarantees because landscapes and identities constitute terrains of struggle. Bulldozing, hut burning, and armed raids are as much part of the fabric of Kaerezi as are planting crops, propitiating ancestral spirits, and rainmaking.

I thus link landscape to historically sedimented practices that mix with environmental milieu. For Lefebvre, "the landscape is an *oeuvre*," the product of located labor.[102] Acts of cultivation at once transform terrain and subjects, both of them imbued with value as bodies of work. Recent metaphors of "scape" in anthropology have creatively remapped the perspectival properties of landscape to novel discursive sites, processes, and practices.[103] Yet when these tropes become radically unmoored from spatial practices, they run the risk of e-scaping ethnographic and analytical precision. John Berger famously termed landscape "a way of seeing," emphasizing the power relations that linked pictorial representations to the politics of class and a propertied view. This hegemony of vision, he argued, obscured the very labor producing material and discursive terrain.[104] A second meaning, denoting an identifiable tract of land, traced to German and Middle English, signifies a material extent of earth.[105] Inherently duplicitous, the term *landscape* refers both to visual perspective and to the geographical territories seized by it. Landscapes articulate culture and nature, seer and scene.

Landscapes, like history, subject people to conditions not of their own choosing. W. J. T. Mitchell conceives the term as a "process by which social and subjective identities are formed." Landscape, in his formulation, does double duty: "It naturalizes a cultural and social construction," and it interpellates a beholder.[106] As prominent studies of colonial discourse argue, imperial explorers, natural historians, and colonial administrators abstracted "natives" out of land-scapes of imperial encounter and contemporaneous history.[107] Differently placed subjects in specific historical moments saw Kaerezi *as* a white farm, a chiefdom, a rainmaking territory, and a postcolonial resettlement scheme. In Kaerezi's en-tangled landscape, no singular spatiality settled a contentious cultural politics of place.

Gramsci termed contingent landscapes of struggle the "terrain of the 'con-junctural' and it is upon this terrain that the forces of opposition organize."[108] Both his metaphors and analysis are alive to spatiality—trenches, terrain, earth-works, wars of maneuver and position, relations between country and city, north and south.[109] Gramsci shared Foucault's insistence that resistance takes place on this terrain, not outside power.[110] "You come to situations with a history," Stuart Hall asserted, "and the enunciation is always in the light of an existing terrain." For this reason, "identities are not given forever, but they're hard to shift."[111] Terrain conjures the historical sedimentation of discursive and material prac-tices, at once locally grounded and translocally embedded.

My perspective builds on a rich Africanist literature on landscape and studies of agrarian micropolitics that emphasize the *simultaneity* of symbolic and mate-rial contestation over terrain.[112] These works understand struggles over cultural meanings not as "merely cultural," as epiphenomenal trappings to deeper struc-tural truths, but rather as themselves constitutive of agrarian politics.[113] In Kae-rezi, women and men cultivate crops, gather firewood, and herd cattle, produc-ing a landscape also shaped by road construction, legal prohibitions on the use of natural resources, and national resettlement policy. Conceived as a contested terrain of practice, landscape becomes less a mute backdrop to human agency than formative to cultural politics and identity.

If landscapes are integrally entangled in power relations, then analysts need to take more seriously the environmental and site-specific materialities enmeshed in rule, unequal resource distribution, and governmental projects. While es-chewing environmental determinism, what conceptual tools enable my analytic of landscape and power? In my vision, *assemblages* displace humans as the sov-ereign makers of history. Humans are not the only entities making mixtures not of their own choosing. Kaerezi is alive with natural-cultural hybrids: SaGumbo's irrigation channel, his wife's neatly planted rows of maize and beans, and cook-hut fires that burn harvested trees. Assemblages arrange provisionally, giving emergent force to contingent alignments of social relations, material substance, and cultural meaning. And like places, assemblages foreground multiplicities irreducible to a single sense, structure, or logic.[114] They span the divide between nature and culture, humans and nonhumans, symbol and substance, marking the "imbrication of the *semiotic* and the *material*."[115] In such a vision, history and politics are inflected with the *consequential materiality* of milieu, of nonhuman entities and artifacts.

Deleuze and Guattari stress three dimensions of the complex constellations they term assemblages: the intermingling of "bodies, of actions and passions"; acts, statements, and representational regimes that enunciate, such as the law, property rights, and social contracts; and "territorial assemblages."[116] In the 1990s, scattered Kaerezi homesteads assembled huts and fields sited near mountain springs, reaped rain-fed crops while drought scorched the *lowveld* (lowlands), and provided subsistence by mixing labor with milieu.[117] State laws, chiefly decree, and memories of burning huts and court-ordered evictions from other times and places also imbued constellations of labor, mud, and thatch-and-wattle poles assembled in a humble dwelling. In turn, the Australian wattle harvested in the 1990s and transported by cattle to homesteads betrayed an earlier era of labor tenants whose embodied acts mixed with seedlings and soil to produce plantations for a white rancher.

Kaerezi speakers of ChiManyika traverse assemblages of *nyika* (territory), *tsika* (culture), *zvisikwa* (environmental resources), and *simba* (power). Rather than seeking an enduring core to these cultural constructs, I trace out their discursive and material deployments. Scholarly invocations of assemblage, however, often occlude power relations, historical sedimentations, and their forceful effects. To avoid this danger, I supplement an analytic of assemblage with one of *articulation*.[118]

As Stuart Hall has noted, articulation carries within it the twin concepts of joining and enunciating.[119] Articulation works through power relations that are historically sedimented and socially reproduced. Like assemblage, articulation brings together disparate elements and relations, giving that constellation a particular form and potential force. However, the historically contingent shape of this formation, the effectiveness of the linkages established among its elements, and the impact it will have on cultural, social, and political processes cannot be "read off" from an underlying structural logic. Thus conceived, articulation challenges perspectives on power that underwrite regimes of rule with a coherent logic or unitary rationality. Instead, articulation opens up questions of how conjunctural contingencies emerge in particular histories and geographies, about the heterogeneity of practices and cultural forms they foment, and about how these linkages inform the cultural politics of place, identity, and subjection.

As an analytic, articulation is open to recognizing that nonhumans produce materially consequential sediments that also inform politics. Yet many who deploy the keyword rely on a self-sovereign humanist subject who articulates, whose agency does the work of enunciating and linking. For this reason, I use *articulated assemblages* to emphasize mixtures of livelihoods, landscape, and environmental resources as well as ancestral spirits, rainmaking territory, and political rule. Unlike assemblage, articulation foregrounds how power relations and historical sediments formatively shape contingent constellations that become materially and discursively consequential.

In this book, the question of *effective articulations*—of provisional linkages that enunciate identities, rights, and political positions—hinges on *contingent cultural politics*. Not all articulations gain traction. Nor do they necessarily enact intended outcomes. Their efficacy depends not solely on agents' assertions but also on assemblages that span the discursive divides of nature and culture, the human and the nonhuman. In C. L. R. James's brilliant rendering of the Haitian revolution, Black Jacobins articulate their historical agency with the tropical rainy season. Insurgents strategically timed revolutionary initiatives to inflict downpours and resulting disease on white Europeans sent to suppress their rebellion.[120] Rainmaking in Kaerezi drew from precolonial practices of ancestral appeasement and postcolonial memories of storms aiding guerrilla fighters during a liberation war. This is neither environmental determinism nor a romanticized vision of human-ecological harmony. Rather, "nature" produces consequential effects, both material and discursive, mingling with humans and nonhumans to make histories in conditions of none of their choosing. Such entangled landscapes thus become crucial to understandings of subjects, power, and agency.

Ethnographic Positioning

Just as Kaerezians' practices are *situated*, so, too, is the production of anthropological insight. In her germinal reflections on "situated knowledge," Donna Haraway elaborated a method of "critical positioning."[121] Echoing these insights, Fabian suggested that an "anthropological attitude" toward ethnography entails a "positional quality of theorizing" constituted "as a praxis."[122] In the text that follows, my hope is for ethnographic insight to emerge through articulations of positioned practices. Amid anthropological attention to the poetics and politics of ethnographic representation, less attention has been devoted to how fieldwork is simultaneously a discursive practice and a located labor process. Ethnography entails acts at once embodied and emplaced. Mine traversed government offices and archives, squatters' homesteads, cattle dips, and plowed fields. As I maneuvered, others' actions governed my conduct, politically positioning me while I also positioned myself.

I arrived for a twenty-six-month stint of fieldwork in 1990, foolishly on a public holiday in the fresh wake of student protests at the University of Zimbabwe. Government research permission took more than a year *after* I received the required written support from two ministries and several university officials who vetted and endorsed my research proposal. Immigration officials at the airport, clearly angered at what they perceived as an antigovernment university that required riot police to restore order, issued me a catch-22 instead of a visa. To enter the country, they insisted, I needed original documentation from my file at the closed university. They vigorously shook their heads as I produced faxes verifying separate documents for research, work, and immigration clearance. After threatening to put me on the night flight out of Harare, they "offered" to detain me until the university reopened and my dossier could be brought to the airport.

A friend from the university intervened, confirming that this was "government hostility" toward the university and not simply fishing for a bribe. "They just want to discipline us," she explained. She did not mention sovereignty. With a seventy-two-hour provisional permit, I reported to Harare's main immigration office early the next morning. After I stood in sullen lines for anxious hours, bureaucrats shuffled me between offices, offering contradictory accounts of my file's fate. My "lost" dossier emerged near closing time, a fetish assembled from myriad technologies and techniques stretching across time and space. An earnest orderly stamped "Government of Zimbabwe" on a dated document that condensed ruling relations that guided my conduct, enabling me state-sanctioned mobility. Yet other sovereignties and territories also awaited me.

Arriving the next month in Nyanga District Center, a seven-hour bus ride from Harare, I was relieved to find District Administrator (DA) Mandisodza who had been supportive during my 1988 research trip. Then a tourist visa had sufficed, but increasingly contentious agrarian politics and my request for research access to government archives and officials, as well as rural constituencies, required his rigorous scrutiny. After checking my documents, including a letter from his Ministry of Local Government's central office, he kindly wrote a letter of introduction to Kaerezi's resettlement officer, Marumahoko. Affixed with the DA's official stamp, this letter effectively served as my research "passport" in Nyanga and proved much more important than the nation-state's documentation that enabled me to reach the district. I carried it dutifully for at least the first year of my fieldwork. As the DA administered relations between subjects and space in Kaerezi, he orchestrated my routes through channels of appropriate authority—practices at once spatial and political.

Weeks later in Kaerezi, I jumped out of Marumahoko's battered Toyota Land Cruiser with a few bilingual schoolteachers. Along with Nyafaru's headmaster and Marumahoko, they brokered a meeting with the acting chief, Magwendere Tangwena. We met at one of the scheme's primary schools, a cluster of asbestos-roofed yellow cement buildings near Magwendere's home. Scattered settlements defying linear grids spread east across pastures, furrowed fields, and thick forest that rolled steeply toward the Jora River that marked the boundary of Mozambique. A curious police officer emerged from a security post, resting his rifle across his lap for the meeting's duration. The year before, armed border-crossing bandits from the Mozambique National Resistance (MNR) had marauded Kaerezi by nightfall and pillaged food, killing several and forcing others to sleep in the bush for fear of attack. One headman, emerging from his hut with a drawn bow, had shot an invader with an arrow, fiercely scaring the rest away. Across Mozambique's lush landscape, Mount Tangwena's distinctive ridgeline rose from the eastern horizon, reminding me of deeper histories of violence, migration, and exile entangling territory.

After a round of handshakes, a dozen of us sat on a grassy knoll near grazing cattle. The headmaster began the meeting by ritually clapping a cadence distinctive to the chiefdom, sonically signaling respect to sovereign and territorial ancestral spirits. Told to leave the speaking to others, I dutifully clapped respect to my handlers, the chief, his son, two headmen, and a few other assembled elders. Despite my fledgling ChiManyika, I followed idioms of education, my infantalization as a "schoolboy," and a robust discourse of development coding my whiteness as a beacon of "progress." A distant federal government in the United States had funded years of my Shona study, but taught me the Zezuru dialect. Wearing a tattered navy blazer and a visored cap with floppy ears that reminded me of filmic images of the French Foreign Legion, the acting chief asked a few questions before launching into a meandering speech. My schoolteacher friends sat poker-faced, though later they ridiculed his rambling rhetoric.

Magwendere's son, Panganayi, in contrast, briskly asked pointed questions while handling the DA's official letter. After an awkward moment, a schoolteacher offered to translate it since Panganayi appeared not to read English. Following a brief discussion, he demanded a small fee and pulled a worn inkpad out of his shirt pocket. He stamped the letter with the chiefly seal, bold ink now proclaiming "CHIEF TANGWENA" next to the DA's stamp and signature. Then Panganayi misspelled the sovereign he claimed to represent. Politely alerted by a schoolteacher, he crossed it out and, with his tongue clenched between his teeth, rewrote authority with a broken ballpoint pen.

Officially stamped by government and chief, that thin sheet of paper enabled my entanglements with Kaerezi's landscape and social relations. From capital to national frontier, a trail of documents, permits, and negotiations interpellated me, as did myriad positioning practices. After negotiations with Headman Mweya in Nyamutsapa, nestled between the Kaerezi River and Nyanga National Park, I met with a gathering of forty. Women and men sat in separately gendered spots on a grassy hillside overlooking the river valley. Children and teenagers, including those not attending school, were conspicuously absent. Before speaking, I was already positioned in a social space gendered, inflected by generation, and saturated with political textures much less visible to the uninitiated eye. The wind whipped the doubly stamped letter I waved as I explained, in my then ChiManyika-Zezuru hybrid, my hope to live and work among neighbors. Weeks of dialogue with individuals and small groups had laid the groundwork for this public meeting's contingent endorsement of my research.

When I pitched my tent at the Gumbos' Nyamutsapa homestead, I sank stakes into ground inside the scheme but outside the planned "villages," becoming an anthropologist among squatters. After weeks in a tent, my unskilled labor joined SaGumbo's able craftsmanship to construct a mud-and-wattle hut. Class, race, citizenship, and experience radically divided us. Yet living in a squatter's homestead located in a chiefdom and resettlement scheme, my own situated practices produced affinities, shifting alliances, and also confrontations. Ethnographic praxis, generative of analytics and politics, made me appreciate more fully the dynamics between positioning and being positioned, the cultural politics of location, and the salience of spatiality for understanding the micropractices of power.[123]

Two trips of several months each in 1988 and 1996 complement my twenty-six months of Zimbabwe fieldwork from 1990 to 1992. Living with squatters in a state-administered scheme made me acutely aware of the effects of precarious and vulnerable livelihoods. Some fissures and gaps mark limits of my understanding; others I consciously carve, guided by concerns about the safety of Zimbabweans amid ongoing political violence, injustice, and violations of rights. I am well aware of governmental surveillance of my own practices, including investigations by the Central Intelligence Organization filed in the state's grid of intelligibility. Several months of fieldwork in 1996 convinced me that detailed elaborations of Kaerezian positions—politically and spatially—in that era are too dangerous to publish at present. Yet these are not the only contingencies that guide the conscious silences that follow.

Just as Kaerezians position themselves in histories and landscapes not of their choosing, so, too, must I. A 1996 car accident had impacts at once embodied, existential, and analytical. More than two years and eight trips to an operating room later, experimental microsurgery targeted a fissured disc in my back. Struggling with bodily impairment and exile from ethnographic engagements in Zimbabwe, I reflected on situated struggles, suffering as a nonsovereign form of agency, and the potential as well as pain of memory work.

Architecture and Argument

The themes of governmentality, spatiality, and entanglements of power and practice suffuse this book's conceptual contours. Yet this framework only emerged out of shifting assemblages of fieldwork, archival research, ethnographic writing, conceptual engagements, and reworked text. An analytic of ethnographic emergence means that "architecture" arrives out of anthropological elaborations, rather than scripting a structurally fixed plan that dictates in advance. My analytic is also an aesthetic, seeking to conjure both multiple spatialities and temporalities at work in precise places and moments. I thus eschew a singular unfolding of chronology. Instead, I juxtapose events from disparate moments since Kaerezians' practices invoke such shifting sedimentations. I pull temporally and spatially distant events into understandings of struggles in the early 1990s to emphasize how their traces, while reworked, remain consequential. Nineteenth-century political violence in Mozambique, twentieth-century anthropology and imperial administration linked to London, and postcolonial development strongly influenced by an American colonial agriculturalist produced unpredictable effects amid Kaerezi's ongoing agrarian struggles.

Part I, "Governing Space," traces tensions between competing modes of power in the spatial ordering of subjects in Kaerezi. I give both ethnographic and historical perspective on the triad-in-motion of sovereignty, discipline, and government. In the early 1990s, who claimed to rule subjects and space in a postcolonial resettlement scheme? I emphasize both the political technologies that produce governed spaces and the spatiality of governing practices, their situatedness in localized geopolitics. Chapter 1 traces ruling relations and spatial striations ethnographically, relating Kaerezians' livelihood struggles in the early 1990s to the scheme's administered spaces. I highlight how practices of postcolonial government, spatial discipline, and modes of subjection became crucial stakes in conflicts over the lines of power.

Chapter 2 places these agrarian micropolitics in the larger landscape of resettlement policy and its colonial precursors: centralization, launched in the 1920s, and the Native Land Husbandry Act of the 1950s and 1960s. These schemes provided powerful grids of intelligibility for seeing the landscape and its inhabitants as amenable to technologies of disciplined management. I trace imperial discourses of "race" and "culture" that traveled through global circuits, influencing grounded governmental development projects. In chapter 3, I elaborate how Kaerezians locate livelihood practices in relation to governed spaces, melding emergent initiatives and historical sedimentations. Scattered agrarian homesteads, I show, were critical assemblages of agrarian practices and material resources. I examine agriculture, cattle dipping, and assertions of environmental rights, including struggles over the meaning and practices of "respecting" territory.

Part II, "Colonial Cartographies," focuses on the production of Kaerezi's colonial geo-body, also examining precolonial patterns of political violence, migration, and territoriality, as well as rule. I argue that a distinct mixture of two territories—the Tangwena chiefdom and Gaeresi Ranch—became especially formative of Kaerezi as a colonial place. I stress the salience of racialized capitalist labor relations and practices of indirect rule that sought to fix ethnic subjects in tribal territories. Hegemony's analytical emphasis on productive inequalities, labor relations, and property rights here complements governmentality's triad-in-motion. Kaerezi's geographies of power, I demonstrate, are both locally distinctive and translocally enmeshed.

Chapter 4 chronicles histories of racialized dispossession and labor relations in the Eastern Highlands. How did Africans understand white arrival and assertions of property claims? In turn, how did administrators and white "owners" seek to rationalize their usurpations? I examine racialized prisms of cultural difference that discursively constructed "communal" land tenure and a corresponding collective African subject, effectively disenfranchising rural cultivators of precolonial rights. Tracking between Rhodesian archives and ethnographic moments in Kaerezi, I trace postcolonial reverberations of a politics of custom. Chapter 5 examines the political technologies that produced a colonial chiefdom and sought to anchor ethnicity in fixed tribal territory. Crowning salaried chiefs, Rhodesian indirect rule deployed anthropological assumptions of "tribes" as governing African society. Administrators understood these polities as representing a relic of an earlier evolutionary moment in human history. In turn, these understandings influenced cultural cartographies produced by colonial administrators whose "ethnographical maps" influenced tax collection, chiefly salaries, and ruling recognition.

Chapter 6 examines conflicts over labor discipline on Gaeresi Ranch that culminated in the era of Tangwena evictions from the late 1960s. Skirmishes on the ranch and in courts underscore how Kaerezians asserted and appreciated translocal relations deeply constitutive of place. These struggles to defy colonial evictions, I argue, demonstrate the need to bring labor discipline into the analytic of governmentality. Spatially distinct divisions of labor also produced gendered geographies crucial to anticolonial protest and postcolonial land claims. In the early 1970s, rising African nationalism and Mugabe's escape to Mozambique during the war wove Kaerezi into the fabric of national liberation.

Returning to ancestral territory after the war in 1980, smallholders claimed land many perceived as a political reward for contributions to independence. In part 3, "Entangled Landscapes," I place localized regimes of rule—chiefs, rainmakers, and headmen—in relation to projects of government administered by officials of the nation-state. I stress the multiple spatialities alive in postcolonial Kaerezi and examine power's provisional alignments among contending practices, sovereignties, and subjects. In chapter 7, I examine rainmaking and chiefly rule to unyoke political theory's embedded assumptions that map sovereignty to states. I use oral histories to complement ethnography, exploring variants of power divided between conquering chief and vanquished rainmaker. Prayer and ancestral appeasement further complicate the spirits inhabiting landscape. Chapter 8 focuses on headmen's rule in relation to Kaerezians' claims to lineage and family land. It shows how commoners' memories of self-settlement represented a populist critique of headmen who invoked "tradition" to authorize their control over allocating land. I foreground the spatial practices of subjection and the emplaced acts of individuals as they establish their own homesteads in territories claimed by headmen, lineages, and specific state officials. Together, chapters 7 and 8 further demonstrate how government *and* sovereignty are unhinged from "the state," grounding the triad-in-motion in Kaerezi's micropolitics.

Chapter 9 positions subjects in relation to postcolonial assertions of rights, inheritance, and identity. How, I ask, do these practices gain *traction* in the 1990s to assert political entitlements earned through struggle rather than patrilineal birthrights to land? Popular assertions of suffering for territory, emphasizing participatory struggle against colonial evictions, critiqued the acting chief by locating him outside this formative moment of history conceived as constitutive of Tangwena identity. Magwendere's postcolonial rule thus contended with multiple mappings of sovereignty and territory. In these conflicts, I focus on the discursive and material *effects* of articulated assemblages rather than the presumed intentions of humanist subjects. I argue that the efficacy of traction depends on both ground and emplaced action, the conditions of possibility shaped by terrain as well as by positioned practices. For SaGumbo and his neighbors, micropractices matter in grounded geographies: daily livelihood struggles, seasonal harvests, and decades of suffering for territory.

The epilogue elaborates an analytic of effective articulations that links my concepts of traction and entanglement to Kaerezi's distinctive cultural politics. I connect legacies of colonial evictions in the 1960s and villagization conflicts in the 1990s to the racialized politics of land during contentious parliamentary debates in 2004. In so doing, I show how postcolonial Zimbabwe's triad-in-motion of sovereignty-discipline-government spans scales from chiefdom to nation-state and remains crucially shaped by the historical sedimentations, at once discursive and material, of racialized dispossession and suffering for territory.

PART I · · · *Governing Space*

1 · Lines of Dissent

Diesel fumes spewed from the white Toyota pickup as Chidumbu downshifted to climb the steep Nyangani range. Eight of us huddled against the cold mountain air amid boxes of cooking oil, sugar, and supplies for the small Nyafaru store he managed. His weekly trips to town for the cooperative saved a fortunate few long walks to the nearest rural bus route. Twenty minutes before, we had pulled out of Nyanga Township's bustling market on a briskly cold 1990 afternoon. Hawkers rushed to buses shuttling between the district's rural areas and two cities—Mutare, the provincial center two hours south, and Harare, the national capital a six-hour ride west. After passing the Nyanga National Park turnoff, the road climbed steeply for more than a thousand feet before reaching Troutbeck, where a luxury hotel attracted international tourists and Zimbabwean elites. A small shop and petrol station in Troutbeck serviced buses, tourists, and the farmers—almost all white—whose properties lay further north on the high range. A few kilometers later, Chidumbu pulled onto a narrow track, passing a small post office, a couple of white-owned cottages, and a lumber mill before winding through thick forest. A smiling grandmother apologized for grabbing my leg as the pickup bounced along the rutted dirt road.

Emerging from the wattle and pine forest, we entered Dazi, the westernmost section of Kaerezi Resettlement Scheme. Barefoot children in ragged clothes scampered from thatched mud-and-wattle huts, greeting us with smiling shouts. Homesteads hugged the road in rows; huts crowded together in long lines. Most of Dazi's 112 settler families arrived in late 1986, having no previous ties to the river valley. Earlier that year, one branch of government had purchased a white-owned commercial farm in the nearby Tsanga Valley, converting it into a state experimental wheat station. Overnight, former labor tenants and farmworkers lost their settlement rights. Police burned huts in Tsanga Valley, one official explained, after "squatters refused to move peacefully." Dazi's disciplined lines thus emerged from the ashes of evictions elsewhere. Kaerezi's resettlement officer told me that Tsanga Valley's newly landless "had no choice. They had to move into the demarcated stands and accept the pegged arables." Far from huts, these blocks of rectangular fields marked the Dazi landscape. Few could afford to fence the three-hectare parcels allocated by government. Some cultivators walked more than a kilometer from their huts to fields. In yet a third zone, cattle grazed.

Chidumbu slowed to let a few oxen clear the road. Plunging down the steep riverbank, the truck fishtailed around a hairpin turn, swerving to avoid a boulder. A stone's throw from the river, a rusted metal sign planted in state property proclaimed: "PRIVATE, NO FISHING. POACHERS WILL BE PROSECUTED." The threat was backed not by the state but "by order, IDFFC," the Inyanga Downs Fly Fishing Club—a private group of white anglers. A decade after independence, the colonial spelling "Inyanga" conjured specters of racialized dispossession, rusted white letters on a black sign. Chidumbu gunned the motor across the narrow cement bridge and engaged the four-wheel drive for traction. Deep erosion channels and rock slides roughened sharp switchbacks climbing east up the steep valley. We were now in Nyamutsapa, the westernmost portion of Tangwena territory where a chiefdom entangled a state scheme.

In sharp contrast to Dazi's dense grids of huts, scattered Nyamutsapa homesteads dotted rolling hillsides. Agrarian mosaics sprouted from clusters of thatched huts, most made of mud and wattle but some of sun-dried bricks. Spatially separated from other homesteads, families lived where they farmed— furrowed fields emerging in multiple directions from residences. Nyamutsapans lived *pake pake*, the repetition meaning "each at their own place," connoting at once scattered settlements and self-selection. "Haphazard" was among the terms favored by the Ministry of Local Government staff.

A decade after independence, government villagization policy sought to resettle those already living in Tangwena territory. Administrators asserted state sovereignty, demanding that Kaerezi residents move into the scheme's concentrated settlement grids distant from their fields. Invoking discourses of development, state officials heralded the advantages of living in lines along a road, thus improving access to transport, marketing opportunities, and government services such as agricultural extension. Spatial concentration, advocates argued, would also increase efficiency of delivering state infrastructure—cement for toilets, future materials for housing, and boreholes. In Harare and Nyanga District Center offices, civil servants spoke openly about resettlement's administrative advantages of surveillance, policing, and enforcement of state regulations. However, officials also complained candidly of political constraints to "implement resettlement" in the ancestral homeland of the anticolonial chief Rekayi Tangwena, Mugabe's intimate ally buried in 1984 as a national hero. They coded local history as an ornery obstacle to the imposition of a uniform national development policy and spatial order.

Shortly after independence, state agents purchased Gaeresi Ranch, anxious to reclaim from whites the homeland of the country's most prominent anticolonial chief. The ranch comprised 80 percent of the main resettlement scheme of 14,500 hectares, initially planned for 296 settler families.[1] Another small property extended the scheme north beyond the chiefdom. Until 1986, Nyamutsapa remained within the Tangwena chiefdom, but on Pulpwood Estates, a white-owned property. Africans living there were technically squatters, and the owner was anxious to unload that portion of the property overlapping Tangwena territory. In 1986, the resettlement officer wrote his superiors to recommend the state purchase of Nyamutsapa: "If this area is bought for resettlement purposes," it would improve crop production and "will boost the morale of the Tangwena people as they hold much sentiments [*sic*] to this area."[2] As he grappled with implementing government policy, the administrator acted on Kaerezians' actions. Recognizing passionate attachments to place, his report acknowledged Tangwena territory as a powerful landscape of affect that linked nation and chiefdom, overlapping areas simultaneously ruled by two sovereigns.

Administrators also encountered the nightmare of competing ministries, often working at cross-purposes within a differentiated state. As early as 1985, staff in the Department of National Parks and Wildlife Management (DNPWLM) in the Ministry of Environment and Tourism sought to extend its estate by annexing a river corridor running through Dazi and Nyamutsapa. Officials in the Agricultural and Rural Development Authority (ARDA) in the Ministry of Agriculture established the nearby Tsanga Valley experimental wheat station, evicting former farmworkers. Employees of the same ministry's planning branch of Agricultural and Technical Extension (AGRITEX) drafted Kaerezi's land use plan. In turn, the staff of the Department of Rural Development (DERUDE) in the Ministry of Local Government sought to administer a resettlement program for those displaced from Tsanga Valley by state evictions. Grounded practices of government shepherded rather than eliminated squatters in Kaerezi. Political processes, not Malthusian laws of nature, produced an emplaced population exceeding what technocrats termed the area's "carrying capacity"—threatening both the river's fragile ecosystem and administrative authority on state land.

The 1986 state purchase from Pulpwood Estates of 4,175 hectares flanking the Kaerezi River's headwaters created Kaerezi Extension, annexed to the main scheme to resettle an additional 200 families. Nyamutsapa, east of the river, lay in Tangwena territory; Dazi, west of the river, was located in the chiefdom of the neighboring Saunyama. One postcolonial resettlement scheme entangled two chiefdoms, two former white farms, and a mosaic of Kaerezians' livelihood practices historically sedimented to place. By 1990, the replanned and integrated scheme was home to 1,000 smallholder families (5,500 official residents) spread across 18,500 hectares. Administrators envisioned forty-three concentrated settlements paralleling dirt roads in Kaerezi Main, seven in Dazi, and five in Nyamutsapa. While the scheme's plan promoted monocropping for market, most families relied on subsistence crops. Farmers planted potatoes in the highest reaches, tobacco and cotton in the lowest, and maize throughout. Despite ambitious government proposals, Kaerezi's scarcity of transport and rugged mountain terrain constrained the marketing of cash crops.

Kaerezi excluded but completely encircled Nyafaru, a private 810-hectare parcel excised from the surrounding Gaeresi Ranch in the late 1950s. A few years later, the progressive white who purchased the excision angered Gaeresi's owner by transferring the title deed to the Nyafaru Development Company, a multiracial cooperative. Nestled inside land legally designated European, Nyafaru's operations defied Rhodesian policies of racial segregation. From the early 1960s onward, blacks and whites comanaged an explicitly socialist cooperative, promoting a social and spatial mixing radically subversive of Rhodesian rule. During the mid-1970s, Nyafaru served as refuge for both Rekayi Tangwena and Robert Mugabe, offering temporary shelter for Tangwena tenants evicted from Gaeresi Ranch and for black nationalists fleeing Smith's security forces. After independence, two of Nyafaru's former managers—Didymus Mutasa and Moven Mahachi—occupied cabinet posts and headed ministries. These nationalist party elites remained among Nyafaru's shareholders in a postcolonial cooperative on private property and separately managed from the surrounding state scheme. The cooperative housed a school, a clinic, and a diesel-powered grinding mill. Daily foot traffic and frequent development meetings linked Nyafaru, part of the Tangwena chiefdom, to the surrounding scheme.

Beyond Nyafaru, all land in Kaerezi was officially state property and administered by a resettlement officer. As in all Zimbabwe resettlement schemes, the official issued permits to a "head of household" on behalf of a family. While widows and divorcees were eligible, married couples received conditional rights vested solely in the husband's name.[3] In the name of government, the administrator allocated three use rights—to a residential stand, to a three-hectare field, and to a shared grazing commons—all corresponding to spatially and functionally separate zones conceived by state planners as mutually exclusive. Packaged as a single bundle of rights, all land access pivoted on settlers' being allocated one-hundred-meter by fifty-meter plots in concentrated linear villages, popularly called "the lines" (*maline*). Rumors of witchcraft, enmity, and discontent in Dazi's crowded settlements floated across the river valley, fueling critiques of villagization.

Distinct yet interlaced spatial histories produced two paradoxes of place. In Dazi, those officially resettled through villagization policy complained of feeling unsettled—enduring crowding and social conflicts in the cramped lines. Across the river, Nyamutsapans felt comfortably settled in scattered homesteads located outside the resettlement grids. For many, resettlement represented displacement tantamount to eviction. In Tangwena territory, "villages" remained uninhabited government fictions, the antithesis of social space.

A lone exception lay near the park border, far from scattered homesteads. This linear anomaly west of the river spilled over from Dazi when, in 1987, fourteen families evicted from Tsanga Valley moved into the grids. By 1991, only four impoverished families resided in dilapidated huts. Spatially and socially isolated, with neither Tangwena kinship ties nor visible wealth, their sad site bore witness to villagization's failure. Initially, I could not fathom why the chief and headman tolerated this sliver of state spatiality trumping their claims to sovereignty in Tangwena territory. But by letting the isolated village hang by a thread, they offered their subjects an object lesson in the evils of the lines.

Eastern Highlands Exceptionalism

In the 1990s, Kaerezi differed from other national resettlement schemes in three important respects. First, nationally, most resettled farmers moved into schemes in which they had no prior ties to place.[4] In contrast, many Kaerezians, claiming ancestral rights, had lived on Gaeresi Ranch prior to the liberation war (1966–79). Moreover, Chief Rekayi Tangwena and his fellow labor tenants defiantly fought evictions in the late 1960s and early 1970s, becoming nationalist symbols for anticolonial resistance to racialized land policies. Robert Mugabe's escape through Tangwena territory to Mozambique entangled local, national, and regional liberation struggles. Some Kaerezians considered local land rights a postcolonial reward for their wartime contributions to national liberation—enabling a president's escape and rallying with their rebel chief to defy racial land and labor laws. In newly independent Zimbabwe, Rekayi Tangwena became national senator as well as local sovereign. Kaerezi, in turn, became the only resettlement scheme with a salaried chief. Government also allowed six unsalaried headmen under the chief, all officially recognized as "traditional leaders" (*vatungamiri ve chinyakare*) with limited powers to mediate disputes but no legal authority to allocate land.

Second, unlike most schemes, Kaerezi was in Zimbabwe's most preferred agro-ecological zone—a high rainfall belt running along the mountainous Eastern Highlands. Average rainfall exceeded a thousand millimeters annually.[5] In 1989, only 11 percent of resettlement land nationally was located in this preferred Region 1 *highveld*, three-quarters of which contained private commercial farms.[6] Third, Kaerezi shares a border with Nyanga National Park, a major international tourist attraction. The clear, roaring headwaters of the Kaerezi cascade from Mount Nyangani's north face, at 2,592 meters Zimbabwe's highest peak. The river's upper reaches flow between Dazi and Nyamutsapa, cascading over waterfalls, through silt-free pools tucked into bends, and over a rock bottom. "One of the best trout fishing rivers in all of Africa, superb," a white angler described to me the upper Kaerezi, a depiction echoed by state officials. In an area perceived to have high agricultural and tourist potential, debates over the most viable land use have been intense.

Kaerezians, officials, and Harare dwellers have all described the area's rugged landscape as remote and transport routes as potentially treacherous. Few vehicles ventured on the steep, rutted road Chidumbu traveled with Nyafaru's four-wheel-drive pickup. The rare larger truck and one rural bus traveled on the scheme's major dirt road, still under construction through 1991. The road entered Kaerezi from the north, a dusty ramble turning east from the paved road that ferried crops, tourists, and troops to northern Nyanga District. After crossing the bridge that spanned the Kaerezi River's slow-flowing, wide lower reaches, the grated road climbed a smooth stretch to Tsatse, passing close to the government-built cement house inhabited by Rekayi Tangwena's widow. Near her Tsatse home, the bus line ended and the road became rougher. During the early 1990s, the driver slept at a small school built a few years before, leaving near dawn for Nyanga and connecting routes to Mutare, Harare, and beyond. The road ascended again to Nyafaru before heading east toward the border, past Magadzire, where the acting chief lived, and then plunged south toward the lower-lying Communal Areas and tea plantations in Honde Valley. Vehicle traffic through Kaerezi was extremely rare, yet administrators invoked security to justify road construction and maintenance. A bulldozer, grater, and culvert crews appeared in what seemed the most inaccessible sites to connect the road to bus and security routes coming north from Mutasa District. With Mozambique National Resistance (MNR) raids making frequent incursions across the border, large army trucks could travel rapidly on the otherwise dormant route.

Common(er) Dilemmas

In the early 1990s, many Nyamutsapans located assertions of "suffering for territory," articulating cultural identities, spatial histories, and political claims. They grounded their opposition to state villagization policy in memories of defying colonial evictions on Gaeresi Ranch. In 1990, the Nyanga District Administrator (DA) explained across his office desk cluttered with piles of paperwork, "Tangwena people epitomized symbolic resistance to the colonial government. At independence, it was almost impossible for government not to support the chief. Tangwena was a 'special case.' Our problem has always been defining just how special." He struggled with the quandary of how postcolonial administrators would govern those whose rights relied on a history of resisting rule. The DA worried that chiefly sovereignty and settlers' autonomy would erode both state authority and the local landscape: "If people are practicing settlement, agriculture, and grazing that degrades the soil, should they be allowed?" The Tangwena people, he underscored, "believe that they should have the freedom to choose their settlement patterns and land use practices." Government struggled with how to rule this freedom.

For years, officials had tried unsuccessfully to persuade smallholders in Tangwena territory of villagization's development advantages. In 1991, the frustrated DA changed strategy, threatening to evict Nyamutsapans whose location left them the most vulnerable. They lived inside Tangwena territory but outside the lines in the scheme's 1986 annex. This detail enabled the DA to distinguish two territories administratively, differentiating policy in Kaerezi Main and Kaerezi Extension. On May 20, 1991, he wrote to ninety Nyamutsapa residents. Stenciled in Shona and bearing an official government stamp, the letters delivered an ultimatum to "Residents of Kaerezi Extension Resettlement Scheme":

> You know that the land you were given was bought by the government in order for you to help yourself and to farm, thus improving your life. From the day you were given this stand in 1986, you have shown that you have not used it. This is not the government's intention. So you are being notified that on June 30, 1991, your name will be crossed out from the book of resettlement stands, and the land will be allocated to those with problems getting land.

The letters' recipients were understandably shaken. In late May, MaiHurudza, a mother of five in her late twenties, echoed her neighbors' concerns: "The way we are settled now, we can be chased away at anytime." By "giving" Nyamutsapans land, the letters stated, government acted on residents' actions, enabling settlers to "improve" their lives. By subjecting themselves to resettlement, farmers' own agency would help enable progress, development, and welfare. How did villagization become a crucial battle line in governing spaces? In turn, what kinds of subjects did these struggles produce?

Since the scheme's inception, Kaerezians living in Tangwena territory had demanded notable exceptions to national resettlement policy. By claiming allegiance to traditional authorities, they wanted official recognition of their chief, rainmaker, and headmen, something not granted other schemes. While usual state policy required full-time residence for all resettlement farmers, Tangwena subjects invoked their militant defiance of colonial evictions in an earlier era of place to argue for both secure land tenure and the right to pursue migrant labor. Almost all of the ninety people who received letters identified themselves ethnically as Tangwena. Many vividly recalled Rhodesian evictions and flight to Mozambique during the war. Their triumphant return at independence, Tangwena smallholders asserted, grounded identities and rights in a chiefdom rather than a resettlement scheme. The DA's letters incited fierce debate about which relations of subjection, sovereignty, and rights would prevail in Tangwena territory.

The day after the DA's threatening letters hit Nyamutsapa, I went looking for the area's headman, Mweya. He had left at sunrise to walk twelve kilometers to the chief's homestead near the Mozambican border. I knew that in the past, such visits signaled seismic shifts in local politics. A few days after returning from the chief's home, Mweya called a meeting in Nyamutsapa. He wanted to collect all the letters and return them to the DA, signifying a unified resistance to villagization. But people voiced mixed concerns at the meeting, some openly opposing the plan.

Roughly thirty Nyamutsapans gathered on a ridgeline overlooking the river valley, anxiously debating their options. Simba, a member of Headman Mweya's lineage, was an influential elder. Arrested by Rhodesians for "aiding terrorists" in the wake of Rekayi and Mugabe's escape to Mozambique, his imprisonment coupled chiefdom and nation—he suffered for both territories. Sitting in the tall grass, Simba reminded his assembled neighbors, "We can be chased away from here. We don't have any other place to go." Angrily he confronted his lineage mate Mweya: "I am moving to my allocated stand because the government told me to. If you do not like it, complain to the DA (*mudzviti*) and get him to write a letter for me to see." Fearing eviction, Simba invoked state power to challenge "traditional" authority. He subjected self and headman to government, supporting a regime of truth written through official letters. Render your power and knowledge visible, he challenged the headman, rather than hiding behind popular discontent. The stakes were high if the state trumped headman; commoners would pay the price in evictions. When I later pushed Simba on his position, he clearly opposed the lines. His move at the meeting had been a tactic to avoid eviction. Kinship and his past political persecution converged to enable not only the voicing of his challenge but also its effectiveness.

The meeting ended without resolution, constituting a standoff between supporters of the headman's proposal and Simba's challenge. Mweya said he would summon the chief to a future meeting, pushing politics up the food chain so that a bigger fish could buttress his authority. Siding with the government against the headman, however, also raised risks. If the DA did not uphold his threat, commoners occupying state-allocated stands risked the wrath of local leaders. SaGumbo, the father of the family with whom I lived, termed this predicament one of living between a rock and a hard place. Nyamutsapans understandably felt increasingly constrained in their room for political maneuver.

Remapping Militarized Spaces

Along Mozambique's border, officials marshaled military arguments for villagization by citing security concerns. Between 1989 and 1991, they attributed more than five hundred civilian deaths nationally to cross-border armed incursions by members of the MNR, although how many attacks stemmed from rogue bandits seemed difficult to discern.[7] In the wake of major raids, officials in 1989 launched a special villagization program that targeted border areas. They argued that strategically placed troops could better protect concentrated settlements. In two years, officials pegged a reported 19,000 "demarcated stands" nationally, 17,000 of which were located in Manicaland Province.[8] Yet by June 1990, Kaerezi's scheme administrator reported to the DA that "the recent plan to use the prevailing security situation in an attempt to establish the villages for better protection has proved to be effectively dead."[9]

Attacks by the MNR, many argued, followed kinship or political networks across the border; reprisals and the settling of old scores produced collateral damage. As one Kaerezian put it, "If Mozambicans are here, the MNR will come to hack you to death." The DA's response to such threats was to have police screen around 150 Mozambican families in 1988, moving them to a refugee camp across the district. By 1990, scheme staff knew of about 40 Mozambican families illegally living in Kaerezi. Zimbabwean citizens who during the war lived as refugees in Mozambique sympathized with the plight of noncitizens. Such legal Kaerezi residents expressed their deep ambivalence, wanting to offer refugees safe haven yet feeling that Mozambicans in their midst attracted MNR attacks. Arguing for their own families' safety, most Kaerezians endorsed the state policy of containing refugees in camps, while lamenting the camps' living conditions.

Many Kaerezians opposed state arguments for villagization, however, fearing that the death toll would rise in concentrated settlements. Some already slept in forests and bush for weeks or months at a stretch, leaving their scattered homesteads empty for fear of attacks by night. As one headman put it, "If we reside together, we will be killed together"; it was a position echoed by many. Some Kaerezians also invoked bitter wartime memories of so-called Protected Villages (PVs) established from 1973 onward. Rhodesian authorities had herded families into crowded compounds cordoned off by razor wire and patrolled by armed sentries. Rhodesian security forces had engineered this spatial technology to cut guerrillas off from food supplies and other support enabled by scattered rural settlements.

Dwellers of such villages had to travel to their distant fields, some as far as ten kilometers from fenced compounds called "the keeps." Curfews meant that those leaving at dawn and returning at sundown had to sandwich agricultural labor between long hours of walking. Such memories fueled Kaerezians' contemporary critiques of resettlement. Officials in several ministries publicly discussed how charged opposition to PVs produced formidable administrative obstacles to villagization.[10] During the war, colonial ranch evictions in Kaerezi left no villagers to protect. While most Kaerezians did not directly experience wartime PVs, memories and perceptions of another district's spatial assemblage of unfreedoms gained traction in Kaerezi. Accounts of PVs were recalled by relatives, friends, and a few migrants, especially those from the neighboring Mutasa District's Honde Valley, where the keeps were widely implemented.[11]

In contrast, Kaerezians had vivid personal memories of MNR attacks from the late 1980s. Across generations, education, and class, most residents called presumptive MNR marauders *Matsanga*. Differing etymologies for the term are telling. A savvy Nyafaru schoolteacher knew the farm near Mutare at which the Rhodesian Central Intelligence Organization first trained MNR counterinsurgents culled from defectors of FRELIMO, Samora Machel's Mozambican nationalist liberation army. The teacher rattled off dates, names, and events, tracing the cross-border traffic linking anticolonial struggles and counterinsurgency campaigns in two nation-states. He knew that André Matsangaissa escaped from FRELIMO captivity to Rhodesia in 1978—becoming the leader, with the Smith regime's backing, of MNR. For good measure, the teacher threw in Soviet regional support of anticolonial movements advocating socialism to explain the past political moment. Raids in Kaerezi during the early 1990s, for him, were the legacies of cold war politics interwoven with revolutionary armies and colonial strategies to undermine guerrilla movements. Whether bandits plundering for profit or armed forces allied with a political movement, Kaerezi's aggressors, he claimed, derived their name from MNR's first political leader Matsangaissa.

The teacher's less formally educated elders told me that *Matsanga* were "people of the reeds" (from *tsanga*, reed; *ma*, a formative marking plural persons). Living like beasts, these brutal bandits were placed beyond sites of human dwelling. Stealing and killing, *Matsanga* lived away from spaces of sociality—deep in the bush, rooted in reeds. *Matsanga* became woven into the fabric of place—so much so that a neighbor's child born during the era of intense raids received that name. For weeks, siblings screaming "*Matsanga*" to call the infant scared the hell out of me, literally causing me to jump. Neighbors who watched me go airborne laughed, humor emerging from the deadly serious violence spanning decades and nation-states.

A Hut of My Own

Shortly after my 1990 arrival in Kaerezi, a group of Nyafaru teachers generously shared their stone-walled and zinc-roofed quarters at Nyafaru Secondary School. Brian Gumbo, one of the teachers, and the headmaster helped me negotiate research permission from the chief. Brian, an eldest son, took me to visit his parents in Nyamutsapa, an hour's walk away. A growing friendship, our affinity as educators, my informal tutoring of his siblings, and my comfort with his family made the Gumbo home a welcoming abode. We approached Headman Mweya to seek permission for me to live in Nyamutsapa. Brian astutely anticipated the headman's desire to lure me to his own homestead, speculating that Mweya sought surveillance of a foreigner, personal financial gain, and increased stature among his neighbors by hosting a *murungu*, a white.

With Zen-like finesse, Brian steered complex negotiations toward a decision enabling me to live with his parents. He brought along an elder neighbor, a close ally of the headman and a strong supporter of education. For good measure, Brian and I carried a history book adorned with Chief Rekayi Tangwena's image—a fetish instantiating our shared educational interests. Mweya knew we had the permission of Rekayi's successor; his strongest option was to direct my place of residence, not to forbid it. Neighbors in Nyamutsapa were receptive to having a *murungu* in their midst. If he strongly objected, Mweya would have to buck both chief and populism. At the time, I did not catch all the nuances of Brian's ChiManyika dialect. But later we laughed at his insistence that my delicate white body would be healthier at the Gumbo's, whose spring was known to be especially clean. *Muchena* is at once a white person and a clean one. Brian punned to persuasive advantage, playing off my "racially" fragile constitution.

After weeks of pitching my tent near the boys' sleeping hut in the family compound, awakening deep in the night to cattle hoofs stomping inches from my head, I gladly accepted SaGumbo's offer to construct my own sleeping hut. We first leveled ground and dug drainage by hoe and steel rod. I then joined two teenage boys and a team of four oxen to chop down shin-sized wattle trees, dragging them back on a wooden sledge. In the 1930s, African labor tenants first planted wattle for the white ranch owner. The Australian import's straight poles yielded strong structures; its bark, when soaked in water and then twisted, securely bound lashings. We sank the poles into a perimeter trench, wrapping them with freshly harvested, thumb-sized saplings and lashing them together with bark. Using a hand ax, we doctored split logs, wedging them into gaps in the wall. Barefoot children marched in place in a deep pit, stomping straw into wet clay soil. Then three generations of women smeared two coats of mud from the pit on the wattle walls. Teenagers jumped in place, pogoing to pack the floor. Animated with laughter, flinging mud, and skillful craft, my hut began to feel like a home.

SaGumbo and I resumed our paired work, erecting a roof frame by lashing

SaGumbo constructing
a hut, Nyamutsapa, 1990.
Photo by the author.

green boughs to ten-foot poles. We jogged for kilometers behind his cattle sledge brimming with bales of thatching grass cut with a hand scythe. I lacked the skill to thatch, so I handed batches to SaGumbo who wove wet bark through bundles, layering and splicing to seal out the heavy rains. He capped the apex with four sharp, chopstick-sized slivers of wood whittled to sharp points. I asked Tewa, a cheerful man in his late sixties, why such sticks sat atop many huts. He explained that the sticks protected against evil, against those who might wish me harm by dispatching owls at night to drop tightly bound packets of ensorcelled "medicine" (*muti*) atop the roof. While witches (*varoyi*) were malevolent people who attacked victims by dispatching occult artifacts, wizards or sorcerers (*n'anga*) could also be healers or diviners, bending occult powers to good or evil. Tewa, like many Kaerezians, told me he was not sure witchcraft or sorcery would work on me because I was white. The sticks were a good protective measure in any event, he added with a chuckle; they prevented birds from perching on, shitting on, and thus rotting the thatch.

My hut emerged through emplaced labor, cultural meanings, and environmental resources. The conditions of possibility that enabled my living with the Gumbos included negotiations across many moments and spaces far from their home. The process of procuring permission to dwell and conduct research linked Harare ministries and officials, Nyanga's District Administrator, Kaerezi's chief, and Nyamutsapa's headman. Throughout, I was an active agent but far from self-sovereign in orchestrating my position spatially and politically. My race and class marked me as a privileged outsider and afforded me security amid Kaerezians' vulnerabilities due to ongoing agrarian conflicts. By living in a hut outside villagization's grids, however, my location placed me squarely inside the homestead of squatters. When the DA's 1991 letter arrived, it was not my choice but rather emergent events that positioned me on Nyamutsapa's frontline of threatened evictions. My subsequent ethnographic elaborations became deeply inflected by these fieldwork positionings, fomenting reflection on the politics of location, as well as on situated knowledge.

Pegging Land and Staking Claims

In 1987, state officials demarcated linear villages in Nyamutsapa while burning huts in Tsanga Valley, trucking the newly displaced to Dazi. Looking across the river, Nyamutsapans saw Dazi's orderly grids emerge in the wake of state force. The seventy families then living in Nyamutsapa offered little resistance to the actual pegging of residential and arable plots for each family. The resettlement officer relied on lists of settlers from the headman, thus incorporating traditional authority into land allocation. During demarcations, surveyors sited villages along rutted dirt tracks, euphemistically called roads, running through the scheme. Recalling the 1987 demarcations to me in 1990, the resettlement officer emphasized efforts to recognize settlers' existing fields:

> When we pegged in Nyamutsapa, first we saw where people were farming on the ground. If it was good arable land, we'd peg three hectares of it for the family. If there was excess land, we'd give it to another family, preferably a relative or a close friend. If there was less than three hectares, we'd give them an additional arable land adjacent to their arable. And if they were farming in an unacceptable area—for instance, along stream banks—we'd assign them three hectares in good arable land we would demarcate. . . . Most people had arables within the land we demarcated as arables, but the holdings were not equal. We equaled the portions, allocating three hectares per family.[12]

Historical patterns of landholding aided this egalitarian ethos. First, the availability of labor limited the amount of land cultivated by any household. In the cash-strapped local economy, hiring workers was a stretch for all but the most resource-endowed households. Second, Kaerezi's remoteness—its distance from tarred roads, the rugged route, and the lack of transport—made getting crops to market logistically difficult and expensive. Wealthier families that could hire trucks from town tended to invest in capital-intensive crops such as potatoes, which required lime and fertilizer, producing higher yields on a fixed land area. Hence class stratification did not translate into unequal landholdings as much as into wealth-accumulation strategies. Third, uneven terrain and steep slopes precluded mechanized tillage in many areas, serving as a further check against capital-intensive strategies to increase cultivable areas. Nyafaru's tractor was the only one for miles, rented out only rarely through private arrangement. And fourth, memories of colonial evictions and the lack of secure postcolonial tenure made residents wary of fixing capital in place. As threats of displacement lingered, the spatial mobility of cattle remained attractive as a more secure investment. Cattle herds, rather than landholding, tended to be a greater indication of relative wealth.

Some settlers whose holdings were reduced by the 1987 demarcations complained to administrators. In a few cases, changes in field boundaries rekindled dormant or ongoing disputes among neighbors. Yet most Nyamutsapans accepted the arable demarcations, landholders experiencing only minor modifications to their boundaries. For most, the state demarcation of each field was a de jure recognition of their de facto farming rights. Many residents saw state pegs as legitimating their already emplaced practices of livelihood.

The demarcated villages, however, represented displacement. Villagization separated residences from arable sites where farmers worked but were prohibited to dwell. Beyond the labor burden and inconvenience, farmers feared increased crop destruction from wildlife—a major concern on the border of a national park. As one headman put it, "We don't oppose the way they are allocating the fields, but only the residential stands." Nyamutsapa's empty grids and Dazi's crowded lines represented the antithesis of *kumusha*. This idiom—literally "at home"—conjured images of intermingled huts and fields, a hearth from which identity emerged. Kaerezians' invocation of *kumusha*, less a literal place of birth or a residential dwelling, mapped affect to place. By nurturing home places, Kaerezians harbored memories while cultivating sentiments of longing and belonging. Idioms of *kumusha* were not merely voiced but practiced on the landscape. Critics of

villagization chronicled the anti-social tendencies that crowded settlements ironically produced, insisting that spatial proximity fomented enmity, strife, and
witchcraft while exposing children to undesirable conduct and dangerous temp-
tations. Nor did the scheme plan include provisions for sacred sites used for
ancestral propitiation that encouraged spirits to protect families and territory.
The lines were empty, in part, because they left room only for huts, not homes.

Villagization policy also opposed how homesteads assembled livelihood practices. Historically, fields emanated from scattered clusters of huts. Families strategically utilized a range of niches, often maintaining several arable holdings in
areas with different soil types, rainfall levels, sun exposure, and slopes. By planting diverse crops on multiple sites, families managed the risk of poor harvests
across space and microecological conditions. Root crops planted in low-lying
vleis (bogs) and on steep ridges complemented the predominant mixture of
maize and beans planted at homesteads. The scheme plan recognized only one
field per family. Villagization separated discrete functions and spaces: arable,
residential, and grazing. In contrast, Kaerezians grazed cattle on maize stalks
after harvests, cultivated diverse crops spread across agro-ecological zones, and
placed huts amid fields to protect crops from wildlife and domestic herds.

Abundant springs and streams, an anomaly in a predominantly semi-arid
country, also encouraged dispersed settlements. The planned grids were far from
waterpoints, some used for generations and reliable during the 1992 drought, the
worst in living memory. Residents were understandably skeptical of state promises to dig boreholes in the lines. In 1992, I spoke with a former planner involved
with Kaerezi who criticized. government's technocratic application of lowveld
logic to the well-watered Eastern Highlands. "Settlers were mostly against the
linear settlements," the planner recalled, "and in a way they had my sympathy
because the chief attraction of the villages was water. There it's ridiculous. Almost
everybody had water at their homes. So promising them a borehole in a village
was just laughable." Nyamutsapa's one inhabited village demonstrated the danger
of unfulfilled government promises. Residents walked more than a half kilometer
to the nearest stream while no boreholes emerged at their parched homesteads.

Villagization oriented huts toward the scheme's dirt roads, ignoring environmental conditions. Residents often situated homesteads to protect huts from
prevailing winds. They faced thatched cook huts north to allow a sheltered
entrance during the cold rainy season. With no chimneys, open doors on huts'
leeward sides provided crucial ventilation as whipping winds drew smoke outside. By day I never noticed the pattern, but on dark nights, as I looked south

A *musha* (homestead) embedded within family fields, Nyamutsapa,
1991. *Photo by the author.*

toward the park, I spied fires that peaked through open doors dotting the valley.
To the north, hardly a single light was visible. Villagization ignored Kaerezians'
enlightened practice encouraged by weather.

As a spatial assemblage of power, the lines articulated history, geography, and
rule. By pegging plots, officials staked claims to govern practices by imbricating
people and resources. Their attempts to implement villagization sought to impose state spatiality. For many Kaerezians, such efforts evoked injustice. In 1990,
even before the DA's threatening letter, a Nyafaru schoolteacher declared, "Basically, resettlement is viewed as eviction." One headman voiced the opinion
of many when he said, "The government promised us that no one will move us.
But when Rekayi died, that's when the resettlement issue started." Two years
after Rekayi's 1984 death, the initial pegging of arable holdings went smoothly.
When officials began demarcating linear settlement grids, however, villagization
sharply territorialized opposition to resettlement.

In 1986, pegging began in the north of the scheme beyond Tangwena territory.
As soon as the demarcation team crossed the river into the chiefdom, they
encountered an angry delegation of Tangwena elders. The contingent threatened
locally hired workers, making them pull up the pegs they had just hammered
into the ground. By uprooting pegs, elders sought to protect people from the
same fate. Most living in Tangwena territory backed the elders' actions, defend-

ing scattered homesteads against the threat of imposed linear settlements. Residents claimed belonging in a Tangwena community they defined by having collectively "struggled together" against colonial evictions and during exile in Mozambique. Such practices of identity linked ethnicity to both locality and translocal displacement, to shared historical experience as well as spatial politics. Agency, rather than essence, asserted an emplaced ethnic entitlement.

Meeting the Chief Halfway

While elsewhere some Zimbabweans used *gavhumende* for "government," Kaerezians used *hurumende*—possibly derived from a related Nguni rendering of the English term.[13] They had no separate word for "state" in either Shona or their ChiManyika dialect, but this did not mute minute debates over practices of rule. "Inasmuch as it is a plural space of interaction and enunciation," Jean-François Bayart envisioned the state, "even subordinate groups shape its contours. The State buzzes with . . . the murmur of social practices."[14] Shifting analytical attention to the practices that produce and rework state power also entails recognizing assemblages of government. If the state is not assumed to be a metaphysical structure, it loses its sovereign status as a unitary, undifferentiated subject that acts on a population. Competing agendas pursued by state actors are not always orchestrated. That abstraction analysts term the state is a discursive effect of power relations, rather than a fixed objective structure determining dynamics of power.[15] Amid popular practices, sedimented patterns of rule prevail. Yet neither representatives of government nor of the state can seal off a self-proclaimed unitary sovereign from popular knowledge of differentiated, and at times contradictory, projects.

"I don't think the government is saying 'get into *maline*,'" SaNyamubaya told me, taking a long swig of tea in front of his Kaerezi Main cook hut. Strong and sinewy in his sixties, he lived a short walk from Rekayi's home in Tsatse. While only Nyamutsapa's residents received the DA's letter, SaNyamubaya worried about its ripple effects throughout Tangwena territory. He accused Marumahoko, the resettlement officer, of "promoting his ministry by forcing people into *maline*." He went on to differentiate the postcolonial state: "Marumahoko's ministry is going to the government, saying the Tangwena people want *maline*, and they are coming to us, saying that the government is telling us to get into *maline*." Rather than adhere to the pronouncements of a low-level civil servant and his politically weak ministry, SaNyamubaya argued, "the government" should tell Marumahoko's ministry "that you have to follow the people's will." His populist rhetoric aligned government and people over and against ministry and civil servant. A smart sovereign, he implied, should articulate the people's will and the art of government, enlisting subjects in the project of their own rule.

Less than two weeks before the DA's deadline and a week after Headman Mweya's failed attempt to mount a collective refusal, Chief Magwendere and a few of his councillors addressed a gathering of sixty people—two thirds of them men. The meeting's location had political implications. Nyamutsapa lay on the chiefdom's western border; the chief lived on the eastern edge near Mozambique. He traveled ten kilometers to the meeting, figuratively and literally meeting Nyamutsapans halfway. In turn, Nyamutsapans walked into the chiefdom's heartland. Lines of sight were also important. Most meeting places in Nyamutsapa afforded clear views of Dazi's linear grids across the river; deeper in Tangwena territory, Dazi was obscured behind ridges. Located at the intersection of a dirt road and a prominent track, the site was a transit point—a place of passing rather than dwelling, movement rather than habitation. The meeting's location ensured that the spatial referent of disputed practices would necessarily be elsewhere, out of site but under scrutiny.

Headman Mweya opened the meeting with the customary clapping of cupped hands as a sign of respect. The syncopated rhythm had a distinctive localized cadence, one I only heard in Tangwena gatherings. "I have called the chief to settle the disagreement between myself and the people of Nyamutsapa," Mweya began formally. He then sat down, turning the floor over to the chief's delegation of four. One of the councillors berated government conduct: "The resettlement officer does not respect traditional leaders. He should have brought the letters to the *sabhuku* [headman] but the *sabhuku* got the letter last." The elder's icon of tradition, *sabhuku* literally means "custodian of the book." The title derives from headmen's role in colonial tax collection—the book at once the tax roll, the rural constituency, and an administrative area. By transgressing channels of protocol, the elder argued, a government official had demonstrated disrespect to traditional authorities (*vatungamire ve chinyakare*), notably the chief and his headmen. Kaerezians across generations frequently invoked respect (*kukudza*) to critique unwanted government *imposition*. By foregrounding respect, the elder rhetorically pushed political authority onto the grounds of culture (*tsika*). Ethical conduct yielded people who "have culture" (*vane tsika*), demonstrated by good manners. Coding government interventions as nasty and brutish, the coun-

Acting chief Magwendere addresses a meeting, Kaerezi Main, 1991.
On the right sit Headman Goora and the rainmaker Nyahuruwa.
Photo by the author.

cillor implied that administrators lacked culture, a crucial component of legitimate claims to rule.

Traditionalists and nationalists alike respected the former chief, Rekayi. In
contrast, many described his successor Magwendere as feeble and weak. A frail
man in his early seventies, Magwendere rose awkwardly and spoke without
introduction—transgressing the custom his councillor defended: "I want people
to raise their hands whether or not they want the lines." A tense silence followed
his ambivalent command—would raising a hand signal support or dissent? The
chief's oratorical antics were legendary. I once sat in a packed primary school
room as he stood before his subjects to address the DA and visiting dignitaries
including a member of parliament (MP). Inverting the formulaic ZANU-PF slogans, he shouted, "Forward with Oppression. Down with Cooperation." Pumping his fist up and then pointing it down, he added emphatic gesture to verbal
blunder. Such displays only increased perceptions, frequently voiced, of Magwendere's incompetence. Many shook their heads and said, "*haagoni kuita*"
(he is unable), a phrase mingling incompetence and impotence, inability with
inaction. The wording itself betrayed disrespect. A worthy elder, even if unable,
warranted the plural verb form (*havagoni*).[16]

Born in 1919, Magwendere in the 1940s worked for the army, but lived most of his life a day's walk south of Kaerezi in the Honde Valley's Mandeya area. He moved to Tangwena territory around 1986, two years after Rekayi's death and when state officials began processing the paperwork for his appointment as acting chief. Five years later, he remained an acting chief not formally installed as Rekayi's permanent successor. By explicitly linking his rule to the anticolonial hero who refused resettlement in Tangwena territory, Magwendere would gain popular legitimacy. Before the meeting, a schoolteacher overheard the chief bragging that he would "win the war against the lines." Magwendere boasted that he would force those supporting villagization to stand publicly, subjecting them to community and chiefly scrutiny. The meeting's location in Kaerezi Main meant that most attending lived beyond Nyamutsapa. Most assembled resented the governing grids; yet only Nyamutsapans were threatened by eviction. Administrative practices disciplined subjects and space differently in Kaerezi Extension from those in the main scheme. Residents of the latter could critique the lines from a position of relative security, remaining insulated from potentially torched huts. The chief knew this. In his premeeting boast, he promised to seize on the gathering's precise location, positioning any Nyamutsapans who obeyed government as opponents of the chief and the majority of his followers. By demanding that individuals stand, he further exposed them to community pressure.

Magwendere's maneuver had a regal precedent. In 1984, prominent nationalist leaders joined civil servants to clarify resettlement policy amid hundreds assembled in Tsatse near Rekayi's home. The teacher who overheard Magwendere's 1991 boast recalled that previous Tsatse meeting: "Rekayi stood up to introduce visitors and topics and then said, 'People have come to talk about resettlement. Before they talk,' Rekayi said, 'those who are interested in resettlement should move there'—he pointed to a spot on the ground—and no one stirred. 'And those who are not interested in resettlement should go there.'" The schoolteacher now pointed to an imaginary spot. "Before he finished his words, almost all the people jumped to the spot where he pointed."

SaGumbo witnessed that wily 1984 maneuver. As Rekayi's loyal follower and friend, he distanced Magwendere's rule from the nationalist hero. When linear settlements were first pegged in Nyamutsapa in 1986, SaGumbo's family was among a few that built huts in them. During state evictions from Tsanga Valley, police had torched the huts of several of his friends. Anticipating escalating force against those defying government, he adhered to villagization. He stopped construction, however, when summoned to Magwendere's court. There he was fined five dollars for defying the chiefly order to "refuse the lines" (*kuramba maline*). Magwendere's edict still echoed, but the ruins of SaGumbo's unfinished mud-and-wattle hut remained visible on the landscape—an artifact of his challenge to chiefly authority.

Responding to the chief's call for a show of hands, SaGumbo acknowledged authority while implicitly challenging it: "Chief, you are our leader. So we follow what you want. Speak first, then the people will say what they think later." His deference had a tactical edge—to force a public position and then work on that terrain to stake a claim. The chief, neither a persuasive orator nor politically savvy, might play his hand ineptly. At a previous meeting, Headman Mweya had demanded that his fellow Nyamutsapans give him their letters. An elder pointed out that all had received the same letter, "so his letter can represent anyone. *Sabhuku* said, 'I do not want to do that.' " The implied critique targeted cowardice and ineffective representation.

Many worried that the headman and chief might not have the mettle to defy evictions. These leaders appeared overzealous in muting public debate and manufacturing consent to a unified position. Guiding conduct by counterthreatening, Magwendere and his minions acted on his subjects' actions. If administrators complained, he could hide behind the popular opinion that his threats fomented as much as echoed. All the while he asserted sovereignty—claiming to control land, Kaerezi's most crucial resource. In turn, headmen—officially barred from allocating land—could yoke their authority to his. Mweya, who had received the DA's threatening letter, was himself a possible target of eviction. He had much at stake in the lines of authority.

After the debate, the meeting's tide turned when one of the eldest headmen—prominent for contesting colonial evictions and actively aiding Mugabe's escape—supported Magwendere. The acting chief seized the opportunity, launching into a monologue claiming state support for his own rule:

> I told you long ago I do not want *maline* in my chiefdom [*mu nyika yangu*]. The member of parliament came with his wife and took me to Harare where I spoke with Mugabe, and he said all the powers are in the hands of the chiefs now. I asked him about this resettlement issue. He said: "We bought that area [*nzvimbo*] for you, Tangwena. You should do whatever you want with your people." I told him I do not want *maline* in my area. When we went to Nyanga . . . the DA said: "Everything in the Tangwena area is under you, Chief Tangwena." . . . So anyone who I see getting into *maline*, I will chase that person from this area because I was given that right by the government.

The chief's claims wove a contradictory tapestry of postcolonial authority. Government, from the chief's perspective, gave him purchased property where he would rule subjects on sovereign territory. But whose sovereignty reigned supreme—that of chief or that of government? The new chief was no national hero. During colonial skirmishes on Gaeresi Ranch, Kaerezians underscored, Magwendere had lived outside Tangwena territory and had struggled for neither chiefdom nor nation-state. By locating the source of his authority in government recognition, Magwendere undermined traditional claims to chiefly rule (*kutonga*) as a rightful inheritance (*nhaka*). Unwittingly, he reminded those assembled that, unlike Rekayi, he had not earned his right to rule.

After a short pause, Mujuru, an elder Nyamutsapa man, spoke passionately. Many recalled him on the frontlines of ranch conflicts in the 1970s. "We will be beaten like dogs," Mujuru warned, "if state threats become actualities." Local dogs, kept as hunting animals and for crop protection, were routinely subjected to brutal beatings. Many also remembered when, during colonial evictions, Rhodesian police set German shepherds on Tangwena squatters. Citing the approaching deadline mentioned in the DA's threatening letter, Mujuru gestured toward the chief: "So what will we do if we are chased away? We will have nowhere to stay. But at your side," he swept his arm toward Mozambique and the chief's home, "you will be living well." He contrasted commoners' vulnerability with Magwendere's security, while reminding the audience that the Acting Chief did not live among his Nyamutsapa subjects. Mujuru mapped the threat of state violence to differentially located spaces, persons, and power relations. His message was clear—politically naive chiefly bravado would render subjects, not sovereign, vulnerable to state force and displacement.

Marketing Morality

Before the chief could respond, Headman Goora, who lived near Mozambique's border, interrupted. Many believed that his homestead's proximity to the chief and their close political ties made him the master behind the feeble chief's puppet strings. He scolded the crowd: "You people in Nyamutsapa, you have troubled us for a long time. What kind of people are you? You do not know **development**. Your job is to be given dry fish [*matemba*], and then you will get into lines. We in this territory [*nyika*], we do not want lines. I want to snuff the issue out while it is in this area [*nzvimbo*]. Listen to us. Do not get into lines." Goora outed a key opposition, constructing an "us," the Tangwena people—

against a "them," you Nyamutsapans who trouble us. Significantly, his desire to contain villagization voiced a fear of spatial contagion. Caught in the cross fire, Nyamutsapans were told that if they submitted to the lines, they were selling out chiefdom and community.

Matemba, small dried fish, were store-bought commodities often arriving with visiting relatives or migrant workers returning on holidays.[17] These products from elsewhere, cheap and common, were bribes of a mere pittance. As icons of increased market dependency, *matemba* condensed in their commodity form threats to subsistence agriculture's relative self-sufficiency. Planners and administrators recommended that Kaerezians increase acreage planted with crops for market while diminishing acreage for subsistence cultivation. Subsistence crops represented a crucial hedge against hyperinflation and volatile markets influenced by distant, invisible, and unintelligible forces. Widespread perception of state failures to provide development in the form of transport, promised infrastructure, and marketing assistance added fuel to fire. *Matemba* and *maline* represented the increased subjection of Tangwena people to disciplines of market and state, both seen as arriving from an outside.

From this perspective, the marketplace of bribes commoditized political loyalty and allegiance. During Zimbabwe's liberation war, guerrillas brutally punished sellouts (*vatengesi*), perceived as informants to the state security apparatus, as traitors to nationalist liberation. A Kaerezi man once explained his reluctance to accept drought relief and other forms of assistance: "People think that accepting 'help' [*rubatsiro*] from the government sells out territory [*kutengesa nyika*]." The semantic stretch of *nyika*—country, territory, land, nation, and chiefdom—moved across scale and sovereignty. Sellouts capitulated to powers deemed to emanate from a spatial site far removed from Kaerezi, thus mortgaging chiefly territory for nation-state.

In a move of oratorical jujitsu at the meeting, Mujuru seized Headman Goora's idiom of Nyamutsapa as a distinct place that troubled chiefly rule: "In this area [Nyamutsapa], we did not know that we had a chief because he has never come here for a meeting to talk with his people. So now he has come. We want to see what he will do." Locating Magwendere as spatially and socially removed from his subjects, Mujuru implied that the sovereign's physical absence from Nyamutsapa weakened his reign there. The chief responded feebly to the shifting terrain: "You must give me your letters to prove definitively that we are united together in not wanting *maline*." A headman echoed Magwendere by airing critiques of the scheme's on-site administrator. Another elder recalled that the first resettlement officer "failed to put the Tangwena people into lines." Kaerezi's first administrator had initially visited for short stretches while based in another resettlement scheme more than eighty kilometers away. After moving to Kaerezi in the early 1980s, his caravan was looted, and he fled. One of his colleagues told me that the inexperienced official "was absolutely, completely powerless" to implement policy in the homeland of a national senator shortly after independence. Another recalled the first administrator showing up at the district offices "like a boy who had peed in his pants."

In 1986, Marumahoko, Kaerezi's second resettlement officer, inherited this legacy along with widespread opposition to villagization. When we first met in early 1990, the MNR's armed incursions had displaced him from the scheme's Rural Service Center—a compound housing a cement clinic, storage sheds, a one-room administrative office, and staff quarters—near Mozambique and north of Tangwena territory. He moved away from the border to a teacher's house at Dazi School, still under state construction. His wife and family lived in Nyanga Township in a modest home that came with his job. Friendly and welcoming, he prepared tea on a single-burner kerosene stove—a lonely beacon in a bare cement house. This vegetarian anthropologist gratefully ate stiff maize porridge that night, passing on the kind offer of tinned beef. Beyond a few pots and plates, a folding card table held a pile of neatly stacked files. Folded blankets sat atop a small, thin mattress on the cold floor. Marumahoko, an embodiment of government in Kaerezi, was displaced, humble, and tired from walking due to the shortage of petrol and an inadequate budget. Well aware of Tangwena opposition to villagization, he later showed me his 1989 research report written for a state course that earned him a certificate in rural development. Villagization, he wrote, "reminds people of compounds or Protected Villages during the war" and many see it as a "revision or revival of colonialist settler practices that involved grouping people into demarcated areas." One line hit hard: "Basically, people hate resettlement implementors." On the frontlines of administration, he regularly encountered open hostility.

Eight months later, I waited near Magwendere's home along the Mozambique border with a small group summoned the week before by Marumahoko who dispatched messages carried by schoolchildren returning home. He could reach all of Tangwena territory by dropping letters at the three state primary schools in Tsatse, Nyafaru, and Magadzire. I walked the ten kilometers west from Nyamutsapa with a few neighbors. When we arrived, a few dozen women and men sat apart on a grassy knoll, gendering the space. Marumahoko pulled up in his truck, personally greeted many by name, and smiled warmly as he shook hands. Before he could explain the meeting's purpose—to discuss a plan to establish trout ponds in the scheme—the acting chief interrupted: "*Maline* same, same *na*Smith." It was the most English I ever heard Magwendere utter, and it echoed what Marumahoko had officially chronicled for years. Villagization represented the colonial legacy of Ian Smith's racist regime.

Despite this mantra, Marumahoko often advocated a rural populism promoting what he understood as postcolonial freedoms. He had lobbied for Nyamutsapa's state purchase in 1987, defending squatters' rights to ancestral territory on what was then white property. In our many conversations and his administrative reports, he blamed "traditional authorities"—the chief and headmen—for "intimidating" those commoners who wanted to occupy the government grids that promoted development desires. In a 1990 official update to the DA, he welcomed "new ideas" from "higher offices" and advocated a "take-it-or-leave-it approach" that would "go a long way in enabling some people who are interested in the rural housing program to benefit."[18] Officials should demarcate concentrated settlements but not force people into them. For Marumahoko, government would provide the conditions of possibility for farmers to cultivate common freedoms in places of their choosing, guiding and enabling their actions while protecting them from traditional despots—Magwendere and his headmen.

Back at the June 1991 meeting in the wake of the DA's letters, the chief's councillor—who attacked Marumahoko's political legitimacy—egged on Magwendere: "The chief has said: 'I have more power than the resettlement officer [RSO].' He will go to Nyanga and talk to the District Administrator. The headman is also more powerful than the RSO. We in this area do not want to be ruled [*kutonga*] by an outsider [*mutorwa*]." The chief seized his councillor's argument: "I am more powerful [*kusimba*] than the RSO, so I will go to Nyanga and talk to the DA. Give me your letters." He pledged to conquer (*kukunda*) Marumahoko by seeking support from the DA. The old colonial trick of divide and rule could also be used to target postcolonial government. Long after the meeting, several reflected on Magwendere's salary as a civil servant, arguing that accepting wages placed him "under" government. Was he shooting his own security umbrella? If he so strongly objected to villagization, a few opined, perhaps he could protest by renouncing his state salary.

Stakes and Axes

"We do not want *maline*," said Gonzo, a man in his late sixties wearing cracked glasses who stood to address the crowd as Magwendere sat back down in the grass. A skilled hunter, Gonzo had grown up on Gaeresi Ranch—joining the multiracial cooperative Nyafaru in the 1960s where he still herded livestock, informally exchanging labor for land rights at a homestead just beyond the ridge marking Nyamutsapa's eastern border. In 1975, Gonzo and his wife Angela had smuggled food to evicted ranch squatters hiding in nearby mountains and had sheltered Mugabe at Nyafaru. In the immediate wake of independence, Rekayi helped Gonzo secure one of the few family parcels allowed on Nyafaru—all farmed by cooperative shareholders. Political contingencies produced conditional rights: a fire destroyed documents, and squabbles at the cooperative rendered his already legally uncertain land claims more unsettled. With his ally Rekayi dead and a severe limp in one leg, would Gonzo be turned off Nyafaru property if he could no longer work? This convergence of events encouraged Gonzo to secure the land rights allocated him in Nyamutsapa by government. Angela already cultivated maize in the field assigned to them by the resettlement officer, commuting from their Nyafaru homestead. Gonzo needed a stable foothold for farming and dwelling. He opposed the lines but might be compelled against his wishes to occupy them.

Magwendere's ruling decree undermined Gonzo's room to maneuver. Worse still, subjects suffered from chiefly bravado while the acting chief enjoyed a relatively secure homestead far from Nyamutsapa's battle zone. Gonzo stood, glaring at Magwendere across the seated assembly, publicly opposing *maline* while angrily demanding accountability. "The chief has definitely promised us he will solve this problem before that deadline. If, however, that day arrives and the government evicts us, we will come to your home, our chief." He pointed a small ax, frequently carried by adult men, at Magwendere. He then addressed his chief directly, "If at that point you don't give us somewhere to live, we can chop each other to pieces."

Gonzo's ax to grind recalled past challenges to chiefly authority. Origin stories for the chiefdom contained enlivened accounts of Rekayi's ancestor arriving from Barwe territory in what is now Mozambique to vanquish a rival rainmaker ruling Kaerezi. Tales of a dramatic struggle, with Tangwena axing the rainmaker, bound together violent conquest, sovereignty, and territory. Generations later, a few families allegedly spent the war hidden in forests on the outskirts of Tangwena territory near Mozambique. Shortly after independence, this group angrily confronted Rekayi. Simba, a lineage brother to both Gonzo and Headman Mweya, informed me that Rekayi "told his people they should not run away during the war but he fled to Mozambique. . . . He was almost axed by them because he lied. But he was forgiven after begging for their pardon." Many assembled in 1991 knew that commoners had called to account the chiefly rule of a popular nationalist hero. Against a less worthy adversary, Gonzo fired his closing salvo: "Let's give these letters to the chief. If we are asked, we will say the chief took the letters from us."

Spurred on by this direct confrontation, Peter, a younger man, pushed the point: "For us to see that the chief is more powerful than the government, the chief should remove the pegs himself and pile them together; then we will take them to the resettlement officer." Rather than a political gesture, Peter demanded a materially grounded demonstration of situated sovereignty. State practice inscribed the lines, marked by rusted pegs. To defend territory, Magwendere should uproot that spatial order. Many believed that removing the stakes, hidden beneath tall grass in dormant "villages," was a punishable crime. Peter effectively called Magwendere to enact his ruling claims on the landscape, exposing sovereign rather than subaltern subjects to state reprisals. "You," the chief pointed a bony finger at his young challenger, "don't behave as if you are the leader of the people here. I can chase [*kudzinga*] you from this area. How long have you lived here?" Mweya intervened, answering "three years" in an attempt to pass off the dissident as a recent immigrant. "You are lying," the young man shot back. "I was born in this area." While Mweya condensed time, Peter stretched place. Born in what became Nyanga National Park, Peter had moved to Nyamutsapa with his family in 1982. When Magwendere moved to Tangwena territory in 1986, Peter already lived in the chiefdom.

Before the side dispute escalated, Headman Goora closed the meeting by demanding the letters from the Nyamutsapans assembled. Reluctantly they agreed, most claiming to have "forgotten" their documents at home. A chief's councillor made vague plans to collect them, but his proposal's lack of specificity opened the possibility of future foot-dragging. Mujuru, still concerned about the rapidly approaching deadline, delivered a defiant challenge to the chief: "If you come late with an answer, you'll see huts erected in those lines." As Kaerezians dispersed from the meeting to their scattered homes, sovereignties of state and chief, as well as the governmental resettlement grids, remained radically unsettled.

Sticks and Carrots

You need both the carrot and the stick. With the Tangwena, it has only been the carrot and the carrot. When you don't have the stick, nothing happens.
—DA MANDISODZA, November 1991

A week after the DA's deadline for Nyamutsapans to occupy the lines came and went, over a hundred people gathered at Tsatse primary school. The spot was almost within sight of Rekayi's homestead where, two decades before, Rhodesian police had burned squatters' huts. Independence had not erected a secure fire-guard. As recently as a few months before, state-sanctioned flames engulfed squatters' homes in Bende Forest. A man in his fifties complained to me bitterly: "This government is made of matches."

Like dry tinder, Tsatse's meeting crackled with tension. The DA arrived in a Toyota Land Cruiser, armed police escorting him in their Nissan truck. I conspicuously avoided exchanging small talk with civil servants and sat in the grass next to Simba whose political antennae I trusted. Visiting officials sat on chairs outside the school. The political commissar, a district representative for the nationalist party, and the police joined DA Mandisodza, resettlement officer Marumahoko, and Kaerezi's field orderly. Next to them sat Elijah Nyahuruwa, ZANU-PF district chairman and rainmaker. Then came acting chief Magwendere and his headman Goora. A few male elders sat on chairs completing the semi-circle. Women, who made up a third of the crowd of more than a hundred, sat on the ground off to one side. Goora, attired in a long overcoat and green tie, outdressed the younger visitors casually attired in leisure suits, jeans, and the latest Harare fashions. He opened the meeting by ritually clapping his hands in a gesture of thanks and respect, *kuombera*. Segueing from wordless tradition to shouted nationalist political slogans, he threw his fist in the air: "Forward with unity!" Then he pumped his arm toward the ground: "Down with oppression!" The audience repeated his words while pumping their fists.

While Goora often referred to villagization as a "lie," that day he urged the gathering to "work together with government." He introduced the political commissar who passed the baton to the resettlement officer who, in turn, asked the chief to talk. Nyahuruwa interrupted sharply: "The one who wrote those letters should speak to us, not the chief." Seated between visitors and chief, his spatial position belied a social and political one. He knew the commissar through nationalist party circles and, unlike the sober chief, occasionally drank beer with civil servants and party members during visits to town. Like his migrant labor experiences in Bulawayo in the 1950s that drew him to nationalist politics, his township forays forged relations that gained political traction in his rainmaking territory.

Implicitly acknowledging Nyahuruwa's authority, the DA stood, respectfully greeted the audience, and queried why no one had replied to his letter. He had come, he insisted, to clarify Kaerezi Extension's status:

The main reason we bought Nyamutsapa and Dazi was for those who had been evicted from Tsanga Valley when it was wanted for wheat farming. That area was not bought to say "it belongs to the Tangwena people," but rather to resettle people. Tangwena has no authority to allocate land to people living in these two areas, but he can rule [*kutonga*] the people at his will. It was mostly eighty-three families that it was purchased for who were to resettle there but, at the time of purchase, there were other people living there. They were also affected by the pegging exercise. Dazi and Nyamutsapa has a law that governs it as **Lot Z, areas A and B.** There were so many people there that while we wanted to give 5 hectares to each family, we saw that there was not enough land for that. So we decided to give 3.5 hectares to each family, accommodating two hundred families, including those already living there. If we had evicted those living there, a war would have erupted [*paimuka hondo*]. If a person is not occupying his or her [residential] stand, it demonstrates that he or she does not want it, so we will give it to someone else. Long ago, Ngurunda was not under Tangwena. But when it was purchased for resettlement, it was given to Tangwena.

Constructing a governable space, the DA carved out a discrete administrative area from the complex histories of shifting legal land categories. All assembled knew that Ngurunda, the main scheme's northern extreme, lay in the land of Chief Saunyama, widely perceived as a feeble colonial sellout. The government "gift" of a portion of his territory accorded with an understanding of Kaerezi as a political reward for Tangwena contributions to national liberation. For the DA, purchase, not historical claims, secured property rights. Law, not liberation, defined ownership; in turn, the rule of law enabled administration. Secure land rights, he implied, are only awarded to those who subject themselves to government on state property. Distinguishing Kaerezi Main and its annex, he targeted administratively distinct disciplines ensnaring subjects and space. State resettlement efforts emerged from land hunger and populist politics, in this idiom, at once gifting and governing national citizens.

The DA supported Magwendere's previous boast to Nyamutsapans that "the government gave me the power to rule," but he also limited it. The chief could rule (*kutonga*) people in Nyamutsapa, but he could not allocate fields (*kugova minda*). Postcolonial government distributed rights: the chief's authority to rule and commoners' access to land. Yet by grounding several sovereignties in legal land ownership, the DA deployed a colonial discourse. On Gaeresi Ranch, white rule had converted conquest into racialized property rights through the enforceable fiction of legal ownership. The DA stood on the dangerous ground of dispossession, his pronouncement perceived more as coercion than as seeking consent, more as threatened force rather than governing persuasion. Would separate state purchases of private property, legal designations predicated on sediments of white conquest, trump claims that Nyamutsapa was an inalienable portion of the Tangwena chiefdom?

Magwendere rose to provide his own charter, entangling his rule in Rekayi's reign:

> I lived in Mandeya and Rekayi came and told me that he and his people had won the area. I came here to inherit Rekayi's chieftainship. When Mugabe came . . . he told Rekayi that nobody should disturb his people. He repeated this at Heroes' Acre again. I don't want *maline* installed in my territory [*nyika*]. We want development [*budiriro*] not *maline*. The DA should bring more agricultural demonstrators who will teach people about good farming—and tarred roads should be constructed, and some buses so that people are able to transport their things.

Thunderous applause erupted from the crowd. Defending his own sovereignty, Magwendere effectively invoked Rekayi's nationalist legacy as an anticolonial chief. The temporal trick also switched spatialities of power, locating the DA under President Mugabe. Magwendere reminded those assembled in Tsatse of Rekayi's televised funeral at Harare's Heroes' Acre, adding an allure of sacredness to Mugabe's pledge to recognize Tangwena chiefly sovereignty. Surprising many in the audience, Magwendere appealed to two camps: those proud that Rekayi lay in a place of national honor; and Kaerezians who objected to the nation-state's claiming their sovereign's body and spirit who argued unsuccessfully in 1984 for Rekayi's burial in the Tangwena royal graveyard.

By foregrounding distinct moments, events, and places, Magwendere reminded subjects, administrators, and visiting politicians of his chiefdom's complex articulation in politics at once national and nationalist. For good measure, he marked villagization's grids as an unwanted imposition. Government, he demanded, should orchestrate development, assembling a package of appropriate infrastructure, capital, and expertise to enable farmers to improve themselves. The frustrated ZANU-PF commissar explained that all parties could arrange a future meeting to resolve the dispute since the chief claimed the president had given him the power to rule Tangwena territory.

As applause faded, Headman Goora leapt from his chair, advancing the chief's argument. He, too, had attended the presidential meeting to which the chief alluded. Supporting two sovereigns, he opposed oppressive state administration:

"Mugabe said there should be **development** in Tangwena's territory [*munyika yaTangwena*] because we were oppressed by whites. . . . We forced the people who pegged to remove their pegs because they were putting people into *maline* instead of development [*budiriro*]. Nyamutsapa belongs [*ngeya*] to Tangwena." The path to development meant opposing the lines of resettlement. Rather than rejecting state power in Kaerezi, the headman sought to shape the kinds of discipline government should provide for the welfare of its citizens. He welcomed productive rather than repressive power.

By demanding development from the state, Goota complemented rather than contradicted the Tangwena refusal of resettlement. The state's failure to provide for the welfare of its population weakened its legitimacy. For the headman, Mugabe's recognition of racialized dispossession supported chiefly rule and populist freedoms, trumping private property and resettlement policy. Governing projects should provide development on terms that respected rights claimed through cultural politics not reducible to deeds and documents. Yet did a Tangwena sense of belonging specify chiefly name or a collective identity? Did Nyamutsapa belong to a chief or a people? In turn, localized land rights, paradoxically, pivoted on an apex of government linked to meetings held in Harare. What underling would dare publicly challenge Mugabe's word?

Even the commissar's body language exposed his shock. He awkwardly attempted to steer the meeting toward a close, but Chidumbu, arrested in 1976 during a Rhodesian raid on Nyafaru, stood to complain about the letters threatening evictions in Nyamutsapa. He voiced the fears of many assembled: "The letters told us that if we do not get into our residential stands we will be chased away. Politicians come, saying that we should not be forced [*kumanikidzwa*] to do what we do not want. We are now confused about what to follow because there are too many preachers." Knowing laughter mingled with humorless gazes focused on visiting officials. Without responding to the call for clarity, the commissar closed the meeting with a plea for people to "cooperate" and "unite" (*kubatana*) with representatives of "government" (*hurumende*), including the DA. He hoped hostilities could be harnessed to fight "a war for development" (*hondo yebudiriro*). "The people" were free to voice their desires. In turn, "members of the cabinet should plan what they are told by the people." In his rhetoric, party pronouncement emerged from populist will. Citizens subjected themselves to government because it represented their interests. By working together, he implied, they enabled government to work through their actions, rather than opposing them, thus securing their own welfare.

The resettlement officer's monthly report concluded on a less upbeat note. It complained that "allocations seem to be static due to illegal allocation by traditional leadership who encourage squatting." Marumahoko wrote that "the people interested in villagisation were demoralized by what transpired" at the meeting. He noted that residents from the main scheme rather than Kaerezi Extension comprised the crowd's vast majority, lamenting the "ululation and applause" in response to the "chief designate" who "strongly objected" to villagization. That vocal support "showed that the traditional leadership was still running the show regarding the opposition." He wrote a lengthy letter to his provincial superiors in Mutare to explain constraints to resettlement policy's implementation.

A week after the Tsatse meeting, I encountered the frustrated DA in his district office. The Tangwena always complain of government attempts to "divide and rule," he chided sarcastically. He voiced exasperation, angrily chronicling wasted time and petrol burned to attend countless Kaerezi meetings. They always met and made a decision before he arrived, he complained. How could he govern when stonewalled by stubborn refusal? Raising his voice, mixing Shona and English, his anger invoked the headman who opened the recent meeting: "You arrive and Goora stands up and says, '*hatidi*' [we don't want it]. Then someone says 'meeting *yapera*' [is over]. And it's over." As I recall the meeting, the chief said "*hatidi*" and Goora proclaimed "meeting *yapera*." Yet the DA's frustrated target remained: a Tangwena refusal to subject themselves freely to government.

2 · Disciplining Development

Legacies of Land and Liberty

Land resettlement represents a crucial terrain for grounding the populist promises of anticolonial liberation. Discursively and materially, government acts to promote the welfare of its citizens, placing them in spaces designed to discipline their social relations and settlement, as well as their agricultural and economic productivity. Planning and administration's technical expertise target the improvement of population by orchestrating arrangements among subjects and space. Crucial to postcolonial agrarian politics are governing claims to redistribute land *racially dispossessed* by colonial rule.

Two forms of freedom fuse in resettlement rhetoric: national liberation from the shackles of colonial injustice joins peasant demand for land. Self-rule and family farming shape this agrarian landscape, yoking together the cultivation of new subjects and new fields. For Frantz Fanon, emancipation from colonialism required the wretched of the earth to articulate a new national culture emerging from the "fight for the liberation of the nation, that material keystone which makes the building of a culture possible."[1] In *Toward the African Revolution*, he mapped terrain where the colonized would cultivate their humanity on fields of freedom: "The logical end of this will to struggle is the total liberation of the national territory."[2] Land in postcolonial Zimbabwe remains a privileged material and symbolic terrain for the formation of national culture and state rule, a critical hinge for the hyphen joining nation and state.

Historically, dispossession has been formative to freedom struggles. Gramsci suggested that both colonies and European metropole witnessed the pillaging of property belonging to "wretched subjects." Popular struggles "raise to the level of a national religion the cult of those who died for the homeland."[3] Gramsci insisted that the complexity of "political struggle" could be compared to "colonial wars." Armies maneuver on conquered territory, but the "struggle continues on the terrain of politics."[4] In 1994, the Zapatistas revived relations between land and liberty in Chiapas, Mexico, articulating twinned southern questions to foment agrarian politics in the global South.[5] Contemporary discourses of globalization, celebrating the frenzied speed of capital and communication, squeeze land out of their reflections on space-time compression. While territorial assertions did not solely dominate the Zapatista agenda, insurgent demands included land rights among populist grievances: the earth's wretched suffered novel dispossessions, new forms of enclosure wrought by neoliberalism and NAFTA.[6] Zapatista leader Subcommandante Marcos's 1996 communiqué from the Lacandon jungle translated Emiliano Zapata's Nahuatl, penned in a prior revolutionary moment, into a new Mexican era: "We must continue to struggle and not rest until the land is our own, the property of the people, of our grandfathers, taken from us by those who crush the land with their stone step, . . . with the strength of our heart and our hand held high, we raise, to be seen by all, that beautiful banner of the dignity and freedom of we who work the land."[7]

Marcos's resurrection of Zapata's rallying cry interwove images of soil and self, cultivated together in the project of individual and national liberation. Metropolitan theory's cosmopolitan sensibilities frequently forget that postcolonial predicaments of rule remain entangled in agrarian landscapes of dispossession. Marx suggested that it was only in "an enchanted, perverted, topsy-turvy world, in which Monsieur le Capital and Madame la Terre do their ghost-walking," and thus bourgeois ideology confused the "personification of things and conversion of production relations into entities." Insisting on "land" as both critical milieu and socially produced space grounding rural livelihoods, Marx appreciated its integral, earthly connection to liberty. Locating land within capitalism's "Trinity Formula," in a triad with capital and labor, he denaturalized histories of dispossession that mapped class privilege to private property.[8] In this vision, property and land are not reifications, but rather the congealed products of social relations of production, power, and exclusion. Property rights become politicized not as sacred principles of Lockean liberalism, but rather as instruments of class reproduction, social inequality, and human injustice. In Zimbabwe, race, rights, and rule became entangled in political technologies targeting land and labor. My analysis of this assemblage, I hope, might critically rework Marx's holy trinity where his gendered couplet of capital wedded to land is anointed through social relations of production. As future chapters elaborate, gendered patterns of migrant labor in southern Africa complemented dispossession of land rights that relied on distinct politics of race and class.

The stubborn refusal of land struggles to recede may speak back to the West, outing the brute force and violent exclusions woven into liberalism's own origin stories of law, property, and free markets. Attending to agrarian questions in the global South may also aid in the project of displacing a settled sense of universal history.[9] The European transition from feudalism to capitalism has often been uncritically exported, serving as a template for measuring third world histories against a universal yardstick of progress, modernity, and capitalist development. To further provincialize Europe, I *ground* land politics in alternative understandings of territories, as well as of histories.

Zimbabwe's National(ist) Resettlement Policy

> Our freedom struggle always recognised the question of land as the principal grievance.—ROBERT MUGABE, "Heroes' Day Speech," 1989

Zimbabwe's national resettlement program emerged at independence after a protracted guerrilla war. Peasants found common cause with nationalists during a liberation struggle rallying to recover the "lost lands" seized by colonial conquest.[10] Forcible dispossession mapped distinct racial identities to the national landscape, segregating space, rights, and cultural practices. In 1894, four years after Cecil Rhodes's Pioneer Column of white settlers trekked from the south into current-day Zimbabwe, they created the first Native Reserves. They relegated more Africans to reserves after defeating the first Chimurenga, widespread uprisings in 1896–97. An order-in-council established Southern Rhodesia as a British protectorate, reducing the British South Africa Company's authority. The colony's legislative powers were further consolidated in the 1923 constitution. In 1953, Southern Rhodesia joined a short-lived federation with Northern Rhodesia (Zambia) and Nyasaland (Malawi). After it disbanded, Ian Smith's Rhodesian Front party announced a Unilateral Declaration of Independence (UDI) in 1965. A protracted guerrilla war and negotiations among black nationalists, white Rhodesians, and international diplomats preceded the 1979 transitional government of Zimbabwe-Rhodesia. The following year, independent Zimbabwe emerged from national elections and with a new constitution.

In the fresh wake of conquest, white "pioneers" who had fought against African freedom received land holdings from the British South Africa Company. Whites claimed not only vast estates, much more acreage than they could cultivate, but also the most agriculturally productive land in the highest rainfall regions. These "conquest lands," as many note, were alienated without "any regard whatsoever for existing African rights."[11] In 1944, the Native Affairs Department defended colonial usurpation's civilizing impulse: "We are in this country because we represent a higher civilization, because we are better men. It is our only excuse for having taken the land."[12] Conquest *racialized* rights to rule and to land.

Rhodesia's sharply skewed dual agricultural economy emerged from the seeds of racialized dispossession, producing spatially separate populations, territories, and rights. Large-scale European commercial farmers benefited from protective legislation, while small-scale African peasants produced on the poor soils of overcrowded labor reserves in the lowveld.[13] In 1901, when Zimbabwe's total population was just over 700,000, African Reserves made up 8.4 million hectares, while whites had set aside 32 million hectares for European purchase.[14] The 1910 Native Affairs Committee of Inquiry recommended the removal of Africans from isolated patches, what would later be termed "black spots" in apartheid South Africa, to larger, consolidated reserves. They received formal legislative backing with a 1920 order-in-council. After 1923, when a self-governing colony's new constitution formally replaced British South Africa Company rule, legal instruments elaborated further protections for racially segregated land.

The 1930 Land Apportionment Act came to be what Machingaidze termed white settlers' "*Magna Carta*," a bedrock of colonial policy.[15] In this formula, "unassigned" land composed 20 percent of the country, "African" areas 30 percent, and "European" areas 50 percent. The act designated 11.6 million hectares for African Reserves, declaring 19.7 million hectares "European" areas, where Africans could only reside under labor tenancy agreements with white owners. Africans who dwelled on these expropriated lands were legally bound to further alienation through labor expropriation. Few could afford to buy land in an extremely small Native Purchase Area, designed as a reservoir to reward the black bourgeoisie and so-called Master Farmers. By 1955, land legislation declared 20 million hectares "European" for a population of 250,000 whites. In contrast, more than 2 million Africans lived on less than 16.2 million hectares of "Native" Reserves,[16] administered indirectly through "traditional" authorities, chiefs and headmen. The 1969 Land Tenure Act permanently protected almost 45 million acres for "European" property while entrenching racially segregated divisions of land "for all time."[17] Apartheid-like policies further supported aggressive evictions of Africans who unlawfully occupied these zones legislated to be racially European.

Rhodesia's Ministry of Agriculture initially conceived of a resettlement program during the late 1970s. Its defining features emerged, however, from the 1979 Lancaster House agreement, when Britain brought black nationalists and Ian Smith's stalwarts to the negotiating table. Smith's 1965 UDI had eclipsed aspirations for African majority rule, provoking international ostracism and sanctions.[18] Abel Muzorewa signed the 1978 Internal Settlement, engineered by Smith's Rhodesian Front party, and became prime minister of the short-lived Zimbabwe-Rhodesia. The settlement reserved white seats in parliament, requiring their vote to amend any provisions in a constitution protecting property rights, the establishment of security forces, and the judiciary. Britain recognized the Internal Settlement. Shortly after Margaret Thatcher's 1979 election, she announced the lifting of sanctions.[19]

But rival Zimbabwean politicians split. While in 1971 Muzorewa led a coalitional umbrella of allied African nationalists, in 1977 his United African National Council (UANC) was seen by many as a party of colonial collaboration. Joshua Nkomo, leader of the Zimbabwe African People's Union (ZAPU) since its 1961 founding, called Muzorewa's signing "the biggest sell-out in the history of Africa."[20] Robert Mugabe and other members of the black elite had left ZAPU in 1963, challenging Nkomo's leadership and forming the competing Zimbabwean African Nationalist Union (ZANU) party. The Patriotic Front (PF) emerged in 1976 as a provisional alliance of ZAPU and ZANU, but remained a strained coalition. The separate parties would each annex the PF to their acronyms in the 1980 elections, but in the late 1970s the front represented a coalitional counterpoint to Smith's co-optation of Muzorewa and other alleged sellouts to African nationalism. In 1978, Mugabe headed ZANU and denounced the Internal Settlement in a speech to the Security Council of the United Nations. He spoke sharply of the "mass killings of our people by the racist Rhodesian regime," the "concentration camps" that constrained African freedoms, and the "genocidal proportions" of "the violence, terror, and brutality that we daily experience from the terroristic despotism that is 'Rhodesia.'"[21] Bombings after the settlement's announcement in 1978 and an escalation of the guerrilla war left Muzorewa with little popular support, increasing the legitimacy of Mugabe and Nkomo as nationalist leaders.

Mugabe's ZANU and Nkomo's ZAPU, the two major nationalist parties, controlled two guerrilla forces. Any binding peace required their collective consent.

The previous year, a ZANU policy statement had identified "land hunger" as "the inspiration of peasants who have rallied behind the movement," providing crucial support for the "freedom struggle."[22] Populist nationalist discourse pivoted on the return of "lost lands" to right a crucial racial injustice of conquest. At the British-brokered Lancaster House negotiations for a constitutional framework for independence, Mugabe rattled his rhetorical sword: "Land is the main reason we went to war: to regain what was taken 89 years ago. There are 6,000 farmers owning seven million black people's rights. Those 6,000 include absentee owners. . . . As good revolutionaries we have already liberated 50 percent of the country. Already 65 percent of the white farms are vacant. We have a right to pass that land on to the people. It is a life and death matter."[23]

Foreign interests also saw land as the lifeblood of a new nation entangled with empire, global geopolitics, and the alignments of African states. Populist appeals for nationalizing land ran into international pleas to protect private property. Amid the cold war, as Mugabe's ZANU party advocated Marxism-Leninism, Britain and the United States sought to counter potential Soviet influence in southern Africa.[24] Leaders of the frontline states, adversely affected by the protracted liberation struggle, also pressured nationalists to negotiate an end to Zimbabwe's guerrilla war. Marxist-Leninist socialism took a backseat to realpolitik and pragmatism.

The Lancaster House negotiations promised British aid to underwrite half of the costs of a resettlement program in return for Zimbabweans' guarantee to protect existing property rights. For the new nation's first decade, land transfers required the formula of "willing seller, willing buyer," precluding compulsory acquisition of land. Market mechanisms and the rule of law, two of liberalism's most hallowed "freedoms," underwrote Lancaster's land provisions. Yet both relied on histories of unfreedom: Colonial conquest converted land seizure from "unwilling" Africans into racialized property rights; laws and markets then secured these dispossessions.

I focus on ethnographic moments preceding Parliament's 1993 passage of the Land Acquisition Act that reversed Lancaster's protection of private property. After years of promises, in 1996 government acts began designating white farms for compulsory state purchase from "unwilling" sellers. In the wake of widespread state-supported land occupations in 2000, so called fast-track resettlement gained ground and ushered in an era of agrarian politics at once distinctly new and haunted by more than a hundred years of land struggles. The agrarian conflicts in the 1980s and 1990s that I analyze in more detail contributed condi-

tions of possibility to subsequent events but did not constitute historicist ante-
cedents that authored inevitable outcomes.

Bureaucratic Nightmares

Resettlement's rhetoric always exceeded its implementation. In 1980, the government proposed resettling 18,000 families nationally on 1.1 million hectares of land
over a three-year period, revising its target to 162,000 families in 1982. By 1989,
however, they had allocated resettlement land to only 54,000 families.[25] A decade
later, the figure was only slightly more than 70,000.[26] Before the explosive agrarian politics of the early 2000s, the vast bulk of land was acquired in the early half
of the 1980s, consisting mostly of farms abandoned by whites during the war and
by those who feared the new policies of a black nationalist government.[27] In 1991,
government plans conceived of an eventual resettlement sector of 8.3 million
hectares, roughly 21 percent of Zimbabwe's total land area, yet only 3.3 million
hectares had been officially "committed to resettlement."[28] In contrast, in 1988,
16.4 million hectares composed Communal Areas—formerly termed Native Reserves and, in turn, Tribal Trust Lands—while the large-scale commercial farm
sector, still almost exclusively white, made up 11.2 million hectares.[29]

In 1980, 6,000 white farmers had owned 42 percent of Zimbabwe's land. By the
end of 1989, less than 4,500 commercial farmers, almost exclusively white, owned
29 percent of the country.[30] By April 2003, an estimated 600 white farmers
remained while, since 2000, government had seized around 11 million hectares,
claiming to resettle 330,000 African households. Others estimated less than half
that number.[31] In the 1980s, the large-scale commercial sector accounted for
about two-thirds of total agricultural output nationally. The overcrowded Communal Areas—where African smallholders farmed—in turn, dwarfed resettlement schemes. Collective cooperatives envisioned near independence did not
proliferate, and the few that survived struggled. By 1991, Model A schemes, where
settlers received title to individual land holdings, comprised almost 80 percent of
all resettlement land and 90 percent of those settled.[32] Despite the resettlement
sector's relative insignificance in national economic production, population, and
geographical extent, it has remained politically potent. The 2000 occupation of
white farms and subsequent government acquisition of land from unwilling
white owners has ushered in yet another chapter in the unresolved legacy of
racialized dispossession.

Resettlement schemes, in particular, have tested administrative capacity and coordination, involving a staggering array of actors, ministries, and departments. In the first decade after independence, the Ministry of Lands identified and purchased commercial farms; the planning branch of Agricultural and Technical Extension (AGRITEX) within the Ministry of Agriculture developed a land use plan; and the Department of Rural Development (DERUDE), within the Ministry of Local Government, Rural and Urban Development, implemented the plan. Where schemes bordered national parks, yet another ministry, the Department of National Parks and Wildlife Management (DNPWLM) entered the fray. The Interministerial Committee on Resettlement met irregularly in the early 1990s, seeking to coordinate the agendas of separate ministries and branches.

During a 1992 interview, a senior AGRITEX official described the forum as rife with "conflicts over invading other ministries' territory." A 1990 World Bank evaluation echoed his opinion.[33] Not surprisingly, turf wars flourished. Staff at AGRITEX complained about a DNPWLM tendency to trump viable agricultural practices with policies that privileged environmental conservation. Speaking in the gleaming new DNPWLM headquarters, nestled in a former white suburb, a senior official described resettlement as a "bureaucratic nightmare." In a downtown Harare high-rise, a senior resettlement planner in DERUDE stressed interdepartmental and interministerial tensions with AGRITEX. The latter advocated "maximizing production," while DERUDE saw "resettlement as part and parcel of development," focusing on its social dimensions.

A walk across town, in AGRITEX's sparse, barracklike, fenced compound, a planner admitted that the branch's reliance on technical principles constituted a major weakness because "we aren't involved in settling the people. We plan in a vacuum. We plan and DERUDE implements. If there is any feedback on the planning, it doesn't get to us."[34] Another AGRITEX planner explained that the "target group" of resettlement farmers is usually not known to them, so they plan for a generic farmer whose arrival to the scheme will inaugurate a new regime of spatial discipline. "The essence of planning," he continued, "is to separate arable from nonarable land." With a BS in agriculture from the University of Zimbabwe, he echoed AGRITEX's emphasis on what he termed "principles": "We use air photos to identify potential arable land. That's the basis of the whole lot." Satellite imaging can also be consulted. In his planning space, calipers, air photos, and sketches lay on a long table. Maps from the surveyor general's office served as blueprints, grounding information inferred from air photos on templates with contour lines. Resource inventories catalogued the total hectarage of arable land

within the planner's scripted schemes. Using these tools, planners made agricultural production recommendations based on altitude, slope, soil type, and
rainfall.

As Bassett suggested, the "technical production of maps based on aerial photographs and satellite measurements reinforces the idea of cartographic truth—that
the objects being represented (bounded land parcels) are real and exist inde-
pendently of the mapmaker."[35] In Zimbabwe, planners' identification of residential, grazing, and arable parcels relied on a technical grid of intelligibility removed from practice on the ground. The land's "objective" qualities, they told
me, determined cropping, pastoralism, and settlement. Agro-ecological and economic criteria dictated the size of holdings and the number of livestock allowed
to not exceed the inherent "carrying capacity" of the land's "natural" properties.[36] Stripped of the historical traces of human practices, the landscape became
a site of undeveloped natural resources. Neither the scheme nor the abstract
resettlement farmers who would inhabit them were accorded a past; placeless
people would arrive to a space without history. Planning produced a regime of
truth, establishing the conditions of possibility for schemes of habitation and
cultivation. The plan became what Latour terms an "inscription device," an
assemblage of instruments, procedures, and practices that visually display representations of scientific truth.[37] The plan as fetish, seen as itself a powerful object
authorizing land use, performs three active erasures: the practices of planning
itself, the previous histories of place, and the past experiences settlers will bring
to the scheme.

The principles of land-use planning dictated the spatial and functional separation of three discrete zones for residence, farming, and grazing. From most
planners' perspectives, following these blueprints ensured the goals of "conservation" and "development," the improvement of sustainable agricultural productivity. Envisioning land use through air photos and maps rather than through
farmers' situated practices, plans performed what Haraway called the "god-trick
of seeing everything from nowhere," an unlocated claim to objective knowledge
that occludes issues of accountability, political position, and historical contextualization.[38] Technocrats and future farmers became normalized through
specific technologies of vision, optical devices, and their affiliated cultural practices that positioned observers as well as observed.[39]

In so doing, the discursive practices of planning assembled technologies and
techniques that constituted a specific "way of seeing" the landscape.[40] Devoid of
human habitation and the historical sedimentations of past practices of place,

these empty spaces were "seen" to have objective properties, not relational histo-ries.[41] Practices of government and political economy *produced* this spatial fetish-ism. Resettlement schemes represented what Lefebvre termed "abstract space," a historical product of capitalist social relations. Explicitly instrumental, a resettle-ment scheme became "manipulated by all kinds of 'authorities' of which it is the locus and milieu." In the process, "lived experience is crushed" and "affectivity" vanquished. In Lefebvre's vision, abstract space is at once "locus, medium and tool" of "technology, applied sciences, and knowledge bound to power."[42]

Attributing uses to the inherent features of the land itself, planners ventrilo-quized the laws of the land. Discursively, "the land" dictates the normative prac-tices to unfold on it. When spatial orders are "seen through the lens of function," Rosalyn Deutsche asserted, they appear to be "controlled by natural, mechanical, or organic laws." Space, "fetishized as a physical entity . . . appears to exercise control over the very people who produce and use it."[43] Principles, rather than the practices of planning, become the cornerstone of truth. Architects of colonial rule in Egypt, Mitchell suggested, "conjured up a neutral surface or volume called 'space'" in their efforts to "enframe" model villages as containers of objects and functions.[44] In this vision, plans reflect, rather than translate or construct, the verities of land use.

Planning, as a discursive practice and labor process, produced an articulated fetish, enunciating and joining space and plan, each conceived as authoring regimes to discipline subjects. Technical expertise, a commanding knowledge of principles, would secure truthful representation in the service of progress and development. Here is a crucial site of planners' agency, for many conceive them-selves as creating spaces whose categorical definition will discipline the practices within them. But whose practices produce these resettlement spaces? Planners, administrators, and farmers all inform the landscapes and their inhabitants.

What kinds of subjects are deemed worthy of resettlement? Near indepen-dence, an array of ministries envisioned schemes as fulfilling a social welfare function, providing land to the most destitute of the rural poor. Selection criteria favored the landless, jobless, and those most deprived of resources. By the mid 1980s, resettlement made provisions for more "experienced" farmers, including those who would give up their land rights in Communal Areas.[45] Shifting from a rhetoric of social welfare, a 1991 DERUDE circular emphasized "productivity." Settlers were still required to be landless and jobless, but "proven agricultural ability," formal education, and adequate draft power—in short, the economic and social capital deemed necessary for market-oriented agriculture—should be privileged. A point system, vaguely modeled on that used in Malaysia, was proposed. A Master Farmer certificate, evidence of attending agricultural training, earned twice the points of being landless. An AGRITEX assessment of "proven agricultural ability" outscored the needs of a landless family with five or more children.[46]

Claims to define authentic needs, as Nancy Fraser has underscored, constitute profound political stakes.[47] Official discourses of policy frequently elide political struggles over the interpretation of needs enabling government to shape not only the field of social interventions but also the kinds of subjects deemed worthy of receiving welfare. Nicholas Rose suggested that "government entails the construction of such technologies for acting upon persons, enrolling initially hostile or indifferent persons and forces in the pursuit of their objectives, enlisting previously oppositional elements . . . and turning them to one's own favor, building durable associations that will allow the exercise of rule."[48] A senior AGRITEX planner told me that "what people need, and they currently lack, is a disciplined approach to management." This *discipline*, he emphasized, was necessary because resettlement farmers "invariably want to grow maize, because they don't know anything else. I call this the mealie mentality." For this planner, prescheme experiences informed subjectivity, becoming constraints to overcome, bad habits to vanquish.

Some technocrats conceived farmers' mentalities, like the inherent properties of land, as part of their nature, not as historical products. I spoke with an AGRITEX field officer visiting Kaerezi to promote fruit cultivation about localized knowledge of agroforestry. Farmers described indigenous trees, which were leguminous, as "strengthening the soil" and "improving pasture." While admitting that such practices improved the soil by fixing nitrogen, the official suggested that "locals" were "too primitive" to understand agro-ecology. The discourse of primitivism ran deep in AGRITEX's furrows of planning and extension. I frequently heard reference to "backward" peasant agriculture. Both colonial and socialist discourses of development invoked evolutionary models of modernizing progress. In both, the difference of subjects' practices from a desired norm became evidence of an ideology or mentality that government could transform by encouraging or coercing conduct.

At DERUDE's Harare headquarters, I asked a planner if his department had a dominant philosophy. "I think, basically, we believe in technology," he answered. Yet rather than locating this technological faith outside of politics, he offered a historical account of its endurance. Just after independence, those who failed to consult peasants in any development project were "lambasted." Civil servants began postcolonial projects making good-faith efforts at participatory planning. A former DERUDE official explained: "But then peasants actually behaved towards them rather like they had behaved towards the previous government. I remember early on, some who had been guerrillas, totally, utterly perplexed at this." Nationalist liberators who became representatives of the postcolonial state found peasants opposing them. As a result, "they concluded that the peasant is backward, and that some people are poor, because—that's one of the arguments, that some people are poor, and you can do and say and help them as much as you like but they will always be—and that there isn't enough time to do the other kind of planning." Here, technocratic planning became a pragmatic necessity and an expedient instrument. At the same time, political opposition was coded as an irrational obstacle to developmental progress.

Following Foucault, Rose has reasoned that since the eighteenth century, the population has been the "terrain of government *par excellence*." The project of developing, improving, and managing the capacities of this population became a principal task of modern rule. New targets of rule emerged, as did new techniques for calculating improvements, regulating efficiencies through "explanatory schemes." Government, Rose asserted, "depends upon the production, circulation, organization, and authorization of truths that incarnate what is to be governed, which make it thinkable, calculable, and practicable."[49] An array of ministries, departments, and discursive practices produced resettlement's regime of truth. Calculating techniques placed the population in schemes of improvement. Yet on the ground, the gap between policy and practice left room for maneuver, among both farmers and administrators, the governed and those governing. In Manicaland, most provincial officials and scheme administrators were well aware of ministerial proposals moving toward what bureaucrats termed a Malaysian model. In the absence of a new binding directive, however, they continued to use criteria favoring landlessness and need rather than productivity. Planners and administrators both complained about the lack of clarity, yet acted as if an agreed template underwrote policy.

According to a senior planner at DERUDE, since 1986 resettlement relied on a legal fiction. When the department moved that year from the Ministry of Lands, Agriculture, and Rural Resettlement into the Ministry of Local Government and Rural Development, statutory instruments were not amended for issuing resettlement permits. Conditional permits, however, remained the legal pivot anchoring settlers to a spatialized bundle of rights to a residential plot, an arable field, and a grazing commons. Noting that the permits were "technically terminable at the will of the government," Roth and Bruce concluded that it "would be difficult to imagine a less secure form of tenure: uncertain duration, broad powers of termination on the part of the Ministry of Lands, Agriculture and Rural Resettlement, and few rights to compensation for investments."[50] Yet the senior DERUDE official admitted that while the permits "were planned to be rescinded and renewable, in practice few if any people have had permits withdrawn for any violation."

Legal ambiguity over the permits' formal status appeared an advantage rather than a liability for government. Most resettlement farmers had only an inkling of what the permits represented. Much as headmen had recorded names in a tax book, resettlement officers recorded settlers on the scheme's roll. Officials demarcated individual village plots and arable fields to farmers who became "settlers." Conditional rights, anchored in specific sites, required smallholders to subject themselves to a distinctive spatial discipline. Those who refused their proper place risked losing this bundled package of land rights: in effect, they faced eviction. Striking in postcolonial resettlement were the lines of colonial land-use planning, its imposed conditionalities, and assumptions about improvement, spatial order, and the disciplining of African agriculture.

Governed by Custom

Government launched centralization, the cornerstone of colonial land-use planning, in 1929. By 1944, nearly a third of the Native Reserves had been centralized.[51] The plan's architect was E. D. Alvord, an agriculturalist and missionary born in the United States who would become director of native agriculture from 1944 to 1950. Centralization relied on the physical and functional separation of three mutually exclusive land categories: residential, arable, and grazing. This triad became the holy trinity of colonial land-use planning. Centralized linear settlement grids, usually straddling dirt roads, divided common grazing land from farmers' individual fields. Trained agriculturalists allocated single, permanent plots for cultivation to married men, subsuming women's land rights under the assumed shared interest of an undifferentiated household. Alvord devised this technical spatial fix to curtail "shifting cultivation" and what he saw as the poor farming techniques that caused environmental degradation.

Alvord disdained African agriculture, attacking cultivators with missionary zeal. "Because of their poor farming methods," he lamented, "the lives of the great mass of our Rhodesian Natives are filled with poverty. They have worn-out lands, poverty-stricken cattle, poorly constructed huts and under-nourished, naked children."[52] Primitive practices produced a package of poverty, inscribing buildings, bodies, and beasts. Alvord never considered the destructive effects of land policies that crowded Africans in reserves, impacting social, political, and ecological relations. In this he echoed and anticipated colonial conservation discourse in Rhodesia and throughout much of sub-Saharan Africa.[53] For Alvord, African agriculture's inherent deficiencies threatened not only the reserves but the entire nation: "Their methods are wasteful, slovenly and unnecessarily ineffective, and, if continued, will be ruinous to the future interests of Rhodesia."[54] Echoing Alvord's sentiments in 1940, Inyanga's Native Commissioner argued that he would "compel" the African to submit to "technical assistance" if "through sloth and ignorance he fails" to preserve the land for future generations.[55] By 1941, the Natural Resource Act legislated compulsory stocking rates, mandated contour ridges, and gave greater legal backing to centralization's ambitions.[56]

Alvord decried the alterity of an African culture "governed primarily by custom, without thought for cause and effect."[57] Witchcraft and superstition rather than the soundness of science ruled African farming practices. Entitling his unpublished autobiography "The Gospel of the Plough, or a Guided Destiny?," Alvord sought to convert Africans to Christianity, thus cultivating crops and souls in the Lord's fields.[58] His religious zeal emulated the nineteenth-century "civilizing mission" preached and practiced elsewhere in southern Africa. Jean and John Comaroff have stressed the assemblage of practices, dispositions, and habits targeted for improvement by agrarian evangelists who envisioned European progress and African modernity through sedentarism, linear settlement and fields, and market orientation.[59] Subjection to orderly discipline would align the exteriority of landscape with the interiority of Christian selves. Drayton suggested that by the late eighteenth century, a European discourse of improvement traveled imperial circuits, providing global reach to an affinity of practices that earlier supported the English enclosures of the commons, as well as Irish and Amerindian dispossession. It "promised that people and things might be administered, in the cosmopolitan interest, by those who understood nature's laws."[60] What Drayton termed "Nature's Government" emerged through the capillaries of imperial rule, seeking to put colonial subjects in their proper place in nature and under a Christian god.

In Rhodesia, Alvord intercropped Christian faith, agriculture science, and a teleology of progress—defined primarily through economic industriousness and market orientation. Fields, however, would be monocropped in line with ten "rules of permanent cultivation" phrased in language resonant with the biblical Moses' receiving the Ten Commandments.[61] Burning bushes, however, was strictly prohibited. After a visit to the US Dustbowl in 1936, Alvord introduced contour ridging, which soon became compulsory.[62] He targeted details—the depth of contour ridges, the spacing of furrows—and recommended a package of practices. Alvord brought "Hickory King" hybrid maize from the United States, a higher-yielding variety than that introduced by the Portuguese two centuries before. His interventions helped establish maize as a staple food and cash crop and advocated the extensive cultivation of cotton and groundnuts for European markets. The gospel of the plough and the miracle of the market cut deep furrows in Rhodesia's agrarian political economy.

Lines of Control

In southern Africa's settler colonies, colonial administrators had long advocated concentrated linear settlements for the purposes of surveillance, control, and the collection of taxes and labor. Government officials first used Native Locations as a conscious administrative policy in Natal in the 1830s and 1840s.[63] They lauded the neatly planned spatial grids for disciplining African residence, market orientation, economic productivity, and cultural conduct within a European order. Locations were designed to be spatially separate from settler society yet integrally articulated to the political and economic imperatives of empire. An 1847 Location Commission report extolled the economic benefits of these regulated sociospatial arrangements, at once developing the capacities of the native population while opening them to global markets: "The native locations will become centres of industry and improvement, the whole of the native population in the district and gradually those beyond it, will become consumers of imported articles and producers of articles for export."[64] Productive African subjects would not only cultivate crops and modernizing selves in these sites but also commute to European areas to provide labor for white farms, mines, and urban industries. Keletso Atkins conceived Natal's Native Locations of the mid nineteenth century as a " 'gate of misery': by placing Africans in such overcrowded, uncomfortable conditions, land hunger and all of the suffering attending the shortage of that crucial resource would compel them to leave the locations to seek work."[65] The

Cape passed ordinances beginning in 1869, following Natal's Native Locations, designed to limit the number of "idle squatters" on white-owned land, and Zululand followed in 1897.[66] In each case, orderly spatial discipline targeted the improvement of racialized subjects and the productive powers of the population.

When a modified version of Alvord's centralization scheme was introduced to South Africa in 1936, its very name, "betterment," conjured images of progress, modernity, and development. Officials forcibly removed Africans from scattered homesteads, placing them in linear settlements spatially removed from arable and grazing zones. Individual tenure on a fixed parcel followed principles first widely applied in the 1894 Glen Grey Act, designed to curb shifting cultivation and sedentarize residence and agriculture. State policies enforcing terracing, ridging, and the construction of grass strips became widespread in colonial Africa, as did cattle culling and rotational cropping and grazing, thus making political interventions in daily livelihood practices.[67] Governmental regulation of rural spaces worked through such disciplining of the details of African agriculture.

Ranger stressed centralization's effect on redistributing land in Zimbabwe's reserves, equalizing holdings and thus influencing agrarian class relations by limiting accumulation through extensive farming. Chiefs and headmen greatly resented the challenges to their authority over land allocation. Much more so than previous policies, the mapping of individual title to a fixed parcel intervened directly in lineage-based practices of land distribution and access.[68] Targeting the point of production and a critical node of rural power, centralization's spatial discipline unsettled Africans in several senses. In his 1943 annual report, the Inyanga District Native Commissioner singled out agricultural improvement as an area of administrative concern: "The Native will not change his slipshod tillage methods except under compulsion and control."[69]

Enforcing Acts, Rising Resentment

The 1951 Native Land Husbandry Act (NLHA) extended agrarian control by requiring Africans to contribute compulsory labor to conservation works. The same year, the Natural Resources Board warned of "heading for disaster," invoking an impending crisis fueled by the Malthusian mix of overpopulation and resource degradation.[70] To counter this dangerous duet, the NLHA would "revolutionize African agriculture" across 21 million acres in the reserves.[71] Boosters ambitiously predicted a 50 percent increase in African crop output within five years. Alvord's holy trinity remained central. Individual farming rights, pegged to a single permanent plot, would be conditional on following recommended farming practices.[72] The act explicitly linked security of tenure to "good farming," seeking to govern agrarian livelihoods through a rigid, orderly spatial discipline.

The NLHA would also produce workers in distant cities. A *dual spatial fix* sought to tie peasants to rural reserves while requiring urban wageworkers to live in townships. Excluded from subsistence production in the reserves, workers would become wholly dependent on wage labor. Officials voiced concerns for securing urban labor and providing housing for married workers. "Good" factory workers, like their corollaries in the fields, needed a milieu oriented toward their productivity.

In reserves, as with centralization, the NLHA allocated fixed parcels to patriarchs. Women's access to land would remain entirely dependent on their relationship to husbands, fathers, and male kinsmen. Fields would be finite, equal in size, and monitored for adhering to the act's provisions. These precisely demarcated rural spaces both required and produced particular kinds of laboring subjects, affixing land rights to a precise site. This arrangement of bodies in space also targeted the details of agricultural practice—furrowing, contour ridging, plowing along regulated lines. The labor demands of digging contours, sometimes under police surveillance, produced bitter resentment.[73] Threats to white land development officers and black agricultural demonstrators were widespread throughout the country.[74]

To surmount opposition, implementors of the NLHA sought to include traditional authorities in demarcation and allocation exercises. The plan's success, they reasoned, required manufacturing the consent of rural leaders.[75] When the act was first introduced in Inyanga District, the Native Commissioner reported the cooperation of chiefs and headmen who procured African labor "free of charge" for a "soil conservation gang."[76] While in 1951 requests for labor were "met with a ready response," a decade later "political agitators" had stirred up "considerable hostility towards the Land Husbandry Act and the agricultural field staff."[77] Complaining that traditional leaders had been "negative during the disturbances" of 1961, the Inyanga official objected to their "sitting on the fence," waiting for authorities to intervene.[78]

Faced with ungovernable subjects, administrators feared that the NLHA would become midwife to rising nationalist opposition. In 1960, when the act was to have been fully implemented, only 60 percent of the reserves were under some of its provisions, while individual tenure operated on only a third of African lands.[79]

The laws of racialized land segregation, not those of nature, produced over-crowding and environmental degradation in the reserves, while white farms remained vastly underutilized. Continuous cultivation of fixed fields depleted nutrients formerly sustained through fallowing and shifting arable sites. Concentrated settlements also degraded resources.[80] Projects of government literally eroded the conditions of possibility for agricultural improvement.

The erosion of state authority also raised serious challenges. In 1962, the Rhodesian regime suspended the NLHA amid mounting African resistance to its provisions. Migrant wage labor powered the colonial political economy, long linking urban and rural spaces. Africans straddled footholds in smallholder agriculture and urban jobs. The translocal circuits of wage labor migration became the channels irrigating nationalist politics. Grievances against the NLHA emerged from the *articulation* of urban and rural routes, the relational spaces produced through migrant labor. The NLHA's dual spatial fix would need to displace routes as well as roots, unsettling translocal links as well as rural homesteads.

Administrators conceived of the reserves as isolated sites distant from the anticolonial nationalist politics they associated with cities, towns, and wage laborers. In this vision, "infiltrators" and "agitators" brought political opposition from the city to the country, a spatial contagion that punctured the presumed quiescence of a rural idyll. In 1948, the Inyanga Native Commissioner reported no interest among natives "in the political situation" and "no feeling of unrest." Four years later, he attributed this political docility to Inyanga's peripheral location: "Natives show little interest in what is going on outside their kraal life; no doubt the district lies too far away from the towns to allow of infiltration of political awareness."[81] By the mid-1950s, an administrator complained of "the half baked city dwelling intelligentsia" who were at "loggerheads" with one of the district's chiefs. He contrasted the political consciousness of a number of "locals working in Salisbury" with the "apathetic and uninterested" masses in the reserves.[82] An official geography of dissent located unrest in urban sites. Like Rhodesian images of state power, political opposition threatened to spill from urban centers to the peripheral reserves.

In Bulawayo, the Southern Rhodesia African National Congress (SRANC) emerged in 1957, members electing Joshua Nkomo as its first president. Its founding manifesto called for "the fullest freedom for the use of land by competent people regardless of race."[83] Banned in 1959 by the prime minister's declaration of a state of emergency to thwart political mobilization deemed dangerous, the National Democratic Party (NDP) quickly emerged in 1960 as a successor. Nkomo eventually became president, and Robert Mugabe also held a prominent office. When the NDP was banned yet again in 1961, in nationalists regrouped as ZAPU. Nkomo took a ZAPU executive council to Tanzania in early 1963 with plans to establish a government in exile from where he hoped to negotiate with British diplomats. He returned later that year, denounced by fellow nationalists. Mugabe, Edward Tekere, and others at odds with Nkomo formed the rival ZANU in 1963, splitting anticolonial opposition into two major parties. Rhodesian authorities banned both ZANU and ZAPU in 1964, sending insurgents both underground and overland. Despite legislation against formal nationalist parties, anticolonial opposition spread through the countryside.[84]

In 1958, the year after the SRANC's founding, officials investigated allegations that its "agents" were active in Inyanga District, attempting to organize meetings.[85] Inyanga's administrator reported in 1961 that African nationalists "caused considerable trouble by inciting lawlessness and civil disobedience." So-called detribalized workers—disarticulated from the social networks and political loyalties of the reserves—threatened rural communities ruled by custom and traditional authority. "The unrest was stirred by young louts from the towns, the Kraalheads and the majority of the older rural Africans embarrassed by events, but silence[d] by intimidation."[86] In this vision, unrest arrived from the outside to rural communities, carried by younger urban workers whose spatial transgressions the NLHA failed to fix.

In many reserves, Africans flagrantly disregarded the allocations and prohibitions of the NLHA. Administrators complained of "freedom ploughing" by those who cut across the act's contours.[87] The year of its repeal in 1962, the Chief Native Commissioner summed up the politicization of government attempts to orchestrate "conservation" and "development": "From the very outset nationalistic organization have made the Act one of their foremost targets, and have done all in their power to bring it into disrepute."[88] In myriad ways, the NLHA represented increased interventions in African agriculture, disciplining the details of livelihoods in regulated zones. It colonized the micropractices of subjects already incarcerated in territories of conquest. Popular resistance fomented anticolonial sentiments as peasants and nationalists articulated grievances against the NLHA's imposition to the wider racialized injustices of colonial rule. When I asked a Nyamutsapan woman in 1991 which current government policies were most reminiscent of her childhood in the 1960s, she did not hesitate: "*Maline* and burning huts, like they did in Bende, remind me of the policies of *mabhunu*," the Boers. With Bende's displaced then huddling in squalor beneath canvas tents that billowed when buses from Nyanga Township barreled past, her pairing of *maline* and *mabhunu* traveled a familiar route to postcolonial Kaerezi.

Postcolonial Planning Hits the Ground

Planners, administrators, and farmers all recognized the lines of continuity between colonial land-use policies and resettlement's villagization grids. In 1981, AGRITEX's ancestor, the Planning Branch of the Department of Conservation and Extension (CONEX) proposed a Model A scheme for 296 families who would farm individual plots in Kaerezi. At year's end, estimating 140 families living in the scheme, they revised their vision, proposing a Model B collective cooperative.[89] At the time, socialist agriculture still occupied the national resettlement agenda, collective production seen to be moving the nation forward in history, away from the shackles of colonial capitalism. By 1985, Kaerezi's architects returned to their drawing tables. They replanned a hybrid scheme, mixing Model A and B, individual and collective holdings. By 1991, the cooperative was a desolate site. A broken-down tractor sat underneath a rusted roof without walls, a few lonely sacks of fertilizer lay in the small storage shed, and the parched field looked unattended, surrounded by a fence sorely in need of repair. Fencing materials evaporated at night, appearing kilometers away on farmers' individual fields. The cooperative had dwindled to twenty-eight official members. All had individual holdings, and few visited the collective field with any regularity.

Bureaucrats and nationalist politicians initially intended Kaerezi's cooperative to mimic landscapes cultivated by Tangwena war refugees in Mozambique's liberated zones controlled by FRELIMO forces. Arriving en masse, the refugees initially lived together at a large field they cultivated communally (*mushandirapamwe*). FRELIMO's security concerns, fearing the possibility of betrayal by unknown refugees, significantly shaped this collective settlement. Emissaries traveled between capital and periphery to sort out whether the new arrivals were traitors, spies, or genuine refugees and revolutionaries. Within a few months, Rekayi negotiated with both FRELIMO and the local chief Nyauchi in Katandika. Tangwena's people were allowed to establish individual homesteads where they farmed family fields "under" (*pasi*) the Mozambican chief. Families worked both household and communal holdings, subsisting from the former while fortifying FRELIMO's granary from the latter. Participation in one production regime or agricultural space did not preclude making claims in the other.

Kaerezians named their Mozambican site *Gonakudzingwa*, a place from which one can be chased.[90] A year before her death in 1992, the elderly Ambuya Tagadza proudly remembered working on those cooperative fields with Mugabe and Tekere, two nationalists for whom she cooked and warmed water for nightly bathing. "When they were going, I gave Mugabe a bag made from tree bark so that he would come and 'liberate' [*kutora*] Zimbabwe." Others invoked memories of picking beans together with Tekere and Mugabe in cooperative fields. Whether more metaphorical or actual, that spatial integration of laboring bodies mixed humble Tangwena grandmothers and nationalist leaders, fomenting a sense of common toil. Kaerezians also nurtured idioms of agency in those collective fields, their agrarian struggles yoking Tangwena survival in exile to national liberation. The future president shared grounded practices with Tangwena commoners in a specific historical moment. In another, that cultivated *communitas* became invoked, spanning nation-state border and the end of colonial rule.

In newly independent Zimbabwe, Mugabe's embodied entanglement with Gonakudzingwa's fields of freedom offered a powerful precedent. When planners initially imagined Kaerezi's Model B collective cooperative, they sought to mimic agrarian experiences in exile. The material terrain could not be transported, but a similar *spatial assemblage* of agrarian livelihoods could travel. Planners would transplant what they conceived as a socialist collective spatiality from Mozambique to Zimbabwe, making newly returned refugees feel at home in a landscape of familiar agrarian production. Yet the official imagination of an exclusive collective order neglected alternative articulations of agrarian practices and cultural identity. Planners' initial models opted for either collective or individual land holdings, mutually exclusive sites mapped to separate uses. Mozambican experiences mixed modes, defying planners' assumption of a single logic binding together spatial, social, and economic relations. Despite populist intentions, the initial scheme's plan for a collective cooperative could not counter Tangwena aspirations for family farming.

Rekayi chaired the Tangenhamo Cooperative from its inception, when members continued to farm individual family holdings, putting in a day's labor a week on a collective field. When his national political duties demanded increasing time away from his homeland, he initially supported a new chairman but then turned against the cooperative. Rekayi's influence remained a shaping force. In 1992, a former planner integrally involved for years in Kaerezi recalled to me advice received during a 1982 meeting from the director of DERUDE: "The Tangwena were the only people who 100 percent didn't cooperate with the Smith Government. Everybody else did to some extent, whether it was 95 percent or 1 percent. But they all did. Rekayi didn't, and therefore I need not worry about policy applying here. This was a very special case. Rekayi had of course direct access to Mugabe. . . . if I did anything wrong I could be quite certain that they would board a bus and go directly to the Prime Minister's Office."

Planning could not unfold on a frictionless, smooth space. In the planner's account, the powerful political alliance between state and chiefly sovereign constrained the powers of government, the implementation of resettlement policy by civil servants. The spatial movement of the boarded bus arcs from periphery to the center of power. Rekayi's ability to connect those points remained critical to a seeming paradox: he kept government at a distance by keeping nationalist politics in the foreground. By remaining integrally connected to centers of state power, he buttressed his own claims to local sovereignty. State president and local chief both claimed sovereignty that routed through their contributions to liberating the nation.

In 1992, the same planner sat with me on a Harare park bench years after leaving government. The former bureaucrat described in great detail a 1984 meeting in Kaerezi. Moven Mahachi, former manager of Nyafaru, was then minister of lands, overseeing the branch of government orchestrating resettlement. In the planner's account, more than the liberation struggle's specter haunted the proceedings:

> When I arrived, I noticed with horror how agencies were working at crosspurposes, and also how the local population exploited this. . . . The chief had long realized that there was a war on between [the ministry of] Local Government and the Ministry of Lands. So he always called on the District Administrator, and I think that was one of the reasons why he wanted the area to be declared a Communal Area, not a Resettlement Scheme—to get rid of this tiresome resettlement policy and the threat to his powers. So to this meeting the entire population of Kaerezi was invited, all government officials were told to attend. . . . The chief addressed the meeting. He was very irreverent to Minister Mahachi, who he never called minister and certainly never by his surname. And sometimes he didn't even remember his name. He often called him "that boy Moven." . . . During the speech—now that's one of the times he spoke out against the projects that were being planned with the cooperative . . . he was not going to have anything to do with them. And if those cattle for the cattle project came up, he would confiscate them and distribute them to those who had been deprived of their cattle during the war. Then the minister spoke and then the *svikiro* [spirit medium], this woman . . . was Rekayi's wife. She went into a trance and

for about twenty minutes, she made these INCREDIBLE noises which were quite sort of spine-chilling. The whole meeting came to a dead stop. Nobody spoke. Nobody moved. And eventually she went away and then she came back again. She sided with Chief Tangwena against resettlement and all its rules. . . . During the time when she made these noises and was in a trance and spoke, I just observed everybody, all the actors that I had been working with. And I could predict very accurately as to whom among the government workers would still work with me.

Spirited politics confounded the technical rationality of resettlement policy. Cultural politics—of chiefly rule and spirit mediumship—defied desires of ministers and planners. Divide-and-rule tactics turned back on state rule as Rekayi positioned his power in alignment with one ministry against another. He infantilized "that boy Moven," who he knew as a young manager of Nyafaru's cooperative during the war. This move subordinated the minister in two senses: in hierarchies of age that buttressed the cultural respect commanded by chiefs; and in a territorial history in which Rekayi's heroic agency liberated the *nation*. Ancestral spirits could also govern subjects, acting on their actions, exercising influence on their habits, regulating their conduct. Planning, in this account, confronted not only the realpolitik of Rekayi's maneuvers, but also the spectral effects of the *svikiro*'s discursive practices.

I was told that after Rekayi's death, his widow journeyed to the district's administrative offices to complain about bureaucratic paperwork delaying her receipt of a pension. An accountant recalled a colleague explaining the reasons for the delay in detail. He became animated, much as had the planner, explaining the tale: "She became possessed and transformed herself into a *svikiro*." She left the office, he added with a wry laugh, with a sizeable portion of the pension she felt entitled to receive.

In the 1980s, petrol rationing, restrictions on mileage, and a shortage of vehicles made visits to the remote scheme infrequent. Some Kaerezians welcomed planners, understanding that donor money flowing into the scheme would need to be channeled through project plans. Technical expertise could be an ally, not simply an oppositional enemy. In 1984, a small group of farmers brought a planner to locate a site for a sheep project. Donors required state approval before funding fencing and purchasing a herd. In the mountain mist, farmers led the unknowing official into Nyamutsapa, then beyond the scheme's boundary but still within the chiefdom. Getting government to establish a donor project on that site would help legitimate land rights for squatters living on what was then a private white farm. The planner almost fell for the ruse.

A decade after DERUDE's director advised a subordinate not to push resettle-ment policy in Kaerezi, a senior planner in the branch's high-rise Harare head-quarters explained the continuing tension between "political will" and "technical planning": "Kaerezi people have always claimed ownership of those properties. If government had in the first instance given the people other land, we wouldn't now have these problems. We allowed people to occupy the land they believed to be their own. That is the source of the problem. We see it as a resettlement project; they see it as a traditional settlement in a Communal Area under their chief." On this point, the bureaucrat and Tangwena commoners agreed.

The District Administrator's Dilemmas

Months after he wrote the letter threatening evictions, I met the Nyanga District Administrator at the Ministry of Local Government offices, a cluster of neatly aligned colonial buildings in the District Center. He lived in the colonial District Commissioner's compound, a spacious house with a veranda surrounded by a barbed wire fence and guarded by dogs. Yet a strained budget made routine repairs and maintenance on these colonial-era houses rare. The compound kept the DA at a spatial remove from his colleagues and insulated him from unwanted intrusions from citizens at his home. Some in Kaerezi still used the English acronym DC, designating colonial District Commissioners, instead of DA. Most, however, called him *mudzviti*, a Shona term spanning the colonial divide that targeted the position of power over a territory. He was *mukuru we hurumende mudunhu*, the head of government *in* an administrative area, Nyanga District. His authority, to commoners, came from the center out, radiating down a chain of authority descending from Mugabe through an imagined abstraction termed government (*hurumende*).

The DA was a local boy with global routes. His grandparents were evicted as squatters from the national park bordering Kaerezi in the 1950s. In the early 1990s, he threatened to evict another generation of squatters from Nyamutsapa. Many there knew the spot, less than a day's walk away, where his grandparents had lived in the park. He had a bachelor's degree from Syracuse University, majoring in molecular biology, an experience sharply setting him off from the rank and file of civil servants. After leaving his state post in 1992, he moved to the capital, eventually working for an international environmental NGO. In 1990, handwritten notes and face-to-face meetings orchestrated our encounters in the

District Center. By the end of that decade, he had posted one of his research papers on the Internet.

In November 1991, however, it was a challenge to secure a phone connection between Nyanga's District Center and Harare. A Zimbabwean NGO, ZIMTRUST, had agreed to bankroll a district workshop I was helping organize with the DA and the ministry of Local Government on "community-based resource management." Kaerezians had asked me to help them propose alternatives to the official land-use plan. Months of meetings and countless conversations with Kaerezians led to a gathering where they chose representatives to attend a workshop they actively endorsed. That had been the condition of my own involvement. The process brought me into candid, collegial, and sometimes critical exchanges with the DA. We openly debated the legitimacy of Tangwena cultural understandings of political rights to land and the ways ancestral claims might exclude more equitable access to Kaerezi's landscape by displaced farmworkers who could not claim a Tangwena identity. What kinds of disciplinary power should prevail in a state scheme overlaid with a chiefdom? What kinds of subjects should government recognize?

"The Tangwena people have been spoiled," the DA shared his administrative predicament. "It's a contradiction. I wouldn't want to be a policy planner. They defined it as a resettlement scheme, but it has a chief." Popular refusal to accept Kaerezi's "status of a resettlement scheme" remained the biggest obstacle to government, a refusal to recognize state spatiality and the kinds of subject that regime sought to rule. The DA was particularly concerned about regulating the relationship between people and place, between settlers and the landscape. Spatial practices, in his view, revealed fundamental relations of power and authority. In several senses, he wished recalcitrant subjects knew their place in an orderly scheme. Complaining of the Tangwena "people's general resistance to authority," he reasoned:

> If people remain where they are and don't move into the pegged residential stands, that is an indirect way of legitimating the authority of kraalheads to allocate land. That is a power that was taken away from them. No kraalheads in Communal Areas or resettlement schemes have the power to allocate land now. That's the government's authority. Finite land, which is pegged, prevents that. Kraalheads cannot allocate land if it is demarcated, and everyone knows which parcel belongs to which person.

From his administrative optic, government allocated land, ruling the *relationship* between subjects and territory. An official grid of intelligibility here maps allocated land rights to the landscape, an orderly space disciplined through governing practices. Official acknowledgment of squatters' rights to remain rooted would unsettle the very authority that might recognize those entitlements. Pegging the land and putting settlers in state-demarcated sites, for the DA, grounded rights that headmen (kraalheads) had no legal authority to grant. Rendering these practices visible on the landscape itself made abuses less likely.

"Planned land use," the DA argued, prevented "random settlement," an obstacle to good government, development, and conservation. From the scheme's on-site administrator to Harare's head office, officials repeatedly complained to me of Tangwena settlement patterns being "scattered," "random," and "haphazard." Concentrated villages, the DA argued, improved administrative efficiency, made surveillance easier, and enabled the delivery of development: agricultural inputs and technical extension; roads to market; boreholes, pit toilets, and grinding mills; clinics and schools. Development both required and inaugurated a specific spatial discipline, one that linked distant sites and practices—the Grain Marketing Depot in the district center, consumers in the capital—to those cultivated by Kaerezi farmers.

Heralding the conservation benefits of villagization, and thus implicitly echoing Alvord, the DA supported the scientific soundness of functionally and spatially segregating arable, grazing, and residential zones. "You can concentrate areas for different land-use purposes, and control things that way." He cited the benefit of reduced erosion. While he agreed that education was a necessary component of any villagization program, he made ominous reference to "necessary coercive mechanisms" at government disposal. For him, coercion complemented consent as part of a project of rule.

Postcolonial government, for the DA, needed to pry apart the principles from the politics of colonial land-use planning: "The Land Husbandry Act [NLHA] was seen as coercive, but it had more than one side." He decried the act's unfair implementation yet defended its sound scientific principles: "It realized that with the limited resources in the reserves, resources will go to waste without a land-use plan. . . . It was right. It's still true today." In the postcolonial period, villagization represented the NLHA "by a different name. But it's the same thing. And it's still necessary." The only change, he underscored, was an emphasis on education and the governmental attempt to secure consent. Living outside Kaerezi Extension's planned inscriptions of order, Nyamutsapan squatters represented sedimented *practices* that defied ruling *principles*.

For the DA, the Tangwena refusal to submit—to the logic of land-use planning, to government regulations, to a specific spatial discipline—was grounded in an alternative understanding of property and power. Claiming to rule themselves, they became ungovernable by the state. This defiance thwarted development. In Kaerezi, because "the Tangwena people feel that it is theirs . . . they are skeptical of government involvement. But if you leave them alone, they can't do anything." Improving Tangwena welfare required submission to government. Only by securing adherence to administration could the capacities of people and place be developed. Crucial to the DA's calculus of coercive mechanisms was knowing when to use them. State sovereignty secured an arsenal of brute force, but government also worked through the discursive construction of *interests*.

Imagined communities of beneficiaries implied a politics of scale. A development project serving national interest could pave over place-specific rights. The DA cited Osborne Dam, near the provincial capital Mutare. When locals opposing displacement realized that national will would steamroll them out, they opted for resettlement. While the DA depicted them as embracing their newly located livelihoods, coercion certainly seemed to trump consent. "In the case of the Tangwena people," the DA concluded, "*they have to define certain interests—are they local or national?*" Government managed the overall welfare of population and nation-state, privileging that geo-body as the paramount scale.

Aware of the traction Rekayi's legacy had in the early 1980s, the DA recognized that government had agreed to "people staying in their historical settlement patterns" in the main scheme. But the 1987 annexation of Kaerezi Extension was different. He sharply distinguished two properties, two land histories, and two different regimes of rule. He knew that Nyamutsapa's half of the extension fell in the Tangwena chiefdom and that war refugees returning from Mozambique had lived there since shortly after independence. Yet his administrative memory represented Kaerezi Extension as an empty landscape. In his vision, plans were to be underwritten by technical principles, not contentious politics. The scheme's officer and farmers alike recalled the 1987 demarcations that recognized preexisting arable holdings in Nyamutsapa. The local headman was involved, and few resented the pegging of fields. Yet the DA told a different story. He tweaked the past to legitimate present administrative agendas, lumping together in one entity two territories divided by the chiefdom's western boundary:

> We did not consult local people on pegging and allocating stands. Dazi and Nyamutsapa were planned resettlements pure and simple. We assumed no one was living there. AGRITEX did all of the land planning without consulting local people. If a person does not move to land allocated to him,[91] he loses his right to resettle-

ment. We have not pushed this notion, although we should have earlier. . . . We are waiting to enforce this provision . . . because the chieftainship is not settled. We might victimize people when it's not their fault.

An array of officials used the language of "concessions" initially granted to Kaerezi settlers. Even AGRITEX's first planning document for the scheme, aware of the volatile situation, urged the recognition of existing arables cultivated by smallholders unless they violated "sound conservation."[92] A senior DERUDE planner's 1986 technical report recommended appropriate crops and livestock carrying capacity, becoming the blueprint for Kaerezi Extension. Since settlers in the main scheme "could be employed and . . . retain their traditional authorities," the report argued, the same should apply to the annex. Using a variant spelling, the plan observed that "Gaerezi is really a 'hybrid' scheme halfway between a normal model A and a Communal Land."[93] The same year, another DERUDE report described how "the Tangwena people resettled on Kaerezi Ranch in 1980 on an accelerated or cooperative basis. The allotment of land holdings was done under the traditional leadership" of Chief Tangwena's six headmen.[94] While both state archives and administrators invoked principles of abstract space and planning, at times they each acknowledged residues of alternative spatialities and power relations in Kaerezi.

Postcolonial government attempts to impose villagization encountered a landscape entangled with territorialized powers that spanned colonial rule. Kaerezians' sedimented livelihood practices also produced both spaces and subjects that defied the orderly discipline of governmentalized settlement grids. I now turn to those agrarian micropractices that grounded Kaerezian homesteads while also attending to emplaced articulations of rights and resources.

3 · Landscapes of Livelihood

Months had passed since the DA's threatening letter. We awoke well before dawn, bolting down a cup of tea in the cook hut as children slept on the mud-and-dung floor close to the fire. Celia, the Gumbos' eldest daughter, rose even earlier, jolting me awake with ax-strokes splintering firewood. I emerged into the chill of predawn air to join two teenagers, Sironi and Patrick, groggily walking through the family's fields to the cattle kraal where our labor would begin. A small pen of wooden poles lashed with bark embedded pastoralism in a homestead. During plowing season, beasts were yoked to till household fields. Manure from the small enclosure fertilized the fenced garden; mixed with mud, and smeared on floors, it dried to form a protective coating. When a lion roamed the scheme, a rarity at Kaerezi's elevation, SaGumbo was glad to have his cattle close where he could guard them. His wife, MaiNyasha, felt safe milking a cow in the kraal even at dusk or before dawn. Security came through this spatial integration of practices and resources.

Ample pasture provided plenty of grazing for local herds, but the closest functioning dip tank was a long haul from Nyamutsapa. State law required farmers to dip their herds weekly during rainy season and every other week during dry months. To reach Dazi's dip tank across the river required driving cattle to the cement bridge and then making a rugged roundtrip climbing up each side of the steep Kaerezi River valley. As a result, Nyamutsapans instead drove their herds to the Magadzire dip tank, close to the Mozambican border, a roundtrip of around twenty kilometers. In 1990, MNR's cross-border incursions killed settlers in the north of the scheme. Army warnings and good sense discouraged travel at night. Yet Nyamutsapans agreed that dipping early, soon after the salaried civil servant mixed chemicals in the tank, protected herds with "strong medicine." If farmers waited until daybreak to journey to the dip, traversing rugged terrain en route, they would arrive late in the dipping process. This meant that hundreds of cattle had already "used up the fresh medicine," lessening its efficacy. Leaving before sunrise allowed farmers to dip early when the medicine was still strong, but risked encountering MNR. Waiting until the relative safety of daylight increased the risk to their herds. That morning, Sironi, Patrick, and I split the difference.

The previous dusk, we had penned MaiHurudza's four cattle in the kraal, adding them to the Gumbos' herd of six. With her husband working for wages at a tourist hotel, MaiHurudza appreciated the neighborly help driving cattle. The two teenagers chose a route up the valley to link with a worn path where we could run more quickly. Reaching the ridge in the dark was the hard part. We began the steep climb on muddy paths out of the river valley, cattle breath steaming in the cool mountain air. The animals' pounding hooves found firmer hold than our sliding feet. Without a moon, we needed to run close to the cattle through thick brush, jumping streams and avoiding gullies. "If you slip and fall," Sironi advised with a smile, "be sure to roll away from their hooves." We almost lost two beasts that leapt across a stream and bolted toward the national park. Patrick sprinted to head them off and cracked his rawhide whip, which I could hear but not see in the dark. "They know where we're going," he explained, "and they *hate* being dipped." Sironi and Patrick knew the tendencies of specific beasts and the collective herd, but they could not predict all escape attempts. The teenagers also knew the terrain intimately, using rock formations, sheer drops, and thick groves to corral the cattle. Thick vegetation on the steep slopes made human ascent exhaustingly grueling work. Patrick and Sironi remembered previous cattle drives where a beast bolted at *that* gap in the rocks or across *that* narrow gully. The landscape's materiality became consequential in an assemblage enabling our cattle drive to the dip: knowledge honed from previous spatial practices, cooperation among running humans, histories of human-bovine relations, and government regulations requiring regular cattle dipping.

As a cross-country runner in high school, I had run on rough terrain and at night, but I had rarely mixed the two. Adrenaline pumped as hoof beats and bovine breathing filled my ears. Following Sironi's sage advice, I rolled the few times I fell. Scampering through brambles near a ridgeline, we picked up the pace on a more traveled trail, eventually joining the scheme's dirt road heading toward the border. We were more than an hour into the journey before sunrise splattered shadows of human and bovine strides dancing together on the landscape. With increasing light and on gentler terrain, the last few kilometers felt downright mellow. We arrived early in the queue of cattle herders. Households with limited labor or more caution waited until sunrise; those who sent the elderly or teenage girls arrived later in line. The availability of gendered and generational labor translated, Kaerezians told me, to stronger medicine to protect a critical family resource.

Separate herds of four to twenty beasts began to mingle in a swarm of cattle. An ox's bellow, thrusting pelvises, horns, and hooves, or a mounted cow's contortions would produce a domino effect rippling across hundreds of cattle. Beasts would bolt from the periphery, chased back into the combined herd by cracking whips and makeshift poles. A large collective paddock narrowed into a small holding pen. Shouts, whips, and heavy blows separated out single herds from the morass, filling the funnel with one registered owner's beasts before sealing them off with a gate. Across the pen, another gate led to a chute, narrowing the animals to single file before ascending a cement ramp. I began to appreciate why cattle "hate" being dipped. The ramp ended over the dip—a narrow strip of water, chemicals, and excrement from anxious cattle. Driven off the dip, cattle plunged more than a meter, ensuring full submersion in water well over their heads. Emerging with loud snorts and bulging eyes, they swam frantically for twenty feet, finally finding a hoofhold on the cement ramp at dip's end. They scampered up and darted to daylight as the paid attendant recorded their passage in his registry.

Dipping was a highly gendered performative practice. While some women herded cattle to the dip, once in the paddock and chute, men ran the show. Neighbors relied on mutual cooperation and coordination. One's cracked whip directed a beast toward another's pole, pushing cattle into the chute. Beasts bellowed, balked, and twisted in the chute, sometimes getting a leg stuck in the wooden fence posts. A huge ox once turned in the chute, splintering wood and toppling the fence. Eight of us lunged, our strained shoulders propping the falling posts to contain the frantic animal. Horns thrust menacingly through gaps in the broken fence. The owner beat the ox ferociously with a thumb-sized pole, drawing blood. Grandmothers shouted directions and critique. Finally, the massive ox named Blackie plunged into the dip, splashing chemicals and cattle shit on our sweating bodies. The exhausted but satisfied owner cursed the beast with the only English insult in his arsenal as Blackie hit the water: "Shut up, shut up."

Even as owners beat cattle, they were careful not to injure their beasts. Force and finesse joined at the dip tank. Effective technique required agility, strength, and a knowledge of both the dip tank's dynamics and the cattle's likely reaction. Men straddled the chute, poking and whipping cattle running beneath them. If a beast balked, men twisted tails and struck tender body parts. Dipping was viscerally intense, physically grueling labor that brought human and bovine bodies into spatial intimacy. The disciplinary practices of dipping gathered in a single site social relations, pastoralism, and nonhuman entities—chemicals, cement, wooden paddocks, and state registries.

Dipping cattle constituted an assemblage of practices—linking human agency and nonhuman efficacy—that government sought to manage in the name of citizens' welfare. Cattle registries, dip tanks, and veterinary officers individuated beasts while monitoring herds of families, communities, and the nation. The health of each beast promoted the collective good. The animals' owners were active agents who subjected human and bovine practices to government regulations. As Kaerezians cajoled and coerced beasts into dip tanks, they participated in the practices of biopower. They helped bring managed care and calculations to life and its mechanisms, targeting the health of a collective population in the name of national improvement.[1] However, disputes emerged over the distance Nyamutsapans traveled to Magadzire's distant dip.

In 1988, DERUDE built new dip tanks in the newly administered Kaerezi Extension. Dazi's dip was far from the river, but the DNPWLM strongly objected to the location of the Nyamutsapa tank, fearing its proximity to the Kaerezi River would leach chemicals into the pristine headwaters of a treasured natural resource. Competing ministries had thwarted initial plans by DNPWLM to annex the property and extend the park estate. Squatters evicted from Tsanga Valley by one ministry became resettled by another in Dazi's grids. Across the river, park officials observed Nyamutsapa's scattered homesteads dotting an ecologically fragile catchment area. They also knew that smallholders in Nyamutsapa—part of Tangwena territory—invoked links to their anticolonial struggles and nationalist chief, to Mugabe, and to prominent members of parliament, including minister of lands Mahachi, who had worked at Nyafaru in the 1970s. The Kaerezi River Protected Area emerged through political compromise. Straddling the headwaters, the five-hundred-meter corridor extending from the park would prohibit grazing and cultivation. Members of a private white trout-fishing club further complicated the situation by writing letters to various ministries. Rumors of a "white land grab" flowed along with rising resentment.

Several state officials advocated a shift to fruit production near the sensitive river corridor. Maize required extensive fields. Decreasing the acreage tilled, the officials argued, would reduce the risk of soil erosion, lessening siltation in the river. Fruit would enable the smooth flow of clear headwaters, and of cash into farmers' pockets. Locals desired cash but were also hungry for quick returns and low investments. Fruit took years to yield marketable harvests. Orchards required management expertise and expensive agricultural inputs. Marketed fruit was a sweet supplement to subsistence production, but not a desired substitute; few wanted fruit to trump maize. At an April 1991 meeting, Mujuru found enthusiastic support among his neighbors: "If we plant fruits and no maize, we will suffer from hunger. The government's approach has been coercive [*kumanikidza*]. . . . We are being forced to grow these crops." Many feared that the protected area, conjoined with villagization, would *impose* undesirable conditionalities threatening subsistence: destocking, prohibitions, forced fruit. Nyamutsapa's dormant dip tank became part of the package of "coercion." "There is oppression [*uzhinyiriri*]," Mujuru told me after the meeting, recalling the ruins of a neighboring white rancher's dip, "if Mabvura had his dip tank near the river but ours is prohibited. Yet ours is far from the river." By implication, he accused postcolonial policy of deploying a colonial double standard, privileging white rights while thwarting African assertions.

In October 1990, the resettlement officer Marumahoko met some forty Nyamutsapans gathered beneath the large *mutororo* tree planted by Headman Mweya's ancestors near his homestead. Marumahoko chronicled the bureaucratic quagmire clogging the dip tank's operation. The national park and a private group of white anglers both objected to chemicals that might seep into the river and kill trout. "So the river's being fought over, and the problem of who will use the river is not yet solved," he explained. His public promise of vigilant labor to resolve the issue provoked an angry response from Mweya who lamented "the distances we travel to the Magadzire dip tank" while the idle dip tank lay less than a kilometer from his home. Mweya angrily accused Marumahoko of shirking his duty. In response, the officer waved letters he had written to different departments lobbying to have the dip opened. Mweya shouted in a rage: "The things they possess are the fish in the river, not the territory [*nyika*] two **kilometers** from the river." To my great surprise, given his blistering critiques of villagization, he also asserted, "This side of the river is for people in **resettlement** [*vanhu ve resettlement*]." Government, Mweya implied, should administer an inhabited landscape rather than protect it for outsiders.

Picking up on Mweya's recognition of resettlement, Marumahoko agreed that "we all know that this area [*nzvimbo*] was purchased by government along with the river." In a subtle switch, however, he countered the headman's *nyika*, a territory bound to a sovereign through practices of rule, with an abstract area, *nzvimbo*, an owned commodity exchanged through the market. In this vision, administration followed ownership, the rule of law reigning over secure property. Yet for Mweya, colonial conquest and white evictions invoked idioms of ownership that did not erase ancestral territory. Mweya pressed the postcolonial government to redress racialized dispossession. Securing legal ownership through market purchase could not liberate the *nyika* of chiefdom or nation. Just rule in both territories required righting racial wrongs.

Mweya challenged the administrator to perform the tasks of postcolonial government. If authority flowed from ownership, then the civil servant needed to struggle on that turf: "You are the one who must go and fight those people. Why are they getting into an area purchased for resettlement? So you want the whites to take the river again." Protect community interests, he pressed. Pushed to defend himself again, Marumahoko chronicled the bureaucratic quagmire his efforts confronted, the slow pace of deliberations, the memos he wrote on farmers' behalf. National Parks wrote a report about pollutants while Veterinary Services, in yet another ministry, had approved the dip tank, verifying that it represented no environmental hazard. Perhaps, Marumahoko reasoned aloud, National Parks wanted to "take over the river." Before he could finish his thought, an elder man jumped into the fray, adding: "The national park wants the river. The dip is not the national park's. They should not control [*kutonga*] what is not theirs." Mweya picked up on the elder's claims, defending locality against predatory encroachment: "We don't want people to drag wealth to their own territory [*nyika*]." Cleverly, his image invoked beasts of burden pulling a heavy load, yoking cattle to a double duty. First, oxen underscored his insistence on smallholder agriculture against alternatives that would prohibit plowing or grazing. Second, all assembled at the meeting knew that oxen-pulled sledges, used to transport heavy materials such as building poles, were illegal in the park. Yet the deep tracks of sledges and cattle hooves cut across the boundary, marking the landscape defiantly with farmers' transgressive spatial practice.

The national park, Mweya complained, was aggressively extending its estate on several fronts. He named several expansions of the border, all secured through purchases of neighboring properties. This spatial extension of claims to control resources ran counter to Tangwena rights to rule territory. In overstretching its appropriate boundaries—spatially and administratively—National Parks was

SaGumbo driving cattle into
a newly opened dip tank,
Nyamutsapa, 1991. *Photo by
the author.*

"making a mistake." While previously Marumahoko had portrayed parks as the
heavy, preventing the dip tank from opening, now he fired back: "National Parks
is a branch of government [*hurumende*]." Without missing a beat, Mweya re-
torted: "Yes, but the branch is bad," threatening the very roots of state power. The
frustrated administrator promised to write yet more letters of inquiry, setting a
date to return and announce the dip tank's fate. When the headman threatened
to go to the officer's superiors if a clear resolution was not forthcoming, the
exasperated Marumahoko pointed to his vehicle: "No problem. The truck is
right there."

At the meeting, headman and administrator traded salvos, enunciating competing claims to discipline people's practices. Marumahoko unraveled and reconstituted complex alliances and conflicts among and within different state
agencies. At times, he represented government as a unified "we"; at others,
branches and ministries divided, pursuing and producing conflicting interests.
De Certeau suggested that tactics describe styles of opposition that "constantly
manipulate events in order to turn them into 'opportunities,'" acting from a
subordinate position to "turn to their own ends forces alien to them."[2] Mweya
appropriated the familiar colonial trope of divide and rule, throwing it back at

the postcolonial state. In so doing, he also challenged the officer to govern—to exercise actions on Mweya's own, thus subjecting the headman to a state spatial discipline Mweya openly opposed. Denouncing villagization, Mweya allocated land in defiance of state spatial designs, allying himself with the chief's claims to "rule territory" (*kutonga nyika*). Yet Mweya enlisted government support in countering the encroaching claims of private whites and the public park. The postcolonial state's failure to deliver the dip tank, a crucial community resource, became its moral failure to redress racial inequality.

While frustrated with Mweya's manner and stubbornness, Marumahoko recognized legitimate resentment over the unused dip tank shared by Nyamutsapans. The morning after the meeting, he dispatched yet another letter to the District Administrator. A permit slowly emerged from the bureaucratic machinery. In late April of 1991, after lying idle for nearly three years, the new dip tank opened. No one complained over the local labor required to fill the tank. Jokes ran along the human chain passing buckets from a nearby water point to mix with chemicals in the tank. Women ululated as the first beast plunged under water. Nyamutsapans celebrated by driving early beasts into strong medicine.

Embodied Earthworks

Villagization separated fields and homes, attacking the spatial and functional assemblage of myriad livelihood practices at a *musha* or homestead. Pursuing this plan, governmental practice cut against the grain of the idyllic "village" it sought to conjure: conviviality, warm hearths and hearts, and a vibrant spirit of community. Farmers located activities and artifacts of their labor—from huts to kraals to furrowed fields—in relation to streams and springs, the contour of terrain, living neighbors and dead ancestors.

Kaerezians' opposition to the lines argued for the pragmatic agrarian benefits of *entangled* fields and homesteads: crop protection from animals, efficiencies of time and task, and the logistics of organizing labor. When fields flowed out from a home, farmers could chase pigs that marauded by nightfall, drive away oxen that strayed into fields at dusk, and keep a watchful eye out for other potential perils to a family harvest. Spatial integration wove daily and seasonal rhythms of agricultural labor into other tasks, accommodating the sun's changing intensity, prevailing winds, neighbors' needs, and social visits. Times near dawn and dusk were coolest for physically demanding tasks, precious windows that daily travel

MaiNyasha, Tewa, and two visitors sit in a *musha*, Nyamutsapa, 1992. Note how fields emerge from the edge of the homestead. MaiNyasha's son and MaiHurudza's son sit near the chicken coop. *Photo by the author.*

to distant fields would deny. Even the logistics of feeding hungry workers far from a cook hut and water source raised challenges, increasing women's provisioning responsibilities.

Kaerezians cultivated in several senses at a *musha*, a term that gathers together the affect and materiality of home, hearth, and huts. Many women and men farmed together in *matambwe*, family fields usually planted with staple crops. Some polygamous households practiced stricter gender segregation, each wife feeding her children from her own field. But most families, including polygamous ones, mixed the labor of genders and generations on their *matambwe*. Gender relations segregated tasks, but not those spaces. Plowing was almost exclusively male work, but women whose husbands worked away for wages and daughters in their late teens occasionally cut furrows with oxen. Women usually planted and weeded, but men and teenage boys sometimes helped. Harvesting demanded all available able bodies, especially if a crop's ripeness lasted a short time.

As a node of livelihood and sociality, homesteads' embeddedness in fields enabled neighbors and relatives to mingle social visits with labor contributions at crucial bottlenecks, especially during planting or harvesting. While some wealthier families hired day workers, most households engaged in a robust reciprocity of labor exchanges usually coded as help (*rubatsiro*). When fields emanated from huts, a neighborly visit could yield furrows planted as well as conviviality; and hospitality could meld with the gracious acceptance of assistance. Spatially integrated homesteads and fields helped poorer families and those with less available labor to benefit from neighborly care. In turn, the less fortunate could also save face, smoothly segueing from receiving a neighbor's toil in their fields to providing a hospitable meal in their cook huts. To orchestrate such labor arrangements at distant fields raised not only logistical challenges, but also social and political-economic ones; it risked shifting idioms that acknowledged the "help" of kin and neighbors toward those that compensated "work" by wages. By realigning the spatial and temporal integration of agriculture, social reciprocity, and neighborliness, villagization raised specters of the commoditizing of labor and the undermining of loose networks of social welfare.

Resettlement policy encouraged monocropping for market, but most families intercropped maize and beans, crucial for subsistence, on *matambwe*. While schoolchildren explained that beans "fixed nitrogen in the soil," their parents knew that beans "strengthened" maize when intercropped because the plants "cooperated." Maize surpluses were extremely rare, since *sadza*, stiff maize porridge, was a daily foodstuff. Most Zimbabweans spoke of *sadza* as a "traditional" African food, fusing cultural preference to national diet. Yet maize only emerged as a staple following its Portuguese introduction to southern Africa. In Nyamutsapa's high-rainfall area, maize dominated family fields. Hybrids, first introduced to the country by Alvord, prevailed. Many families harvested enough to forego expensive store-bought maize meal or locally purchased maize.

The shock of inflation on staple foods shaped desires to keep a strong foothold in subsistence maize production. As the price of maize meal spiraled far beyond Kaerezians' purchasing power, consumption from their own granaries protected against market-oriented reforms. Foregoing the monocrops for market recommended by government, those who planted maize and beans could retreat into subsistence, relying less on purchasing food commodities from scarce cash wages or meager crop sales. In 1991–92, as southern Africa suffered the worst drought in living memory, even families with cash could not always find marketed maize meal. Those in Kaerezi's mountains, where the rains fell long and hard, were among the best suited to weather the long absences and astronomical price increases of store-bought maize meal. For most Nyamutsapans, subsistence agriculture represented a lifeline amid Structural Adjustments' double trouble: skyrocketing inflation and frozen wages. In retrospect, subsistence strategies appeared even wiser as Zimbabwe's inflation rate topped 500 percent in 2003.

Marketing opportunities were limited, but those lucky enough to reap a good bean harvest could carry a bucket or sack some twenty kilometers to a small market at Troutbeck, near the workers' quarters at a tourist hotel. I would often encounter adult women and teenage boys and girls carrying these heavy loads in recycled tins atop their heads, and would marvel at their balance and strength in negotiating steep, rugged trails. Vegetables, usually grown in a fenced garden, provided the daily "relish" to complement maize porridge—greens, vegetables such as squash, and the occasional seasonal tomato. Skillful cooks could stretch two small tomatoes in a relish complementing *sadza* to feed more than ten people.

Like those of most homesteads in Tangwena territory, the Gumbos' fields flowed outward from a cluster of a few mud-and-wattle sleeping huts and a large cook hut made from sun-dried bricks, all thatched. A few paces from the huts lay the ruins of a stone pit (*khuwira* or *kuwira*), a remnant of settlement that predated any Kaerezians' memories of their ancestors' migrating to the area. Across Nyanga's Eastern Highlands, such evidence of centuries-old agricultural and settlement practices remained visible on the landscape. A short walk from the Gumbos' home, ancient terracing—dating to before the fourteenth century according to some archaeologists—cut parallel horizontal lines across steep slopes, while, at lower altitudes in the district, tourists marveled at the ruins of ancient stone aqueducts, walls, and other structures. In the sixteenth and seventeenth centuries, African agriculturalists built stone fortresses and pits—which may have sheltered livestock as well as humans from raids and animal predators—spread across the landscape in Nyanga's higher ranges. Forts were strategically sited, usually on or near peaks, while the many pits suggest a deep history of scattered settlements in what is now Kaerezi and the adjacent park.[3] In the 1990s, Kaerezians used these pit ruins as storage areas, for garbage and recycling, and as hiding places.

Across the Gumbo homestead from the stone pit, a small mud-and-wattle granary protected stored crops from predators. On those nights when wild pigs dug their tusks into husks of corn near harvest, a sleepy patriarch sprung into action, driving the animals from the fields. Spatial proximity of sleeping huts to fields enabled ears as well as eyes to keep watch, piercing the darkest nights. When SaGumbo knew that pigs were on the prowl, he burned a horrific mix that smelled like torched rubber, strategically placed around crops to thwart raids. Beasts, MNR bandits making incursions from Mozambique, and occult forces all were known to traverse Kaerezi's landscape after nightfall making some fearful to venture out past dark.

On hot days, Tewa sometimes napped under the shade of a raised drying rack, topped with cobs of maize, beans, and other crops out of reach of cattle and other threats. Born on Gaeresi Ranch in the 1920s, he in 1991 moved to live with the Gumbos, his longtime friends, to undergo treatment for his failing legs. Angry spirits, Tewa felt, caused his physical disability. He hoped the Gumbos' faith healing would drive away ancestral anger lodged in his body. Sometimes he sat in the shade weaving hunting nets, hiding them in the granary in case National Parks game scouts decided to search his hut.

The garden's proximity made it near enough for Tewa to hobble to, a hoe slung over his shoulder, on makeshift crutches—an impossible journey from the family's assigned residential plot in the lines. He would carefully fasten the garden's rusted barbed wire gate behind him, surveying as if to remember his last visit. After choosing a spot to sit or lie sideways, his skillful hands made dirt dams, designing channels to redirect water. Atop the garden, Tewa's skillful strokes of the hoe directed water from an uphill spring through newly crafted channels irrigating patches below. Cultivating with care, he reaped humble harvests and solace for an ailing soul. Mixing gravity, perennial spring water, soil, seed, and human labor, the garden assembled distinct qualities of nature and culture. The saddle below a steep incline also provided shelter from storms. Yet with good sun exposure especially to the west, its gentle slope hosted well-tended rows of beans, tomatoes, and squash. In season, even lettuce and beets grew, a treat for the Gumbos' anthropological ally. Decades before, SaGumbo had worked as a cook in a tourist hotel, those acquired skills now informing his garden's cropping.

The Gumbos' cattle kraal was a stone's throw from their garden, sited downslope so manure did not contaminate a spring. Cattle effluence made good fertilizer, and it was handily stored meters from fenced furrows. Subsistence agriculture relied on draft power, bovines integrated into livelihood mosaics. At the edge of a fallow field lay *matambwe* soon to be planted. A slick trail dropped down a steep path to a stream used for washing but never for drinking. Uphill neighbors and upstream pasture dictated this use. Drinking water came from a spring across the homestead, away from fertilized fields, cattle dung, and bathing sites. Hoes and hard work carved a small pool near the spring, affording clean access to clear water that MaiNyasha and her daughters drew with buckets. They washed clothes in an aborted fish pond nearby, carefully keeping soap away from the spring.

Men and older teenage boys performed work around the kraal, wielding shiny sterilized pinchers with an Italian imprint to transform a bullock into an ox. Beasts were rarely slaughtered, but the occasional feast for weddings or celebrations brought somber crews of men to the kraal where a hapless bovine bayed, tethered tightly to the yoking post. I saw both pick and ax used, striking atop the skull. I remember when Simba brought an ox to its knees with a few strokes. He pulled hard on a rawhide tether around its neck, wrapped around the yoking post and running under his foot, to pin twisting horns against the ground. Avoiding flailing legs and horns, he severed the neck from the front with a knife. After letting blood and breath drain from the ox, Simba cut the tail to verify death before letting teenage boys pull it toward a grassy spot for skinning and butchering. The hide became a rug while the meat fed scores at a large church feast.

Sironi, a burly seventeen-year-old, made plowing look easy. The son of a family friend who could not afford boarding school fees at Nyafaru, he lived with the Gumbos so he could commute the few kilometers each day. Like Tewa's, his residence did not align with his location in resettlement policy's logic. The slighter Patrick, a few years younger, cracked the whip near the ear of the lead oxen, shouting "Transport, Transport." I long thought this was a common plowing command, only later realizing it was the *name* of the black ox with a broken horn. His yokemate was called London. Sironi and Patrick knew the oxen's every trick, heading them off with skillful whip strokes, most striking air rather than hide. At furrow's end, as the team came out of the U-turn, Sironi pulled the plow chain taut, jumping the blade to a new furrow. He muscled the heavy plow, while the slender Patrick deployed finesse, leveraging its handles, steering like a one-handed bicycle rider. While my technique borrowed from both, I paled in comparison. Contour ridges, higher and wider than the furrows they paralleled, ran across slopes, channeling water to avoid sheet erosion caused by the heavy mountain rains. We steered the oxen carefully so they did not stomp down bunds of tilled soil, and to lessen the labor of hoes that would sculpt and pack the contours.

Sironi and Patrick tried to plow around rocks if they spotted them in time. If not, they dulled the blade with a thundering crash. The young men were not simply adept at steering, but they could read the lay of the land, including invisible traces I did not see. They often remembered from past seasons where submerged rocks remained. Avoiding rocks was only part of the challenge. In theory, lifting the plow's handle deepened the cut and slowed forward momentum. In practice, there were no brakes. Skillful plowing was an ensemble of embodied skills. Quality furrows demanded concentration, body control,

Patrick is plowing while Sironi and neighbors drive a team of oxen, Nyam-utsapa, 1991, with the Kaerezi River and Mount Nyangani in the background. *Photo by the author.*

strength, and quickness. Constant adjustments for terrain, soil quality, ground cover, and the tension of the chain affected the depth, angle, and straightness of lines. Knowing oxen's habits and capabilities helped. Feeling the lay of the land melded the visual and the visceral: the plow's path, the chain's tension, the oxen's heavy breathing, my strides. I strained after a few furrows, but Sironi could literally plow all day.

While women rarely plowed, wives married to migrant laborers had little choice if relatives or friends did not lend a hand. Some Kaerezians hired and loaned oxen for a price, charging either by furrow or day. Young men frequently plowed neighbors' and relatives' fields, helping (*kubatsira*) rather than charging—especially widows and the wives of labor migrants. Cattle might be "kept" at a friend's or relative's home for periods, enabling their use. Just as often, friends might pool cattle, mixing beasts between personal herds to form matched teams. While kinship oriented obligations of lending labor and capital in times of need, social relations coded as friendship shaped the daily practices of sharing work and the pleasure of neighbors' company. Plowing, planting, and harvesting together cultivated friendships and fields—reciprocal flows of labor and affinity as well as of furrows and contour ridges.

The fifteen-year-old Celia helped her mother in the fields, planting, weeding by hoe and hand, and harvesting. Both women wielded a mean ax. Celia's strong back helped her carry huge bundles of firewood, countless metal buckets of water, and a washing tub filled with manure and ash to spread in fields or clay mud to mix for smearing hut walls. She did the bulk of cooking the daily staple of maize porridge. I could hardly stir the maize porridge that her strong arms and quick strokes expertly brought beyond boil to a paste thick enough to eat with our fingers. During harvest seasons, Celia and her mother roasted fresh maize, peeled boiled yams and fresh potatoes, and scraped the skin off two different root crops, *madhumbe* and *tsenza*, grown exclusively by women. After her younger sister had fallen asleep by the cook hut fire, Celia ventured into the night, drawing water to warm by fire for dishes and the evening bathing.

One form of homework displaced another. Celia's schoolwork suffered, she confided, because chores cut into study time. Lacking cash for candles or paraffin, her only after-sundown light source was the cook hut fire where constant demands on her labor jostled with bustle. She relished the pens, pencils, and candles I brought for her from town, taking a warm blanket into the dark chill of a sleeping hut to seek refuge with her books. Her eldest brother, too, a headmaster living in the district's dry lowveld, worried about the labor demands at home dragging his sister's education down. Celia's younger sister had already been sent to help care for one of her mother's relatives in another part of the district where she also attended school. But her brother told me she spent much of her time doing chores for an ailing elder. While all the Gumbo children attended school, poorer neighbors or those with different budgetary priorities removed girls from school while paying fees for their brothers.

Parents cited bride wealth and patrilocality. Most women at marriage moved to their husbands' homesteads, the woman's labors for subsistence or wages usually going into the husband's lineage's coffers. Younger couples, especially those with secondary education, might pool or divide income more equitably. Especially for the poorest and least formally educated, however, "investing" in a girl's education was coded as contrary to her movement. Spatially and socio-economically, a girl's life trajectory arced away from her natal homestead toward a husband's lineage. A new wife was *mutorwa*, literally "the taken one." The Gumbos would eventually send Celia to live with her headmaster brother several long walks and bus rides from their home. His watchful eye, they hoped, would keep her away from testosterone-fueled teenage boys and would give her more time to study, including a room of her own in cement teachers' quarters.

At seven, Tsitsi, the youngest Gumbo daughter, already planted, hoed, and

Celia and Patrick cook dinner, Nyamutsapa, 1990. *Photo by the author.*

harvested in the family fields. She was the one usually slightly out of rhythm as a line of around six women coordinated their steps, bending at the waist in synch to place seed or fertilizer, fingers agilely blending seed and soil while bodies moved gracefully across freshly hoed fields. Tsitsi hopped on the offbeat, sometimes stumbling, demonstrating not her clumsiness but the difficulty of acquiring the skill of proper planting. She carried twigs rather than logs on her head when women gathered firewood. Old enough to carry her neighbor's infant, bound by cloth to her back, she had not yet acquired the skill to smear a coating of mixed mud and dung on hut floors. Her wrists were too weak to stir the large cast-iron cooking pot filled with thick maize porridge. Nor could her brother Moses, a few years older. He spent much of his time running errands, delivering messages to neighbors, or bringing food to adults and older siblings working in fields. Herding cattle only under duress, he was too young to handle them alone.

Another brother, an "untrained" teacher, lived in the far north of the scheme where he taught at a state primary school. Certified teachers required at least a year's training course, and they were scarce. Those with an O-level education who had finished grade 11 could teach for a modest salary. Yet another brother, then an A-level student living at a mission boarding school, was on his way to university, the first in the family to do so. On holidays, he preached in the church and tilled the Lord's fields. Brian, the eldest son and a certified teacher in his late

Tsitsi hoes *madhumbe* (yams) with her mother, MaiNyasha,
Nyamutsapa, 1991. *Photo by the author.*

twenties, bankrolled much of his younger siblings' school fees since he was the
first in his generation to earn wages. He turned down the opportunity to go to
Cuba for educational training, feeling responsible for his family. He sent home
money for school fees and to buy seed, fertilizer, and clothes.

Flora, the eldest sister, lived several hours' walk north. Her husband worked all
but holidays at a distant army base, and she was chronically short on labor. Celia
and her younger teenage brother frequently lent a hand in her fields around
planting and harvest. Sometimes Flora left her children with their grandparents,
where the granary was better stocked. When she passed away in the mid-1990s,
her children eventually moved permanently to their grandparents' home. Beyond the family tragedy, this added an extended economic burden to the elder
Gumbos. After years of struggling to pay their own children's school fees, they
would now pay their grandchildren's, a fate shared by an increasing number of
Zimbabweans in the wake of AIDS.

As faith healers, SaGumbo and MaiNyasha paired ensouled and embodied
practices. They blessed water and laid prayerful hands on the afflicted who
visited. Receiving no monetary compensation, and hosting "patients" who stayed
for days and even weeks, their subsistence production needed to feed many more
than their extended family. The couple often worked side by side hoeing and

harvesting in their fields. MaiNyasha and her daughters tended to plant and weed together, while SaGumbo spent longer periods alone in their fenced garden. Harvests utilized everyone's labor, but spread it unevenly across siblings depending on their abilities—both to gather crops and to foist delegated duties onto their juniors. As in most families, their gendered divisions of labor were most pronounced around men's plowing and managing cattle and women's responsibilities for cooking, cleaning, and gathering firewood.

Wood fueled cook hut fires were at the physical and symbolic center of homesteads. Women usually stoked the morning fire, often before dawn, sometimes then sweeping the ground outside with branches. Expeditions to procure wood consumed arduous hours, but they also kindled gendered spaces and social relations. Literally, "searching for firewood," *kutsvaga huni*, involved localized knowledge of tree species, their hardness to an ax, their burning properties, and their density. It also required skillful negotiation of mountain trails with lashed logs balanced atop women's heads. Women who married into the area spoke of learning about local trees from their neighbors. Neighborly practices recognized the rights of those who piled together fallen or chopped limbs to return another day to carry them home. While searching for suitable wood, women also gathered wild fruits, snacking on and stuffing their bounty into a sack. Viewed from the homestead's hearth, the forest can be a wild and dangerous place where animals and spirits dwell beyond spheres of sociality. Yet a vibrant gendered community came alive through firewood gathering as women joked, gossiped, and shared tribulations and critiques beyond the watchful gaze of patriarchs and kinsmen. On my few forays with women in the woods, I noticed that they became much more subdued on entering their homesteads, returning to respectful roles as matrons, wives, and daughters. I do not wish to romanticize the gendered valence of what Marx termed the "silent compulsion of economic relations," the onerous daily task of procuring fuel for cooking. Many women, however, emphasized the sisterly solidarity they experienced while gathering firewood.[4]

By firelight stoked with the harvest of her labor, MaiNyasha cut and fried greens for relish. Moving coals with her bare hands, she adjusted the heat. Asbestos-like fingers picked out glowing embers, filling the iron that pressed school uniforms and church robes made from white sheets. The children usually drew water, but MaiNyasha often heated it for bathing in the evening, especially if she wanted her daughter to have more time for studying. Homework and fieldwork often carried the additional burden of a grandchild or neighbor's infant bundled to MaiNyasha's back. The proximity of huts to crops made easier the task of nurturing young children and enlisting older ones in labors orchestrated to sustain a family's livelihood.

Agrarian livelihoods assembled embodied labor and environmental milieu, social relations and subsistence, pastoralism and crop protection spread across a mosaic of landscape uses, meanings, and sites. State proponents of villagization advocated the separation of mutually exclusive zones mapped to distinct uses. In contrast, Kaerezians *situated* their practices in hybrid spaces where agriculture, residence, and pastoralism mingled in a rich mosaic. Spreading their livelihoods across diverse social and environmental spaces, Kaerezians located homesteads as a node of nurturance—a site of pragmatic materiality, affect, and articulations that conjured opposition to villagization's lines of spatial discipline.

Plotting Micropractices of Cultivation

More than a half hour's hike from most homesteads, small plots of *tsenza* dotted steep ridges throughout Tangwena territory. Seasonally, this chalky root crop's verdant leaves shot out from dark, tilled soil. Tended exclusively by women, these grounded, gendered spaces inscribed sites outside the scheme's officially demarcated arable zones and far from farmers' fields and homesteads. The resettlement officer cited "conservation regulations" that prohibited cultivation on steep slopes, and his concerns were echoed by AGRITEX officials in Nyanga and Harare offices who argued that such practices promoted soil erosion. But he openly admitted to tolerating *tsenza* cultivation, as did visiting officials. Visible from long distances, these patchworks stood out on prominent ridges. Why were state prohibitions against *tsenza* cultivation not enforced?

First, *tsenza* plots were far from the scheme's dirt access roads. Visiting officials, the rare technical expert, and NGO workers rarely walked far from a road or spot accessible by four-wheel drive. Spatial remove and rugged terrain thus insulated *tsenza* from on-site policing. Second, most administrators agreed that *tsenza* cultivation was relatively environmentally benign. Third, Kaerezi's administrators, visiting state officials, and the rare NGO worker were almost exclusively male, while *tsenza* cultivation was exclusively female. A tone of "Well, women are ignorant" and a shrug of the shoulders often accompanied official explanations for tolerance. The gendered shot often came with a chaser: benevolent patriarchal authority and gendered government should not persecute women who "don't know any better." Such explanations, however, should not neglect the *agency* and *effective articulation* of grounded micropractices. Assemblages on steep slopes mingled labor, soil, rain, and planted root crops. At the same time, agrarian practices articulated with ongoing cultural politics of rights, place, and power.

While most claimed that a meal was not a meal without *sadza*, two seasonal crops helped stretch families' maize supplies: yams (*madhumbe*) and *tsenza*. Yams required boiling, but *tsenza* could be simply peeled and consumed raw. The root's crunchy texture provided tactile variety in a diet almost exclusively boiled or soft-fried. For all these reasons, Kaerezians deemed *tsenza* a treat. Planted in bogs, along waterways, and sometimes lining stream banks, *madhumbe* were moisture hungry. Kaerezians termed these sites "fields" (*minda*), regardless of their location. Some *madhumbe* patches adjoined homesteads, separated from fields of maize and beans by the width of a single person. For those families located far from soggy soil, *madhumbe* fields might be a long walk away. Girls cultivated *madhumbe* with their mothers who "gave" the fields to both daughters and daughters-in-law—practices that cut against the grain of patriarchal inheritance. Social memory rather than physical demarcation and the resettlement registry mapped these plots.

While *madhumbe* might grow near other crops, I never saw *tsenza* near fields or fallow sites. An agricultural expert told me that *tsenza* depleted nitrogen from the soil and attracted nematodes to potatoes, but admitted that "technical knowledge" on the crop was scarce. Kaerezians spoke of the plant's "poisoning" the soil, "robbing" its productive power, and "weakening" the land. *Tsenza* "steals" and "impoverishes" soil while "confusing" and "disturbing" crops planted near it. In contrast, beans "cooperate" with maize, "strengthening" soil. Such understandings recognized the consequential materiality of mixtures of crops, soil, and labor both embodied and emplaced.

Informally organized groups of women, usually ranging in number from four to eight, selected and allocated an initial spot for *tsenza* as MaiRuvimbo, almost forty, told me: "We are not getting permission from anyone because that is the way our ancestors [*madzitateguru*] did it." Headman Mweya's niece, a young mother, explained that in *tsenza* groups, "There is no leader, but everyone says what she thinks, and we plan together to make the fireguard, and then to burn. We think together that we want that particular place. Then we go there." Groups emerged out of already existing social networks and friendships. MaiRuvimbo expressed her preference for farming together with members of the same church "because we already share a conversation." Minor disputes within groups were extremely rare and, by all reports, resolved among the groups themselves. The elderly Ambuya Clarissa stressed that women "farmed freely" (*kurima madiro*) on *tsenza* plots, an idiom many invoked. Rather than asking the local headman for permission, women "divided the area among ourselves."

In her late fifties, MaiHungwe lived in Tsatse, the epicenter of colonial ranch evictions. She once belonged to a group that inadvertently cultivated on *mabinga*, sacred sites running along the rainmaker's ridge. Nyahuruwa demanded a payment for their offense but was not angered. MaiHungwe explained: "We simply cultivated without authority from anyone, so we did not know that there were *mabinga* there. We paid, but Nyahuruwa told us that you may cultivate *madhumbe*. The ancestral spirits [*vadzimu*] do not like *tsenza*." To rectify the "mistake," the rainmaker asked that the group "respect the land" (*kuremekedza nyika*) by paying a bucket of *njera*—a grain brewed for rainmaking—and a chicken, a relatively minor fine. Cultivating "freely" did not preclude subjection to a rainmaker's rule.

"We cultivate each on our own [*pake pake*]," MaiHurudza explained, "but all at the same place. At the times we plow, we call each other together, then we apportion the plots [*huma*]. . . . Those who have cattle provide them, and those without, there is no problem." Getting cattle and a heavy plow up steep slopes represented a challenge, but procuring beasts and labor for opening plots was not. Other women spoke of sharing arrangements, describing the pooled agricultural labor for clearing the fields to plow as a *gumwe* (cooperative work arrangement). The women's teenage boys burned, cleared, and plowed the land while their daughters helped plant, weed, tend, and harvest by hoe and hand. On land flat enough to accommodate yoked oxen, a husband or adult male relative might plow. Male labor "helped" (*kubatsira*), but laid no claims to produce emerging from *tsenza* plots. In these sites, contrary to Locke, males' mixing of labor with land engendered neither exclusive property rights nor patrilineal inheritance.

Among small groups, women apportioned tilled soil into a patchwork of parcels (*huma dze tsenza*) demarcated by hoed ridges. Each woman claimed perhaps three to five small *huma* scattered across the group site. If a woman had all of her parcels grouped together, I was told, she ran the risk of a poor harvest due to the variations of soil quality, water flow, slope, and crop damage from animals and pests. Distributing the plots spatially, women emphasized, spread risks evenly. Heavy rains might favor one section of the mosaic, a drier-than-usual season another. The unpredictability of weather, blight, raids by animals from the nearby park, and other threats could not be controlled; but it might be managed.

Once individual portions were distributed, women cultivated, weeded, and harvested individually, rather than collectively. Cecilia, headman Mweya's niece, lived as an unmarried mother with her parents in Nyamutsapa. "When cultivating," she explained, "everyone has her portion. When you harvest from it, you may use the money in any way you feel. I may dig a portion in the name of Tatenda or Nyarai [her young sons] and when we sell the crops, the money has to be given to those children." In this manner, women's cultivation inscribed the landscape with domestic budgeting as gendered desires for family provisioning mapped onto mountainsides. Careful accounting allocated money earned from a particular plot for a specific child's school fees, clothes, or bus fare to visit a relative. Children might contribute labor to plots designated for their own school fees, but they also labored on behalf of crops earmarked for relatives or neighbors. Adult accounts relied on the fiction of children's free labor. Cash from selling *tsenza*, more than from any other marketable produce, became subject to women's discretion within household budgeting. *Tsenza* provided an important source of relatively autonomous income in cash-strapped homes. As feminist scholars have stressed, such resource access improves women's bargaining position within the "conjugal contract" through which household economic decisions and provisioning responsibilities are negotiated.[5]

Sedimented practices meticulously *graphed* the landscape with a complex patchwork of plots, household budgets, and women's rights to harvest. To read these "maps," officials needed knowledge specific to place and practices. Viewing agricultural plots on steep slopes, official optics could not discern the nuances of micropractices and their articulations with cultural politics. Individualized rights and household budgets, etched on the landscape, were at once visible and indecipherable. Visibility did not guarantee legibility, and far from the landscape constituting a text, its markings pointed to situated practices and knowledge not captured in any single way of seeing. Government officials could not interpret identifiable individualized claims—household accounting and a woman's or child's crop—and thus could not hold individuals accountable for transgressing conservation prohibitions.

Women's *tsenza* cultivation produced spaces tolerated by patriarchal and state power yet entangled with both. Alvord's centralization in the 1930s and the Native Land Husbandry Act in the 1950s and 1960s, by allocating a fixed parcel of land to married males, sought to subsume women's land rights solely within patriarchal households. In *tsenza* plots, women "farmed freely" (*kurima madiro*) on state-owned land spatially beyond their government-allocated fields legally registered in their husband's names.[6] Women cultivated sites not outside state space, but entangled within it. Their practices proclaimed freedom while recognizing subjection to a rainmaker's sovereignty. Gendered assertions of rights, grounded in root crops harvested from precise plots, entangled hoeing and harvesting with deeply rooted territorial politics future chapters will detail: the traces of a rainmaker's claims to precolonial rule, memories of women's defiance of colonial evictions, and subsequent challenges to an appointed acting chief many perceived as a postcolonial puppet.

An Encroaching National Park

In early 1991, I gazed across fireguards, strips of burned grass that marked the park's boundary, near MaiHurudza's home as she shucked maize to roast for her five children. The forested landscape south of Nyamutsapa had been white property buffering Kaerezi from the park. State purchase in 1987, amid complex land transfers that also acquired Nyamutsapa and Dazi, effectively extended the park estate. Why, I asked MaiHurudza, did she think the park expanded? "Greed" (*mbayo*), she responded scornfully, pulling hard on a green husk to emphasize her anger. Some spoke of the park's extension as "seizing land by force"; others called it "plunder" (*kupamba*). MaiHurudza's neighbor echoed such sentiments: "We are no longer free [*rusunguko*]. When we went to get permission to gather wood, we had to kneel down and beg." She mimicked kneeling in the direction of the nearby park and then pointed to hillsides in the park where she used to gather freely whenever she wanted. Parks staff had been allowing the scheme's residents to harvest pine and wattle trees, planted when the estate was private commercial forest. Most could not read the English on park signs that proclaimed an "Exotic Species Eradication Program" next to freshly clear-cut pine swatches. An employee told me a "shortage of manpower" dictated a policy that limited Kaerezians' access to "exotic" species to one or two specified days of the week. During these set days, women could chop and gather firewood, but not disturb "indigenous" trees. Men could cut wattle or pine for fencing or building materials. Yet the park prohibited cattle and the sledges they pulled to transport heavy loads. Cattle could be impounded and fines levied. Ferrying firewood and lumber legally thus required exhausting labor, and people replacing oxen as beasts of burden. As a result, park officials' "offer" held little attraction and, for some, increased resentment.

Most women I knew feared greater surveillance of all their harvesting practices, including fruit and reeds, and more rigid enforcement of regulations in the

Nyanga National Park game guards on armed patrol, Nyamutsapa, 1992.
Photo by the author.

scheme due to the neighboring park. Angela, a forthright woman in her late fifties, critiqued the park's policing of livelihood practices that violated her sense of local "freedom": "Long back we fished and hunted, but nowadays it's no longer possible. Nowadays there are **National Park**s. When you are seen going to the river, they check whether you are going there to fish. Long back you moved at your will [*madiro*]. . . . The **National Park** was there long ago, but the laws were different. We knew that animals had to be preserved, but we did not know that they would put soldiers all around." Her defense of activities usually gendered male, hunting and fishing, suggests that she perceived these livelihood practices as critical to family and community well-being. The "soldiers" were uniformed game scouts conducting armed patrols. Most appreciated the patrols pursuing the pride of lions that preyed on cattle in late 1991, but the weapons also represented an extension of state force. Some staff personably nurtured friendships with Kaerezians; others appeared to enjoy the authority of gun and uniform. When a drunken game scout became belligerent at a neighbor's homestead, I was not the only one nervously eyeing his brandished weapon. A shrewd mother of nine whose youngest children were in eyesight immediately suggested a meal of maize porridge, her hospitality muting his apparent anger.

Park staff disagreed on how to reduce the problem of poaching. The term constructed hunting and gathering as a theft of property, effectively criminalizing customary practices. One game guard had been the former head of security for a large tea estate. I was hiking in the park with a couple of schoolboys when I encountered him near the confluence of two small rivers. Once convinced that we had not set the snag line he just found rigged in the river, he detailed his plan to "capture poachers," showing me his "stakeout" spot. Some of his colleagues, however, favored "education" rather than rigid enforcement. One local officer admitted to a problem with game scouts who searched Kaerezians' huts for animal skins and other signs of poaching "with no legal right." Hospitality and suspicion mingled in the scheme. Some feared visits to homesteads might lead to searches; others offered meals and tea in exchange for news and gossip from the District Center. A policy of stationing staff far from their homes minimized kinship connections. Yet friendships formed, as did grudges.

Angela accused game guards of poaching salaries while letting wildlife, well, run wild. She lambasted the guards for letting animals escape by nightfall to raid her crops. The border's permeability, from her perspective, should flow one way, letting residents hunt and harvest firewood while keeping animals from poaching crops. Residents debated the relative merits of a wire fence on the park perimeter, a highly unpractical and unlikely prospect. MaiHurudza, often the sole adult in her homestead while her husband earned wages at a tourist hotel, bemoaned the crop predations from wildlife. "I'm a woman and alone. I'm scared to go outside in the fields at night." Women and men who wanted a fence cited two advantages: the reduction of crop destruction from marauding animals crossing by nightfall from the park; and the prevention of cattle straying into the park where they could be impounded and ransomed for an official fee.

Many women feared losing access to reeds growing along the park's streams and riverbanks. They harvested, processed, and wove them into handicrafts for sale. For women from poorer households, the handicrafts represented a relatively autonomous source of income. Many were able to decide how to spend the money from their sales, usually on children's school fees or clothes. Women could weave by firelight in the evening without taking time away from expected household labor. Friends or relatives would market rugs, bags, and weavings near the district's tourist hotels. Waiters, bellboys, and kitchen workers home on holidays collected crafts for sale. White tourists, by some accounts, preferred the informal markets to the tourist shops in the District Center. They could purchase "rural authenticity" along with a local handicraft, getting a story from a hotel employee about his mother, aunt, or sister who wove the fruits of nature into a desirable commodity.

Tewa sits with his wife, MaiFarai, MaiNyasha, and Celia who are weaving reeds, Nyamutsapa, 1991. *Photo by the author.*

Beyond the legal gathering of firewood and building poles, or reeds and herbs, some claimed customary hunting rights in defiance of state law prohibiting unauthorized hunting of wildlife. SaGumbo asserted these rights by invoking what Marx called, in the context of resource conflicts in nineteenth-century England, "the customary rights of the poor" to harvest the "alms of nature."[7] Poetically, he mused: "*Mhuka dze sango inhaka ye povo*" (The wildlife in the forest is the poor's inheritance). Claims to inheritance, echoing chiefly Tangwena claims to a *nyika*, here extend to wildlife populating the landscape. Yet these localized rights deployed global discourses to justify environmental entitlements. SaGumbo eloquently explained his rationale "The Bible says 'cattle is meat, goats are meat, and a buck is meat.' That's why people should eat all different kinds of animals, except those prohibited in the Bible such as pigs. Meat, I want it, but National Parks doesn't allow us to hunt. . . . But it's *our* wildlife, the animals are *ours*." Fascinated with a headlamp I sometimes used to walk at night, he asked to borrow it late one evening. I was speaking with his children and wife around the cook-hut fire when we were all startled to hear a musket shot ring from the dark of night. His wife and I exchanged knowing glances and a grin as she crafted creative explanations for the noise, assuring the children that MNR bandits were not on the prowl.

Several men spoke of their *shavi*, a personal patron spirit, who required habitual appeasement through hunting. Denied the pursuit of game, a *shavi* risked becoming an angry "avenging spirit" (*ngozi*) dangerous to self and kin. A local schoolteacher recalled a teenage hunt with Gonzo, at least forty years older and almost a foot shorter than the athletic young man. Gonzo walked with a limp, usually aided by a cane or ax handle and wore glasses thick as a bottle. Yet he was known for his hunting prowess. I knew the schoolteacher well enough to sense both surprise and earnestness as he spoke of Gonzo's heated pursuit of a buck, bow and arrow in hand: "He sprinted past me as though I was standing still. I was running as fast as I could, but he was possessed by his *shavi*." Even the District Administrator recognized that for many men this gendered patron spirit needed to be considered when planning wildlife conservation projects. Hunting spirits forcibly made idle, like dormant dip tanks, fomented anger and raised rural discontent.

My one experience of joining an opportunistic hunt emerged while plowing in a neighbor's field. Women gathering firewood flushed a buck from the forest by daylight. They yelled to a man herding cattle. In turn, neighbors relayed the buck's path by shout, gesture, and fleet-footed children, word reaching us many links from the hunt's originators. Among my fieldmates was Sironi, the secondary school's fastest runner, who cleaned up at the annual field day. He grabbed a small bow and quiver, handed me a hand ax, and my strides followed his toward neighbors' shouts. After scampering through brambles after the bounding buck, we marveled as it sailed over a surprised boy running toward us before it leapt a deep gulley and bolted up a hillside toward the park. A fateful combination of adrenaline and luck placed us on its return path when another neighbor's pack of dogs bore down from a ridgeline. With the buck exhausted and cornered by dogs, Sironi shot a hand-tooled arrow into its throat at close range.

My hand ax had been but a running baton, but the dogs' owner jokingly told me, "Your *shavi* will be pleased," as he came on the kill and called off his pack. While cutting up the carcass, he carefully reviewed the respective labors contributing to the hunt, apportioning shares to all, including the women who flushed the buck and those who shouted its path. For having pulled the fatal bowstring, Sironi received the heart and liver, presented as a couplet to us both. Knowing I was a vegetarian and that we shared the same cook hut, Sironi played to the elder's insistence on honoring my lame contributions. Later, the schoolteacher who once watched the possessed Gonzo sprint past him, joked: "You're a hunter's dream—long legs, swift when possessed by your *shavi*, and a vegetarian."

Zvisikwa

The national park and state legislation stressed the "conservation" of "natural resources"—rivers and streams, valleys and mountains, forests, game, and fish, the scenic terrain and wildlife that attracted tourists to Nyanga National Park. Most Kaerezians used the term *zvisikwa*, literally, "things created," to refer to these environmental features. *Zvisikwa* do not posit an ahistorical essence excluding human imbrications from milieu. They transgress a clear boundary between the natural and the cultural.[8] By reminding users of the historical process of creation, they invite reflection on human and nonhuman agency in their formation. The term accommodated a range of cosmologies and religious idioms: a supreme being, a Christian deity, ancestral spirits of lineage and family (*vadzimu*), and guardian spirits for a particular territory (*mhondoro*) can all hold responsibility for creation. So, too, can ecological processes. *Zvisikwa* have become imbued with use-values and meanings through daily livelihood struggles: the collection of firewood, pasturing of cattle, drawing water from springs and streams, and hunting and fishing. As Headman Mweya put it: "People must use *zvisikwa*. When we see an animal, we say we have seen meat, and when we see trees, we now have firewood."

Angela's ax strokes, ancestral spirits, SaGumbo's cattle, and the river's headwaters all shaped the terrain of territory (*nyika)* and environmental resources (*zvisikwa*). Many Kaerezians expressed befuddlement at clear-cut swatches of pine-and-wattle plantations in the park. They knew from experience as colonial tenants the backbreaking labor of establishing plantations on white property. Some shook their heads, claiming white tourists *wanted* to see trees in the park. Evergreens, Kaerezians told me, reminded Europeans of home, making African landscapes familiar. Park officials targeted invading exotics, Australian wattle and Mexican pine, hoping to return the ecosystem to its indigenous roots. Yet locals remembered African labor *producing* that landscape. Colonial evictions uprooted African tenant farmers from the park; postcolonial "exotic eradication" targeted the mixture of African labor and Australian and Mexican trees.

Mwari created *zvisikwa*, Angela explained, "without saying that they had to be protected [*kuchengetedza*]." Her God also created environment, and she resented park-imposed regulations. Yet Angela actively practiced many forms of "protecting resources" (*kuchengetedza zvisikwa*). She walked further into forests to search for dead trees, leaving live ones untouched by her ax. She spared specific trees amid pasture because they "made the soil strong." Angela drew water to wash pots rather than putting dirty ones in streams or the river. She applied cattle manure in her fields, intercropping maize and beans. Angela knew to avoid mixtures of organic matter and embodied labor that "confused" or "robbed" soil. Students taking agriculture courses at Nyafaru's secondary school explained that the leguminous trees Angela let stand "improved pasture," charting nutrient cycles and nitrogen flows. I frequently walked the landscape with their teacher, who pointed out both "ecologically sustainable" and "harmful" agricultural practices that dotted Kaerezi's hillsides, valleys, and ridges.

Kuchengetedza wove together notions of nurturance, guardianship, preservation, and intimacy; caring for, looking after, and valuing. The verb's cognates kept children close, imbued affect in social relations, and emphasized emotional and spatial intimacy. Neighbors and kin could be asked to care for fragile pots and people, fields and friendships, cattle and cash. Each obligation required a blend of wise management, ethical use, and skilled practices. Conduct deemed dangerous created cracks, fissures, and possibly even irreparable damage. This assemblage *produced* a collective interest in protecting resources, just as it shaped political sentiments critiquing park prohibitions. Hall's elaboration of Gramsci's notion of hegemony has stressed the production of emergent cultural formations: "It entails a quite different conception of how social forces and movements, in their diversity, can be articulated into strategic alliances. To construct a new cultural order, you need not to reflect an already-formed collective will, but to fashion a new one, to inaugurate a new historic project."[9] Kaerezians' cultural practices surrounding *zvisikwa* fused with the consequential materiality of nonhumans as well—the flows of rivers, the growth of forests, and the erosion of soil.

Animated spirits that dwelled in the landscape encouraged care in relating to resources. I knew schoolboys and adults afraid to swim in particular pools along the river for fear of *njuzu* said to live in their depths. These water spirits, less mermaids than predators, seized children whose drowned bodies, I was told, were not always found. When I dove deep into a dark pool in the bend of a river, two teenagers refused to swim, explicitly citing their fears of *njuzu*. They were not timid. Both traveled trails at night when they knew a lion was killing cattle in the scheme. And both had braved possible MNR attacks by leaving to dip cattle near the border well before sunrise. Neither would point at Nyangani, a sacred site (*nzvimbo inoera*).

Tales of magical mist and enveloping clouds haunted the mountain range where people claimed to have seen unexplained lights. Many agreed that Nyangani was a place where "strange things happened and people disappeared," making it a bit like Zimbabwe's Bermuda Triangle. In Kaerezi, the prohibition against pointing to Nyangani's peak was widely followed. Some used their elbows rather than fingers to gesture toward landmarks in the park just to be safe.

Such cultural practices should not be romanticized to suggest that "traditional" or "indigenous" environmental knowledge and practice *necessarily* nurtures nature in sustainable ways. Some Kaerezians cultivated on stream banks, quickening siltation, while others dutifully avoided the practice. Some flushed fertilizer in shared waterways. Others went out of their way to keep downstream neighbors assured of clean drinking water. Some walked longer distances to find fallen tree limbs for firewood. Others, scarce on incentive, patience, or embodied energy under the burden of difficult livelihoods, chopped live trees knowing they were contributing to deforestation. Kaerezians had no essential bond with nature that produced inherently ecological practices.[10]

Yet in Kaerezi, the cultivated conduct of caring for landscape refracted through the cultural politics of belonging to both a community and a landscape. Many practiced *kuremekedza nyika*, respecting, honoring, and appreciating territory. Menstruating women did not wash in rivers, while sacred sites precluded tilling or burning. Spectral powers demanded thanks for rains and harvests, whether through church prayers or ancestral propitiation. Members of African independent churches contributed a small token of grain to the rainmaker for a ritual to summon water from sky to fields, but they spoke directly to heaven, asking their God to bring rains and healthy harvests. Christians and animists disagreed on the ethics and efficacy of spiritual practices, but they largely shared a sense of what constituted an offense to *nyika*.

Headman Pabwe proudly pointed across his neighbors' fields and grass-filled hillsides as we walked his territory. The absence of unsightly burns, he explained, rendered visible that people were *kuremekedza nyika*. Almost as an afterthought, he acknowledged that they obeyed the laws of state as well as those of territory. Children learned early not to wash pots in streams or rivers, drawing water from springs with a clean bucket so as not to pollute drinking supplies. Some admonished youngsters not to wear red in the fields during harvest to "respect territory." Others cited state regulations that precluded stream-bank cultivation to stem the tide of soil siltation. Both state and local sovereigns had laws (*mitemo*) regulating resource use. Both laws and micropractices of *zvisikwa* produced particular kinds of subjects.

Postcolonial conservation prohibitions bore traces of concerns voiced by E. D. Alvord, the American agriculturalist and missionary whose "gospel of the plow" invoked apocalyptic images of the US Dustbowl. *The Rape of the Earth*, influenced by US fears, circulated widely among colonial conservation officials throughout Africa from the late 1930s onward.[11] In 1987, Bernard Chidzero, Zimbabwe's minister of finance, economic planning, and development, was a member of the Brundtland Commission that put sustainable development and environmental politics firmly on the global policy agenda.[12] In the 1990s, posters adorning schools and government offices promoted national conservation strategies by proclaiming the importance of *kuchengetedza zvisikwa*, encouraging a participatory population to secure the welfare of nature, nation, and their respectful inhabitants. Repressive forms of power excluded access to fragile ecological landscapes, forbid land use deemed degrading, and arrested transgressors while impounding their cattle. Yet cultivating subjects also policed themselves, producing landscapes while procuring livelihoods.

In postcolonial Kaerezi, the concepts of "protecting resources" and "respecting territory" were shot through with localized sedimenations of global routes. A hunter invoked biblical verse to argue for environmental entitlements that secured customary access to wildlife. Angela critiqued soldiers of fortune whose armed patrols enforced park prohibitions, their salaries suggesting illicit forms of wealth grounded in denying local resource rights. And Sironi yoked oxen named London and Transport to plow contours bearing the traces of Alvord's American agricultural missionization, finding fertile ground in colonial land policies. All considered *sadza*, the staple stiff-maize porridge, their most "traditional" food— sewn by Portuguese empire but adopted as a nationalist native meal. As *bricoleurs*, Kaerezians harvested idioms from multiple meanings of *Mwari*, from agricultural science and customary agro-ecology, from the local roots of indigenous trees and the global routes of maize, markets, and conservation discourse. Neither purely local nor global, sole product of chiefly rule or state power, the (agri)cultural practices that grounded subjects in territory produced entangled landscapes.

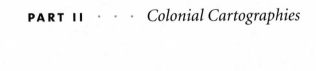

PART II · · · *Colonial Cartographies*

4 · Racialized Dispossession

First, white folks discovered Africa
and claimed it fair and square.
Cecil Rhodes couldn't have been robbing nobody
'cause he said there was nobody there.
—GIL SCOTT-HERON, "Black History," 2000

Many Kaerezians used the Shona *mbayo*, greed, to refer to whites having ex-propriated more land than they actually used (*kushandisa*). Stemming from *kushanda*, the verb for arduous manual work, *kushandisa* evokes a terrain that is the target, product, and ground of labor. On white farms and ranches, African tenants toiled on landscapes with vast stretches unworked, void of visible "improvements." A man in his fifties displaced by 1986 state evictions from Tsanga Valley to Dazi, where he was resettled, recalled the vast stretches of the Inyanga Block, once a single European property. Sweeping his arm dramatically to convey the huge historical acreage owned, he quipped angrily in English: "Too much fucking land for one man."

In this chapter, I link racialized dispossession and labor discipline. Rather than conceiving of capitalist labor as outside the project of governmentality, I locate the politics of productive relations within the triad-in-motion of sovereignty, discipline, and government. How did racialized rule shape the twin projects of dispossessing Africans of land rights and bonding them as labor tenants to white farms? To ask the question is not to assume that colonial administrators, as representatives of the state, always acted in ways functional to capital accumulation by white farmers. As an analytic, governmentality can help displace the often exclusive pairing of the politics of land and labor solely with the couplet of capital and state. *Racialized dispossession*, I argue, constituted one of capitalist labor discipline's conditions of possibility in the Eastern Highlands. I focus on the projects of producing laboring subjects, of governing their conduct, and of disciplining their practices on white farms.

These technologies of rule, extremely localized in their applications on specific parcels of land, drew from imperial circuits of power, knowledge, and colonial administration. Capital flowed through these transcontinental routes, but so, too, did discourses—of sovereignty, ownership, property rights, and laborers on estates. Crucial to tenancy arrangements was the legal fiction of a "labor agreement" that contractually stipulated terms of employment and dismissal. Hegemony's twins of coercion and consent fused in efforts to impose supposed agreements on Africans in the name of protecting their labor rights. Kaerezians invoked idioms of rights that challenged Rhodesian policies and white owners' practices. Yet colonial administrators, at times, sharply disagreed with white farmers, arguing for government policies more accountable to the claims of African citizens and subjects.

Absentee Owners and African Unrest

Colonial authorities installed Dzeka Tangwena, Rekayi's father, as the first officially recognized Chief Tangwena in 1902, the year of Cecil Rhodes's death. His rule lasted until the late 1920s. A man in his eighties told me that during Dzeka's reign, "whites came begging [*kukumbira*] for grazing land." Local residents generally gave them permission, providing labor to tend their cattle herds. In contrast, colonial assertions of white land rights invoked imperial property laws. In 1654, white settlers near Cape Town received their first land grants. Through the Cape Dutch system of land tenure, "Europeans were virtually given a free hand to peg out their own farms."[1] The laws of Europe's Low Countries traveled far up southern Africa's slopes. White settlers arrived in Nyanga to peg farms in 1893; six of them had been members of Rhodes's 1890 Pioneer Column.[2]

Following in his brother's furrows in 1870, the seventeen-year-old Rhodes arrived by ship in Durban and began farming cotton in colonial Natal. North America's Civil War shaped British metropolitan demand for colonial cotton from other sites. Discourses of race and freedom linked violence in one former colony to land expropriation in another. "What strikes you here most," Rhodes wrote his mother that first year, "is how little cultivated the land is."[3] Before eventually purchasing land from the British Natal Land and Colonisation Society, he tilled his brother's farm. Eyeing an adjacent parcel in 1871, he noted that a chief had cleared the land. Since it was in an area not reserved for Africans, the chief could be evicted and "the fruit of his labours turned to a white man's advantage." It might not be "right," but it was white; and it was "legal."[4] Over the next decades, Rhodes accumulated a vast fortune through mining, reaping capitalist profit and governing empire as an elected official. He became prime minister of the Cape of Good Hope Colony in 1890, the same year he attempted to orchestrate white colonization of the territory that bore his name.[5]

Rhodes himself visited Nyanga for the first time in 1896 en route to the port of Beira on Africa's eastern coast. Struck by the spectacular landscape and concerned about white landgrabbing, he contacted his real estate agent: "Inyanga is much finer than you described. I find a good many farms are becoming occupied. Before it is all gone, buy me quickly up to 100,000 acres and be sure you take in the Pungwe Falls. . . . Do not say you are buying for me."[6] Rhodes's agent could not acquire the Pungwe Falls, but he purchased 96,000 acres (a little under 40,000 hectares) that eventually comprised the core of Nyanga National Park's 47,100 hectares.[7] When he died in 1902, Rhodes willed his estate "for the instruction of the people of Rhodesia," entrusting his property to benefit his namesake nation.[8]

During the early decades of the twentieth century, experimental fruit production and stock raising of cattle and sheep benefited white farmers, clarifying the racialized imagined community Rhodes's estate envisioned. As with many farms in the district, however, vast pockets of the estate remained idle; these sections were described in a 1902 report as "Occupation nil. Stock nil, improvements nil."[9] For decades, such absentee ownership was widespread.

Throughout the Eastern Highlands, whites used legal instruments to claim vast tracts they neither occupied nor operated themselves, speculating in real estate, running cattle, and collecting African rents. By the 1920s, 60 percent of the district had become alienated by Europeans.[10] Characterizing the situation in 1934, however, the Inyanga Native Commissioner reported on the "scanty" occupation of land by Europeans: "Most of the landholders are absent and the agents do not live on the property."[11] Initially, land alienation concerned less white on-site presence than a need for cash for the district's estimated 20,000 Africans.[12] Dispossessed of land rights, Africans living on white farms had their labor doubly alienated—in tenancy agreements with white owners who allowed them a subsistence smallholding, and through migrant wage labor to procure cash for taxes and rents.

Hut taxes were collected as early as 1899, and Kaerezians reportedly paid their first taxes in chickens to a civil servant collecting in Rhodes's name.[13] To enlist chiefs in the project of indirect rule, officials paid them a small allowance, in the words of a 1897 report, "whilst they remained loyal and carried out the orders of the NC [Native Commissioner]."[14] The following year, the Inyanga NC recorded district chiefs' "decided objection" to private farms. Noting that natives "seem quite content" working under labor agreements, he argued that "unless the chiefs work them up they will soon be taught to see that the act is a protection to them and not a burden."[15] Government, in this vision, secured national wealth by managing, in Foucault's terms, the *imbrication* of "men and things."[16] It oversaw the welfare of laboring subjects, ensuring protection from potential predation by white capital while using laws to secure production for private farms.

Chiefs who riled up their subjects, however, threatened this project. So also did African objections to absentee owners who demanded rents. African popular and regal resentment to private rents on alienated land became a major administrative concern. In 1907, the Inyanga NC argued: "They cannot understand why they should pay rent when, to their idea, the land is lying idle and there is no visible owner. Briefly, on occupied land they see a reason for paying but not so on unoccupied ground on which they have been living for generations past."[17] Rents paid to absentee owners unsettled Africans in several senses, inciting grievances and encouraging migration across the colonial border.

Private rents diminished state revenues. Roughly 10 percent of the district's population fled to Portuguese territory in the year ending in 1906,[18] causing, by 1909, a dip to levels below those of 1904.[19] The vast estates in the Eastern Highlands were especially hard hit, hemorrhaging rent fleers whose taxes had been the lifeblood of colonial coffers. By 1906, the NC expressed concern regarding lost tax revenue, noting that "most of [the] Tangwenas" had moved over into Portuguese territory fleeing hut rent. He contemplated Inyanga's "huge block" of "practically unoccupied ground" from a "business point of view," suggesting its conversion to a rent-free reserve to attract tax payers back across the border.[20] Dzeka Tangwena was among three chiefs whose majority of followers ran from "double taxes" on white land, "passing over to Portuguese Territory to evade payment" in 1906.[21] When Dzeka lodged a formal complaint against rents in his territory the following year, he provided more fuel for arguments already made by Inyanga's NC.[22] The NC sought earnestly to convey populist and chiefly complaints to his superiors, unsuccessfully lobbying for "an ordinance, compelling [white owners] to occupy the land, before demanding rent from Natives."[23]

To aid administrative efforts, the NC invoked a metaphysics of white presence.

White absence on private property impeded tax collection and administration that enlisted headmen and chiefs in governmental practices. In turn, Africans needed to *understand* their subjection so that state power could act on their willful actions. To enlist Africans in the projects of government, he implied, they needed to inhabit a territory where white presence rendered visible racialized dispossession. At times, Inyanga administrators attempted to *defend* African rights from rapacious capitalist accumulation. African unrest on unoccupied farms prompted a lengthy 1906 report to the Chief Native Commissioner chronicling the "case as put by the natives":

> We have lived here and held the ground. The Government has taken our money in the form of tax and promised us protection. We remained loyal in the rebellion. Those who rebelled are still in possession of their ground and ours have been sold. The Government has thrown us away they don't want us. We don't want to go to Portuguese Territory but we are not going to stay here and be eaten up. (The Government Tax is £ 1 plus 10/- for each wife; the rent tax is £ 1 per individual and £ 1 for each wife). . . . We have too many chiefs. . . . how can one man own all the ground (They of course cannot realize that Bullock is agent for various companies). . . . The feeling in general throughout the district (and among the natives) is open and bitter: it is the grievance rent: at every beer drink it is the subject. . . . All the natives want is a reserve and an assurance that it will be theirs and not be sold.[24]

In the century's first decade, the NC defended Africans' "natural" resentment at the "option of moving on to Government Reserves should they refuse to pay the 'farmers' tax' (rent)" since "they have lived undisturbed on the land now occupied by them for so many years."[25] He recommended that all government land in the district's lowveld be "thrown open" for Africans refusing to pay rents on private land.[26] Those *practicing* the administration of Africans sometimes objected to a rationality of rule conceived far from the point of power's application. The Inyanga NC's implicit desire to recognize African rights emerged from his pragmatic attempts to govern. Protecting Africans from greedy capitalists also meant filling the state's coffers and making tribal subjects less likely to rebel. Administrators also claimed benevolent paternalism, supposedly safeguarding Africans from patriarchs. In 1906, the Inyanga NC suggested raising the tax age for males from fourteen to eighteen since fathers and senior relatives laid claim to money earned by younger teenagers.[27]

By the 1920s, Inyanga's commissioner bemoaned the "great misfortune that so much land was alienated to private companies in the early days."[28] Increasingly, men migrated outside the district in search of more favorable wages to pay both rents and taxes. Between 1940 and 1957, the number of Africans living on alienated European land dropped from 12,000 to 7,000, while those living on state land almost doubled from an initial 20,000. Some farms only charged rent to married resident males, enabling couples to avoid taxes through the long-term absence of men whose wives farmed and managed homestead parcels.[29]

In the early 1950s, more than half of the district's tax-paying males were "to all intent permanently away from home, in employment in the larger centers."[30] Wages sent home or directly paid by mail became the core of tax revenues. In the middle of the century, private white farms like Gaeresi Ranch and the nearby Rhodes Inyanga Estate relied on labor agreements with tenants, but they were short on labor.[31] Male absence worried administrators who reported that in the early 1960s, "Most of the land holdings are left in the care of women who are quite incapable of farming properly on their own."[32] As social historians have documented, however, women capably managed family fields in the long-term absence of labor-migrant husbands, bearing the major agricultural burden of this spatial distribution of work.[33] Gendered relations of production tapped women's daily and seasonal running of family parcels and the holiday visits of men to plow and transact livestock. When in 1992 MaiHurudza farmed in Nyamutsapa while her husband poured drinks for tourists in a hotel bar, the couple echoed more than a century of gendered geographies of labor shaped by a regional political economy.

Bankrolling Brothers

Loosening the top of his overalls in 1992, Mudhara sat in the tall grass overlooking the Kaerezi River Valley. He was one of the only Dazi residents with deep historical ties to the valley and its surrounding ranges. Self-identifying as Tangwena, he was also one of only a few Dazi families who refused to live in villagization's linear grids. His plowed fields emanated out from a cluster of huts near the park border. Sweating from our climb up the river valley, we sat on the steep slope; across the river, we saw scattered homesteads mingling huts and fields in Tangwena territory. Dazi's tightly packed settlements inscribed visible lines below us.

Born in Kaerezi in the first decade of the century when a Johannesburg-based syndicate owned the land, Mudhara herded cattle in 1921 for a white policeman stationed in the district center. Perhaps the absence of syndicate presence allowed the official to skim some grazing off property where he represented the principal form of white surveillance. Located in mountainous terrain along the colony's frontier, Kaerezi's relative isolation from white presence enabled corruption on multiple fronts. In the late 1920s, the white employee collecting rents for his Johannesburg office had his hand in the till. The syndicate sought government assistance, asking the Nyanga NC to send a native "through the block telling tenants that they are no longer to pay Macrone."[34] Translocal capital, racialized rule, and native assistance—as well as both white and black subversion—all infused practices of government. At the time, officials saw most of Inyanga Block as "empty country" with African settlement grouped around its borders.[35]

Mudhara recalled the arrival of the white owner to what became Dazi: "We were given *Manungo* in 1930." Tales of the rancher's being carried in a hammock by Africans may have been apocryphal, but his nickname literally means "the lazy one." *Manungo* was born Charles Hanmer in Britain in 1899, the year after white settlers forcibly put down major African uprisings across Rhodesia. He left Europe by ship in 1922 and traveled by train from the port of Beira to Rhodesia, where he began farming. During a trip to the Transvaal in 1927 to buy merino sheep, he spotted an advertisement for the Inyanga Block's sale in a South Africa farmers' weekly. The next year, Charles first walked a portion of the property with his younger brother William.[36] According to one of their friends, they were "enthralled by its beauty and its bountiful promise." They feared, as had Rhodes three decades earlier, that other whites would snatch up the property. Using the same imperial ingenuity pioneered by the colony's namesake, they deployed deception, telling the hotel manager on Rhodes Inyanga Estate that they had been prospecting, unsuccessfully, for chrome and asbestos. They did not want to get burnt. Charles boarded the next ship from Cape Town bound for Britain, seeking financial backing. Family connections proved helpful. Their great grandfather's brother had been governor of New Zealand, and imperial circuits had long linked family fortune to global routes.[37]

In 1905, the Anglo-French Matabeleland Company had purchased the vast Inyanga Block consisting of 73,600 morgan (approximately 67,000 hectares) from the British South Africa Company.[38] In the mid-1920s, around two hundred "native Africans" living there paid rent.[39] By 1930, the multinational imperial corporation, based in Johannesburg, sold 94,000 acres of its 162,000-acre Inyanga holdings to the Hanmer brothers for £9,000.[40] Inyanga's NC wrote to Salisbury's head office to request a "Private Location Ordinance," including an application to contract labor agreements with tenants.[41] The Hanmers enlisted twenty-six "Tangwena" laborers living on the property.[42] Charles began establishing pine and wattle plantations as early as 1930, the year Africans built his first homestead on the property. His initial plan to float logs down the Pungwe River to sawmills near the Mozambican port of Beira proved unfeasible, so he established his own sawmill, beginning operations in the early 1950s.

Mudhara recounted his 1927 marriage and *Manungo*'s arrival three years later. He then earned good wages in Harare, while his wife managed their smallholding on the Inyanga Block. His father's elder brother's funeral brought him home. While he never detailed the lineage claims on labor this might have entailed, he implied the loss tethered him more closely to home (*kumusha*). He knew that the property had been "the same farm with the tea estate of Igoe," naming the man who had sold a portion of his property to the national park in 1987, extending its own estate. "In 1930 *Manungo* bought the farm," Mudhara recalled. Charles Hanmer was among a large gathering in the District Center attended by other whites who had recently bought farms. Mudhara elaborated, mentioning the "books" (*mabhuku*) of tax payers kept by Chief Tangwena's headmen (*masabhuku*): "We were told that the seven books should be shown to the white person who had taken the land. We were told that we used to pay three dollars rent per year, but now we were going to pay two dollars. Everyone was happy, and we clapped hands. Long back it was very difficult to get two dollars. We were working, and to us it was not a problem. We sent the two dollars home so that parents would keep it for next year's rent."[43]

His vividly detailed memory of an event more than fifty years before stressed the intergenerational flow of urban wages to his parents on the ranch. Translocal migrant routes secured his parents', as well as his own, tenancy roots. Mudhara remembered *Manungo* at his arrival less as an oppressor extracting labor than as a generous landlord lowering rent. Perhaps the Inyanga Native Commissioner's plea to lessen the double burden of a "Farmers' Tax" finally found cooperative ears. Concerned about securing labor on his new property, Hanmer may have wanted to appear benevolent to administrators and tenants alike. Regardless, Mudhara's memories of ritual clapping (*kuombera*) acknowledged gratitude for the landlord's actions.

However, a tenant born on the ranch three years after *Manungo*'s arrival seemed less nostalgic. In 1951, when he became a labor tenant, he remembered that "people were afraid that if you stopped working you would be evicted from here. That was because *Manungo* used to say 'I bought this land.' So people followed what he said to avoid being chased away." The elder puzzled over the contradiction: "When *Manungo* arrived, there were already people living here. I don't understand how the area could be sold when the land already had its 'owners' [*varidzi*] living here." Letting *Manungo* stay did not mean accepting his claims to rightful ownership. State laws might require tenants to pay labor and rent to white landlords; white capitalists might claim ownership of alienated land. Yet neither white commodity conversions nor legal instruments displaced African moral and political assertions of land rights in Kaerezi.

Fences, Neighbors, and Rappers

In the late 1960s, chief Rekayi Tangwena, much like Mudhara in the 1990s, recalled that Charles Hanmer had "asked for grazing rights, and we granted them." When the white rancher's brother, William, arrived in 1948, he established a presence east of his brother. Yet Rekayi had his own interpretation of boundaries, rights, and idioms of ownership:

> He left a manager there who later went to the tea estates. Mr Hanmer then defined what he thought were his boundaries by putting fences around. His first fence left our people out of his area. We were not worried because it meant that his cattle would not come into our crops. It seemed a good thing. We thought it was done to prevent our cattle straying among his. We were surprised later when a second fence was put up which included our land. We thought it was to prevent our cattle from straying.[44]

"Good fences make good neighbors," wrote New England poet Robert Frost. Rekayi appeared to share the sentiment. The spatial separation of cattle and the ranch's plentiful grazing common open to African access may have contributed to tenants' understanding of a continuation of African land rights. In 1992, I interviewed Fergus Gilmour, the ranch manager mentioned by Rekayi, in a Harare suburb. He sat in a worn armchair in a modest bungalow brimming with old furniture, dust, and memories. A widower, Gilmour showed me pictures of his daughter's family, doting over his grandchildren. He had left Ireland for Southern Rhodesia in 1949, reaching Kaerezi the same year, twenty years after Mudhara married there. He became the only white then living east of the Kaerezi River, a recollection shared by Kaerezians. William Hanmer moved to the property in the early 1960s after Gilmour departed in 1954 to run a tea estate in Honde

Valley to the south. Gilmour stressed Kaerezi's remoteness and the rugged terrain: "When I got there, there was no road, no bridge. I put in the first bridge across the Gaeresi in the area, with gum plies, and then later with iron pegs." He oversaw the construction of the first buildings at Nyafaru. Gilmour recalled that the "main settlement was down at Tsatse's kraal," but he was unaware that several Tangwena chiefs and the ruling rainmaker had homesteads there. Kinga Tangwena, the only chief he knew, lived *off* the ranch near the Mozambique border.

"The stock was separate; it didn't mix," he noted, confirming Rekayi's recollection. No paddocks were needed. "They weren't any limits on herd size," the manager remembered. William Hanmer's cattle herd began with around 300 head, never peaking beyond 1,000.[45] Gilmour remembered that the neighbor, "Wyrley-Birch, had around 3,000 head of cattle and they were all over the place. He used to drive them across the river and graze them in Mozambique." Locals named Wyrley-Birch *Mabvura,* derived from the verb "to singe" (*kubvura*) and evocative of his harsh treatment of workers. In the 1990s, Headman Mweya and many Kaerezians elongated the syllables in *dzakawanda* (many) to emphasize the numeric and spatial extent of *Mabvura's* herd. The Hanmers, in contrast, hired their tenants' cattle to plow furrows for tree planting, establishing plantations.

The ranch manager recalled few Africans living east of the Kaerezi River in Nyamutsapa, but a number on the west side in Dazi. While Gilmore offered no explanation, Kaerezians did. A man who worked for both brothers told me that when "*Manungo* sold this land" to William, Charles told tenants to move to his western half of the property. A number of people moved, later returning across the river to find that William had destroyed their huts. In an area where labor remained scarcer than many white ranchers desired, the brothers at times competed for tenants.

Sibling rivalry and diverging interests subdivided the property into two parcels. Charles became the managing director of the Pulpwood Company of Rhodesia in the western half, land including Dazi. William managed Gaeresi Ranch, east of the river, overlaying Tangwena territory. A man born in 1931 described Charles as "kind; he liked to help people." Many told me that he brewed beer and slaughtered cattle for feasts, although he was "troublesome" in demanding hard labor. In contrast, his brother William earned the nickname *Chimhini. Nyamini* is a vicious ant with a venomous sting; the prefix *chi* marks a thing. Kaerezians agreed that *Chimhini's* labor discipline stung sharply. Frequently voiced memories emphasized that he was "harsh," "oppressive," and rude (*haana tsika,* literally, "without culture").

For more than half a century, practices in Kaerezi constructed property not as an object owned in deeds, but as effect, at once material and discursive, of power relations. Kaerezians remembered a landscape where ownership did not map discretely to property boundaries. At times, the Hanmer brothers shared labor tenants, even after they divided the property. Yet they also competed for relatively scarce labor, drawing tenants away from each other. In the 1990s, the Nyanga DA asserted administrative differences between Kaerezi Main Resettlement Scheme and its annex, grounding them in separate property purchases. Colonial "owners" and postcolonial administrators, despite rhetorical invocations of fixed policies mapped to discrete parcels, blurred boundaries. Property and power had no singular logic, but rather complex and contingent practices that cut in several directions at once.

Kaerezians frequently invoked the farms of *Manungo* and *Chimhini* as ongoing geographies to locate contemporary events. As a result, I quickly learned to map the brothers' Shona names to respective sides of the river. Yet in Harare's National Archives and the district's offices, documents used their English names. I often crossed wires, and thus the river, in translation. In 1991, I pondered this problem with Maxwell, a savvy young Kaerezian who had recently passed his O-level English exam, an extreme rarity in the scheme.[46] We were sitting in Nyamutsapa, looking across a landscape scorched by a recent brush fire that shot up the valley, burning pasture and coming dangerously close to homesteads. In Shona, I floated, "It looks like I imagined the ranch of *Mabvura*," the Scorcher. Maxwell laughed at the lame pun. He asked about Amnesty International, pointing to the group's logo affixed to my clipboard next to a World Wildlife Fund sticker. His bright orange World Wrestling Federation visor cap, I pointed out, shared an acronym with the prominent environmental NGO. They wrestled with large beasts, too, he fired back. I registered the touché. Conversation turned to *njuzu*, the water spirits living in pools that dragged children into the river's dark depths, to rainmaking, and to his family's appeasement of their ancestral spirits. He gestured with his elbow toward Mount Nyangani, dominating the horizon to the south, avoiding the prohibition against finger-pointing. Rare fires visible at night near the peak, he insisted, could not be explained by lost hikers or lightning strikes. Respect the range's sacred power, he advised.

I confessed that while I remembered where *Manungo* and *Chimhini* lived, I consistently confused their English names. How could I translate my Shona certainty into English, the language of colonial records? "You live near Oakland, don't you?" Maxwell asked in Shona, showing off an impressive geographical knowledge of California. "Isn't that the home of that **rappa**, MC Hammer?" he switched to English with *rapper*, changing inflection to mimic his version of a US "homie in the hood." "Well, *Manungo* was Charles Hanmer." He paused for effect: "Get it, MC Hanmer." (I now live in Oakland. Fremont, MC Hammer's hometown, is a short transit ride.) Global circuits of hip hop helped clarify the intensely localized histories of land, labor, and resource rights. Can't touch that.

Disciplining Labor

Colonial legislation defined squatters as Africans living without formal labor agreements on land designated European by the 1930 Land Apportionment Act, amended in 1941. As early as 1948, Charles Hanmer wrote to the Native Commissioner complaining about the means to procure and *discipline* labor on his ranch. He sent copies to his member of parliament and the Rhodesia National Farmer's Union, hoping for action. At the time, Hanmer used "village headmen" to call on tenants whose "rent is paid in the form of work for a period each year." Yet he noted that these elders "cannot (or do not) have any real authority over the younger men," most of whom are "away for work, returning to their wives and kraals intermittently." Migrant labor and weak African authority, he worried, eroded his ability to secure a compliant workforce: "This lack of discipline leads to friction."[47] Feeble headmen were only part of the problem. They were "handicapped by having over them an equally weak and ineffective and uninterested chief. This man, TAUNGWENA [*sic*]," Hanmer wrote, "lives just off this property, and so I have no authority over him. The only legal pressure I can bring to bear on tenants is to turn them off the property. But I do not wish to do this, except in extreme cases."[48]

Evictions would remove needed labor along with unwanted squatters. As ranch manager Gilmour told me in 1992, "the labor agreement just said that you could recruit labor from the kraals on the farm. But if there wasn't any labor there, you couldn't recruit it." Writing to officials for assistance with labor discipline, Hanmer invoked both white ownership rights and the responsibilities of government. Gilmour recalled beginning ranch operations with only five African laborers, but expanding to scores because "usually people came and asked for work; we didn't usually have problems finding workers." "Lots of men were working away in Harare as cooks," he explained, "and the government didn't interfere with the wives who stayed home." Unbeknownst to him, Kaerezians spoke of concealing marriages to evade being "called for work" on the ranch. If workers failed to fulfill tenancy stipulations, he requested one of the Native Commissioner's staff to demand compliance. Before "the troubles with Tangwena," Gilmour recalled, "the Africans were very quiet, they never interfered with us." After moving to a tea estate, however, he did threaten a headman who refused to bring his people to work. "I told him that if they didn't come to work for me, I would bring a bulldozer and knock down all of their huts. Of course, I wouldn't really have done it, but he didn't know that. And it worked. They showed up with plenty of workers."

Targeting adult men, ranch labor discipline relied on an unstable interweave among white capitalist farming, threats made to traditional authorities, and state enforcement of tenancy contracts. A man born in the late 1920s expressed the predicament of most male migrants:

> There was nothing we could do. We worked so our families would have some-where to stay. . . . If you worked full-time in town, your family would be evicted. You were supposed to work three months a year on **duty**. A person was supposed to sign what they called the **Labor Agreement**. If you refused to sign, you would be evicted [*kudzingwa*]. You were free [*madiro*] to do anything as long as you showed up for work.

When Hanmer received no district-level action in 1948, he requested a meeting in the capital with the Chief Native Commissioner to discuss two pressing concerns. First, "Bringing pressure to bear on chiefs and headmen to exercise their authority more effectively over their rank and file, to oblige the latter to fulfill their obligation of service under their tenant's agreement with my company." Second, Hanmer wanted help "encouraging the women to work on the farm, particularly those whose husbands are away at work." He complained that the district's Native Commissioner "has not seen his way to help me."[49] Hanmer wanted government to act, obliging Africans to work under labor contracts. Indirect rule should modify African conduct even as it harnessed it. Hanmer lobbied colonial officials to *direct* indirect rulers, the chief and headmen, who would discipline productive subjects on white property. Government here braided together a tapestry of ownership, rights to persons, and command over subjects.

In the capital, the Chief Native Commissioner expressed concern that he had no record of any labor agreement between African tenants and Hanmer on Inyanga Downs, the mid-century name for the property. "The Natives are there illegally," he wrote to the secretary to the prime minister handling Native Affairs, "and unless Mr. Hanmer wishes to enter into a Labour Agreement they should be given notice through the Native Commissioner, Inyanga, to move off. I'm afraid the Chiefs have no more powers than we have to turn out Natives to work for Mr. Hanmer."[50] The Provincial Administrator clouded the waters a bit, finding records of natives who "live on the property under tribal conditions," approximately 150 to 200 of whom had entered into labor agreements with the owner. Noting the huge stretch of Inyanga Downs, he surmised, "I doubt whether its boundary with Crown Lands to the east has ever been correctly defined."[51] The white owner's appeal to law produced an *unintended effect*: surveillance of his own actions. He made administrators aware of Africans living on his property who violated racial land laws. Government, rather than procuring Hanmer labor, would require that he evict squatters who refused to sign agreements, purging his property of its workforce. If he attempted to stretch his boundaries to bind Africans in the neighboring reserves into tenancy agreements, he would also violate the law.

A few years later, Hanmer informed the Chief Native Commissioner that he "recently entered into a new labour agreement with tenants on this property." While some were "unwilling to sign," Hanmer hoped they would soon change their minds, and he expected them to stay. He complained that he had to "deal harshly" with younger men "for disciplinary reasons." He critiqued Rhodesian policy that required government to "find room" in a reserve for tenants before their legal eviction from European property. "In England, before the war," he argued, neither landowners nor government were responsible for evicted labor tenants. Those displaced subjects simply had "to find a new home." To mimic their motherland's modernity, colonial owners needed more freedom to evict tenants at their will. Government interference, he implied, coddled Africans in the name of welfare and paternalistic protection while constraining capitalist production. Owner-orchestrated evictions without government interference would, he argued, offer "hope for an improvement in the efficiency and discipline of the Africans."[52] For Hanmer, owners' threats of eviction should be an instrument to improve white land, the working conduct of the nation's population, and the economic security of the colony. Responsibility to find new homes should devolve to displaced workers, whose indiscipline on the ranch would render them both jobless and homeless. Labor tenants would thus become self-disciplining in the service of both state administration and white capital accumulation.

Marx famously critiqued the oppressive "ossified particularizations" that removed "all fixity and security in the situation of the laborer" in industrial Europe. Capitalism created a "monstrosity, an industrial reserve army, kept in misery in order to be always at the disposal of capital."[53] In Rhodesia, racial land laws provided a powerful prism to refract class relations onto subjects and space. Race was at once a legal, spatial, and social marker of difference produced through the imperial encounter. Rather than a prior ontological essence, "race" emerged from the political technologies that produced landscapes of dispossession and bonded labor, radical *unfreedoms* ushered in by colonial government and a capitalist political economy. As officials engineered Native Reserves as reservoirs for an industrial army, taxes made male migrant labor an economic necessity. In a colonial political economy dependent on these rural-urban articulations, labor discipline on white ranches thus targeted relational routes that linked distant sites.

While Hanmer frequently wrote to state administrators requesting their assistance in enforcing laws—especially those regulating tenancy contracts on his property—he also sought to keep government at a distance. A former tenant explained to me: "He didn't want the government's police to arrest anyone on his farm. If someone committed a crime, a policeman would go to *Manungo* to seek permission to arrest that person. If police came onto the farm without his permission, he would force them to free that person. He said, 'A person who works for me should not be troubled.'" Kaerezians shared several stories of the Hanmers' "chasing away" police from their property. They used the term *kudzinga*, the same verb used to describe the eviction of squatters. On white ranches, both state officials and property owners asserted claims to sovereignty, the enforcement of laws, and the contractual conditions of tenancy.

En-forcing Agreements

In the middle of the century, tenancy arrangements on both Hanmer properties allowed men's seasonal wage-labor migration to mines, farms, towns, and cities as far away as Johannesburg. Their wives farmed smallholdings with family labor, and government policy never supported Charles's earlier efforts to compel women to work for the rancher. By the 1960s, when William moved to Gaeresi Ranch, he demanded longer periods of "duty" from his laborers to expand wattle plantations. In 1964, when the "agreements" came up for renewal, he sought to convert tenants into full-time farmworkers, bonding their labor to locality. William's *spatial fix* would remove seasonal migration in pursuit of more favorable wages. If administrators and the ranch owner euphemized the instrument of labor discipline as an agreement, Kaerezians did not misrecognize its "symbolic violence."[54] They exclusively used the English term *agreement*. I almost never heard any Shona terms that traversed the semantic terrain of *agreement*, *promise*, *oath*, or *pact* to refer to this crucial labor law.

In October 1991, I joined Mujuru and his two wives in their Nyamutsapa cook hut when another potential eviction loomed. More than three months had passed since the DA's threatening letter. Mujuru recalled that during the mid-1960s, only one large extended lineage and a few other families lived in Nyamutsapa when Hanmer imposed the new tenancy contracts: "You will sign, certifying that forever I will work for you, and you will not be allowed to go and work anywhere. There will be nothing like working for **six** months and then going. You have to be at work *always*. . . . **Thirty-six** of us refused. . . . Policemen were sent but they did not find us. . . . I had run from the **labor agreement**." Those refusing, another elder recalled, "were to be chased away because *Chimhini* was saying we are giving others a bad spirit." Conduct in defiance of government policy represented a dual threat—challenging an administrative decree and encouraging others' refusal.

Kaerezians' constant use of the English term *labor agreement* ironically marked their refusal of its transcultural legitimacy. Rather than accepting the legal fiction of mutually consenting parties entering into a binding contract, for Kaerezians this device represented an instrument of *coercion*. They used the Shona terms *basa rakamanikidzwa*, forced labor, and *chibharo* or *chibaro*, the more widespread term with variants used throughout southern Africa for "forced labor, contract labor, and slavery."[55] *Chibharo* cut across state and private extractions, including forced labor for colonial conservation works such as Alvord's centralization scheme, as well as periods of "duty" on white farms.[56] While reticent to discuss the semantic linkage explicitly, Kaerezians used the same term for rape. Social memories in Barwe, the Mozambican territory from where Chief Tangwena had migrated to Kaerezi, melded forced labor and recollections of the rape of young women by African soldiers and police in the early twentieth century.[57] The gendered metaphor of sexual violence was more metaphorical in Kaerezi, suggesting that the emasculation of bitterly resented labor extraction was a moral affront as well as a bodily violation.

The Portuguese term *trabalho* (work) becomes *chibalo* in several southern African languages, and the slippage from *l* to *r* is a common one in Shona. The Portuguese Native Labor Code of 1899 gave legal backing to compulsory labor for any project deemed "public improvement."[58] Atkins traces "the hated system of forced labor, *isibhalo*" in nineteenth-century Natal to the Zulu verb *ukubhala*, to write down or register, used both for labor tenancy arrangements and for long-distance migration engineered by South African officials who negotiated directly with Portuguese authorities to "recruit" workers forcibly.[59] Such practices of *chibalo* were widespread through southern Africa. By 1895, by their own admission, half the Native Commissioners in Southern Rhodesia were "forcing natives . . . to work sorely against their will."[60] Use of the terms *isibalo*, *chibaro*, and *xibalo* traveled regional routes, signaling differing forms of forced labor in mines, farms, cities, and rural reserves. Whether compensated through wages or not, *chibaro* was always coerced.

In the 1990s, Kaerezians appreciated their relative freedom to farm, settle, and pasture livestock beyond villagization's spatial discipline. They frequently contrasted their farming or living "freely" (*madiro*) with government's efforts to "force" (*kumanikidza*) people into the lines against their will. These arguments conjured memories of forced labor (*basa rakamanikidzwa*) on two colonial ranches. But even the oppressive white ranchers, Kaerezians asserted, allowed labor tenants a great deal of self-determination concerning their homesteads, fields, and spatial practices. In 1991, an elder elaborated the lack of regulations over African agriculture. "They talked about pegging people's fields" around 1947, he recalled, but "it was not actually done. People refused." *Chimhini* did not even entertain the talk. "People were sent by *Manungo* to peg, but people refused, so he abandoned it." Simba, born in the early 1930s, recalled an absence of regulations imposed on tenant *farming*: "What the Hanmers wanted from people was labor. They didn't examine people's livelihoods." In contrast, postcolonial villagization represented an unwanted intervention, assembling livelihoods against a remembered ranch landscape of relative freedom amid coercive labor relations.

"How many months a year did tenants work for *Manungo*?" I pressed Simba. "Five weeks was one month," he responded soberly. Many invoked Hanmer's elongated "time of duty." He was contractually bound to pay tenants a set wage, yet he paid a month's wages for five week's work. Labor discipline turned the annual three-month duty into almost four, tying male migrants to the ranch for longer periods. Stretching time, Hanmer squeezed out more labor mapped to place.

Tenants wanted both a secure land right on the ranch *and* the relative advantage of better wages from long-distance labor migration. Reworking Marx's ironic freedoms that marked the historical transformation from European feudalism, Kaerezians wanted to be linked, but not bound to land. They sought the "freedom" to sell their labor to distant capitalists, but demanded a subsistence foothold for family agriculture. Tenants refused the owners' efforts to convert them to full-time bonded laborers. In so doing, they challenged hegemonic processes that struggled to code coercive labor as consent. The Hanmers both enlisted and critiqued government for its practices of African subjection, arguing that those evicted should themselves be responsible for finding a place to dwell. For Kaerezians, *chibharo* conjured unfreedom—the expropriation of their labor in conditions of neither their choosing nor their acceptance. As a cultural category, it cut across public and private. Capitalist labor discipline, racial land policies, and government "agreements" all converged on Gaeresi Ranch.

Freedom's Routes

These localized legacies of land and labor provide critical ground for reflecting on the spatial routes traversed by liberated subjects. Marx and Foucault offered influential accounts of modern power that probed the critical category of freedom and pivoted on relations among subjects, territory, and modes of subordination. I want to stress a convergence between Marx and Foucault that few appreciate—their shared insistence on forms of subjection that work in freedom's name. In the wake of free market triumphalism and the increasing hegemony of neoliberal capitalism as an integrated global system, the points at which Marx's and Foucault's accounts of power converge may offer both analytical and political purchase. Both authors query the exclusions, removals of rights, and disenfranchisement of dignity that dwell on the dark side of modernity, saturating the shadow of Enlightenment legacies.

Often unappreciated, however, is how both stress the *cultural politics of territory and subjection* in their analyses of Europe's historical transformation. In their accounts, empire echoed rather than shaped Eurocentric history, yet they acknowledged colonial relations of power. Both conceived violent conquest *inside* Europe as crucial to material and discursive practices that linked domination, rights, sovereignty, and freedom.

What might travel to the global South from these accounts of European origin? In turn, what insights might Kaerezians' grounded struggles offer for an understanding of processes of spatiality and subjection often occluded in Eurocentric accounts? Zimbabwe's conjoined southern questions—agrarian struggles in the global South—provide powerful tools for the project of provincializing Europe.

They stress the plural spatialities and temporalities of agrarian struggles. At the same time, they highlight the political technologies of racism that produced governed subjects and spaces.

What, in skeletal form, is the thread of power, force, and land woven through Marx's account of Europe's transition from feudalism to capitalism? He likened the might of feudal lords to those of the sovereign, both predicated on the number of their subjects. Serfs were subjected to masters who controlled territory. Neither wages nor markets mediated this subordination or the forms of exploitation they authorized in the name of lordship. In England, by the fourteenth century, serfdom segued to free peasant proprietors who enjoyed usufruct to common land, providing pasture, timber, and agrarian resources to supplement their family fields. At the beginning of the sixteenth century, a "mass of 'free' and unattached proletarian was hurled onto the labour-market by the dissolution of the bands of feudal retainers." Feudal lords, at times challenging both king and parliament, enacted the "forcible driving of the peasantry from the land" and "the usurpation of the common lands."[61] The Reformation infused this "forcible expropriation of the people" with a "new and terrible impulse," as church and state conspired to dispossess peasants from common lands to which they had enjoyed customary access.[62]

In stark contrast to the freedoms proclaimed by proponents of capitalism and the so-called free market, Marx conceived the emergence of "modern private property under circumstances of ruthless terrorism." Crucially, these processes "conquered the field for capitalist agriculture, incorporating the soil into capital, and created for the urban industries the necessary supplies of free and rightless proletarians."[63] Marx conceived these patterns as extending to the colonies through the seventeenth century. "Brute force," exemplified through "the colonial system," hastened the transformation from a feudal to a capitalist mode of production across the globe.[64] By the eighteenth century, "the law itself becomes now the *instrument* of the theft of the people's land," a "Parliamentary form of . . . robbery."[65] By criminalizing custom, the state stole peasant property rights, producing dispossessed proletarians in need of wages to subsist.

Marx's condition of possibility for European capitalism, the creation of a proletariat, required a doubly ironic sense of freedom. Peasants were freed from feudal bondage through their dispossession from customary access to land and rural resources. Power inscribed property rights on the landscape as those who exercised class privilege excluded peasants from private estates. The enclosures sealed off former commons, cordoned off from peasants by force and law. In this sense, evictions endorsed by the state "freed" serfs from their feudal bonds. Liberated from dependent ties to land and lord, a fixed spatial and social location, these new workers were now "free" to sell their labor power to competing capitalists. These wages of freedom supplanted feudalism's bonded labor as serfs subjected themselves to wages.

A specter then haunted Europe—*dispossession* from land. Lords became capitalists securing profits. Capitalism's historical development entailed political, economic, social, and spatial movement. Social relations of production tied together working subjects, sites of labor, and hierarchical dependencies of economic subjugation. What for liberals represents an *emancipatory* moment—breaking the bonds of feudalism, opening workers to the benevolent free market—remains for radicals crucial to capitalist *exploitation*. Liberal laws legitimated this history of evictions, dispossession, and novel forms of economic subordination, celebrating all of them under the emancipatory banner of freedom.

Foucault also found ironic tales of freedom in the emergence of distinctively modern forms of power, sharing Marx's mapping of modernity to a European epicenter. The problem of government "explodes" in the sixteenth century at "the crossroads of two processes: the one which, shattering the structures of feudalism, leads to the great territorial, administrative and colonial states"; the other, with the Reformation and its counterimpulses, raises the question of "the manner in which one is spiritually ruled."[66] In Foucault's reading, Machiavelli's prince pursued a particular objective in his exercise of power: to strengthen "the prince's relation with what he owns, with the territory he has inherited or acquired, and with his subjects."[67] As the art of government developed historically in Europe, sovereign monarchs succumbed to increasingly administrative regimes of rule.

Government targeted new relations between subjects, territory, and their mutual cultivation. Improvement of this assemblage, rather than isolated domination, oriented ruling practices. For Foucault, government became an "ensemble formed by the institutions, procedures, analyses and reflections, the calculations and tactics that allow the exercise of this very specific albeit complex form of power." In this new formation, territory was no longer a defining feature of rule, but one of the "component elements" entangled with the complex qualities of population.[68] Echoing Marx even amid criticizing his analytics of power and economy, Foucault stressed that in Europe "the fact of domination in all its brutality remained." Domination, Foucault elaborated, was "not sovereignty in its one edifice, but the multiple subjugations" entangled in diffuse power relations.[69] Rather than erasing sovereignty, emergent modes of power produced a triad: sovereignty-discipline-government. My analytic of entanglement eschews the erasure of historical sedimentations and emphasizes their imbrication with emergent practices of power.

Like Marx, Foucault focused on *relational powers*, historically emergent ensembles that articulate subjects and territory through their mutual disciplining. In sharp distinction to Marx, however, Foucault's diffuse power defied location in the structural reproduction of class, the possession of productive economic resources, or the dominating apparatuses of the state, either ideological or material. Marx's manifesto united workers in the struggle against the shackles of unfreedom, the chains of capitalist oppression. Capitalist power thwarted the progressive impulses of working subjects, repressing their potentially emancipatory agency through social relations of production. In contrast, Foucault's insurrectionary move was to insist that modern forms of power do not repress liberatory subjects from realizing their thwarted freedom. Rather, power works through forms of freedom that *produce* the subjects of modern government. For Foucault, agents are not self-sovereign authors of their own consciousness, but rather subjects in several senses—active subjects who exercise agency, but only through their subjection to relations of power. Marx and Foucault share an insistence on the critical role of both *relationality* and *production* in their conceptualization of power. For both, historical practices rather than abstract properties reproduce ensembles of relations—political, social, and economic—through which power flows.

While Marx began *Capital* with a binary opposition between capital and labor, he closed the third volume of his magnum opus with a "Trinity Formula" of capital, land, and labor.[70] What generative spatialities emerged from this shift? Lefebvre underscored that the semantic fields Marx plowed with the terms *earth* and *land* reached far beyond agrarian furrows. Their extent included the underground riches that fueled mining and petroleum development in the global South, as well as environmental resources enveloping the countryside. For Lefebvre, Marx's conceptual terrain of land included "the nation state, confined with a specific territory. And hence, ultimately, in the most absolute sense, politics and political strategy."[71] Land's inclusion in capitalism's critical trinity brings territory into history while spatializing productive relations and political practices. Land cannot be abstract empty space, a passive container awaiting the dynamic duet of capital and labor. Rather, the three are integrally entangled along with property and power. Instead of universals, Kaerezians' struggles suggest sin-

gularities where land, labor, and capital have long articulated in distinct formations. So, too, have sovereignty, discipline, and government—all imbricated in
struggles over territory.

Spatial subjection and the cultural politics of freedom have emerged through
political technologies, not unchanging essences. In the late seventeenth century,
Locke located a key to liberal freedom's routes in the contradiction between
natural rights and political rule. *Territory* became the terrain that mediates this
tension: "A man is naturally free from subjection to any government, though he
be born in a place under its jurisdiction."[72] The state of nature had no territory,
only land devoid of political power. Subsequently, natural birthrights defied
spatial incarceration. Humans enjoyed two foundational freedoms: to one's own
person and to patriarchal property through inheritance. Yet territorial conquest
confounded Locke's tale of the freedoms of liberal government. "Conquest may
be called a Foreign Usurpation," he argued, insofar as it removes a right possessed
by another without consent.[73] Tyranny on top of dispossession added another
transgression to the natural rights of man. Even sovereign monarchs "owe subjection to the Laws of God and Nature."[74] Slavery represented a fundamental
usurpation of the natural right of all humans to the freedom of their own
persons. Land expropriation attacked the material and discursive ground for
estates of property. Violating both foundational freedoms, colonial conquest
raised double trouble for Locke's liberalism:

> The *Inhabitants* of any Country, who are descended, and derive a Title to their
> Estates from those, who are subdued, and had a government forced upon them
> against their free consents, retain a *Right to the Possession of their Ancestors,* though
> they consent not freely to the Government, whose hard Conditions were by force
> imposed on the Possessors of that Country. For the first *Conqueror never* having
> *had a Title to the Land of that Country,* the people who are the Descendants of, or
> claim under those, who are forced to submit to the Yoke of a Government by
> constraint, have always a Right to shake it off, and free themselves from the Usur-
> pation, or Tyranny, which the sword hath brought in upon them, till their Rulers
> put them under such a Frame of Government, as they willingly, and of choice
> consent to.[75]

Locke's key to government was consent given by a freely choosing self-sovereign
subject not "forced to submit" to a sworded sovereign. When Locke wrote *Two
Treatises on Government* in the 1680s, he spoke directly to the English civil war of
the 1640s that followed rebellions in Scotland and Ireland. Yet in an imperial

world, colonial conquest unfolded across landscapes spatially distant yet integrally connected to Europe. A few years after the publication of Hobbes's 1651 *Leviathan*, white settlers near Cape Town received their first land grants. Forceful seizure became legal right, refracted through the prism of race.

More than two centuries later, in the wake of Rhodesia's forcibly imposed colonial conquest, administrators were anxious to turn swords into plowshares. The spirit medium Nehanda urged Africans to rebel against the twinned evils of European usurpation and tyranny the year before the widespread *Chimurenga* or uprising of 1896. Possessed by ancestral spirits, she decried the dispossession of ancestral lands. Loyalist chiefs like Umtassa helped subdue such insurrectionary specters. Yet more than eighty years after she was hanged by Rhodesian authorities, Nehanda's spirit was raised from the dead by nationalists to rally guerrillas in the second anticolonial *Chimurenga*. Force answered force, serving freedom's cause. A popular liberation song, "Mbuya Nehanda," urged armed resistance because "the gun seized our territory" (*gidi rakatora nyika yedu*).[76]

During Zimbabwe's guerrilla war, freedom fighters sought the liberation of land and subjects from unjust laws forged in conquest's crucible. White Rhodesians termed these liberators "terrorists," enemies to the rule of law and state, ungovernable subjects. Since 2000, when "war veterans" occupied more than a thousand white farms, property owners and opposition parties have used the same trope to attack these forcible seizures. As a global discourse of the "war on terrorism" gained traction in the wake of the September 11, 2001, attacks on the World Trade Center and the US Pentagon, an old colonial vocabulary found new uses.

Police, ZANU-PF youth brigades, and state-directed campaigns of brutal violence have targeted both persons and property. Those supporting such violations of rights have deployed powerful discourses of national liberation. In contrast, white privilege has been defended by recourse to the sanctity of the "free market," protecting rights to private property. Both positions—white farmers and the ruling nationalist party—use race as a prism of dispossession. They reserve their most insidious forms of violence for those most vulnerable in the articulated oppressions of race, class, and gender. Black female farmworkers, displaced and disenfranchised, many of whom are noncitizens, have been raped and beaten in numbers far exceeding the highly publicized attacks on white women and men. Beyond the horrors of bodily violation remain the forced removals of farmworkers in the wake of occupations by "war veterans." The victims of the victims are here displaced from occupied territory.

Racialized dispossession remains written into Zimbabwe's property map. The constitutive exclusions of liberalism's rule of law fueled forced removals in the name of freedom from tyranny. Yet I also want to oppose state violence and its human rights abuses. Two racial wrongs do not make a regime of rights. Despite populist rhetoric, Mugabe's cronies and strongmen have seized vast farms, while leaving millions of smallholders in dire poverty. No justice can endure without addressing this legacy of conquest. At independence, Lancaster's liberal invocation of market-mediated transactions muted militant claims for radical land reform. British and US officials insist the free market and liberal democracy should now orchestrate Zimbabwe's land redistribution. Such visions ignore the radical *unfreedoms* constituting the liberal rule of law.

In Zimbabwe, the constructed cultural difference of *race* became a fulcrum for land dispossession. Racialized dispossession violated rights in persons and property. Imperial discourses, however, supported violent conquest in the name of enlightened emancipation. Colonial rule inverted this usurpation. Its advocates asserted that colonial power liberated Africans from their unfreedoms as serfs under chiefs. In this vision, Africans prior to conquest had no individual freedoms to violate since they lived in collective societies ruled by kinship and tradition. Personal property rights in land, colonial officials argued, were uniquely modern. Africans were premodern. From this perspective, benevolent colonialists imposed forceful subjugation to move Africans in the direction of civilizational progress. Africans became both encouraged and conscripted to participate in governmental practices through indirect rule.[77] I now turn to those political technologies that targeted governing "customs" and mapped essentialized identities, at once racial and ethnic, to tribal territories.

5 · The Ethnic Spatial Fix

Tracking Tangwena on Rhodesian Radar

Shortly after European settlers forcibly defeated widespread African rebellions across Rhodesia's fledgling colony in 1897, officials anxiously mapped the location of influential chiefs within an imperial topography of rule. The 1891 Anglo-Portuguese Convention demarcated a border between two colonially created territories: Rhodesia, then controlled by the British South Africa Company, and Portuguese East Africa.[1] However, ongoing diplomatic negotiations and boundary skirmishes kept the border unsettled in Inyanga District where Africans and administrators contested its precise location and meanings. The district's mountainous frontier zone was then ruled from Umtali, the provincial capital more than one hundred kilometers to the south. In 1899, Inyanga's administrator asked his superiors for clarification on "the boundary line between this and Portuguese territory," reporting that the "paramount Chief Tangwena is most eager to belong to this territory and complains to me of the Portuguese officials worrying him."[2] Tangwena's placement—social, political, and geographical—also worried colonial officials. They anxiously charted Tangwena's politics of location—mapping relations between ethnic identity, political allegiance, and territorial homeland—within an emerging apparatus of British indirect rule.

By locating Tangwena's origin east of the border, officials grounded his authority *geographically*—territorializing his reign and identity beyond the international boundary. An administrative regime of rule sought to incorporate territorially fixed tribal polities within a colonial cartography of power. As Foucault asserted, "*Territory* is no doubt a geographical notion, but it's first of all a juridico-political one: the area controlled by a certain kind of power."[3] Rhodesian administrators charted chiefly movements to incorporate African power into indirect rule. Spanning two colonies, African mobility unsettled assumed ethnic and tribal roots. Straining to accommodate African spatial practices in their own geographical imaginaries, officials folded the foundational fiction of Tangwena's Rhodesian arrival into their legitimization of British indirect rule. Administrators saw themselves as welcoming a refugee fleeing injustices of both Portuguese and African rule east of the border. The project of *fixing* Tangwena's tribal territory sought to anchor ethnicity to a bounded locality in the new colony's sovereign space. "Discipline fixes," Foucault contended, because "it arrests or regulates movement; it clears up confusion; it dissipates compact groupings of individuals wandering about the country in unpredictable ways; it establishes calculated distributions."[4] For Fanon, "culture . . . fixed in the colonial status, caught in the yoke of oppression," remained crucial to the power relations of racialization and racism.[5] Fixing also suggests repairing the torn fabric of a social order, an African body politic damaged by displacement.[6]

Rhodesian narratives of Chief Tangwena's arrival echo what Paul Carter identified as imperial history's classical trope of reducing space to a stage—a site for the unfolding of events. Yet in opposition to Carter's at times universalizing optic on imperialism, Rhodesians struggled with a partial recognition that "cultural space *has* a history."[7] Some early colonial administrators realized the crucial importance of how space is historicized, by whom, and to what effect. Indeed, officials sought to appropriate precolonial spatial histories, authorizing them through indirect rule. African mobility and situated practices unsettled the fixity of colonial categories. Administrators responded in a variety of ways: with elastic interpretations of tribal taxonomies, with remappings of territory and ethnic identity, and with steadfast assertions of sedentarist sovereignty. All infused a "cartographic anxiety" surrounding landscapes of African rule.[8]

In this chapter, I examine the colonial project of attempting to fix ethnic identities in tribal territories. These administrative efforts, I argue, reveal echoes of Enlightenment understandings of Africa's imagined geography as a place beyond history where radical alterities of race and culture dwelled. I explore the often neglected *territorial* assumptions embedded in teleologies of historical progress. At the same time, I stress the production of racial difference through imperial practices. Use of indirect rule's tribal template offered both colonial administrators and anthropologists an ethnic order to map African culture and govern subjects. Europeans converted forcible seizure to a foundational freedom for Africans, arguing that their superior "race" brought civilizational progress to space and subjects devoid of history. Tribal administration racialized space and spatialized race. Moreover, Rhodesia's national spatial matrix emerged along with ethnicized geo-bodies. Thongchai proposed the geo-body as a concept describing the "technology of territoriality which created nationhood spatially."[9] I rework and rescale his notion, tracing projects that administered ethnicized enclaves. In so doing, I link geo-bodies of tribes to those of colonies.

If race represented for Europeans a fundamental difference from Africans, ethnicity was understood as integral to ordering African societies and polities. The exclusions engendered and the dispossessions deployed by colonial political technologies attest to the inequalities constitutive of liberalism's founding freedoms. Yet the historical contingencies of cultural politics in Kaerezi defy assertions of a singular rationality of rule or of a homogeneous colonial discourse of power. Government worked through fictions of fixity, yet it struggled with the uncertainties of contested micropractices. The ethnic spatial fix was a project of indirect rule, never a secure and settled accomplishment—producing at times effects not intended by colonial administrators.

Placing Paramounts

In the first decade of colonial rule, officials plotted Chief Tangwena's location in relation to stable points of reference. They located his homeland, cultural identity, and political authority in Portuguese East Africa. They also placed him socially, in kinship and political hierarchies, as subordinate to two powerful paramounts. Their respective reigns, officials believed, extended to opposite sides of the international border "laid down" on Nyanga's periphery in 1898.[10] As the brother-in-law of Umtassa (also Mutasa), Tangwena was related to a chief whose loyalty was firmly folded into colonial conquest. In 1902, the year Inyanga District became a distinct government territory with its own on-site administrator, the new Native Commissioner described Umtassa as "the paramount Chief of this and Umtali districts." Heralding Umtassa's having "remained loyal through the Mashona rebellion of 1896," the NC praised the paramount's "valuable service" to white farmers whose stock he tended when Europeans fled during the widespread uprisings. The report recalled Umtassa's "voluntarily supplying large gangs of boys" to construct the railway from Umtali to Beira on the coast.[11] As a paramount ruler whose sovereignty became enlisted in the service of colonial rule, Umtassa was understood to be a military ally, a labor provider, and a trusted aid to administrators and white settlers alike.

In 1897, Umtali officials recorded the movement of Umtassa's son Chambadzo who "trekked across the boarder [*sic*] into Portuguese Territory to his brother-in-law Tangwena under Makombi."[12] By mapping Tangwena's kinship to this proven loyalist, the colonial regime charted ties that might bind. Rhodesian officials could exert pressure on Tangwena through this relationship. Affinal allegiances between ruling lineages, officials believed, provided the mortar of marriage, cementing African political alliances through kinship. In this reasoning, Tangwena's social subordination to the paramount Umtassa (also Mutasa) domesticated potential threats within this loyalist's royal house. Rather than cause for alarm to officials, Umtassa's son's visit to Tangwena represented the possibility of containing the spatial extension of cross-border threats to British rule within a vertical topography of power. The key to thwarting Tangwena's potential threat to colonial security was to place him under the social authority, bound by kinship, of a trusted colonial ally who influenced his affine's *conduct*. Yet as politically subordinate to Makombi, whose attacks plagued Portuguese outposts, Tangwena represented an ungovernable risk to imperial regimes on both sides of the border. Colonial cartographies could not contain the complexities of African agency when ethnic identity, kinship affinities, and political loyalties pulled in different directions. These contending influences produced unstable subjects whose interests were plural, potentially shifting, and at times contradictory. When these entanglements transgressed the boundaries of colonies claimed as sovereign territory, relations with competing European rulers further complicated the mix. Kinship ties connected spaces across the international border, as did Makombi's predations that refused to recognize colonial sovereignty on either side.

Makombi (also Makombe) was the dynastic title of a Karanga paramount who had ruled Barwe territory, once part of the Mutapa empire, since the fifteenth century. The vast bulk of Barwe (also Barue) lay in what became Portuguese colonial territory, west of Sena and extending over a swath between the Zambezi, Ruenya, and Pungwe Rivers. Barwe rulers' influence reached into the Nyanga highlands, including Kaerezi, through the late nineteenth century.[13] A succession of paramounts such as Umtassa claimed Manyika territories to the south in present-day Mutasa District, while Makoni rulers claimed a reign to the west, around present-day Rusape. In Barwe, slave raiding, ivory and gold trading, and African and European militarism infused a volatile historical geography. Eighteenth-century Portuguese documents chronicle repeated disruptions of administration, the burning of settlers' houses, and the extraction of tribute from traders passing through Barwe.[14]

Following their own experience with widespread African uprisings in 1896, Rhodesian administrators carefully monitored what they termed the Portuguese-

Makombi conflict east of the border. White farmers feared the potential contagion of rebellion, reporting "rumors of various chiefs of our own district joining Makombi who in turn would aid them against us."[15] As late as 1918, a year after he spearheaded a major rebellion, Makombi remained "uncrushed," while his followers robbed and extorted food from Africans in Rhodesian territory.[16] Makombi's predations transgressed the foundational fiction of a colonial border securing sovereign space, raising the specter of translocal anticolonial resistance.

Violent geographies fused with geographical imaginations of just rule. British administrators constructed their side of the border as a safe space providing a secure haven for loyal African subjects who would provide labor and taxes. In this vision, Rhodesian space offered Africans a flight to freedom from the injustices of Portuguese colonialism and from Makombi's reign of volatile violence. For Rhodesia's administrators, nationalist visions of empire's moral geography hinged on a distinctive civilizing mission.[17] Britain's superior rule represented a judicious application of might and the art of government. After defeating the uprisings of 1896–97, the British bemoaned "dominance without hegemony" east of the border.[18] Their own imperial agenda, they believed, fused force and consent. In 1889, Lord Frederick Lugard, who would later become governor of Nigeria and Hong Kong and an influential architect of British indirect rule, advised: "Thrash them first, conciliate them afterwards; and by this method our prestige with the native tribes would be certainly greatly increased, and subsequent troubles with them would be less likely."[19] Beyond the British border lay a territory of troubles. Portuguese rule was a target of critique both for its coercive methods, especially forced labor and corporeal punishment, and its administrative incompetence. Portuguese rule thrashed without conciliation.

From the British perspective, Makombi's rogue reign articulated with Portuguese plunder. Territory east of the border represented a dangerous geography: simultaneously moral and political, African and Portuguese. Rebels could rile natives across a national border, encouraging insurrection against Rhodesian rule. The cross-border traffic of people, goods, and information raised fears of contagion as well as rebellion. The health of the body politic depended on securing the boundaries of an emerging colonial nation-state.[20] When news of the spread of bubonic plague in Portuguese territory reached Salisbury in 1905, orders to "stop all natives entering this territory" were dispatched to Inyanga.[21] A few years later, the Inyanga administrator complained that no Portuguese official was stationed east of the district.[22] A more secure border would only come about through efforts on the Rhodesian side.

Colonial officials confronted formidable challenges in attempting to fix Tangwena's territory, his followers' ethnic essence, and their geographical location. In 1899, NC Hulley visited remote areas of Inyanga District by horseback from the provincial capital:

> I am pleased to be able to report that the Chief Tangwena with whom I had some difficulty has sent his son in with the hut tax of those natives who are living in BSA [British South Africa] Territory. The chief himself lives in Portuguese Territory. His son informs me that it is the intention of Tangwena to remove with all his people during the next season onto BSA Territory. I have not encouraged him in this but informed him that I will communicate with the Government and send him word later. The difficulty as far as our own part goes, is that part of Tangwena's country which falls into BSA Territory is to the best of my knowledge private property.[23]

The power geometry of British rule relied on a particular understanding of the relationship between sovereignty, ethnicity, and territory.[24] Administrators strained to reconcile conflicting territorial understandings of chiefly rule, national belonging, political allegiance, and private property. Tangwena was geographically *outside* Rhodesia's sovereign space yet insinuated *into* British indirect rule. He resided as a Portuguese colonial subject east of the international border, yet he was responsible for collecting the hut taxes of his followers in Rhodesia. NC Hulley also recognized a preconquest Tangwena territory that transgressed separate sovereign colonies; yet its bearing on administration remained ambivalent, further complicated by private property. Despite its peripheral location, political technologies of rule made Kaerezi a heterotopia, "juxtaposing in a single real place several spaces, several sites that are in themselves incompatible."[25] While administrators conceived Tangwena ethnicity as essentially bound to Barwe, their efforts to remap cultural identity to Inyanga acknowledged a sovereign's claims over followers and territory in Rhodesia.

Territory's Teleology, Racialized Rule

Administrators' efforts to fix a distinct Tangwena ethnic territory revealed the "distressing links between raciology and statecraft" forged in the crucible of colonial power.[26] Achille Mbembe asserted that "characteristic of the colonial mode of exercising power was the conflation of the tasks of governing, commanding, and civilizing."[27] Lugard's legitimization of the violence of colonial conquest invoked a civilizing mission deeply enmeshed in evolutionary understandings of a singular teleology of Universal History. Those who enjoyed the highest rung of civilization invoked both the moral duty and political right to rule subject races. Lugard's influential Dual Mandate of the 1920s argued that imperial states had the "grave responsibility of . . . 'bringing forth' to a higher plane . . . the backward races" that were "so pathetically dependent on their guidance."[28] Southern Rhodesia's influential 1944 Godlonton Commission similarly argued that it was whites' location in "stages of development" that gave "European races" not simply the right but the moral duty "to assist backward peoples to progress and for that purpose to enforce discipline without oppression."[29] For British rule, African cultural alterity represented a *racial* difference. By incorporating "traditional" authorities into modern government, British indirect rule would bring Africans into Universal History's teleology of progress.

This evolutionary passage required *spatial* as well as temporal progress. Bringing Africans forward into modernity simultaneously required incorporating them into a European construction of territory. Recall Hegel's insistence that the "true theatre of History . . . is the temperate zone."[30] Africa's geographical location was temporally as well as spatially beyond Universal History: "It is no historical part of the World; it has no movement or development to exhibit." When history appears, Hegel attributed this dynamic force to Asiatic or European influence rather than any African agency.[31] In Hegel's imagined Africa, its inhabitants reflect the essential qualities of place, of an isolated geography beyond historical development. He located cultural difference geographically and temporally, reading it as developmental distance.

Such Enlightenment formations influenced colonial rule. Administrators conceived of African alterity as dwelling in an evolutionary moment prior to European modernity. As Igor Kopytoff suggested, frustrated nineteenth-century European nationalism informed evolutionary assumptions about African tribes representing "the embryo of the nation."[32] Ernest Renan's influential late-nineteenth-century reflections on nationalism traced an evolutionary teleology moving from the tribes of Roman antiquity to modern European nations.[33] Henry Maine's 1861 classic, *Ancient Law*, pegged the evolutionary shift from polities organized around shared "blood" to those of shared residence in a fixed territory as a key marker of a modern society. "Local contiguity" was "utterly strange and monstrous to primitive antiquity."[34] Nineteenth-century social theory across the Black Atlantic complicated the situation, but it echoed an evolutionary understanding of modernity's teleology of territory. Lewis Henry Morgan highlighted how a "territorial plan" unknown by primitives "fixed the boundary line between ancient and modern society." Evolutionary progress marched forward through history from social organization based on sex to that of kin and, finally, territory.[35]

Colonial understandings of tribes, where tradition reigned, were modeled on Europe's feudal societies. An 1898 Umtali Native Commissioner's report, written when Inyanga fell under Umtali's jurisdiction, outlined the "Laws and Customs" of chieftainships: "The chiefs are supported on the old feudal system. Each petty chief supplies his emidiate [*sic*] chief with either grain or labour to a certain amount. His lands are all hoed for him by his tribe."[36] Inhabitants of the "Dark Continent" dwelt in the Dark Ages before the Enlightenment of European freedom. Administrators read the landscape and labor relations for signs of feudal fetters and subjugated serfs that mimicked Europe's earlier evolutionary moments. From this perspective, fixing tribal boundaries would bring Africans into Morgan's "territorial plan" of British indirect rule.

Anthropological Tribes

Twentieth-century anthropologists struggled with their nineteenth-century evolutionary baggage. A. R. Radcliffe-Brown's 1940 classic, structural-functionalist introduction to *African Political Systems* rejected the "confusion" engendered by Maine and Morgan. Their mistake was to distinguish between societies based on kinship or lineage and "societies based on occupation of a common territory or locality," presuming that the former were more "primitive." To correct this evolutionary bias, Radcliffe-Brown proposed the study of "political organization," "the maintenance or establishment of social order, with a territorial framework, by the organized exercise of coercive authority through the use, or the possibility of use, of physical force."[37] Weber's influence proved forceful; coercive authority became sharply territorialized. Durkheim provided the rules of a comparative sociological method—structural functionalism's concern with the social regulation of order in functionally integrated systems. Anthropological allies from the same era, Myer Fortes and E. P. Evans-Pritchard, explicitly rejected evolutionary assumptions in their emphasis on the "territorial aspect" that distinguished political systems. "Primitive states" and "stateless societies" were not defined by their locations along a unilineal evolutionary trajectory, but rather by the degree to which they had "centralized authority, administrative machinery, and judicial institutions."[38] Chiefdoms and modern states shared the same discursive time, but they distinguished themselves territorially in distinctive structures and func-

tions: "The administrative unit is a territorial unit; political rights and obligations are territorially delimited. A chief is the administrative and judicial head of
a given territorial division, vested often with final economic and legal control
over all the land within his boundaries. Everybody living with these boundaries is
his subject, and the right to live in this area can be acquired only by accepting the
obligations of a subject. The head of the state is a territorial ruler."[39]

Prominent anthropologists argued about the social evolutionary trappings of
the competing conceptualizations of tribes.[40] At mid-century, Bronislaw Malinowski claimed "a primitive tribe is always a body of people related by bonds
of kinship and relationship, by clanship and age-grade," emphasizing shared
"blood" and affined connections.[41] Isaac Schapera sharply criticized this reasoning, countering the claim that "'political union' is based solely on kinship in
primitive societies and on 'local contiguity' in civilized societies." Working in
southern Africa, he was particularly critical of implicit oppositions that contrasted biological ties of blood among so-called primitives with civilized society
that transcended kinship through modern forms of territoriality. "Even in modern Western society," he argued, "appeal to ties of 'common blood' have featured
prominently in doctrines of racial supremacy and in laws against miscegenation.
Both kinship and locality serve everywhere to link people together."[42] As Archie
Mafeje underscored, both colonial administrators and anthropologists had conceived of "tribal institutions and values as the explanation for the *failure* of
Africans to embrace modernity."[43] Deploying the powerful fiction of tribes, colonial rulers located African culture in a time and space distinct from Europeans.

More recently, Mahmood Mamdani has located the crux of colonial power in
organizational oppositions embedded within a bifurcated state. The tribal template, for him, became a structural principle shaping the project of administering
Africans in mutually exclusive, ethnically discrete spaces. Mamdani views this
ethnic incarceration as a constitutive feature of British indirect rule throughout
colonial Africa: "Encased by custom, frozen into so many tribes, each under the
first of its own Native Authority, the subject population was, as it were, con-
tainerized." By granting colonial chiefs sweeping authorities, he argued, policies
of indirect rule institutionalized "decentralized despotism."[44]

In his conception, structural binaries separate exclusionary spaces removed
from processes of historical articulation. Citizens and subjects, the urban and the
rural, law and custom, force and power become ideal types reified as historical
facts mapped onto discrete institutional and geographical sites. Use of this analytical separation between politics and culture authorizes an occlusion of the *cultural
politics* that shape the discursive and material contours of custom and state, and

the production of governable citizens and subjects.[45] Mamdani's brilliance has been to chart the condensation of chiefly powers inaugurated by the colonial institution of indirect rule. Yet his institutional analysis pivots on ideal types of power, identity, and space that obscure both African and administrative practices.

Much Africanist ink has been spilled debating the "politics of custom," "inventions of tradition," and constructions of ethnicity fomented by colonial projects that deployed tribes as a foundational territorial and administrative unit. Analysts have highlighted the functionalist fit between anthropology and administration in the institutional structures of indirect rule.[46] From the 1920s onward, an articulation of anthropology and administration reinforced an "official view of African societies as clearly bounded and coherently organized."[47] However, fissures also emerged in competing agendas—one seeking administrative solutions, the other practicing anthropological research. In Sara Berry's formulation, " 'custom' embraced both a set of constitutional principles and an ongoing practice of historical narrative and interpretation."[48] While custom might morph through time, a historical hermeneutics held together its fiction of cultural continuity. The interpretive authority granted to custom relied greatly on assertions that it *governed* African conduct.

Colonial administrators and ethnographers often purged contentious practices from the cultural politics of custom.[49] Rather than *discovering* timeless tradition, administrative efforts codified a constellation of principles, thus *producing* custom much less flexible and dynamic than the heterogeneity of African practices often gathered under a single tradition. Yet, as Berry contended, "colonial regimes imposed themselves on societies already engaged in struggles over power and the terms on which it would be exercised. By announcing their intention to uphold 'traditional' norms and structures of authority, colonial officials were, in effect, declaring their intention to build colonial rule on a foundation of conflict and change."[50] Orchestrating improvements, governing conduct, and promoting developmental change became crucial to rule predicated on racialized cultural differences conceived as distinct evolutionary stages on a unilineal trajectory of historical progress.

Rhodesian Routes

In 1932, two years after Charles Hanmer moved to his property west of the Kaerezi River, W. H. Stead began a course in native administration and anthropology at London University. Twelve years later, he was the Inyanga NC called to testify before the 1944 Godlonton Commission, an influential inquiry into the political, social, and economic conditions of Africans in the colony. Stead objected to a questioner's assertion that "the Native today" was "undisciplined." The problem, Stead suggested, was that "he lacks a clearly defined organization with which he can obtain a livelihood and carry out his social undertakings."[51] Colonialism, not African culture, was the culprit. A coherent system of "organization and Chiefship" among "the Shona" had worked well for two thousand years, Stead argued. "The breakdown of Chiefs' authority" was due to changes in "their constitutional and economic conditions as a result of the advent of Europeans."[52] On this point, he echoed Malinowski, whose anthropological authority shaped Stead's London course of study.[53]

Stead singled out that chiefs grounded their authority in land allocation. When administrative officials—rather than African authorities—allocated land in the reserves, colonial rule "strikes at the traditional powers of Chiefs."[54] He called it a "mistake" to treat chiefs as separable from their people. As an "embodiment of the tribal wish," chiefs represented "a democratic institution."[55] Colonial rule erred by imposing administrative agendas that did not articulate with African cultural practices, principles, and the customs that molded conduct. Stead suggested that by engineering the institutional powers invested in chiefs, making them instruments of what Mamdani termed "decentralized despotism," colonial policies purged African polities of democratic impulses.[56] Unfreedoms, from Stead's perspective, emerged from European intervention, rather than from a timeless tradition of African indolence and indiscipline. Good government, Stead implied, produces citizens and workers guided by democracy and engaged in economic development.

The MP W. M. Munro, who presided over the Godlonton Commission, rebuked the anthropologist-cum-administrator for having "steeped yourself in Native folk lore and wisdom." He criticized Stead for having "lost sight of the practical side of things." Munro challenged the administrator, invoking the civilizing mission of empire underwritten by anthropologist Morgan's unilineal evolutionary script: "Isn't it because of that backwardness that we must endeavor to pull them out of semi-barbarism?"[57] Stead responded by endorsing a doctrine of "development," but he demanded that it "use the customs and institutions which are inherent in the people." "Simply to impose things on Natives because they appeal to Europeans," he cautioned the commission, "will result in chaos amongst the people."[58] Development required improvement, not forcible imposition. Officials should nurture the inherent capacities of a population, encouraging their directional movement by acting on actions embedded within African culture.

Stead endorsed the ethnographic study of chieftainship, land tenure, and land use "so that the Native Commissioners are tied down to a constantly progressive system of development."[59] Administration, informed by ethnography, should be bound to the benevolent burden of good government. In this view, effective rule would work through the principles of African custom, securing consent among the citizens subject to the chief and to the Native Commissioner. Emphasizing the dynamism and agency of "African culture," Stead confidently answered the query whether native custom had ever been static with "No, never. It isn't in any community."[60]

Munro responded by charting a unilineal evolutionary model of *racialized* stages of development. "In their present relative stages of development," he proclaimed, "the European races may in general be classed as forward peoples and the African races as backward peoples." The "intrusion of European civilization" required the African to "adapt himself." Hegel's script for historical agency, in which Europeans erect stages on which Africans (re)act, haunted this teleology of civilizational progress. Europeans' *racial* location in a universal unfolding of social evolution gave them the moral duty and legal right to, in Munro's words, "enforce discipline without oppression" and assist "backward peoples to progress."[61]

This evolved European temporality underwrote a reconfiguration of African spatiality. "The occupation by the Natives of lands in Southern Africa," Munro argued, "has not given them a natural or indefensible right to retain such lands and their mode of life in them for all time against all comers."[62] Racialized dispossession became the basis for national development. Teleologies of racial progress, in this vision, suggested superior spatial discipline, reconfiguring rights to land. "Development" required improving the relationship between population and wealth. To pursue this project, government subjected Africans—at once citizens and workers—to temporalities and spatialities of progress.

Such civilizing discourses could also be turned back on colonial policy. When Lugard was not thrashing first, he argued in 1893, that Africans living in protectorates should enjoy "certain well-defined rights and privileges pertaining to British subjects." In late-nineteenth-century Madagascar, he noted, colonial rulers granted to Africans "the rights of French subjects. To our disgrace, we do not deal thus with ours." Imperial rivalries encouraged debate regarding the relative superiority of European as well as non-European civilizations. Lugard compared at length the civil rights of British Indians, Arabs, and Africans in different jurisdictions, asking: "By what right do we thus differentiate between races, and deny to the Africans their just rights as subjects?"[63] In this imperial discourse, civil rights are conferred on *subjects* rather than solely on *citizens*. Imperial subjection traveled spatially beyond the boundaries of any African state. For Lugard, "a native of a British protectorate, when found outside the limits of that protectorate, should be amenable to English law, and not to the law of the State in which he happens to be." Concerned about unfreedoms engendered by the translocal slave trade, especially raids of capture, he wanted protectorates to *protect* Africans. Imperial rights should thus travel with those forcibly displaced against their will from their territories of birth. "Thus a Nyasa slave found in Zanzibar should claim the privileges not only of a British subject, but that his case should be tried by English not Zanzibar law."[64] Yet colonial rule also deployed discourses of imperial progress and protective laws to dispossess and disenfranchise. In the name of "recognizing" native rights to communal land tenure, administrators constructed a powerful fiction eclipsing individualized African rights, thus abetting land expropriation. Lugard's imperial pronouncements authorized African rights by virtue of citizenship and subjection—all entangled in practices of government.

Communal Subjects

Rhodesian administrators saw African landscapes through the prism of "communal tenure," both a way of seeing and a way of administering. In 1928, Charles Bullock, then Native Commissioner and examiner in native customs and administration for the government of Southern Rhodesia, confidently concluded: "The Mashona societal system has grown from the family to the agnatic group or gens, and so to the tribe." Tribal structure and land rights emanated from the patriarchal principles of kinship and chiefly rule. "For the family is part of the tribe," Bullock argued, "and owes allegiance to the Chief who is the 'father' of its own patriarch. In Government, there is a stepping-stone between them in the shape of the *muchinda*, the headman or deputy over a portion of the Chief's country; but, in theory and in practice, the tribe is really a further enlargement of the enlarged family." Bullock depicted a benevolent sovereign with echoes of *oikos*, the managed household Foucault proposed as a crucial organizing idiom for the art of government in Europe. *Musha* (home), perhaps with a pinch of *mhuri* (family), implied spatial as well as kinship ties. Tribal subjects, for Bullock, acknowledged their chief as the owner of territory, "so long as they tilled the land which he owned as the earthly vicar of the controlling spirit whom he and his people acknowledged and made sacrifice to." His evolutionary perspective was explicit, charting the "organization from its beginnings" and tracing a developmental path from family to tribe.[65]

Morgan's formulation resonated through Bullock's reflections on the evolutionary emergence of primitive society. So, too, did echoes of European serfdom—a lord, the tribal chief, who "owned" territory where his feudal serfs toiled under his control. By placing African subjects in an earlier evolutionary moment, administrators could subject them to collective rather than individual regimes of rights. Communal tenure offered an effective instrument used to *dispossess* Africans of individual rights that government could then claim to *grant* in Native Reserves. Beginning with centralization in the late 1920s, the pegging of individual fields became part of a project to "modernize" African land tenure. Rhodesian administrators saw themselves as bringing tribal subjects into a modern teleology of territory, co-opting chiefs and headmen to governmental rule while protecting citizens from the dictates of African despots. In this vision, government granted individual and collective land rights through a tribal template, subordinating rural chiefs and their subjects to Rhodesian rule. In the process, however, Africans were subjected to competing sovereigns.

In late eighteenth-century India, British officials pondered principles of property invoked in ancient texts, oral accounts, and cultural practices.[66] In that context, "colonial governmentality consisted of bureaucracy," argued Nicholas Dirks, with a "form of sovereignty abstracted from even the most minimal conceits of political representation. Sovereignty was to perform itself through the extension of landed property and state security."[67] More than a century later in colonial Africa, administrative efforts to establish official idioms of ownership became an obsession. Rather than discovering "communal tenure," colonial administration produced it. "The official search for the owners of all land" in colonial Africa, asserted Colson, "encouraged the confusion of sovereignty with proprietary ownership and the creation of systems of communal tenure which came into being with precisely defined rules." While administrators cited the authority of alleged traditions and "immemorial custom," the rules they invoked were "a reflection of the contemporary situation and the joint creation of colonial officials and African leaders."[68] Structural functionalism and colonial administration both codified governing principles. Sovereigns and serfs represented a familiar model. Europe's feudal estates offered no freedom for laboring subjects on landed property. If African alterity represented an evolutionary time before Europe, then African spatiality inhabited that premodern temporality in which tribal subjects resided in a single sovereign's lands; he owned the territory they cultivated.

Invoking Malinowski's 1935 quip that "communal tenure" was "the undying fallacy of anthropological work," Paul and Laura Bohannan attributed the reification of tenurial rules and principles to Western political ideologies rather than African cultural practices. "Land, whatever else it may be, is for Westerners a measurable entity divisible into thing-like 'parcels' by means of mathematical and technical processes of surveying and cartography." Emphasizing that property is a *relational* concept, they stressed that tenure implies "rights *in* land *against* or *with* other persons." A semantic slippage, they suggested, creates powerful discursive effects: "In European languages, with the particular notions of land they reflect, 'rights in land' can become attributes *of the land*."[69] Communal tenure is exemplary of what Lefebvre termed "spatial fetishism."[70] The technical architecture of centralization in the 1930s, the Native Land Husbandry Act of the 1950s, and postcolonial resettlement policy all *located* laws in the land, using the inherent qualities of soil and slope to regulate settlement, agriculture, and pastoralism. Use of expert knowledge coupled with administrative imperatives translated the laws of the land into those of state.

The chairman of the 1944 Godlonton Commission denied precolonial Africans individual property rights through the prism of incommensurable cultural difference. "Private ownership of land was," the chairman Munro declared, "until the British South Africa Company commenced to rule, a possessory conception incomprehensible to the Mabele and Mashona who, tired of impoverished gardens, troubled by their insanitary habits, or haunted by superstitious fears, frequently changed their gardens or kraals. Fixity of tenure, if it had been offered to them, would have been a burden not a privilege."[71] Because Africans lacked a cultural understanding of private property, they could not possess it. European arrival, in Munro's version, inaugurated individual property rights mapped to specific parcels of land.

Private property, racialized at its roots, became an instrument of discursive and material dispossession targeting Africans. It gained ground through hut burnings, evictions, tax collection, and rent seeking. For Munro, government should promote the free movement of white bodies, populations, and capital while recognizing the rights of white settlers to anchor wealth in land. Yet Africans should not shift sites of cultivation nor claim bundles of resource rights for individuals and families—rights Munro denied that precolonial Africans either understood or exercised. This powerful colonial fiction of a premodern collective subject underwrote policies of racialized dispossession. As Chanock has argued, the colonial expropriation of communal land was easier to justify than was the dispossession of individual rights.[72]

Refuting Munro's vision, historical accounts of individual usufruct prior to colonial conquest abound. Patterns varied widely. In some areas, despots' whims denied smallholders secure land rights. In others, lineages and families established strongly recognized claims. Holdings were often highly uneven, especially in scarcely populated areas where large lineages could expand their cultivated acreage without encroaching on others' land rights.[73] Cheater pointed to an 1873 missionary account to argue that "the overriding rights of expropriation of political rulers come *after* individuals have established inalienable rights of usufruct over particular portions of land."[74] Indeed, Ranger suggested that the very "idea—and to some extent, the practice—of 'traditional communal tenure' grew up in a sort of rural power vacuum during early colonialism." Until the 1920s, when the colonial state intervened more directly in land allocation, authorities were "content to leave emergent peasant production to itself." As a result, smallholders allocated land to themselves throughout the countryside.[75]

Evolutionary assumptions influenced colonial understandings of chiefdoms as analogs of feudal estates in precapitalist Europe. In turn, administrators and anthropologists tried to identify principles of a presumed premodern African culture that they conceived to rule relations among sovereignty, spatial discipline, and political rule. Like Alvord's interventions in agriculture and land-use planning, the government of custom articulated global discourses and localized cultural politics, imperial entanglements and contentious contingencies. These legacies remained alive in postcolonial Zimbabwe, offering uncanny echoes amid administrative invocations of the enduring relevance of colonial anthropology.

Inscriptions of Authority

I rolled into Nyanga District Center on a hot, dry day in 1991, gratefully catching a ride to town with a half dozen others in the back of Nyafaru's Toyota pickup. I jumped out at the junction to the district offices, a couple of kilometers from the market, bus hub, and the few stores giving life to a black township. I was still patting off dust when Chenjerai, a friend working as an accountant for the Ministry of Local Government, greeted me outside his office. Nearby, he lived with his wife, a primary school teacher in the township, in a spacious but run-down colonial-era government house surrounded by a high security fence. Cracked walls and ripped screens betrayed years of state budgetary priorities; as a tenant rather than an owner, Chenjerai refused to invest private earnings in public property. Both stove and refrigerator were broken and power was unpredictable—electricity sometimes going off for minutes, hours, or even days at a stretch. His wife usually cooked over an open fire outside the kitchen. On that room's tile floor, Chenjerai's nephew once wielded an ax, chopping an ox carcass recently slaughtered by a group of Nyanga civil servants who could not afford meat from the township butcher and had purchased the beast from a nearby Communal Area. Through such resourceful practices, they struggled to stretch meager salaries while making new uses of colonial infrastructure.

After catching me up on his family and work, Chenjerai pointed at my still dusty clothes, jibing: "You're one of the *povo* now, *Mukoma* Moore." *Mukoma* is a respectful term for brother; *povo* is a Portuguese term for "the people" or impoverished masses, a staple of nationalist rhetoric. He invoked fictive kinship sincerely while mocking my perceived populism as an anthropologist living among squatters that his boss, the DA, was threatening to evict. We often discussed the intricacies of state policy, debating and sometimes radically disagreeing. But he saved me from floggings by drunks looking for fights who found me, an anomalous white in the black township, a convenient target. Revisiting a brawl he witnessed the night before, Chenjerai described a drunkard's feeble punches as "scuds," riffing off media coverage of Iraq's ineffective missiles. Even local fights became understood through vocabularies invoking global geopolitics, a topic we frequently discussed along with legacies of US imperialism, Vietnam, and the ongoing Gulf War.

In Chenjerai's small, sparsely outfitted cement office, a uniformed orderly served tea. Most workers oriented tasks around this imperial tradition, tea breaks becoming tantamount to sacred. Chenjerai pulled out a book, one of only a few amid scores of government files. "I thought you'd be interested in this," he offered. "Borrow it while you're in town, but don't let anyone know you've taken it out of the office. It's our only copy." I had last encountered a copy of J. F. Holleman's 1952 classic, *Shona Customary Law*, years before in a California library. Then it seemed a colonial relic, immersed in a structural-functionalist vision of society ordered by underlying rules and institutions. Influenced by the *volkekunde* vision of anthropology deployed to legitimate South African apartheid, the text remained haunted in my reading by an Afrikaner-inflected understanding of culturally distinct ethnic essences. There were hints of an appreciation for the dynamism and flexibility of custom, but they were always embedded in an anthropological agenda deeply wedded to administrative desires for ruling principles. When Chenjerai handed me the text, commenting on how insightful many of the observations remained for governing in the 1990s, I realized how much my own customary baggage shaped my perspective on postcolonial governmentality.

A lively traffic among different temporalities—precolonial, colonial, and post-colonial—and African and European understandings of tradition, custom, and culture saturated projects of government. A few offices away, I read postcolonial administrative files citing, in the wake of Rekayi's 1984 death, colonial constructions of the Tangwena chiefdom. Referencing "facts" dutifully recorded in the Rhodesian archives, administrative files chronicled arguments excluding the rainmaker Nyahuruwa's claims to sovereignty in territory ruled by his precolonial ancestors. Postcolonial headmen in a state-administered resettlement scheme claimed "traditional" authorities over land allocation, citing colonial constructions of salaried duties. Emergent rationalities and micropractices of postcolonial rule did not occlude, erase, or eclipse previous historical sedimentations. Rather, a robust recursivity among temporalities and spatialities intertwined with regimes of rule and assemblages of power.

Anthropological formulations encouraged enduring governing customs. Holleman, the influential anthropologist who died in 2001, was a prominent architect of Rhodesian policies. Employed by the Rhodes-Livingstone Institute in Northern Rhodesia (now Zambia), he later held research posts in South Africa and in Southern Rhodesia's Department of Native Affairs.[76] He served in the early 1960s on the Magwende Commission, established in the wake of a chief purged from his post for behavior deemed "obstructive and detrimental to good order and progress."[77] The commission sought to make indirect rule less susceptible to subversion. Widespread opposition to the deeply resented Native Land Husbandry Act in the late 1950s provoked the possibility for anticolonial resistance within the channels of indirect rule, especially when popular resentment targeted chiefs and headmen whose duties included the recruitment of forced labor for public conservation works. Chief Magwende opposed attempts to implement land policy in his area, provoking his dismissal. Refusing to endorse the Rhodesian project of government, he became excluded from it. Holleman discussed such controversies in his 1969 *Chief, Council, and Commissioner: Some Problems of Government in Rhodesia.* At the time, the Rhodesian Front campaigned to integrate chiefs more effectively into Rhodesian rule, firmly folding anthropology into colonial governmentality.

Imperial circuits deeply informed these administrative and anthropological views. Holleman was born in 1915 in colonial Java. His father, a judge and magistrate working for the Dutch colonial service, later taught ethnology and law in the Netherlands where he held a prominent university chair. His father's footsteps cut deep tracks, pioneering the Dutch formulation of *adat* law—what colonial officials conceived and codified as "indigenous" or "customary" law in the Dutch East Indies.[78] Holleman's grandfather had lived in South Africa, heading to the Netherlands after supporting the losing side in the Anglo-Boer war. Following patrilineal paths, the grandson studied anthropology and law at the University of Stellenbosch.

In South Africa, Holleman became schooled in *volkekunde*—the Afrikaner-inflected version of a Herderian vision of each *Volk*, a people or *ethnos*, bearing a spirited cultural tradition. Distinct customs governed the conduct of separate peoples. *Volkekunde* infused apartheid's administrative agenda, promoting the spatial separation of distinct races and their government through a regime of racialized rights. Fundamentalist proponents of apartheid found a Christian God's creation of distinct ethnicities as divine legitimization for state policies of "separate development." If each ethnos or Volk had a god-given cultural essence, government must strive to administer its ordained progress separately. *Volkekunde* helped provide officials with a pseudoscientific gloss on apartheid's multiculturalism.[79] The so-called Bantustans mapped distinct African ethnicities to governed territories while denying subjects full rights as citizens of the South African nation-state. In southern Africa, Holleman remapped the rich ironies of his childhood in Java. Like his father, he labored under the white man's burden of fixing "indigenous law"—an edifice conjured to accompany indirect rule. Under Rhodesian employ, Holleman's governmental work drew from multiple imperial and national traditions of anthropology, administration, and jurisprudence.

Competing African interests and inequalities entangled indirect rule. Holleman's informants were primarily elder males with social prestige invested in gaining official legitimization for their visions of custom.[80] Through armchair anthropology and brief field visits, Holleman "discovered" ruling principles that structured enduring hierarchies of authority. "European administration has imposed a few new duties upon the headman," Holleman wrote in 1951. Tax collection was pivotal in transforming "his position as a tribal official":

> It has not only resulted in the substitution for the traditional term *samusha* of the new title *sabhuku* ("keeper of the book"), which is now most commonly used, but the custody of a village tax-register has, in fact, become a primary badge of the

headman's office. Where, in the past, *kudzikira bango* ("planting the peg") marked the formal recognition of a community as an independent *musha*, the granting of a separate tax-register to a person would nowadays be regarded as concrete proof of his being a headman (*samusha*), and to entrust the head of a village section (*samana*) with his own tax-book would have the effect of creating a new village community under his control, independent of the original village unity.[81]

Holleman's classic structural-functionalist account of the *sabhuku* is strikingly resonant with contemporary formulations of colonial governmentality. In his vision, a new title, *sabhuku*, supplanted and displaced the previous functional duties performed by a *samusha*, or traditional authority. In the indeterminate and implicitly unchanging past, new communities became recognized by planting pegs to mark formal territories. Indirect rule embedded this traditional institution within a new rationality of government. The tax register, in Holleman's vision, became the sign and basis of the *sabhuku*'s authority. History marched forward into modernity, leaving tradition in a timeless past. New technologies of government occluded previous practices of rule. Less appreciated, even in structuralist terms, was what Fallers termed the "headman's dilemma" in colonial Africa—an official subjected to the multiple burdens of tradition and modernity. Fallers positioned headmen on the one hand as salaried civil servants with obligations to a government bureaucracy, and on the other as authorities embedded within community networks of kinship and patronage.[82]

Holleman's description is less one of tension or competing power relations and more one of progressivist history—a unidirectional shift toward a more modern form of government. Headmen, as agents of indirect rule, helped govern African subjects. Yet missing in Holleman's account, as in influential renderings of colonial and postcolonial governmentality, are the multiple temporalities and spatialities of power that haunt any singular moment. In postcolonial Kaerezi, *samusha*—what Holleman conceived of as the evolutionary antecedent for *sabhuku*—lived on as a term for an individual exercising authority over a homestead or compound. Administrators recorded a *samusha* on the scheme registry as a "household head," including married men, widows, and the rare divorcees living with their children but not in their parents' homes. Some elders recalled planting pegs at a new *musha* as young married couples established their own homestead. But *samusha* and *sabhuku* described two different roles—one a lineage patriarch and head of a homestead; the other one whose authority was mapped to territory and social relations, but not always through kinship. A *samusha*'s authority within a household and an extended family shaped patterns of labor and conduct at once gendered and generational. A *sabhuku* conjured memories of tax collection, labor discipline, and liaisons between colonial ranchers and administrators.

Holleman's structural categories implied both a fixed hierarchy of power and modernity's teleological displacement of tradition. His "village" constituted an administrative unit, a term for social life carved out through a colonial cartography of tribal rule. Alvord's centralization in the 1930s, the Native Land Husbandry Act in the 1950s and 1960s, and postcolonial villagization all sought to settle African subjects in linear grids of intelligibility—disciplining people in governed spaces through taxes, censuses, and legislation over land and labor. Viewed through this administrative optic, vertical hierarchies increased African authority as jurisdictional territories expanded. Headmen were under kraalheads, who were under chiefs, who in turn were under the British Crown—the biggest chief of all.

Crucial to racialized dispossession was the remapping of traditional authority under the British Empire's umbrella. By linking chiefs and headmen administratively to the fiction of "communal tenure," Rhodesian officials encouraged their Enlightenment baggage to be seized by African customs. If inhabitants of the "Dark Continent" were denied precolonial rights to land, *racialized rule* would govern subaltern subjects through communal fictions. Headmen became, in this model, located in channels of government that grounded their subordinate power in imperial sovereignty.

Kaerezians remembered headmen as conscripts of colonial rule who toiled alongside tenants on Gaeresi Ranch and who also migrated to earn urban wages. Born in the 1930s on the ranch, Tewa reflected in 1992 on the headman's predicament during colonialism:

> Everyone was forced to go and work for the whites. *Sabhuku* was given the responsibility to force his people to work. He was also a worker. He was not given money. He was asked to take people from his area to help the whites. What they said was: "*Sabhuku*, your people are living in my area that I bought. So by command your people must come and work for me. If anyone does not come, *sabhuku*, you are the one who will come and work on his/her behalf." So *sabhuku* had the power to force everyone.

For Tewa, colonial discipline and government—represented by white farmers and administrators—imposed force (*kumanikidza*) on African subjects. A *sab-*

huku's power, *simba*, became subordinate to this repressive force. As a result, Africans became subject to colonial labor discipline. In this version, headmen did not choose or refuse; they became folded into the same apparatus deployed to recruit African labor. Many Kaerezians echoed Tewa's perspective. Another elder told me that "people understood that the *masabhuku* were being forced" to recruit labor and collect taxes.

After independence, when villagization efforts in Kaerezi incorporated headmen within land demarcation exercises—echoing colonial policies of centralization and the Native Land Husbandry Act—the planting of pegs pierced the illusion of a unilineal evolution of traditional authority. On a former white farm purchased by the postcolonial state, a black resettlement officer recorded settlers' names in the scheme's registry as headmen witnessed. Hired casual labor hammered iron posts into quadrant corners, inscribing contours of spatial discipline. Yet popular opposition suggested that the lines of custom were anything but settled. With wry grins, many noted the uncanny echo of the resettlement officer's name, *Marumahoko*. Literally, it translates as "you bit the peg."

Imperial Articulations

As Holleman did, early colonial administrators looked locally for vertical topographies of power contained in what they conceived as tribal territories. They often ignored translocal and transcultural relations baring traces of other empires.[83] When in 1890 the British South Africa Company entered the scene, several chiefs in or near Nyanga were paying tribute to a powerful Portuguese trader and warlord, Manuel Antonio de Souza, popularly known as Gouveia.[84] He made a fortune in the ivory trade, amassing a private army of hunters—extending his regional influence while providing crucial military support to Portuguese campaigns.[85] Commissioned as a captain major of Manica by the Portuguese in 1863, Gouveia rallied a reported 10,000 men against a Shire rebellion. In 1875, he intervened in chiefly succession disputes, claiming the submission of the Manica kingdom to his overlordship, an assertion later disputed by Manica chiefs and the British South Africa Company.[86] Gouveia journeyed along a route of Portuguese empire, arriving from South Asia to Zambesia in 1853 to help administer his uncle's holdings. "In Portuguese parlance, he was a Canarin, an Indian from Goa."[87] Shortly after the Indian "mutiny" against British rule in 1857, Gouveia formed uneasy alliances with colonial officials in southern Africa.

While Gouveia's military clout helped thwart Gaza Ngozi attacks in Portuguese territory, his ruling ambitions provoked concern from the governor of Manica in 1890, six years after the administrative district's founding. "Manuel Antonio's people today reside almost totally in the former kingdom of Barue [Barwe], a land which he calls his own, exalting his vanity to the point of calling its inhabitants his vassals. And he even now wants to be crowned *king of Barue*."[88] Gouveia married a daughter of the Barwe royal house. When one of the Makombe chiefs died in 1880, he laid claim to the chieftainship. His five African wives were strategically located across Manica territory, helping him maintain considerable influence.[89] Portuguese racialized discourses dubbed Goans who settled in the Zambesi Valley after 1750 the "Jews of the East," allegedly for their role in controlling commerce. Gouveia's intermarriage with African royalty turned the derogatory Portuguese term of *kaffir lovers* for Goans into a political idiom for constructing alliances through kinship that troubled racialized boundaries.[90] While British imperial rule in Rhodesia oriented itself around a binary opposition between European and African, Portuguese imperialism produced much more fluid, flexible, and hybrid racial identities.

Gouveia was among several Afro-Portuguese and Indo-Portuguese warlords Newitt termed a "three-headed monster," fusing multiple modes of power in a single individual—Portuguese official, African chief, and successful bandit.[91] While his claims remained disputed, his influence extended widely across what would become British territory. In the late 1960s, a Tangwena elder born around 1885 recalled Gouveia's passing through the Kaerezi vicinity before Rhodes first arrived.[92] In 1890 Rhodes's police criminalized Gouveia's predations in their new colony, capturing and imprisoning him. By the time of his release the following year, Rhodes had encouraged a Barwe revolt against him.[93] While historians differ on the details and timing of his death, his political and economic ambitions were deeply entangled with those of African chiefs.[94]

At the turn of the century, Rhodesian attempts to govern African subjects and administer territory on Nyanga's frontier confronted the historical sedimentations of what Doreen Massey called a "global sense of place."[95] On the Inyanga Block, Africans paid rents to employees of Johannesburg syndicates with financial backing in Europe, paid taxes to British colonial officials, and recognized a Tangwena chief who may have once paid tribute to an Indo-Portuguese warlord. Chief Tangwena's insertion into indirect rule connected Inyanga to the capillaries of the British Empire circulating from India to Africa. Lord Lugard traveled these same circuits, grounding his legitimation for "thrashing first" on his experience as an army officer in British India. When Lugard served as high commissioner of

Northern Nigeria in 1902, the year of Rhodes's death, he chided British reluctance to use force by reminding those in England's Exeter Hall that "the way our Raj has been established in India or elsewhere" did not abide a "policy of trying to make omelettes without breaking eggs."[96] Across Rhodesia's international border, where Tangwena also claimed land and loyal subjects, a rival imperial network also linked South Asia and southern Africa. Gouveia, a privileged migrant born in Goa, competed with African and Portuguese authorities for power, profit, and territorial claims.

Deep histories of regional and transcontinental trade linked localities to distant sites. Archaeological evidence in Nyanga suggests contact with Arab traders as early as the eighth century. Barwe groups may have served as middlepersons between Arab traders near Mombasa on the Kenyan coast and the gold-mining kings of southern Africa's interior.[97] By 1512, according to one noted historian, the "eastern Shona territories of Barwe and Manyika" were established, suggesting their linkage as entities within a larger whole.[98] Nyanga became surrounded by prominent political formations: the Manyika kingdom to its south, the Makoni to its west, and the Barwe to its east. Chief Makoni joined the 1896 uprising against white settlers. Umtassa, the Manyika paramount, remained loyal to the agents of indirect rule. When Tangwena received official Rhodesian recognition as a chief in 1902, he had long negotiated regional spatialities of power. Tangwena's complex entanglements articulated with Kaerezi's, positioning the chief and this Nyanga territory in relation to overlapping European and African assertions of contending polities and sovereignties.

Much as Hegel did in his insistence that historical traces in Africa signaled non-African agency, Europeans saw Nyanga's archaeological record as evidence of distant civilizations.[99] When two German travelers visited at the turn of the century, they attributed the stone ruins of forts and terraces to "ancient Semitic origin." Around the same time, the curator of the archaeological site at Great Zimbabwe attributed Nyanga's ruins to "Arabs."[100] Most Europeans believed that Africans were culturally and technologically incapable of producing civilizations characterized by complex irrigation and ancient architecture. Summers suggested that the uplands of Inyanga remained uninhabited until the late fifteenth century, when people sought refuge "in the inhospitable mountains of the Inyangani range."[101] The labor required to produce ancient terraces in the highlands could be read not as African ingenuity and technical expertise, but as evidence of the inherent undesirability of the landscape itself. Much like postcolonial planning technocrats who reified land categories conceived as scripting agricultural activities, archaeologists and colonial administrators saw Africans living in the highlands out of natural necessity rather than out of cultural preference. Rhodesian rule invoked this presumed natural affinity between Africans and the lowveld to legitimize their forced removal to Native Reserves, securing the highlands for white capitalist farming.

Competing Coffers

In 1902, the year of Cecil Rhodes's death, Inyanga's NC welcomed Chief Tangwena's migration "into our territory," offering him Rhodesian refuge from Makombi. "I told him he could remain and was to remain quiet and give up his guns," the NC reported, thus curtailing any threat in the form of armed rebellion. Incorporated in important ways on the state's periphery, Tangwena offered an extension of state surveillance beyond the international boundary by reporting on Makombi's strongholds in Portuguese territory,[102] perhaps seeking his own revenge on the ruler who exiled him. Officially installed by Rhodesian officials in 1902, Chief Dzeka Tangwena received an annual salary of twelve pounds and began hosting occasional police patrols. However, the broken terrain, distance from the District Center, and location on the periphery made on-site visits difficult.[103] By embedding Tangwena within an administrative grid of intelligibility—of space, sovereignty, and cultural identity—officials sought to subordinate African power to their own rule. Rather than as eclipse or erasure, this agenda can be better conceptualized as *articulation*—understood in its dual sense of joining and enunciation, producing emergent alliances as well as tensions.

At times, the administrative archive suggests a metaphysics of presence haunting African space and sovereignty: a chief must inhabit the territory he rules. In this reasoning, the migration of the sovereign's body transforms his territory. African subjects, officials reasoned, needed this embodied and localized presence to understand their *spatialized* subordination. Much in the same way as administrators complained about the difficulty of collecting rents on properties with absentee owners, they saw absentee chiefs as obstacles to rule. Taxes and rents were more easily procured on territories where African sovereign and white owner resided.

These two flows of payment charted separate routes of power. Taxes paid to chiefs and collected by their subordinate headmen traveled up the hierarchy of indirect rule to the Native Commissioner and the colonial state. Rents, while regulated by colonial laws, flowed to private accumulation of distant speculators in Johannesburg offices or to whites on highland farms. When chiefdoms entangled farms, Africans paid both rents and taxes. Administrators balked, however, when white ownership strained against chiefly reign harnessed to tax procurement. These competing administrative and commercial agendas reveal the "tensions of empire" that linked localized skirmishes over rent and taxes on white farms to imperial arguments about indirect rule, benevolent paternalism, and predatory capitalism.[104]

Private greed could complicate colonial administration, extractive rents riling the natives. Yet public-private partnerships gave cash-strapped administrators leverage to make demands on commercial syndicates to help provide public services. Africans living on bordering reserves, the NC suggested, should use dip tanks on the Inyanga Block constructed by the property owner.[105] The "shoestring" budgets of early colonial regimes in Africa, Berry proposed, encouraged the use of African authorities within the structures of indirect rule.[106] Administrative incapacity and economic constraint, rather than an invincible imperial power, informed the conduits of indirect rule. Resourceful administrators invoked the burdens of empire, enlisting private commercial support for the funding of government provisions.

Use of the Inyanga Block dip tanks by Africans in the neighboring reserves suggests the permeability of private property boundaries to the movement of people and livestock. Many Africans were acutely aware of the precise locations of boundaries demarcated by physical beacons. Despite vocal protests, boundaries' relative traction hinged less on their visibility and precise locations and more on how boundary assertions might adhere to claims on resources, notably land and labor, thus regulating African spatial practices. When Inyanga Block was parceled out in 1930, Africans complained that one European purchaser settled in their Native Reserve. "The natives living on the border are very upset and I think it would be advisable to have a Surveyor as early as possible to fix the line," the NC reported to his superiors in Salisbury.[107] Africans living outside the border wanted a Native Reserve with secure boundaries—to thwart encroachments from white neighbors, as well as the potential obligations of labor tenancy and rents on private property.

Chiefs had significant economic incentives to encourage settlement in their tribal territories since their salaries were linked to the number of taxpayers residing in their areas. While they might claim followers across the international border, only taxpayers in Inyanga District's four chiefdoms counted in colonial rolls. In 1912, Tangwena brought in a tenth of Saunyama's revenues and a fourth of Katerere's. All were dwarfed by Shiovu's tax procurement, collected in the name of the paramount Umtassa.[108] In the 1920s, Tangwena's salary equaled that of his two paramount peers. But by the 1950s, as his contributions lagged in chiefly comparison, Tangwena was paid less than a sixth of what his next closest competitor received. Umtassa's loyalty during the 1896 rebellions continued to reap rewards through tax rebates channeled to Shiovu's salary, still much greater than those of chiefs Saunyama (also Sawunyama) and Katerere (also Katerera).[109]

At the turn of the century, with the fresh memory of African uprisings, administrators looked at the number of followers chiefs claimed as potential military threats or allies. Military intelligence reports also estimated the number of men capable of bearing arms, keeping tabs on potential threats to state security. In the mid-1920s, the Tangwena made for the smallest tribe with 385 men, 80 of whom were armed. In contrast, Saunyama's Wawesa tribe had 2,256 members, and Umtassa's Manyika—with 16,050 in their ranks—had the potential to dispatch 3,500 men to armed conflict.[110] Decades later, a tribal topography differentiated chiefs by their followers' contributions to tax revenues. If swords did not become plowshares, spears and muskets became labor and taxes.

Cultural Cartographies

Ethnographical Maps initially contained administrators' descriptions of four separate ethnicities in the district, each specific to a territory and chief.[111] They chronicled each chieftainship's history, installing an origin story. A written narrative graphed a territory, demarcating its boundaries in relation to prominent landmarks—rivers, ridges, and rock formations—and offering a cursory sketch of tribal custom. Officials mapped kinship connections through tribal totems and subclan praise names. They saw ruling patrilineages as key to organizing political, cultural, and social identities. By conceiving the inheritance of a gendered sovereign substance—a tribal totem—as constitutive of chiefly succession, administrators wrote one of Locke's foundational freedoms into colonial policy. Marriage alliances could also create affinities and potentially enduring allegiances across lineage such as Dzeka Tangwena's presumed loyalty to his father-in-law Umtassa.

Through written reports, administrators both echoed and anticipated geographically grounded governing practices. As a political technology, Ethnographical Maps spatialized ethnic identities, locating Africans in discrete tribes. The 1912 classification of chiefs ordered the district's four salaried sovereigns. South of Kaerezi, Shiovu represented Umtassa—the prominent loyalist during the 1896–97 uprisings—ruling over the Manyika people whose large numbers spilled south across his territory, extending beyond Inyanga District. Sawunyama, an "independent paramount," ruled over "tribe Waunyama," located north and west of Kaerezi. Katerere reigned over his own "tribe Wawesa" in the district's northwest lowveld. The classification report described Tangwena as "a refugee paramount in charge of a small number of Barwi Natives."[112] Repeatedly, administrators stressed the Rhodesian refuge offered to Tangwena when he fled violent predations in Portuguese territory.[113] In contrast to Tangwena's movement, Chief Katerere's Warwesa tribespeople were anchored by the most deeply rooted form of sedentarism. A 1923 report noted that they "were always there."[114]

For administrators, tribally distinct identities, marked by totem, charted the path of spatial movement and political subordination. The colonial archive tracked the Tangwena tribe from refugees to assimilated migrants. In 1913, Inyanga's NC explained that "the leopard is not really a Manyika *mtupo* (totem) but belongs to a small tribe who broke away from Portuguese Territory and paid tribute to Umtassa."[115] Chief Tangwena's marriage to a daughter of Umtassa's lineage produced an alliance among unequals and a son-in-law's subordination to a prominent paramount. By 1923, while still "tribe Barwe," the "Tawungwena" became "intermixed with Wamanyika," the ethnicity administrators understood to comprise more than two-thirds of the district's population. As the sharp edge of ethnicity began to blur around its boundaries, the Inyanga NC charted Tangwena's cultural and spatial mixing as the erosion of a separate tribal identity. He divided the district into only three tribes—the Warwesa, the Wanyama, and the Wamanyika—folding Tangwena into Umtassa's people. Explaining the evaporation of a distinct tribe, he reasoned: "The Chief TAWUNGWENA, who occupies the strip of territory lying between the Jora and Gairezi Rivers is also of the WABARWE tribe having left Portuguese Territory some twenty years ago, owing to trouble with the European authorities there, and come to his present location as an early refugee. However, Tawungwena brought with him but a small following: most of his people are now of the WAMANYIKA tribe, and I am including them as such."[116]

The NC repeated his administrative predecessor's claims to have provided, in a new British colony, refuge for a chief fleeing another empire's *European* authorities east of the international boundary. A couple of years later, Tangwena reportedly still stressed his refugee status, claiming that "the larger part of my country is in Portuguese Territory and the smaller in this district. I cannot live in Portuguese Territory."[117] Official archives repeated these accounts of a displaced sovereign who sought Rhodesian refuge, thus inaugurating a Kaerezi "tribe" and bringing an ethnic history to a territory understood as previously culturally empty.

Administrative accounts noted that before Tangwena's migration to Barwe, the tribe "originally came from the West, whereabouts unknown and travelled through NOE (Mrewa District) and settled in Portuguese East Africa."[118] While administrators accorded fleeting recognition to a Tangwena origin located between what became Salisbury and Inyanga, they conceived another moment and place as foundational to tribal history. Barwe exodus and Kaerezi arrival, for officials, inaugurated a governable chiefdom.

Officials conceived Tangwena and his followers as ethnically distinct on their arrival, but spatial and social mingling in Rhodesian space eventually melded his people into a "Wamanyika" tribe. At the same time, however, administrators recognized a residual cultural difference. In 1923, they continued to distinguish Tangwena's totem (*ingwe*, leopard) from that of Makombi's Barwe tribe (*hunga*, wild pig), using the patrilineal descent of respective royal houses to carve out a cultural difference between ethnic groups.[119] While demonstrating obsessive concerns about Tangwena tribal totems, territory, and ethnicity, officials failed to acknowledge any alternative African identities or spatialities in Kaerezi. Rainmaking eluded Rhodesian radar, as did the affinities of inhabitants who recognized a rainmaker's territorial rule—both before and after Tangwena's arrival.

In contrast, administrators and the Hanmer brothers acknowledged the chiefdom's entanglement with white property, a spatiality that imbued colonial archives and administrative practices on the ground. In 1948, when Charles Hanmer complained about weak African authorities exacerbating problems with labor discipline among Tangwena tenants, authorities found Chief Kinga Tangwena guilty of failing to assist a native runner in apprehending an offender pursued by police in his tribal territory.[120] The following year, a report noted that the guilty party was "a chief, in this colony, of a small section of a larger tribe which was divided by the boundary between this colony and Portuguese East Africa." An administrator precisely mapped the location of "Tangwena's people" on "a portion of Crown Lands which lie to the East of Inyanga Downs." Despite its peripheral location, this area "east of Inyanga Block" was "fully occupied."[121] Around the same time, the state purchased the private Holdenby Estate abutting the Crown Lands to the south and converted it to Tribal Trust Land.[122] Administrators described their challenge in this rugged frontier: "Owing to the broken nature of the country and the thick tropical vegetation the settlement of the natives into this area will take some years because the country will have to be 'tamed' as it were."[123] Tangwena's territory, as well, was "inaccessible except by foot."[124] Geographically and administratively remote, Tangwena territory became enmeshed in overlapping claims of property and power, British Crown and African chiefdom, colonial government, and white capitalist farming.

Amid these entanglements, officials continued to chart a distinct Tangwena identity allegedly claimed by those "who are not of Barwe tribe, but call themselves WANEWA or WANYANGA." By 1950, Tangwena's previous totem, *ingwe* (leopard), had become a *chidawo*, a subclan praise name.[125] While officials mapped tribal demise, an emergent ethnicity—Wanewa or Wanyanga—entered administrative ethnography. Patrilineal inheritance of tribal substance continued to define cultural and political identity, excluding both the totems of wives who become mothers, as well as of migrants who might claim allegiance to a chief through a process of historical becoming rather than essential being. Within the Tangwena royal lineage, administrators conceived a rotation of "houses" to regulate an orderly succession of chiefly rule. A 1948 family tree delineated Nyamariodzo as the founder of the Tangwena dynasty, passing the reign to his royal successors Kubinha, Tsatse, Gwindo, and, finally, Dzeka, whose 1902 installation in Rhodesian territory appears as the first recorded date. Dzeka's younger brother Mudima ruled from 1928; and Kinga (also spelled Kenya and King'a) became installed in 1938.[126] By mid-century, Internal Affairs administered a tribal territory ordered by established ruling traditions.

Tribal tradition, however, could be trumped by state concerns about tax revenues and economic efficiency. As early as 1950, administrators in Salisbury's Native Commissioner's office recommended the "abolition of redundant chieftainships" on bureaucratic and economic grounds, using low tax revenues to direct the budgeting ax. "The present Chief Tawungwena, an old man," the Inyanga assistant NC recommended, should be "allowed to continue as Chief until his death, and the post then be reduced to a Headman" because he had "too small a following to warrant a chieftaincy." Underscoring the elderly chief's physical frailty and feebleness, the official suggested waiting until regal death to avoid "a considerable amount of ill-feeling."[127] The art of government required the appearance of goodwill. Apparently the centralized colonial administrative apparatus swallowed several letters concerning the fate of the Tangwena chieftaincy, leaving those in Inyanga to question the archival regimes of truth on which later policies built. Internal tensions within a differentiated state surfaced as angry administrators fired memos between center and periphery.[128]

By 1965, Internal Affairs had left a notable blank space under the category for Tangwena's "Area" on the district's Delineation Report, signifying what Homi Bhabha called a "site of ambivalence. Its representation is always spatially split— it makes *present* something that is *absent*."[129] In the colonial imagination, how could a chief not have a territory? In a bureaucratic mix of English and Shona, Internal Affairs reported: "Kraals *tonga*'d at this dare but living outside the tribal area: Some on European farms." *Kutonga*, to rule, is also the verb for presiding over a customary court, or *dare*. Chief Tangwena's jurisdiction, the report suggested, transgressed private property boundaries and extended to an area where he did not reside. Echoing the 1950 position, it concluded: "It seems this chief-tainship is no longer functional and should be abolished upon the death of the present incumbent."[130] Again it stressed economic and administrative efficiency.

The Internal Affairs proposal would purge Inyanga Downs of the complica-tions of a chieftainship while assimilating Tangwena's followers into the tribal jurisdiction of either Umtassa or Sawunyama, the neighboring chiefs.[131] State sovereignty would giveth and taketh away tribal territorial rule. A civil ser-vant chief would be structurally adjusted, laid off the tax-driven payroll, and turned off his tribal territory. He would be demoted to a headman subordinated to another chief. Vertical descent went with horizontal movement as Tangwena's spatial dislocation would accompany his downgrading within a vertical topog-raphy of rule. This administrative agenda, however, encountered entanglements colonial rule promoted. Rhodesian attempts to disarticulate the white ranch, Tangwena ethnicity, and tribal territory could not secure segregated spaces through governing practices. Sovereignty (of state and chiefs), government (the orchestration of a field of action obliging African subjects to abide), and disci-pline (the ordering of bodies in space) did not form a stable tripod. The triad-in-motion, shifting with explosive potential, became fiercely contested.

6 · Enduring Evictions

> To articulate the past historically does not mean to recognize it
> "the way it really was" (Ranke). It means to seize hold of a memory
> as it flashes up at a moment of danger. . . . The danger affects both
> the content of the tradition and its receiver.—WALTER BENJAMIN,
> "Theses on the Philosophy of History," 1940

In 1957, William Hanmer sold off a parcel of land in the middle of Gaeresi Ranch and the Tangwena chiefdom. A few years later, John Oram donated the property to a multiracial cooperative society whose members enlisted friends and distant supporters, soliciting capital from whites in Switzerland, England, and southern Africa to launch Nyafaru Development Company in Kaerezi. Established on land legally designated European, its origin echoed the familiar pattern of absentee white ownership. Yet from its inception, blacks and whites comanaged the farm cooperative and the school for ranch tenants' children. In an era of apartheid, Nyafaru integrated blacks and whites—spatially, socially, and politically—becoming a node of antiracist nationalism. Multiracial alliances channeled not only overseas capital but also networks of managers, workers, and supporters to similar cooperatives. In 1965, Nyafaru welcomed new codirectors, Guy Clutton-Brock and Didymus Mutasa, whose mere cooperation defied governing intentions of racial segregation.[1] That same year, chiefdom, white ranch, and nation-state all became further entangled as chief Kinga Tangwena and his son both died; Hanmer attempted evictions; and the Rhodesian Front announced the Unilateral Declaration of Independence (UDI), provoking international ostracism and sanctions. Tangwena's terrain of the conjuncture became a contentious ground of struggle.

In 1991, I sat with Chidumbu in a cold Nyafaru stone farmhouse that, like much of the cooperative's equipment, was in dire need of repair. Born in 1948, he recalled boyhood memories of Fergus Gilmore, Hanmer's first on-site manager, who built Nyafaru's first house when the property was still part of Gaeresi Ranch. "Didn't African workers actually build it?" I pressed earnestly. "Yes, but he *directed* them," he clarified in ChiManyika, letting loose a belly laugh. Chidumbu now ran the cooperative's small store, ferrying supplies by four-wheel-drive truck from town and tending the counter in front of sparsely stocked shelves of candles, cooking oil, sugar, and small food tins. Bottled beer and soda were a rare treat, cement and rock rather than a refrigerator providing coolant. The "store" was more a site of social mingling than commerce, where Chidumbu's infectious laughter echoed off stone walls along with visitors' gossip. A shout away, his family occupied company quarters a stone's throw from the building where his wife coordinated a women's weaving group that produced handicrafts from sheep herded by yet other cooperative members. Laughter stopped as Chidumbu detailed his 1976 arrest when he was charged with "aiding terrorists" at Nyafaru. He emerged from prison around independence, returning home to chiefdom and cooperative. In the early 1980s, he worked for the American Friends Service Committee, coordinating food relief and social services for Tangwena war refugees returning from Mozambique. His record keeping gave him an ear and eye for numbers.

Chidumbu spoke slowly, his voice resonating the cadences of events he conjured from more than twenty years before: "In 1969, the Tangwena were evicted [*kudzingwa*] by the government. Huts were burnt starting on the eighteenth of September, 1969." Jumping from his chair, he dramatically swept his arm to trace movements of people, vehicles, and events. He *embodied* memories, mimicking different actors, using his body as a prop. English words peppered his ChiManyika rendition of what he called "the Tangwena war": "All the people had gathered at Tsatse. They were waiting to see what was going to happen. **1969**, around **4 am** one night, there came **Land Rovers**. We counted them, there were **thirty-four** new **Land Rovers, five lorries,** and one **bulldozer**. They went down to burn Tangwena's huts."

Chidumbu located events and his own perspective precisely. "I was standing *there* when the Land Rovers cleared *that* ridge," he once pointed to the spot as we walked near sundown. Like most Kaerezians, he placed skirmishes in relation to Chief Rekayi's huts, familiar homesteads, ridges, streams, and other prominent landscape features. Memories became mapped onto assemblages that spanned

The Nyafaru school and cooperative, 1991. *Photo by the author.*

time and space. The rocks near the grove where we both knew Mujuru still appeased ancestral spirits had afforded, twenty years before, a lookout to spot approaching evictors. Tenants toiled in one site and moment to establish wattle plantations, later harvesting and transporting poles they then mortared with mud to build homes. Police torched those huts in yet another time-space. While Rhodesian soldiers fought nationalist guerrillas, violence visited a chiefdom and ranch. The era of evictions marked what Veena Das termed a "critical event," a culturally marked historical hinge generative of transformation and constitutive of identity.[2] Walter Benjamin suggests that some places become so entangled with events that the two cannot be unraveled.[3] During what Kaerezians call the Tangwena war, critical events became *emplaced*.

Stoking her cook-hut fire in 1991, MaiHurudza conjured memories from a Rhodesian raid. Her children sat low on a reed mat, drawing in flames' warmth but not their smoke. I sat on a bench built into the wall, made from sun-dried clay bricks and smeared with a mixture of soil, straw, and manure. Helped by neighbors, MaiHurudza assembled products of cattle, earth, and organic processes. With an absent husband pursuing migrant wages, she carried the daily burden of agricultural and domestic work. We spoke over tea while trying to make a small dent in her endless task of chores. Sitting in a squatter's humble hut, I reflected on how her sedimented labor was also the condition of possibility for my own.

MaiHurudza's strong fingers removed maize kernels from the cob as she spoke. I feebly worked at less than half her pace. Friction on my fingertips heated what would become blisters, heightening my awareness of gendered embodiments of labor in multiple modes of fieldwork. The male task of plowing, as well as hoe and ax work, had roughened my hands yet left my fingertips soft. My field notes left their embodied trace, too, producing a graphic callus on my writing finger. "You write too hard, brother," the nine-year-old Serina once exclaimed while running her small fingers across my palm. As Serina's mother spoke, a tape recorder picked up the sound of dried maize hitting the hut floor, and my fingertips added a tactile echo to other senses. Her animated gestures pointed toward places she named, locating them relative to her home, to spots where she witnessed pivotal events. Like Chidumbu, MaiHurudza's movements mimicked those of two decades before: a policeman pointing a gun; a schoolchild scampering; a white administrator ushering edicts, hands placed on swaggering hips.

The children gazed raptly as she enacted her mother-in-law's escape. When soldiers descended on the ranch during a 1972 helicopter raid, MaiZiko hid behind a waterfall, leaving them cursing at her empty cook hut, its fire still-smoldering. We all knew the waterfall from visits to that homestead. And we all knew the young man, once a baby bundled on MaiZiko's back, who had not cried out from their hiding place. Glances exchanged across one cook hut fire conjured images of another. MaiHurudza wove airborne maize kernels, their resistance to her fingers on the cob, and the arc of maize into embodied memory work. Words, gestures, and flashing memories emerged amid labor oriented toward current livelihood. Remembered images joined harvested firewood and crops around the cook-hut fire she stoked.

Herded into a government truck during a 1972 raid, MaiHurudza recalled, children were terrorized by armed police: "Rings with our names on them were put around our necks. We were told that we were being taken to slaughterhouses to be killed. As children, we did not want to move from the area. We were terrified to see our homes being demolished by bulldozers. When soldiers told our parents that they wanted to kill us, we cried." "*Kudzingwa upenyu hwedu*" (to be chased away is our way of life), MaiHurudza lamented, throwing a dried maize cob into the fire. Yet loss can be a paradoxically productive pathos for senses of community.[4] For MaiHurudza, dispossession and displacement *constituted* her relationship to place. Culture does not sit in place; nor is landscape merely a backdrop, a stage for grounded practices. *Lieux de mémoire*, Pierre Nora suggested, are "hybrid places, mutants in a sense," at once the sites of enacted

MaiHurudza and two of her children in their cook hut, along with Tsitsi,
Nyamutsapa, 1991. *Photo by the author.*

memories as well as a crucial ground shaping identities.[5] When memory work
rekindles conflicts over fields, land allocation, and political entitlement, the contours it carves in the local landscape are more than merely metaphorical. The
production of locality consists not in the establishment of a seamless web of
cultural meanings in a single site, but rather in contested processes through
which sedimented yet not settled practices animate landscape, horizons of belonging, and the imagination of community.

Jonathan Boyarin ventured that the "politics of memory" does not posit memory as an autonomous force, but rather directs attention to "rhetoric about the
past mobilized for political purposes."[6] Such a vision, however, has the danger of
presuming that sovereign subjects are fully formed prior to memory. Conscious
choices then steer instrumental deployments as Machiavellian actors with inten-
tional goals strategically pursue a politics of memory. In contrast, Kaerezians'
practices caution against the notion of a calculative political rationality that self-
consciously marshals memory. As Natalie Zemon Davis and Randolph Starn
argue, "memory is indeed polymorphic and historically situated," operating
"under the pressure of challenges and alternatives."[7] The cultural politics of
"memory work" draws attention to how work performs, reproduces, and re-
molds memories; at the same time, memories work to produce materially and
discursively consequential effects.[8]

In October 1991, I sat with Mujuru and his two wives in their Nyamutsapa cook hut, built shortly after independence when they returned from Mozambique as war refugees. Lush fields sprang out in several directions from their cluster of huts, defying villagization's vision. Mujuru and his wives had been at Rekayi's homestead in 1969 when the convoy of government vehicles pierced the predawn sky. "We saw lights like a town drifting toward us," he recalled, invoking icons of urbanity to mark the administrative invasion of his remote rural home. Police arrested and threw him in a fenced Nyanga Center compound where they set German shepherds on defiant labor tenants. "They put some of the dogs inside the fence with us and locked the gate," he recalled. "People were attacked by dogs and by the police. If you ran to one side the dogs would follow. Poles reinforced by concrete bent over on the fence posts. Trousers were torn," he leaped from a stool to tug on his overalls. "Nyakurita was beaten," he singled out one of the prominent headmen who actively resisted the evictions. One of Mujuru's wives interjected as she stoked the fire: "*Mai*Nyakurita was beaten on her breast," reminding us of the violence visited on the headman's wife.

Such enlivened memories complement an "event history" of evictions, constructed from press accounts, human rights reports, and colonial records.[9] As localized land and labor politics became enmeshed in Zimbabwe's liberation struggle, "suffering for territory," *kutambudzikira nyika*, wove both nation and chiefdom into landscapes of belonging. Skirmishes spilled beyond the ranch to courtrooms, the district center, administrative offices in Inyanga and Salisbury, and even overseas.

A Chieftainship without a Chief

In 1962, William Hanmer ordered twenty families off Gaeresi Ranch.[10] It was the same year a government land inspector's flight observed "excessive damage to natural resources" on the property. In December 1963 and January 1964, a ground inspection confirmed the initial appraisal.[11] In the words of a later report, "erosion, the fore-runner of famine, was plainly evident." Noting that most of the African cultivators in question were illegal tenants, officials pressured the landowner: "Although he was not morally responsible for the erosion, the landowner was legally responsible and faced possible criminal prosecution for the negligence in the land husbandry methods adopted by the tenants."[12] Also in 1963, officials oversaw the evictions of "all African families resident on the Rhodes Inyanga National Park," moving them to be "resettled" in one of the district's

Tribal Trust Areas.[13] State conservation concerns fused with labor politics and racial land policies.

In 1965 alone, Hanmer purged 76 families from his ranch.[14] At the time, only 290 families reportedly lived on it.[15] The following year, the secretary of Internal Affairs noted the termination of labor agreements on Gaeresi Ranch. As a result, "tenants who failed to take up full-time employment with the Hanmers were required to quit and move elsewhere."[16] Followers of Chief Saunyama, whose territory overlapped the north of the ranch, agreed to move "voluntarily" to reserves.[17] But 152 families refused, making them squatters who comprised the majority of "tribesmen under the Tawungwena Chieftainship."[18] The title of a 1966 memorandum aptly captures the splicing together of chiefdom, labor relations, and colonial land policy: "Tawengwena Chieftainship: Land: Removal of Squatters: Gaeresi Ranch."[19] By 1969, administrators estimated that approximately 300 ex-tenants moved off the property in the wake of Hanmer's termination of labor agreements.[20] Yet stubborn squatters remained, throwing a wrench in ranch and governmental operations.

The 1965 Internal Affairs Tawungwena chieftainship report noted that "the chief no longer has a tribal area," citing meager tax roles to justify its disbanding.[21] Since 1961, Chief Kinga Tangwena's son, Marijeni, had been deputized to carry out his elderly father's duties.[22] Dying a month after his father at the close of 1965, Marijeni's official appointment as acting Chief Tangwena came posthumously, the new salary paid to his estate.[23] Timing was crucial. The deaths of two chiefly civil servants occurred the same year Smith announced UDI and Hanmer evicted squatters. Articulating previous historical sediments, in that moment the chiefdom's colonial geo-body became embroiled in local, national, and international politics of race, rights, and justice.

In February 1966, a delegation trekked to Inyanga District Center. Kraalheads had met in the wake of Kinga's and Marijeni's deaths, choosing Rekayi Tangwena—the son of Dzeka, the first colonially recognized Chief Tangwena installed in 1902—as their new leader.[24] After kraalheads had selected him as sovereign, they approached the District Commissioner (DC) to inform government of their actions. The DC told elders that only after Hanmer's labor conflicts were resolved would a decision be made on the chieftainship's fate. Tangwena kraalheads returned the next month "with their chief to be crowned."[25] Again the commissioner refused to disentangle chiefly politics from ranch labor struggles. Reporting to superiors, the DC speculated: "In view of the fact that five of the six kraals controlled by this chief are likely to disperse far and wide, as they are resident on

Gaeresi Ranch, it is probable that this chieftainship will become redundant." While acknowledging that Rekayi was "recognised by the tribesmen as their leader," and that "the administration has worked with and through this man when discussing the Gaeresi Ranch problem," he took pains to clarify that "this has always been as the tribal spokesmen, and not as the chief."[26]

After another unsuccessful attempt to gain recognition in March 1966 at the district level, Rekayi traveled to the secretary of Internal Affairs office in Salisbury, "claiming appointment as the new Chief Tangwena." Administrators from the center, unaware of Marijeni's death months before, fired off an angry memo to the periphery.[27] As late as 1972, the acting DC in Inyanga answered a query for historical documentation supporting arguments for disbanding the chieftainship with the assessment that "somewhat sketchy information is all that I have been able to glean."[28] Both the Provincial Commissioner and the National Archives reported similar futile searches for the 1950s discussions over abolishing the Tangwena chieftainship.[29] What Nikolas Rose terms "government at a distance" circuits through technologies of rule yet also encounters obstacles of transmission.[30] Crossed signals as well as administrative apparatuses linked Salisbury, Inyanga Township, and a white ranch.

Nationalist Routes

Born around 1915 in his father Dzeka's homestead on the ranch's Tsatse kraal, Rekayi grew up in a royal family. His wife farmed a smallholding in Tsatse, while he earned wages in Bulawayo from the 1930s as a waiter, later working for the railroad. In that distant city he joined Southern Rhodesia's African National Congress (SRANC) shortly after its 1957 founding. Government had banned the SRANC in 1959, and its successor, the National Democratic Party (NDP), in 1961. Rival nationalist parties—Nkomo's Zimbabwe African People's Union (ZAPU) and Mugabe's Zimbabwe African National Union (ZANU)—emerged in the wake of the NDP's legally decreed demise. Around 1963, the year before ZAPU and ZANU were banned, Rekayi returned from Bulawayo to full-time farming and ranch residence as Hanmer tried to coerce "agreements" from Kaerezi labor tenants. Nationally, the Rhodesian Front's victory in white elections that year paved the way for Smith's 1965 UDI from Britain. More rigid racial rule ensued as apartheid-style politics detained so-called political agitators. Fighting for his father's chiefdom, Rekayi produced an administrative nightmare: a subversive populist and self-proclaimed chief who fused nationalist politics, land rights, and labor militancy. As kraalheads selected a new chief in 1966, a small band of Zimbabwe African National Liberation Army (ZANLA) guerrillas fired on Rhodesian troops in Chinoyi (Sinoia). Helicopter gunships killed seven of the twenty-one, bringing a bloody end to the 1966 skirmish nationalists claimed as the military launch of Zimbabwe's liberation war.[31]

Anticolonial nationalism animated both the history and geography of Tangwena terrain. Whig histories often suggest progressive teleologies that unfold, inexorably, toward triumphalist futures. Metaphors like the "rising tide of African nationalism" lend nature's inevitability to history's progress. Kaerezi's situated struggles, in contrast, emerged from contingency rather than certainty. A *historical* moment created the conditions of possibility for a subversive chief's anticolonial nationalism, but so did Rekayi's *spatial* routes, linking nationalist aspirations, migrant labor, and ancestral claims to Tangwena territory. In 1966, Rekayi journeyed by foot to Inyanga District Township, and later by bus to Salisbury to assert his claims. That same year, Josiah Tongogara led a small ZANU contingent to China for revolutionary training, returning to Tanzania to prepare them as exiles for revolutionary warfare.[32] Struggles on an Eastern Highlands ranch entangled localized, regional, and transcontinental networks.

Digging Heels, Hiring Lawyers

William Hanmer first took legal action against Rekayi before Kinga's death, giving him an eviction notice in September 1965. The following year, Hanmer targeted twenty-six men and thirteen wives whose husbands were away working.[33] Eviction orders usually stipulated an August removal date, after the annual harvest and before the planting of a new crop. Yet when the Provincial Administrator visited in September 1966, he "gained the impression that they would probably dig their heels in and see what we were going to do about it."[34] Kaerezians recalled in the 1990s that Hanmer had chased low-level civil servants off his property in the late 1950s and early 1960s, claiming that he was "the law" on his land. By the end of that decade, Hanmer gave power of attorney to the Inyanga DC to "act on my behalf and in my interest in respect of the removal of these persons, their belongings and dwellings."[35] A decade after chasing government officials off his property, he welcomed state intervention.

Recall that colonial legislation defined squatters as Africans living without formal labor agreements on land designated European by the 1930 Land Apportionment Act. Section 93 of the amended 1941 act stipulated that Africans who occupied a piece of land *before* it became European could legally continue to reside there. In order to remove them, a Government Proclamation naming specific Africans was required.[36] In the wake of the Native Land Husbandry Act's spectacular failure, officials feared the anticolonial impulses fomented by unpopular land policies. The 1962 report by the Select Committee on the Resettlement of Natives, dryly opined: "The Government would incur the great displeasure of the people if it up-rooted them for no apparent reason."[37]

In May 1967, an Inyanga judge convicted Rekayi of contravening the Land Apportionment Act. Hanmer claimed the squatter had moved to the ranch a year and a half before. Rekayi pleaded not guilty and "maintained that the land was an African area and has been from the 'time of our ancestors.'"[38] Losing his case, Rekayi paid a fine of thirty pounds. He returned to the ranch, dug in his heels, and hired a white lawyer, R. H. B. Pringle. Together they returned to Inyanga's magistrates court in November. The defense argued "that at the time of the original grant of land by the British South Africa Company in 1905, Rekayi's family was living in the kraal he now occupied."[39] Continuous ancestral residence, they asserted, predated European alienation. Rekayi lost, again being found guilty of contravening the Land Apportionment Act in January 1968. Defiantly, he took his case to the appellate division of the High Court in Salisbury. Later that year, in a nationally publicized case, he won an appeal from the High Court overturning his conviction.[40]

Despite the temporary legal victory, officials responded by issuing a proclamation evicting Rekayi and thirty-six fellow squatters in January of 1969, ordering their resettlement to Holdenby, east of the ranch. A Ministry of Lands public statement euphemized the maneuver: "Today's proclamation provides for the resettlement of the group in the adjoining Holdenby Tribal Trust Land only a short distance away. Their new home is identical in character to the area they will leave, the soil is good with abundant natural water, there is a good grass cover and the protected slopes are well wooded."[41] Internal memos spoke more bluntly, outlining "Tangwena's eviction to Holdenby Tribal Trust Land—i.e. dump him in the vicinity of the late Chief's kraal and if he returns in contravention of the order criminal action will then be taken."[42]

At the time of the 1969 proclamation, Rekayi's position was emphatic: "I will not be moved. This is our home and I shall die here. They can kill me if they like."[43] In memos, press releases, and court cases, the Ministry of Internal Affairs repeatedly mapped Tangwena as a subordinate subchief of the paramount Makombe, always orienting the source of sovereignty east. In contrast, Rekayi insisted that Makombe "whose area lies in what is now Mozambique, was not paramount Chief." Rather, he asserted, "Makombe and Tangwena were friends and equals" allied through marriage. The mother of the Makombe who rebelled against the Portuguese in 1917 had been the daughter of Nyamariodzo, a Tangwena chief. For Rekayi, Makombe's dynasty was to the east, but Tangwena chiefs or their designated representatives had once ruled as far west as Macheke, more than one hundred kilometers away. Makoni and Mutasa chiefs, he argued, came later into the region, respectively west and south of Kaerezi, establishing their territorial influence—either by dominance or negotiation—across portions of what had once been Tangwena territory.[44] Officials' orientation east occluded this spatial history, while their proposals for resettlement constructed spaces as exchangeable—in their terms, objectively "identical in character." In contrast, Rekayi recognized qualitatively different characters of *place* spread across Tangwena territory, stressing agricultural and cultural distinctions. He sharply differentiated portions of his reign overlapping Gaeresi Ranch from *Machena*, the name for the section of Holdenby Tribal Trust Land designated for Tangwena resettlement, derived from the white stones dotting the landscape.[45] "It is a barren, unfertile area and very rocky. . . . It is useless for farming," he argued. Moreover, he underscored, "the place is sacred; it is a graveyard. No one can be asked to go and live there. People in England are not asked to go and live in graveyards."[46]

Rekayi compared his own rule, and notions of inheriting dominion over people and place, to the reign of Queen Elizabeth, the sovereign of the United Kingdom. During negotiations over Rhodesia's settlement with Britain in 1971, he asked a reporter whether the Queen of England would agree to be moved to Italy by the British government.[47] Declaring that "the Queen is overall and the Rhodesian Government should be punished," Rekayi claimed that "the child of the Queen is doing very much wrong." "If the people could not inherit," the press depicted his reasoning, "what was the Queen doing on her throne? Why could he not inherit his land?"[48] In 1991, sitting outside her cement-block and asbestos-roofed house in Tsatse, Rekayi's widow proudly recalled to me his argument: "Rekayi was saying it is his rightful inheritance [*nhaka*]. He was saying Queen Elizabeth inherited her post, so if she is removed, he will do the same thing." Invoking the sovereignty of imperial rule, Rekayi positioned Smith's state as a "rebel" refusing the principles of good government.

Rekayi similarly targeted the brutality and injustice of Rhodesian land alienation, the discourse that converted forcible seizure to legal property rights. "When
the Europeans came they found me here," he asserted his rights: "When a nice
place is seen it is said 'this is ours'—a nice fertile place is said to be 'ours' while we
blacks are stacked in the hills. Is it not killing us? . . . These people recognized by
Smith . . . they are thieves; they steal, they are robbers. The DC is not a ruler (or
judicial officer). I consider he is more a robber, who wants to steal the whole
country like a snake."[49] For his explicit resonances between reptiles and Rhodesian rule, Rekayi received a subversion charge in 1971.[50] Twenty years later, the
Nyafaru headmaster recalled journeying to Harare as a standard 6 schoolboy to
see his chief's day in court: "*Hurumende inyika inouraya zvaisingadyi*, the government is a snake which kills what it doesn't eat. That's what Rekayi said." For
him, the spectacle of subversion produced pride in his chief, the thrill of witnessing defiance in a court of law, the righteousness of speaking truth to power.

Many stressed the progressive politics of multiracial alliance. In 1991, Headman Goora, one of those who accompanied Rekayi on his initial visit to Inyanga
to claim the chieftainship in 1966, echoed many of his peers in lauding Guy
Clutton-Brock's instrumental activities at Nyafaru: "He worked like a lawyer. He
could ask us, 'What do you want?' What are you thinking about your country
[*nyika*]? We answered and he helped." Chidumbu positioned white contributions in relation to African agency. "In 1970, the Tangwena war was hot and the
school was closed," he told me in 1991. Africans, he stressed, were the on-site
orchestrators of operations at the multiracial cooperative:

> The farm was not under whites. The white who was here mostly lived in Harare
> at Cold Comfort, and he was **Mister** Guy Clutton-Brock. This white man politi-
> cized the Tangwena people so that they knew about the right [*kodzero*] to stay in
> their area. It's the same with hunters. They may have a dog that does not hunt, and
> when they give it a share of the meat, it will feel that hunting is good. Then it will
> start biting goats and other animals. Then it starts hunting. Guy was giving the
> Tangwena a portion so that they knew that they have the right to stay in the area.
> The Tangwena started to fight for their land.

Other whites offered legal advice, enabling assertions of ancestral rights on a
ranch to gain traction in distant courts. When police destroyed the huts of those
not named in the legal proclamation ordering evictions in 1969, lawyers sued two
ministries—Internal Affairs and Justice, Law, and Order—for unlawful destruction of property.[51] Others followed suit, most receiving more than half of dam-

ages claimed. While the law isolated individual offenders and beneficiaries, a communal ethic shaped Tangwena assertions of rights and responsibilities. They pooled funds from court cases to share with those not compensated for destroyed property.

A frustrated Inyanga administrator complained that "the whole procedure is incredibly clumsy with the onus on the Administration all the time to enforce the law rather than upon the squatter to obey the law."[52] He highlighted the politics of scale. Government at a distance, the machinations of bureaucrats, a legal apparatus, and pronouncements emanating from Salisbury contradicted his on-the-ground attempts to administer order on a ranch plagued by squatters. After Headman Goora and others named in eviction orders received only fines in 1971, he wrote angrily to the Provincial Commissioner: "I am frankly tired of the whole business. The rest of the machinery of our form of Government seems totally disinterested in anything but frustrating what is done at a local level. Why myself and the local police should walk hundreds of miles for the dubious satisfaction of securing occasional $25 fines I can no longer comprehend and see little point in continuing operations on Gaeresi Ranch."[53]

The Inyanga DC decried the "rebellious" actions of the Tangwena who were "prepared to flout the law." Echoing Lord Lugard's dictum—thrash first, conciliate afterward—he concluded that "the destruction of all huts by the authorities within a few days cannot but have an intimidatory effect advantageous to the forces of law and order."[54] Meanwhile, the Provincial Commissioner emphasized the need to "strike while the iron is hot," citing public opinion that demanded swift government action to " 'fix' the Tangwena." He recommended distributing leaflets with seven days notice to destroy dwellings instead of waiting "for publication of a notice which would take 3 months before we could act again."[55] The head office in Salisbury, however, did not want Internal Affairs to be "caught with its pants down" and stressed the need for the publication of eviction notices. It ordered those destroying huts to first remove all property and money before torching them to "avoid the chance of any liability."[56]

As different branches of government debated the ruling merits of intimidation, force, and legal instruments of dispossession, squatters clung defiantly to the ranch. Within a week of the September 1969 raid bulldozing charred huts in Tsatse, Rekayi and his followers were back on the ranch rebuilding. The following month, police again demolished huts, seizing nineteen men with their possessions and dumping them on the sliver of state land east of the ranch.[57] They, too, returned to rebuild in explicit defiance of court orders. A year later, police impounded 658 head of cattle and plowed under crops cultivated by squatters.[58] Fearing arrest, many families never returned to claim their cattle. As a result, over 200 head were auctioned by the state.[59] Kaerezians eluded capture by hiding in thick mountain forests bordering the ranch. In November 1970, Rekayi claimed more than 1,000 men, women, and children living "like baboons" in hiding.[60] Living in a makeshift thatch-and-wattle lean-to, one woman told a reporter given access to some of the hideouts by Rekayi: "We are living like animals but we will not go where the Government wants us to go."[61] Twenty huts were again destroyed in a highly publicized raid in late November 1970. Photographs on *The Rhodesia Herald*'s front page depicted triumphant white Rhodesians in shorts and knee socks overseeing the destruction of huts.[62] Little more than a year later, however, Rekayi claimed a following of 150 still living on the ranch.[63] Moving clandestinely from mountain hideouts by nightfall, they snuck back to cultivate crops and rebuild. To avoid leaving signs of a well-worn trail, they chose novel routes in and out of the forests. They sprinkled pepper across paths to confuse tracking dogs used by soldiers and police. Forest dwellers carefully obscured fires, burning only at night to avoid smoke's daytime visibility.

Mujuru, born in Kaerezi in the early 1930s, recalled that after officials destroyed huts, "we would go as a group during the night to rebuild homes. The next day the soldiers would be surprised to see huts built. We would divide ourselves into groups, saying that groups would go to build at such and such a home. They were surprised to find a hut they burnt yesterday standing up with a cooking fire going inside it today." In 1972, Rhodesian security forces descended from helicopters, arresting ten, while around two hundred, including Rekayi, escaped.[64] Those captured were mostly the elderly unable to run. Police dogs brought down one of the fleeing men, who appeared for sentencing covered in bandages.[65] Around a 1991 cooking fire, Mujuru remembered the same German shepherd attack. Recall, also, that he reminded neighbors opposing villagization that they could be "beaten like dogs" by state officials.

Nyafaru's multiracial cooperative became a critical conduit, providing food, information about police raids, and aid for those sleeping in mountain forests. While more than a thousand fled to surrounding mountains, many families sent young children to be cared for at Nyafaru, where Swiss donor funds and African educators constructed a small school. In the major 1972 raid, police seized 110 Tangwena children—claiming they had been abandoned by their parents—and loaded them into trucks bound for a "Social Welfare repatriation camp" outside Salisbury.[66] Police charged managers and members of the cooperative with aid-

ing Rekayi to occupy European land.⁶⁷ Officials also suspected that Nyafaru
residents harbored and guided nationalist guerrillas to and from rebel camps
across the Mozambique border. Chidumbu became one of those imprisoned for
his support of "terrorists."

Liberalism's Global Reach

Media coverage of skirmishes on Gaeresi Ranch pondered how images of defiant
squatters challenging Rhodesia's racialized land policies might travel. In a 1969
editorial, the *Rhodesia Herald* worried: "The Government future land policy,
whatever its validity, seems to contain risks of creating the beginnings of an
embittered rural proletariat."⁶⁸ "What began as a private squabble between the
Tangwena tribe and a company that apparently wanted them off the land," another editorial wrote amid increasingly militant African nationalism, "has been
allowed to develop into a harmful clash between a few hundred primitives and
the State."⁶⁹ However, the domestic press failed to appreciate how official refusal
to recognize Rekayi's chiefly rule fanned the fires of popular support by squatters
and nationalists alike. Press reports followed government practice of denying his
status as a legitimate chief, referring to Rekayi Tangwena as the "self-styled chief
of the Tangwena,"⁷⁰ the man "who claims to be their chief,"⁷¹ and the man
"whom his people call chief."⁷²

   With the help of advisors at Nyafaru and elsewhere, Rekayi wrote letters to
prominent British newspapers, seeking to lobby transnational public opinion. In
1966, the *Guardian* published Rekayi's claim: "When the first European came
here my ancestor, the Chief at that time, allowed him an area." African hospitality
bestowed use rights to white colonists. But colonists mistook generosity for
ceding of legal land title. "Our claim is older and should be recognized," Rekayi
insisted, "we have never released it." The letter pleaded against evictions from his
ancestral homeland, reminding responsible fellow citizens of empire that "the
final settlement of the Unilateral Declaration of Independence accepted by Britain does not allow this treatment of the African to continue."⁷³ Later that year in
London, a letter appealing to universal justice and attributed to Rekayi appeared
in the *Times*: "We will never voluntarily leave our country, but the might of their
arms is irresistible and as a peaceful people we do not want to fight. Our numbers
are only about 1,200 but justice should be for the few, as for the many."⁷⁴ Such
subversive invocations of liberal humanism alarmed the secretary of Internal

Affairs enough to brief the prime minister's office on the political implications of Tangwena evictions gaining overseas press exposure.[75] Internal Affairs opened surveillance files on domestic and international press coverage of "the Tangwena Issue." Another dossier chronicled correspondence penned in support of Tangwena's position by Rhodesians and Europeans.[76] When film footage of Rhodesian officials burning Tangwena huts reached Britain in 1971, editorials worried about international opinion.[77] Press reports raised concerns that the Tangwena conflict would enter into negotiations between Rhodesia and Britain.[78]

SaNyamubaya neither spoke nor read English. Yet he astutely understood the power of media images to convey the graphic texture of Tangwena struggles to the minority community of progressive whites in Rhodesia, as well as to Americans and Europeans. All criticized racist injustice in a country targeted by international sanctions for violating human rights. After Rekayi's forcible seizure during the September 1969 raid, SaNyamubaya walked with a group of squatters toward Inyanga District Center to protest their chief's arrest. At a tense standoff with police at the Kaerezi River, SaNyamubaya recalled a "friendly" white who "came from the back of the police and hid behind them. One of the police produced a gun and pointed it at us, and the white man took a photograph of the policeman, accusing him of producing a gun in the eyes of civilians. He defended himself by saying he was trying to intimidate them. The white man said: '. . . Release them.' And we arrived at the offices." In SaNyamubaya's memory of this battle of progressive white against might, camera trumped gun.

Chidumbu's brother, headmaster of Nyafaru School in 1991, recalled the cooperative's white comanager passing news onto the BBC. "We did not know how he did it. Let's say this morning huts are being burnt. By 12 noon you could hear BBC saying something about the Tangwena's huts being burnt." Many Kaerezians emphasized how progressive whites transported the Tangwena struggle across transnational mediascapes. Rhodesian authorities recognized their role as well, seeking to depict primitive tribespeople as the dupes of subversive outside agitators. A 1966 Internal Affairs memo reported that "certain elements (mainly European) are inciting these people to defy Government and the law and hence the inflated and exaggerated position that is being canvassed overseas."[79] Letters to British newspapers were similarly seen as "inspired by a certain European element which operates at Nyafaru Farm."[80] By 1969, after a series of court battles, Internal Affairs alleged: "Communists and fellow travellers at Nyafaru were to blame for manipulating Africans, encouraging their defiance of the Land Apportionment Act."[81]

Stanley Keeble, who worked as a farm manager on Nyafaru in the 1960s, became a "Prohibited Immigrant," barred in 1969 from entering the country. He wrote to the *Rhodesia Herald* from his new post in Limbe, Malawi. Technically, he stated, Hanmer had only *managed* Gaeresi Ranch, which was owned by shareholders in Britain. Keeble outed the capital circuits of empire on which Gaeresi depended, while attacking racialized rule:

> I have written to all the Gaeresi Ranch shareholders in England and Ireland. Six have replied. All of them express concern and sympathy for the Tangwena and wish them to remain. As one put it: "Anything was preferable to having been used by the Government for their racialist and unimaginative policies." . . . Is there any other country in the world where a responsible government would deliberately dispossess their own people from ancestral land to give the land to absentee foreign landlords who don't want it? Or does the Rhodesian Government not regard the black majority as its "own people"?[82]

The same white circuits of capital that enabled Hanmer's evictions could challenge them, absentee owners wanting to recognize African land rights denied by a racist regime.

Complex networks spanning race and space converged at Nyafaru. The cooperative's comanagers first met in 1949 at St. Faith's Mission near Rusape. There, the schoolboy Didymus Mutasa benefited from agricultural classes offered by Guy Clutton-Brock. Born in England a few years after Rhodes's death, Clutton-Brock had his imperial connections gain progressive ground in another era. A Cambridge graduate, he headed Oxford House, a community center with a board run by Anglican bishops, university academics, and philanthropists, in down-and-out East London. Christian idioms of social justice melded with national duty as bombs rained on Britain. Having sheltered impoverished East Enders during air raids, after the war he did a stint in bomb-ravaged Berlin as a religious affairs officer with the occupying government before taking a ship to Cape Town in 1949. When Mutasa met him near Rusape later that year, Clutton-Brock embodied access to capital, knowledge, and support that spanned countries and continents. His wife ran a clinic, while he focused on an agricultural cooperative—first at St. Faith's and, later, near the capital at Cold Comfort Farm, again working with Mutasa.[83]

In stark contrast to E. D. Alvord's gospel of the plow, Clutton-Brock's biblical inspirations guided racial and spatial *integration*, despite enduring inequalities. Idioms of socialism melded at St. Faith's with what has since been called Libera-

tion Theology. Oxford academics, Irish Anglicans, and curious African nationalists from Salisbury visited what was, in 1950s Rhodesia, an extreme anomaly:
whites and blacks co-owning machinery, mingling together in soccer and maize
fields, and holding community meetings chaired by Africans. Clutton-Brock was
a public intellectual, writing editorials and booklets, while his travels to Nyasaland supported striking plantation workers who deployed explicitly Gandhian
tactics. Networked through the African Development Trust, transnational circuits connected Clutton-Brock's projects with cooperatives established in Tanzania and elsewhere.

Drawn into multiracial politics, he helped draft the SRANC's first antiracialist
constitution in 1957, becoming the only white imprisoned during the 1959 banning of the group. A decade later, no less than the minister of Internal Affairs
denounced him as a communist in Parliament. That same year, the Rhodesian
press described him as "a welcome guest in the home of practically every black
politician in Central and East Africa" and his home as a "mecca for Africans who
believe themselves victims of injustice."[84] Tanzanian president Julius Nyerere
would eventually claim the white Christian for socialist humanism, recognizing a
fellow traveler in the "struggle for total African liberation."[85] Mugabe first read of
Clutton-Brock's activities when teaching in Nkrumah's Ghana in the late 1950s,
and thirty years later celebrated the white's "socialist-style life," crediting his
"active assistance" to the Tangwena people.[86] The complex contingencies that
routed a future president's 1975 escape to Mozambique through Tangwena territory included Mugabe's experience in Ghana, where he learned about Clutton-
Brock's exploits in yet another place, at St. Faith's. Mugabe flew to Britain in 1995
to attend Clutton-Brock's memorial service and to collect his ashes, returning to
scatter them at Heroes' Acre on Harare's outskirts. That North Korean–designed
monument honors contributions to Zimbabwe's postcolonial nation. Clutton-
Brock's remains are those of the only white to share that soil with the graves of
black comrades—claimed by the national sovereignty of his political affinities
rather than of his birth; in death, his struggles against racialized segregation
endure.

At Nyafaru, Clutton-Brock was among the conduits of African nationalism's
transnational histories. Crucially, he fused discourses of Christian humanism
and citizenship. Refuting claims that Rekayi and his followers were dupes of
outside agitators, he wrote to the *Rhodesia Herald* that "those who have helped
him have done no more than the duty of any Christian or citizen."[87] "Like all key
contested political concepts," Hall and Held argue, citizenship can "be appropri-

ated within very different political discourses and articulated to very different political positions."[88] They stress how citizenship entails struggles over the cultural politics of community, belonging, and membership. Clutton-Block gave white backing to Tangwena's ancestral assertions of rights due tribal subjects who were also national citizens. He fired off editorials challenging Rhodesia's illiberal *exclusions*: "It raises serious issues for the ordinary citizen when such a judgement, given in the High Court, is apparently not accepted or is disregarded in a statement subsequently issued by a Government department—when something declared lawful by the High Court is declared to be illegal by a Ministry."[89] Fed up with his protests, Rhodesian officials deported him in 1970.

Didymus Mutasa defended his friend against charges of communism. Their common cause, Mutasa argued, hung on a Christian humanism dedicated to racial equality. He stressed the sins of Rhodesian rule, countering allegations that it was atheists who opposed apartheid policies: "Their identification with the problems of the African people in this country is based on the Christian belief that all people are the same in the sight of God; and the desire to live up to moral justice and good human relationships. If this is Communistic, Christ was a Communist, and so are those who declared independence illegally, allegedly to preserve Western Christian standards."[90] Rekayi also proclaimed his faith in Christian citizenship: "We are not afraid to be arrested nor to suffer; we are Christians and this is the way of the Cross."[91] Officials detained Mutasa for translating an interview with Rekayi for the *Struggle*, a publication of the African National People's Union, also fining Tangwena for subversion. Declaring that "God will come to us if we seek his grace," Rekayi alleged that the Inyanga District Commissioner "wishes to destroy the African here on earth if this were permitted by God. . . . He is a racist." He stressed the brutality of Rhodesian force: "They arrest us and toast us on fires. They hit us with the butts of their guns." Yet he concluded by advocating pacifism: "Basically I am not a violent man and I will not commit myself to violence. What we want is a just peace. What we want is social justice. The people must tell the government to stop their cruelty."[92] Human rights reports similarly stressed Rekayi's counseling his followers not to be violent if they were forcibly moved.[93] A 1970 letter to the editor entitled "Organized Terrorism" compared Rekayi to Gandhi.[94]

Emphasizing his Anglican affinities, Rekayi met with the bishop of Mashonaland, telling the press that "as a member of the Anglican Church my problems are also the Church's problems."[95] From overseas, the Christian Movement for Peace wrote directly to Hanmer, asking him to "consider the facts from a Christian and

Humanitarian point of view."[96] Domestically, *Moto*, a Roman Catholic periodi-
cal, included editorials supportive of Tangwena's cause. In the face of government
evictions, a *Moto* editorial wrote: "The representatives of the world Press will be
waiting and it would be too embarrassing for Mr. Smith and his men to have
photographs of what could be a minor Sharpesville splashed across the pages of
the world's newspapers."[97] Reference to unarmed civilians massacred by apartheid forces in South Africa linked global circuits of human rights to regional
histories of racialized violence. Two London-based Christian organizations published booklets sympathetic to Tangwena and highly critical of human rights
abuses. In Rhodesia, the Catholic Commission for Justice and Peace actively
disseminated information supporting Tangwena and countering government
claims.[98]

These discourses of Christian humanism, citizenship, and the liberal rule of
law articulated effectively to embarrass the Rhodesian state. One editorial compared the Tangwena confrontation to US involvement in Vietnam.[99] Another
lamented: "We can think of few more asinine actions politically."[100] Over five
hundred students and staff at the University College of Rhodesia signed a petition registering "their solidarity with and support for the Tangwena people and
held that it was unfair and morally indefensible to evict them from the land that
was their birthright."[101] The same year, *Moto* proclaimed, "Whatever happens,
Rekayi Tangwena has already been assured a prominent place in this country's
history."[102]

Among white Rhodesians, however, Tangwena supporters constituted a distinct minority. Since 1962, the white electorate had supported Smith's Rhodesian
Front. Garfield Todd, former prime minister of Southern Rhodesia, was a prominent dissenter in the national newspaper: "What happens in the mountains of
Inyanga is our responsibility, for all political power is white." Todd warned his
fellow whites of the African unrest their own policies fomented: "Is it really
surprising that all through Rhodesia, even if we whites remain largely uncon-
cerned, Africans become increasingly resentful and angry at the picture of 1,000
of their people fleeing into the mountains because they refuse to leave their
traditional lands? The homes they leave behind are now being destroyed and
their cattle impounded."[103] Hanmer's neighbor, *Mabvura*, wrote back a sharp
rebuke. He criticized Todd's attempt "to wring people's hearts on account of the
Tangwena people, and rouse wrath against the Government."[104] Viewed in the
context of UDI and the racial apartheid policies of the Rhodesian Front government, however, the mobilization of fragments of domestic support, along with

international press and human rights pressure, struck resonant chords with hearts and minds.

Unwon Hearts and Minds

When Tangwena squatters refused to be resettled on Holdenby, state land adjacent to Gaeresi Ranch, the Ministry of Internal Affairs proposed several alternatives. One plan would move the Tangwena as a group to Gokwe, in the semi-arid lowveld of northwestern Zimbabwe, some four hundred kilometers away.[105] Another proposal in the late 1960s advocated relocating the "tribe," again as a group, to Bende, a parcel of land carved out from state forest reserve thirty kilometers away. When the Inyanga DC tried to persuade Gaeresi squatters to move to Bende, one of Tangwena's headmen spoke fiercely: "They are unwilling to comply with your orders. They know that you have built a road to deport us and they therefore also know that the road will kill us. Use it for your lorries and soldiers and kill us. We will not leave."[106]

Sitting at his Kaerezi home in 1992, that same headman's bony finger etched the course of the same road. He mimicked shoveling and swinging a pick. As he spoke of assembling at Rekayi's homestead in anticipation of the major 1969 raid, his arms encircled the remembered gathering before standing to point toward the site where Rekayi's widow still lived: "We saw Rekayi as a good leader because he had joined the NDP in town. NDP was followed by ZAPU, then ZANU." He used the English acronyms for the National Democratic Party and its successors. For this postcolonial headman, Rekayi's radical anticolonial nationalism was a chiefly virtue.

In the late 1960s, press reports and government statements lauded Bende as offering comparable living and farming conditions. An internal memo, however, surmised that "they will find existence on this land pretty precarious and I think, will drift off to other areas, including Portuguese East Africa."[107] By the end of 1969, only four families, described by a human rights group as "strangers who had lived only a short time amongst the Tangwena and had not made kinship ties with them," remained at Bende.[108] Ministry of Internal Affairs declared "no squatters left" on Gaeresi Ranch in February of 1971, noting that fourteen families had moved to Bende.[109] By year's end, however, Rekayi was among those tilling on the ranch by hand since his cattle had been seized. He claimed only five fewer families than before the forced removals. Despite interviews with the press on the ranch, Internal Affairs insisted that there was "no truth in the rumour" of any

Tangwena still resident on Gaeresi Ranch.[110] Years later, Internal Affairs blamed resettlement's failure on people being "intimidated. . . . There is no doubt given freedom of choice in the matter most of them would willingly settle within the area of Bende."[111]

Conscious of the symbolic stakes in a propaganda war, Manicaland's Provincial Commissioner recommended the paying of children's school fees at Bende to promote an image of government's pastoral care: "This known as 'winning their hearts and minds.' Payment might avoid another slanted and unfavorable press campaign."[112] State officials also promised to recognize Rekayi as an official chief, giving him a government salary. He denounced such offers as scandalous bribes.[113] "I cannot be bought," Tangwena defiantly stated. "Government agents offered me 300 pounds plus full title of a chief, but that I rejected and will reject. I and money do not mix."[114] In 1970, he told the Inyanga District Commissioner, "I am not bought. I want my land not money. Land is more valuable to me than money. Land will keep me and my children's children. Cash will only keep me and my wife. I am a chief with people."[115]

Rekayi's refusal to be "bought" challenged two colonial forms of commoditization: land and chiefly rule. Neither his ancestral territory nor his sovereignty was for sale. State offers of a salary would make him a beneficiary of indirect rule in a regime he openly challenged. Cash implied the conversion of his homeland into a commodity. Rekayi had refuted Hanmer's property claims by asserting ancestral rights predating European land alienation. His chieftainship bound together territory, subjects, and sovereignty in an inalienable assemblage. Gokwe's reserves and land excised from the Bende state forest converted abstract space into yet another commodity possessed by government. This calculus of market exchange occluded the violence of eviction euphemized as resettlement. Moreover, cash was central to a nexus that severed Africans from ancestral lands—as labor migrants and tenants paying rent. Those who betrayed the nationalist struggle, "sellouts," traded loyalty for riches and privileges. Rekayi's refusal of government bribes thus bolstered his popularity among squatters and anticolonial nationalists alike.

The Epicenter of Resistance

Many mapped memories of collective defiance to Rekayi's Tsatse homestead. Chiefly compound melded moment and milieu, representing a time and place when "we all struggled together" (*takashingirira tese*). *Kushingirira* carries the

connotation of perseverance through adversity, of courageous suffering, enduring hardship for a just cause. Angela added that "the Tangwena people were
united in everything, even eating together." After several skirmishes on the ranch,
squatters moved to makeshift shelters surrounding Rekayi's chiefly compound, a
relatively modest cluster of thatched huts. Mujuru was among those thirty-six
squatters named for eviction in the 1969 Government Proclamation. Twenty-two
years later, he remembered as his two wives boiled tea by fire. Gesturing frequently, and even leaping airborne to animate events, he recalled the standoff:
"We refused saying that we were born in this area. Our ancestors died in this area.
This is Tangwena's area (*nzvimbo*)." A defiant "Rekayi said you may kill us if you
want. We will not go to Holdenby or Nyangui because this is our territory (*nyika
yedu*). Mr. White went to Nyanga, and we heard rumors that an army was being
planned to deal with Rekayi." In Mujuru's rendering of racialized removals,
District Commissioner Wyatt morphed, appropriately, into "Mr. White." Mujuru continued: "Rekayi said that we might be destroyed so 'all the people must
come and stay at my home [*musha*].' We left our livestock. We built temporary
shelters and were told to stay because 'the DA is coming with his family to destroy
your huts.' How many months did we stay? [turning to his wives] I think it's two
months. [His wives nodded in assent.] We could only go to put our livestock into
kraals during the day, then we came back. No one was then living at home."
Traces from the present slid into renderings of the past as Mujuru used the
postcolonial title, District Administrator, to refer to the colonial District Commissioner, Mr. Wyatt, to whom Hanmer had given power of attorney to super-
vise the evictions in September 1969. In that moment, legislation enabled state
administrator and property owner to fuse.

Kaerezians stressed the tactical advantage of strength in numbers and the
political salience of demonstrating unity at their chief's home. Rekayi's compound held additional appeal. While some squatters could claim generations of
ancestral residence in Kaerezi, others had shallower local roots. Most adults knew
the location of a sacred site designated for chiefly graves, and many could recite a
number of Tangwena's chiefly predecessors. White lawyers pushed arguments
that relied on testimonies of "tribal elders" who recalled the boundaries of the
Tangwena chieftainship, providing oral evidence of Dzeka's sovereign presence
prior to white conquest. Tenants, including those who descended from lineages
who lived in Kaerezi prior to Tangwena arrival, gained more traction by claiming
land rights harnessed to a "tribe," echoing the colonial fiction of communal
tenure. Rekayi's reign, the inalienable birthright of his *nyika*, became a collective
claim assembled out of labor militancy, ancestral ties, and legal arguments.

In 1991, SaGumbo and I sought a patch of shade beneath the overhang of thatch outside his cook hut during a break from work in his fields. He dispatched his youngest son to fetch a mimeographed form letter from the District Administrator, bearing his name written in hand. His residence, the letter reminded him, remained legally conditional on following the owner's laws of the land. Refusing to do so branded him a squatter. More than twenty years before, SaGumbo had been among the thirty-six squatters named for eviction in the 1969 Government Proclamation. "We agreed that we wanted to die for our land," SaGumbo told me in 1991, weeks after the DA's letter threatened another eviction. We spoke while weeding rows of vegetables in his garden. He carefully patted the soil around a shoot of healthy greens, pausing to reflect: "If our children had been killed, they, too, would have died for this land." Days before, he had lamented the possibility of losing harvests that emerged from sediments of earth, toil, and crops, like those he recalled losing during colonial evictions.

His mother, a member of the Tangwena lineage, had returned to her parents' home pregnant in the midst of marital problems that eventually led to divorce. She gave birth to SaGumbo in 1933 amid the same cluster of huts where Rekayi was born at Dzeka's homestead. When SaGumbo assembled with his fellow squatters in 1969 in Tsatse to await Land Rovers, trucks, and a bulldozer, he also returned home, *kumusha*. "The government," he explained, "was encouraging the destruction of the 'book' under Tsatse," referring to those settled in Headman Tsatse's territory. He outlined government's spatial strategy: "They knew that if they are able to chase away people from Tsatse, then the rest would be easy to evacuate. It was Rekayi who by then was leading the kraal. They knew that the chief lived in Tsatse kraal. They saw that it was the one which was powerful, but they found no way to eliminate it."

As eviction efforts intensified, localized knowledge became a weapon of the weak. SaGumbo recalled that when the District Commissioner arrived, those *not* named in the proclamation surrounded him, letting others escape. When the DC read the list of squatters' names, no one came forward. Rekayi and Headman Tsatse refused to point them out. The usual conduits of indirect rule, a chief and his headman, thwarted government. Short-circuiting the link between power and knowledge, these tactical maneuvers produced ruling mistakes: the destruction of property of those not named in eviction orders, the evasion of those named, and public embarrassment. When Salisbury's Internal Affairs officials bypassed his district office, Inyanga's DC complained to the Provincial Commissioner that it was "embarrassing to be ignorant."[116] Government at a distance required the participation and coordination of scales, levels, and modes of authority that at times produced fractures *within* the project of colonial rule. Exploited by savvy squatters and subverted by a defiant anticolonial chief, Rhodesian rule also encouraged ungovernable subjects.

Both the area's spatial remoteness from administrative infrastructure and its rugged terrain frustrated surveillance and eviction. Vehicles could only approach over the slow, winding road expressly built for evictions, rendering raids visible in advance. Kaerezians listened for the warning of a trumpeted animal horn to signal arrivals. Carefully placed lookouts sent visual signals along a series of hilltops, enabling squatters who cultivated fields to flee before government vehicles approached. Even after police seized cattle, borrowed beasts from Nyafaru plowed furrows before being snuck back to the cooperative through narrow paths weaving through the steep valley, hidden from views afforded by the lone dirt road. Thick mountain forests obscured hiding places, while affording views of those approaching from below. Localized knowledge and ingenuity mixed with the materiality of landscape to produce potent places of defiance.

While labor tenants wove Rekayi's Tsatse homestead into the heart of the Tangwena chiefdom, William Hanmer invoked a competing cartography, mapping the chiefdom beyond the ranch's boundary. He testified in a 1967 court case that the "Chief Tangwena who I knew did not live on Gaerezi Ranch but on land known as Crown Lands East. The Tangwena tribe was mainly on Crown Lands East and most of the Tangwena people lived on Crown Lands East and Mozambique." To further distance Tangwena ancestral claims from his property, he added: "I understand that a great part of the tribe lives in Mozambique."[117] Orienting the chiefdom east, Hanmer echoed colonial administrators. He remembered Chief Kinga's homestead on state land east of the ranch, not Chief Dzeka who, like Rekayi, lived deep inside the ranch in Tsatse. Hanmer's vision occluded shifting sites of sovereignty, the homesteads identified with specific chiefly reigns. In opposition, Rekayi invoked boundaries that long preceded white presence:

> My people are living in the same place where they were living whilst I was a small child—partly in the Tribal Trust Lands and partly on Mr. Hanmer's Farm. There is one headman under me in the Tribal Trust Lands and 5 under me living on Mr. Hanmer's property. I don't know if there are any members of the Tangwena living in Portuguese East Africa—as far as I know we are all living in Rhodesia. I have traditional links with the land where I am living—these links are: I have to live there and appease the spirit of my deceased ancestors from time to time. There is a traditional burying ground at the kraal—one for chiefs and the other two for the

other members of the tribe. There are now 9 chiefs buried in the chiefs' burial ground. I have all along believed that there has been a boundary between the lands where I live and the land owned by Mr. Hanmer.[118]

Officials continued to emphasize Tangwena ties to Mozambique, hoping to push the contentiòus chieftainship across the border. In 1966, Internal Affairs sought the help of Portuguese officials, describing six kraals, five on private land, that "wish to remove en bloc to settle in Mozambique. They are of the Newa or Nyanga Tribe, of which the majority are understood to live in Mozambique across the border, and they want permission to settle in that area as complete kraals."[119] A handwritten note alluded to a phone call from "Head Office," presumably Salisbury, reporting on a delegation of three who wanted to move to Portuguese territory where they "still wish to retain their identity as a chieftainship."[120] A week later, Rekayi visited the Inyanga DC "armed with a note from Head Office," allegedly seeking assistance to approach Portuguese authorities across the international border:

A few people have formally moved to other kraals. Those remaining want a "*nyika*," but this is not possible in this district. They do not want to disperse to different kraals, nor do they wish to try and move as a group to some other district, such as Gokwe. They now seek to be given a letter authorizing them to approach Portuguese East Africa authorities with a view to moving to Portuguese East Africa where, I understand, an even larger portion of Tangwena followers reside. If these people can move to Portuguese East Africa it might solve a difficult problem for us.[121]

For his part, Rekayi claimed that the Inyanga DC himself "suggested that 12 of us, whose names he gave me, should go to Mocambique to see a Portuguese official to discuss our movement to Mocambique."[122] While Rekayi's 1966 motivations for a possible Mozambique maneuver remain a mystery, a few years later he refused to budge.

Multiple mappings haunted ranch and chiefdom. A handwritten sketch, dated 1972, delineated the "Gazetted Extent of Chief Tawungwena's Tribal Areas" by government notice 519/68 of 1968. Seven years after one official disbanded the chiefdom, another recognized Tangwena territorial boundaries. While onsite administrators in Inyanga tried to move a tribe off a ranch, denying an African sovereign land claims, another branch of government gazetted his tribal territory. Notes scrawled at the bottom of the sketch describe the "northern tip of Holdenby TTL [Tribal Trust Land] cut off and converted to National

Land."[123] This spot looked suspiciously like *Machena*, the burial grounds for Tangwena chiefs.

Asserting ancestral ties to place, Rekayi deployed his own ethnic spatial fix, arguing for African customs that rooted an authentic identity in tribal territory: "If I leave this area, I cut off all ties with my past and my ancestors and there is no one who can carry them on. . . . It is not according to our custom to move. Our whole life is based on land."[124] Propitiation rites engendered property rights: "Our ancestors died here and were buried here. This country is our inheritance left for us by our ancestors. Our hearts and our spirits are here."[125] "Africans have a deep spiritual feeling for their traditional land," he told a human rights group. "I will only leave this land if the graves of my ancestors, the sacred hills and the valleys are transferred to the place where they want me to go."[126] Through such statements, Rekayi further entangled Tangwena squatters in an inalienable assemblage of landscape, spirits, and ancestral inheritance. "They will have to move the land with us," he told reporters.[127] In 1991, Tewa recalled that many echoed his arguments, saying, "if you want us to go, first of all dig up the bones of our great-grandfathers who were buried long ago in this area. We will carry the bones."

Physical burial materializes ancestors in the earth, as decomposing bodies morph into soil, joining *nyika* in substance and symbol. Yet bones also remain, their stubborn materiality testament to historically prior claims buried beneath colonial conquest. Severing squatters from graves, displacement conjured specters of desecration, of cultural as well as political dispossession.

Engendering Tactics

Mujuru's two wives were both shy in my presence, deferring to their outspoken husband. Yet their memories of ranch evictions animated voice, gesture, and a vivid sense of detail. Elders had instructed women to put children on their backs, fastening them tightly. Rekayi, they all recalled, told men not to fight but advised that women stand between armed police and those named in eviction orders. When police manhandled Rekayi, loading him into a Land Rover, women clung to his legs. "They were holding the vehicle," both wives told me in unison. Baton-wielding police beat women, pushing them to the ground, and sped away with Rekayi. "We thought of going to the DA's office in Nyanga to burn his books," Mujuru recalled. His wives were among those who marched more than thirty miles over a mountain range to the District Center to protest Rekayi's arrest.

Like neighbors who had also experienced that era of evictions, Mujuru and his wives remembered women's courage, resourcefulness, and savvy maneuvers during such moments of danger. As armed troops descended by helicopter on Nyafaru during one raid, a group of women cleverly spread blankets across a preferred landing area. Both astute Kaerezians and the pilot knew that the force of the rotor wash would kick blankets into the air where they could entangle vulnerable blades. Both also knew that Nyafaru's uneven terrain afforded few level landing spots close to the cooperative's buildings that also blocked escape routes to nearby mountain forests. After several failed attempts to land, the pilot opted for a flat area at safe remove where soldiers jumped to the ground and sprinted after fleeing men. The delay enabled many to escape, unarmed women with blankets holding off rifle-toting troops in a helicopter. The efficacy of women's action relied on Nyafaru's rugged landscape, a tactical weakness specific to helicopters, and Kaerezians' wager that Rhodesian soldiers would not fire on unarmed women.

Women's prominence in confrontational protest and defiant resistance to ranch evictions revealed a recurrent Tangwena tactic. Squatters expected colonial violence to make gendered distinctions. Many believed police would hold gunfire with women on the front lines, though they had not expected to witness officers bludgeoning women with batons. Some claimed Rekayi formulated the idea; others credited his headmen. In turn, a headman told me in 1991 that "the white person at Nyafaru told us that women should lead because men may be shot." Yet many women spoke of their own initiative in placing themselves in harm's way as a means to lessen risks of escalating violence. Migrant labor routes extending to South Africa also positioned women on the front lines. Thirteen of the thirty-six families targeted for eviction in 1969 were female-headed households whose husbands sent wages from afar. While subservient in patriarchal homesteads, women anchored family parcels by cultivating on the ranch while men sought distant wages. As more squatters succumbed to evictions, women bore the brunt of providing for displaced families living clandestinely in mountain forests.

MaiHungwe, a widow in her sixties, returned to Tsatse after the war, occupying the homestead where she had lived with her husband, among the thirty-six named for eviction in 1969. She was born in Nyamutsapa, near the well-known *mutororo* tree planted by the locally prominent lineage and a landmark for meetings. We sat amid her cluster of huts one afternoon, a hot wind picking up across the ridge that rolled north down the river valley. Outspoken and forthright, she had no formal schooling. "Long ago," she explained, "our fathers said only boys should go to school because women will learn prostitution there. We were oppressed [*kudzvinyirira*] that way." She recalled colonial evictions:

> When fighting, we were ahead and the chief was behind. We spent seven months at Rekayi's home after we had been told that war is coming. They later came, and the police fought with women until Rekayi's clothes were tattered and he was taken to Holdenby and we went to Nyanga naked. We went with whites who were helping us with food. Rekayi always encouraged us, saying that we will not be killed. If he had not encouraged us, we would have surrendered. . . . He always told *Chimhini* that we were about to have independence [*rusununguko*].

Placing themselves between armed forces and their husbands, kinsmen, and neighbors, women helped *produce* gendered spaces of tactical defiance. The very vulnerability of women's bodies shaped a politics of embarrassment. Facing armed police, women stripped off their tops, exposing bare breasts. These body politics rendered more visible government's violence. By marching to the district center in protest, they brought the turmoil on the ranch to town. Internal Affairs decried "unseemly behavior of the women of the tribe who stripped off most of their clothes, urinated in the road in the tourist village of Inyanga and made lewd gestures and remarks to the Police."[128] Playing deftly on European notions of sexual propriety and assumptions about women's deferential disposition, women disturbed the orderly site of administrative control at the District Commissioner's office. Bare-breasted, throwing dirt at armed police, and marching in protest, their practices embodied those of ungovernable subjects.

In 1991, Angela echoed MaiHungwe's memories, again recalling Rekayi's "respect" for women. Moments before, she had milked a cow in the kraal nestled next to her fields. Drinking tea boiled over firewood she had gathered, we tasted multiple moments of her labor's mixture with fluid, fire, and forest. Angela emphasized women's agency during evictions:

> We were told not to fight. Instead, we removed our clothes. It surprised many people. All ages were naked. Rekayi respected women, and in his *dare* [court] there were women. Rekayi was also advised by women. We at times covered Rekayi with children's clothes so that he would not be seen by his enemies. So he saw that women can help, and he respected us. . . . Women usually cooked maize porridge all night during the war, and men could wake up to food. Women are hard workers.

For Angela, Rekayi ruled as a wise sovereign, receiving women's counsel while encouraging their agency. He governed, acting on the actions of his subjects, through power rather than force. Respect remained crucial, a reciprocal relationship between ruler and subject. In contrast, Rhodesian officials failed to appreciate the political savvy of Kaerezian women. Administrative assumptions about African women could be turned to tactical advantage: "The colonial government did not suspect women involving themselves in politics. One day, Rhodesian soldiers arrived at our hut, and we covered our chief, Rekayi, with grass. When the soldiers saw that there were only women, they saw us as 'politically helpless,' and they went away." Soldiers' assumptions of female docility became the condition of possibility for women's more efficacious political agency. Many Kaerezians told me that during the height of evictions, when police cordoned off Gaeresi Ranch, they "elected" women to "war councils." Women's travel was less policed, enabling their conveyance of crucial messages and information. Their experiences gathering firewood in mountain forests proved especially valuable when those sites provided refuge in the wake of evictions. Remembering the hardships there, Angela reflected: "The Tangwena people are brave because it's no game to live in the forest."

On the ranch, patrilocal marriages placed wives on parcels away from *their* ancestral homesteads. A *musha*—at once hearth, home, and family fields— anchored livelihoods that combined male migrant wages and tenancy with women's subsistence cultivation. Women's agricultural practices inscribed the landscape, materially and discursively, with claims to place earned through territorialized toil. These emplaced assemblages were both plot specific and collectively claimed, articulated through both shared citizenship in a colony and common subjection to an anticolonial chief. Rights telescoped out: individual, family, tribe, race, nation-state, and, ultimately, universal humanism—all refracted through gendered prisms.

For colonial officials and African male elders, *samusha*, the head of household, remained male—he was named on eviction notices and recalled in oral histories. Yet women's subordination in patriarchal households did not eclipse widespread recognition of their crucial role in suffering for territory during the era of evictions. Indirect rule, patrilocality, and patrilineal inheritance weakened women's land rights. Centralization and the Native Land Husbandry Act, by allocating land rights to a patriarch on behalf of his household, assured women's legal subordination. Yet in postcolonial Kaerezi, recognition of women's agency during the Tangwena war produced a complex gendered politics of rights and territory. Claims to a collective chiefdom pivoted on patrilineal power, yet women also staked claims to territory through situated struggles. Sediments of women's micropractices of place would become reassembled during another era of spatial discipline—government efforts to impose villagization.

Near sunset in 1991, Angela returned home carrying a large bundle of firewood on her head. I was helping her nephew unyoke a team of oxen. Green bark bound the bundle to her ax, a steel blade wedged in a handmade handle. In dusk's dull light, she led me to a spot where she had concealed Rekayi beneath thatching grass as Rhodesian soldiers searched her homestead. She also proudly pointed to spots where, fifteen years before, she had hid Mugabe's books during his escape. "Mugabe had come with many books written R. G., R. G.," Chidumbu had told me weeks before at Nyafaru, repeating the initials of Robert Gabriel Mugabe. "Chief Tangwena asked him why he was taking the books as if he were going to town," Chidumbu recalled Rekayi's closing salvo with a smile: " 'You're going to war, not to university.' " Months before, I had failed to appreciate the bittersweet humor of a Nyafaru schoolteacher chiding his younger brother for not studying more: "Where are your books?" he shouted in mock anger at the schoolboy. "You want to go to university, not to war, don't you?"

Chidumbu recounted Rekayi's scolding him for harboring Mugabe in a stone Nyafaru structure, one likely to be searched during a raid. In 1975, both Nyafaru worker and future president recognized the rural rebel's leadership. Rekayi's realpolitik fused discourses of chiefly rule and anticolonial African nationalism, labor militancy and Christian humanism, ancestral spirits and legal rights. Contingent constellations *placed* Chidumbu, Mugabe, and Rekayi in that shared Nyafaru time-space in April 1975. All refused Rhodesian rule. All were active agents, yet none controlled the assemblage of chiefdom, ranch, and cooperative that provided the condition of possibility for an escape from racialist Rhodesia into Mozambique's newly liberated territory. Enabling tentacles stretched as far as Britain, paralleling circuits of capital, knowledge, and personnel that flowed through imperial governmental technologies.

Amid the brutality of evictions from a white ranch, squatters' defiance of *government* fomented Rhodesian deployments of illiberal force. Colonial governmentality sought to align sovereignty, discipline, and government through the circuits of indirect rule, a salaried civil servant, and chiefly ruler subordinate to state power. On Gaeresi Ranch, capitalist discipline relied on indirect rule, yet tribal territories unsettled white occlusions of ancestral land rights. Administrative attempts to dismantle the ethnic spatial fix encountered a stubborn knot governmental technologies had entangled. Migrant labor routes fomented nationalist anticolonial politics, while a chief rallied labor tenants and shepherded enemies of state. Rhodesian refusal to recognize a rebel chief met Kaerezians' refusal to accept the coercive fiction of a labor agreement's consent. Neither governmentality nor hegemony held as violent force transformed squatters into forest dwellers and, later, exiles in Mozambique.

Postcolonial histories and territories emerged that articulated chiefdom, cooperative, ranch, and independent nation-state. After almost eleven years in jail, as Ian Smith made concessions to regional politics, Mugabe walked out of Salisbury Prison in 1974. Apartheid South Africa, seeking to show regional influence to more moderate black governments in Zambia and Tanzania, pressured for his release. Under close surveillance and likely to be imprisoned again, Mugabe fled the capital in 1975.[129] A white nun helped a ruse that used decoy cars under cover of night to sneak Mugabe into a car driven by Moven Mahachi to Nyafaru, the multiracial cooperative he managed. With security forces in hot pursuit, Mugabe's escape through a window of a plain stone building at Nyafaru on April 5, 1975, remained the stuff of nationalist lore. Nyafaru schoolchildren pointed to the actual metal frame, while teachers reflected on the metaphorical "window" that refracted a national liberation struggle. After his own release from prison, Chidumbu returned to live within eyesight of the structure.

By aiding Mugabe's escape amid their own evictions, Rekayi and his Tangwena people became linked to nationalist politics. Returning from exile, the book carrier became president, the chief became senator, and the prisoner became cooperative store manager. Mahachi shuffled through Mugabe's cabinets, moving from minister of lands, to minister of defense, and to minister of home affairs. Didymus Mutasa would become secretary of the ruling ZANU-PF. Nationalist politics entangled Tangwena territory, connecting a remote chiefdom to president, parliament, and ruling party. Yet legacies of precolonial conquest also unsettled postcolonial power in Kaerezi. I now turn to entanglements of chiefly rule and rainmaking that grounded selective sedimentations of rival sovereignties in Tangwena territory.

PART III · · · *Entangled Landscapes*

7 · Selective Sovereignties

Mbuya Clarissa sat near her cook hut on a reed mat surrounded by her cooking pots, arrayed under the morning sun on faded cloths. Nearly blind, her movements bore the traces of age, her hands and feet calloused but her spirit strong. She spoke a deep ChiManyika dialect, rarely using the Zezuru and English terms that melded into vocabularies of migrant workers and schoolchildren. Teenagers confessed they also had difficulty understanding her, a challenge exacerbated by missing teeth revealed through her gracious smile. Mbuya Clarissa always received my small packets of sugar and tea with deep appreciation and enthusiasm, mapping her warmth of affection, I suspect, less to me than toward the family with whom I lived. We spoke while government health workers sprayed DDT on her cook hut's thatch, mist emerging from canisters strapped to their backs. It was September 1991, and a national malaria control program included a pesticide spraying campaign. Workers mixed powerful "poison" with water, the elderly widow explained, killing mosquitoes in order to protect human lives. Rings of dead insects rained down from the thatch, encircling huts and covering floors.

Agrarian acts molded milieu. Citizens could eliminate stagnant pools around homesteads where mosquitoes bred, promoting their own welfare by helping to transform the environmental conditions conducive to another organism's healthy habitat. Mbuya Clarissa explained various forms of conduct the government (*hurumende*) deemed helpful in reducing the risk of malaria. The nearest health clinic was a difficult walk over rugged terrain, and she appreciated the workers' attacking the disease at her homestead. We both remarked on the rarity of seeing government workers, beyond the resettlement officer and his assistant, in Kaerezi. Strained budgets, a shortage of staff, and the logistical difficulties of servicing thousands of poor families scattered across rough country made an official's visit rare. The spraying team concentrated its efforts along the scheme's main road, producing an uneven geography of managed care. As the workers moved onto Mbuya Clarissa's neighbors' huts, I contemplated the biopolitical scene: government workers killed insects to let the human population flourish, seeking to manage an environmental milieu where subjects could also improve their own welfare.

This state-orchestrated spraying campaign also encountered alternative forms of caring for a population. In Kaerezi, citizens of the nation-state were also subjects of a chief and rainmaker. Where government workers mixed chemicals, chief and rainmaker brewed beer to propitiate ancestral spirits, promoting the welfare of land and people, bringing rain, and encouraging healthy harvests. Kaerezians also expected acting Chief Magwendere to conduct similar ceremonies. Those who prayed to a Christian God also asked for rain. All these subjectivating practices imbricated population and territory.

Mbuya Clarissa described a division of labor between chief and rainmaker: "Nyahuruwa is the rainmaker [*musikamazi*]. Tangwena rules the people [*vanotonga vanhu*]." Like many older Kaerezians, she contrasted two tropes of power, emphasizing that the chief "ruled *people*" (*kutonga vanhu*) while the rainmaker "ruled *territory*" (*kutonga nyika*). Her own life traversed these forms of rule. She lived in the rainmaker Nyahuruwa's compound, where he "cared for" (*kuchengetedza*) her as the widow of his lineage brother. Yet as the patrilineal granddaughter of Dzeka, the first Tangwena chief installed by Rhodesian authorities in 1902, she recalled tales of another reign maker. Like Nyahuruwa, chiefs also brewed beer to propitiate ancestral spirits.

Mbuya Clarissa proudly recalled Chief Rekayi Tangwena, her father's brother: "He defeated the whites when they wanted to evict us to Gokwe. He refused to go and live in Holdenby. We lived in the forests while some fled to Mozambique. Now, we are ruled by Mugabe." Just as the critical verb "to rule," *kutonga*, shifted across rainmaker, chief, and president, so, too, did the crucial construction of territory, *nyika*, move from rainmaking area to chiefdom to nation. No single sovereign mapped absolute authority to territory or populace. Each mode of rule targeted *relations* between people and place, subjects and territory.

These relational regimes of power remain crucial to understanding not only Tangwena territoriality, but also modes of subjection. I use the phrase "selective sovereignties" not to suggest that subjects freely choose which sovereign power to recognize. Such a perspective would ironically smuggle the sovereign self, a fully formed and conscious agent of willful action, into an analytic of agency. Rather, my notion reworks Raymond Williams's formulation of a "selective tradition," what he understood to be a *hegemonic* process through which specific cultural features, practices, and meanings become selected as emblematic of an authentic, authoritative tradition. In his conception, this contingent process ratified one selective, partial construction of the past as "the tradition."[1] Tradition is not ruled by an underlying structure of continuity. As Williams stressed, hegemony is not a stable state, but always a contested process of struggle. Selective traditions thus contend with residual and emergent strains, challenges that fracture any singular source of authority. Never finally fixed, tradition itself constitutes the ground of struggle.

In this sense, as Talal Asad proposed, tradition is a "complex space" saturated by contingent constellations of power relations and cultural practices. By emphasizing the multiple temporalities and spatialities of tradition, he suggested, anthropologists can better appreciate "how overlapping patterns of territory, authority, and time collide with the idea of the imagined national community."[2] Neither the times nor spaces of all traditions, Asad asserted, translate into a homogenous time-space of national politics. Precolonial Africa, Mbembe likewise suggested, was an "imbrication of multiple spaces" and a "multiplicity of allegiances and jurisdictions" that "corresponded to the plurality of the forms of territoriality."[3] Greater sensitivity to the spatial and temporal textures of the cultural politics of tradition, I argue, helps illuminate the production of selective sovereignties. By challenging a universalizing assumption of sovereignty bound to the nation-state, I unhinge them, thus provincializing both concepts.

As Bartelson's magisterial genealogy emphasized, far too frequently "sovereignty is taken to be a political or legal fact *within* an already given and demarcated territory," usually a bounded nation-state.[4] Political theory often conceives the state as a "spatial container" of political community, asserting the self-evident coupling of state and sovereignty.[5] In contrast, my provincialized notion of governmentality explores the mutual *production* of power, subjects, and territory, elaborating the kinds of selective sovereignties articulated through Kaerezi's geobodies. *Nyika*, as I previously argued, maps the semantic terrain where no single sovereign is specified. Far from stable, sovereignties shift, realigning relations with government and discipline. I thus eschew a search for an authentic precolonial origin for sovereignty that would ground a traditional truth granting rights to subjects. Instead, I track effects of practices that deploy sovereignties at once selective and situated.

Crucially, such a genealogical approach does not seek an African essence be-

yond histories and geographies of empire but, rather, the distinctive articulations of place, power, and cultural politics. My provincialized notion of governmentality also explores relations among *kutonga*, *kuronga*, and *hurumende*
(ruling, arranging, and government). But rather than simply translating terms of
a triad—searching for respective slots to designate sovereignty, discipline, and
government—I stress the landscape of practices that entangle subjects, territory, and modes of power. Power (*simba*) in Kaerezi involves *kupira vadzimu*
(ancestral propitiation), *kuremekedza nyika* (respecting territory), and rivalries between chiefs and rainmakers. In the 1990s, these cultural politics were
also entangled with governing technologies of colonial rule and postcolonial
administration.

Prevalent models of sovereignty tend to neglect imperial relations of power that
linked Europe to its constitutive outside. In turn, as Bartelson underscored, they
occlude the *spatialization* of alterity and government's targeting of cultural difference as a threat to control and manage. Conventional theories of the state rarely
note how both "race" and "cultural difference" are *constitutive* of selective sovereignties, including those that map to nation-states. "Racial sovereignty" is thus
not an aberrant offshoot of modernity, but woven into its very foundation.[6]
Through administrators' racialized vision of cultural difference, the Tangwena
became—like other southern African groups—"portrayed as a people governed
by the primal sovereignty of their 'custom.'"[7] However, colonial reports reveal
scarcely a trace of Kaerezi's rainmaker Nyahuruwa. Fusing together anthropological and administrative models of polity and social evolution, indirect rule constructed one sovereign slot, a chief, mapped to a singular African landscape, a
tribal territory. Postcolonial administrators largely followed this institutional
occlusion even as they acknowledged the highly respected rainmaker Nyahuruwa.

This chapter complements scholars who have denaturalized universal assumptions about state and sovereignty. Recently, analysts have probed "graduated sovereignty" and zones of regulatory management that striate state space; "shadow
sovereignty"; and reconfigurations among nationalism, sovereignty, and biopower not contained by the nation-state.[8] In these visions, a normative nomadic
subject, and often a particularly classed metropolitan one, tends to traverse these
imagined theoretical landscapes "increasingly unrestrained by ideas of spatial
boundary and territorial sovereignty."[9] In Saskia Sassen's influential formulation
of globalization, sovereignty is "reconstituted and partly displaced onto other
institutional arenas *outside* the state and *outside* the framework of nationalized
territory."[10] The spatial metaphor *outside* suggests a scaling up, a global reach. Yet

what about reconfigurations that rework historically sedimented relations of power at once translocally routed and deeply localized *within* specific territories?

Transnational capital flows, labor agreements based on European models, and customary law with adat influences from colonial Java all affected Kaerezi's colonial politics. For more than a century, Kaerezi's sovereignties have worked in tension. Practices of chiefly rule and rainmaking counter the mantra insisting that sovereignty has become *deterritorialized*. Left largely uncharted in such accounts is the *production of distinctive relations among sovereignty and space*—not new "sovereign spaces" but, rather, specific articulations of multiple forms of sovereignty and hybrid spatialities that coexist in the same geographical territory. If the analytic of governmentality displaces the state as a privileged container of power, so also it denaturalizes sovereignty as the possession of states. Sovereignty's cultural practices pivot on the production of scale, subjection, and territory.

In Africa as elsewhere, sovereignties have been reterritorialized rather than deterritorialized. In the Chad Basin during the 1990s, Janet Roitman argued, sovereignty has been transformed through "new spaces" saturated by violence and economic crises where "the state" does not control modes of appropriation, figures of authority, and institutions of social welfare.[11] In Nigeria, petro-politics has fueled the ongoing federal fomentation of ethnicized violence in the Niger Delta, as well as reworkings of chiefly, federal, and democratic "governable spaces."[12] Unable to subdue rebel forces in Sierra Leone during the so-called diamond wars of the mid-1990s, government allies hired Executive Outcomes, a South Africa–based private security firm. States may no longer monopolize the legitimate use of violence (if they ever did completely); or they may subcontract police, security, and the tasks of governing to private firms.[13] In short, states are neither the sole agents nor the sole arenas of violence and sovereignty.

In southern Africa, such recent patterns have striking historical resonances with conflicts in the late nineteenth century. In the 1880s, Portuguese government officials relied on Gouveia's private army to defeat Shire rebels even as they rebuked his assertions of sovereignty and extractions of tribute that enraged Barwe chiefs. The following decade, Rhodes's police—private security forces enlisted in imperial rule—arrested Gouveia. Under British South Africa Company charter, Rhodes's own forces also launched incursions into Manica and Barwe territory. Both Portuguese and British imperial policies granted territorial concessions to transnational companies—especially for mining, timber, and other resource extraction—whose agents vied with warlords such as Gouveia, African sovereigns such as Makombe, and European government officials. Each group asserted rights and jurisdictions, mobilized alliances, and influenced the deployment of violence in ways that shaped both subjection and spatiality.

Colonial governmentality's administrative impulses further complicated territory. In Kaerezi, Rhodesian tribal administration installed Tangwena chiefs, unwittingly lending the support of colonial conquest to an African one—Tangwena's military defeat of the rainmaker Nyahuruwa. Chiefly and colonial conquest became entangled in territory claimed by several sovereigns. During Zimbabwe's guerrilla war, anticolonial liberation movements sought to construct an independent nation-state as a singular, supreme sovereign. Postcolonial rule, however, emerged from sediments of sovereignties in the plural. In Kaerezi, tensions between *kutonga*, to rule, and *nyika*, the territory ruled, remained radically unsettled.

Regimes of Rule

SaNyamubaya was born shortly before "Hitler's war" in the Honde Valley, a day's walk to Kaerezi's south. After his parent's eviction from the nearby national park, his father sought work on one of Honde's vast tea plantations. Following his father's death in the late 1940s, SaNyamubaya moved to Gaeresi Ranch to live with his father's sister, married to a labor tenant. In the early 1990s, we sat outside his Tsatse cook hut as he rolled a cigarette in torn newspaper. SaNyamubaya pointed down the river valley toward both Nyahuruwa's and Rekayi's homesteads in Tsatse—a place bearing the name of Dzeka's paternal grandfather. He recalled a deep history of contested territory, rule, and rights: "Before Tangwena arrived, Nyahuruwa was the 'owner of territory' [*muridzi we nyika*]. Here there were only a few homesteads." SaNyamubaya contrasted the rainmaker's small family (*mhuri*) with Tangwena's extensive one. Indeed, Dzeka had "waged war with his relatives in Mozambique," fleeing to a spot east of the international border near Mount Tangwena.

Fearing that "war approached," Dzeka arrived in Nyahuruwa's sparsely settled domain, proclaiming: " 'I am Tangwena and I come from Barwe. I am fleeing war and want to go live in Mutoko,' " a region one hundred kilometers northwest of Kaerezi. "Nyahuruwa said, 'Stay here,' " telling Tangwena that the war would not spill out of Mozambique into another person's territory. 'I will put my soldiers on the border.' " Nyahuruwa honored his promise, hiding the refugee near the Kaerezi River. The rainmaker's "soldiers" convinced those pursuing Tangwena "not to enter this area." Eventually, Tangwena "was given a place to live" by Nyahuruwa. SaNyamubaya brought his historical vision into the present, reminding me that John Tangwena, a descendant of the chief who sought refuge, still lived there. He then jumped back to the historical era of Dzeka's initial arrival:

> Tangwena told Nyahuruwa, "Where I come from I am a chief." He was told by Nyahuruwa: "When you are in my territory [*munyika mangu*], you are a *muranda* [a subject or vassal]." Tangwena said he wanted the chieftainship. Nyahuruwa saw that he would be defeated and that war was coming, so he ran to Chionde in Rusape [one hundred kilometers west of Nyanga]. For three years, there was no rain in this area. Tangwena tried to make the rain, but we could only see mist. People started to quarrel with Tangwena, asking him why he had chased Nyahuruwa. So Tangwena sent a delegation of people to go and bring him back. Nyahuruwa came and lived in Dazi and refused to enter the area saying, "I will not come there because there is war."
>
> Nyahuruwa later came and Tangwena said: "You rule the *masango* [literally, forests; here, resources] and I will only rule the people [*vanhu*]." Nyahuruwa had a sister who had rain magic [*makoma emvura*], which she had swallowed, and it was only Nyahuruwa who knew how to make the rain. They took finger millet for the beer and put it outside instead of washing it in the river. Rainwater would wash it, and then beer would be brewed. Tangwena and Nyahuruwa were now getting along well, and if Tangwena wanted to brew beer he would inform Nyahuruwa. Nyahuruwa brewed his beer first and Tangwena then brewed his later. They cooperated. It is only recently that Nyahuruwa wanted to take the chieftainship.

Many elders related differing versions of Tangwena and Nyahuruwa's division of powers. Debates brought an enlivened past of selective sovereignties into the contemporary cultural politics of territory, rule, and rights. In several respects, narratives of a division of powers between a conquering chiefly lineage and rainmaking autochthons shared basic features with other southern African sites and peoples.[14] Kaerezian understandings of Tangwena's political authority as ruling people also suggest similarities with Africanist scholarship exploring the cultural meanings of "wealth-in-people" as a basis of social capital, economic accumulation, and political control.[15] Feierman's study of discourses of *kubana shi* and *kuzifya shi*, to harm the land and to heal the land, in northeastern Tanzania similarly offers provocative parallels.[16] Many Kaerezians invoked the cultural idiom of "respecting territory" (*kuremekedza nyika*). Both the rainmaker's and chief's propitiation of territorial ancestral spirits (*kupira vadzimu*) were, in this idiom, required to secure the "health of territory" (*upenyu hwe nyika*) and hence the livelihood of its inhabitants.[17]

In SaNyamubaya's account, Tangwena migrated to Kaerezi to flee conflicts with his relatives, most likely including Makombe, a powerful paramount in Mozambique's Barwe territory. SaNyamubaya portrayed the rainmaker Nyahuruwa as a benevolent host, providing safe refuge and sending soldiers to protect his border. Tangwena, not content with his subordinate status as the subject (*muranda*) of another ruler, used his larger following and the threat of force to chase Nyahuruwa away. Nyahuruwa fled rather than fight. Failing rains bore witness to Tangwena's illegitimate seizure. Territorial ancestral spirits required Nyahuruwa's propitiation, refusing pleas by a conquering chief. Drought's hardship aligned the living and the dead in a critique of the chiefly sovereign. The welfare of population and territory was at risk. Popular unrest pressured Tangwena to seek Nyahuruwa's return. Ruling (*kutonga*) is much more than the brute force of seizure (*kupamba*). Power (*simba*) hinged on relations among ancestral spirits, living subjects, and the local landscape. Nyahuruwa's return brought the rains back to Kaerezi. Despite Tangwena's command of superior physical force, he remained dependent on the rainmaker's spiritual power.[18]

In this version, "the people" become subject to more than one sovereign. Commoners recognized multiple modalities of power within contending regimes of rule. Military might could not rule without culturally specific skills and authority. Nyahuruwa mediated the living and the dead, linking people and place. Historical time jumped borders. Tangwena's pursuers stopped at the edge of Nyahuruwa's territory. Yet SaNyamubaya mapped this to the nation-state's boundary. In this account, a colonial spatiality animated precolonial histories of chiefly rule and rainmaking. Familiar places dotted SaNyamubaya's tale of territorial power, and his pointing finger etched paths in the landscape. He included translocal routes in local history. Nyahuruwa's negotiated return from exile shaped the historical division of labor between ruling people and ruling territory. A spatial history inaugurated a division of powers. In this version, two regimes of rule once at odds complemented one another, negotiating a balance of powers. Conflict surrounded the bookends of the chiefdom's history—when Tangwena first arrived, and the recent past, after Rekayi's 1984 death, when the rainmaker sought to claim the chiefdom.

Embedded within SaNyamubaya's narrative is a further dependence, that of Nyahuruwa on his sister (*tete*), implying a particular gendered understanding of complementary roles in ensuring the prosperity of people and place. *Vanatete* (paternal aunts) have a recognized role as intimate advisers to chiefs, and more generally as wise counsel to younger relatives regardless of their lineages.[19] Both men and women echoed the claim of one elder man: "The *vanatete* in a chief's family can nominate a chief." In 1991, amid popular challenges to Rekayi's successor, a member of the rainmaker's lineage argued that "we don't know who Magwendere's *tete* is" to challenge the acting chief's rule. Shared social relations made kinship connections public knowledge; not knowing this crucial relationship coded Magwendere as a social and geographical outsider. At the same time, the claim implicitly queried the good judgment of an elder denied the wise counsel of his *tete*.

SaMaridzo, in his sixties when we spoke in 1991, added a further colonial twist to postcolonial authority: "Long ago Tangwena became the chief and Nyahuruwa was only responsible for rainmaking. When Rekayi Tangwena died, it could have happened that Magwendere failed to become the chief because Elijah Nyahuruwa went to Nyanga for the chieftainship. But they were told that there is no book which says that Nyahuruwa holds the chieftainship. 'You are only responsible for rain.'" For SaMaridzo, the state administrative apparatus, a continuity of the colonial regime, remained a critical arbitrator of tradition. The rainmaker, in this version, lacked official government recognition, implying that rainmaking resided beneath chiefly rule in a hierarchy of powers. In 1991, SaMaridzo invoked the colonial technology of a government "book" to prop up assertions of a precolonial division of power between chief and rainmaker. Despite the differences between SaMaridzo's and SaNyamubaya's accounts, both versions *located* modes of subjection in two senses. They foregrounded both the legitimate basis for political power and its territorial dominion.

Spaces of Subordination

Lazarus was one of the oldest Kaerezians I knew. A veritable oral archive, he pointed out his father's birthplace, recalled the precise sites of ancestral homesteads, and chronicled where members of his extended family had migrated to and from Kaerezi. Despite his claim that "I have forgotten when I was born," he had an amazing memory for dates and events. "The war which started in 1914 and ended in 1918," he reflected, "I was already there by that time. By then I knew many things." In 1991, we sat in tall grass along a pasture's slope. Taking a break from herding cattle, Lazarus explained: "Nyahuruwa was responsible for making (*kugadzira*) rain. Traditionally, we call him *sachiuri*, the custodian (*mugadziri*) of a territory. He is not a chief."[20] He continued his tutorial: "Until today, Nya-huruwa is a *sadunhu* of Tangwena." Most Kaerezians spoke of a *sadunhu* as an ambiguously positioned custodian of a distinct geographical territory. For some, a *sadunhu* implied subservience "under" (*pasi*) a chief; for others, territorial power not vertically subordinate to chiefly rule.

Lazarus placed Nyahuruwa under Tangwena, illustrating the hierarchy by in-voking the practice of distributing meat after a successful hunt: "When you killed a big beast in Pabwe's land, you sent a forelimb to him, and if you killed it in the Nyahuruwa area, you did the same with SaNyahuruwa. You sent it to the *sadunhu* of the area where you killed the beast. You also send another forelimb to the chief. Children nowadays are confusing things." Lazarus acknowledged two forms of territorial power here: a horizontal expanse where the chief ruled a greater spatial extent; and a vertical topography that conceived of chiefly power as positioned above that of a *sadunhu*. Lazarus divided the *nyika* of the chiefdom into *ma-dunhu*, or subsections, administered by *masadhunu*. Much as a *samusha* is re-sponsible for both the people and place of a homestead, a *sadunhu* ruled rela-tionally over an extended realm. Colonial officials used the Shona term *dunhu* to refer to "wards" of subchiefs as administrative demarcations.[21] Lazarus subordi-nated rainmaker and Pabwe, one of Tangwena's headmen, to chiefly rule. His tale articulated a custom grounded in place and enduring through time. Yet by lamenting that younger generations were now "confusing things," he also marked a rupture—between generations, historical moments, and cultural practices.

Most Kaerezians referred to the current rainmaker as *munayisi* (from the verb *kunaya*, to rain). Some elders called him *musikamazi*, a more esoteric Chi-Manyika term for "creator of rains." Both terms emphasized his ritual specialty of appeasing territorial ancestral spirits. Knowledge and interest in these subtleties were strongly gendered and aged, elder men having the most detailed esoteric understandings. For many younger women and men, *sadunhu* was a term of the past; for others, it represented a variant term for *headman* or *sabhuku*. For Lazarus, Nyahuruwa's *sadunhu* status subordinated the rainmaker to another authority.

Lazarus embedded tradition in precolonial cultural customs. Yet he also en-tangled chiefly rule, rainmaking, and colonial history:

> Tangwena ruled a vast territory [*nyika*], families there [gesturing toward Mo-zambique] all the way to here. . . . The two sides had been taken by different whites so it was difficult to rule. . . . He was not happy about the laws of the Portuguese.

The Tangwena people came to live at Tangwena Mountain [visible from Kaerezi, in Mozambican territory]. . . . Before Tangwena physically arrived to settle here, it was his territory [*nyika*]. When he had something he wanted in the area, he would send his "police" [*mapurisa*]. He stayed with his families [in Mozambique], but this was his territory. He did not come here to seize this land.

His account differed markedly from those of colonial officials who conceived Dzeka's 1902 installation as inaugurating a new territory of rule. For Lazarus, prior to chiefly arrival, people and place were subject to the rainmaking power of *sachiuri*, the territory's custodian. In the official colonial origin story, the physical arrival of the sovereign's body gave birth to a singular form of rule. In contrast, Lazarus interwove two spatialities of power in the same area. Moreover, these overlapping landscapes did not rely on a singular metaphysics of presence embodied by a sovereign. Chief Tangwena ruled (*kutonga*) territory in Kaerezi despite his residing (*kugara*) in a geographically distant site. Lazarus located Kaerezi in a wider realm, the historically vast expanse of Tangwena territory: when colonial officials established a chiefdom in the early twentieth century, they demarcated only a province in a larger region ruled by a powerful chief.

Older Kaerezians such as Lazarus recognized traces of precolonial rule in postcolonial space. Many elders pointed to a ridge in Mozambique—east of Aberfoyle plantations and thus south of Kaerezi—that they called *Gomo reTangwena*, Mount Tangwena, near where Dzeka had lived before moving to Kaerezi. The landscape itself bore material witness to sedimentations of another era's body politics when Tangwena sovereignty spanned what later became the international boundary. Mount Nyanga was a peak just west of the international border near Holdenby's northernmost boundary, but with its bulk spilling eastward into Mozambique. The mountain's southwestern ridge hosted *mabinga*, sacred areas that composed a burial ground for Tangwena chiefs. White stones dotted this barren area known as *Machena*. Rekayi, whose body lay in Harare's Heroes' Acre, had claimed that nine of his chiefly predecessors were buried there. In contrast, most elders recalled fewer chiefs' graves in *Machena*, but echoed Rekayi's insistence that the burial of these sovereign bodies established at once historical depth and territorial breadth for Tangwena claims to rule land extending east from the Kaerezi River far into Barwe territory in Mozambique. Both the colonial and postcolonial international boundary fractured what once had been claimed by a single Tangwena sovereign.

Lazarus's translocal vision saw place as produced by social relations, cultural practices, and political processes that linked Kaerezi to sites elsewhere. Like many elders, Lazarus recounted the tale of Nyahuruwa's flight from Kaerezi. This severing from locality of Nyahuruwa's practices of ancestral propitiation brought drought, imperiling landscape and livelihoods. The rainmaker's return from exile promoted Kaerezians' welfare. Lazarus recognized the historical role of "whites" who "took sides" in competing regimes of Portuguese and Rhodesian rule. Yet these two colonies did not inaugurate spaces and powers. They entangled those already interwoven through rainmaking, chiefly rule, and the forms of subordination practiced by *masadunhu*.

Guns and Rain, Force and Power

Born in Kaerezi in the late 1920s, Tewa loosened his overalls to ward off the midday sun. In 1992, Zimbabwe was suffering its worst drought in living memory, yet he tilled moist soil in the Gumbos' garden thanks to a nearby stream. Tewa spoke vividly about fleeing Rhodesian soldiers during the war. He tugged on his overalls' strap, explaining how a previous pair saved his life. While running into the bush, he snagged them on a tree, tripping just at the moment a bullet whizzed by his head. "This close," he emphasized for dramatic effect, raising his hand a few inches above his hat. Others also told me the tale.

Tewa also recalled a precolonial era when the Tangwena were "people who liked war." Like most Kaerezians, he often slid "Tangwena" across the semantic terrain of a single chief as well as a sovereign's extended family, lineage, and subjects. As in the 1960s, when labor tenants recognized Rekayi's rule, *Tangwena* conjured political allegiance, historical relations to place and people, and senses of belonging rather than an ethnic essence. Tewa described the rainmaker's flight in the wake of chiefly conquest: "A chief came from Mozambique and said: 'I have come to take my chieftainship. Whatever you want to do, you can. You do not concern me.' Nyahuruwa did not like it. He said: 'I cannot be controlled by a foreigner [*mutorwa*].' He decided to leave the area. He said, 'They have guns and I do not, so they will kill me.'" Drought followed Nyahuruwa's flight. Tangwena kept his guns but paid a goat to the exiled rainmaker, who returned, initially only to teach people how to make rain. But "people begged him to stay until he agreed, and Nyahuruwa began living together with Tangwena and working together again."

For Tewa, Tangwena's arrival became conquest through force. The defeated rainmaker contested Tangwena's authority, refusing submission to a *mutorwa*.

Mutorwa, literally derived from the verb *kutorwa*, to be taken or taken in, referred to a foreigner, outsider, or stranger who lives among those who are not kin. The term marked spatial and social movement as well as embeddedness. In extended discussions, Tewa stressed that Tangwena arrived armed and arrogant, fleeing Makombe's political violence. For Tewa, Nyahuruwa welcomed a refugee, offering safe haven; Tangwena betrayed his generous host. A gendered subtext also haunted Tewa's accounts. *Mutorwa* was a common term for daughter-in-law; in principle, she moved from her natal home to live with her husband's lineage. Some Kaerezians added adultery to the tale to explain Tangwena's fears, flight, and inability to return to Barwe while Makombe ruled. Nyahuruwa welcomed Tangwena, but he refused to submit. The chief's claims to sovereignty did not translate into governing because the rainmaker refused to subject his conduct to chiefly rule. Conduct was also crucial for Tangwena's historical passage from *mutorwa* to *mugari* (resident), the latter marking cultural belonging, friendly social relations, and respectful residence.

For Tewa, force rather than power pushed Nyahuruwa off the land. Yet Tangwena's superior firearms, his soldiers, and his command of physical force found complement rather than competition in Nyahuruwa's propitiation of ancestral spirits who brought rain. Tewa's tale suggested that guns alone did not make a chieftainship. By honoring ancestral spirits, ritual practices promoted the territory's fertility and rains. Nurturing crops, these practices also cared for the local population. Crucially, Nyahuruwa's promotion of welfare remained sharply territorialized. He could not appease from afar; his exile threatened the healthy imbrication of people and place.

Tewa's lineage brother, Robert, born in the early 1930s in Tsatse, underplayed the theme of conquest, focusing on complementary powers exercised by chief and rainmaker. Robert told me that Tangwena fled the Makombe war and was offered sanctuary in Nyahuruwa's territory. During a break from our herding cattle, Robert shared his rendition of Kaerezi history: "Tangwena asserted: 'From where I come I am a chief. I rule in Mozambique.' Nyahuruwa responded: 'We can live together because here I am a chief [*mambo*].'" In Robert's version, Tangwena then declared: "I have a chieftainship over soil and wildlife and ruling people." Nyahuruwa answered: "My chieftainship is different because mine makes the rain when plowing season has arrived." According to Robert, this initial encounter produced mutual recognition and respect since "Tangwena said: 'You rule your way because our chieftainships are different.' They agreed and began living together." After an elaborate narrative, Robert concluded: "The original owner [*muridzi*] of this place is Nyahuruwa." Few Kaerezians conceived of Nyahuruwa as a *mambo* or chief. Yet Robert's rendition accorded the rain-maker rule over *umambo*—a chieftainship of sorts—stressing that qualitatively distinct powers entangled the same territory. Tangwena ruled soil, wildlife, and subjects—all nurtured by Nyahuruwa's rainmaking.[22]

At his Nyamutsapa homestead, I asked Robert about conflicts as well as cooperation. "There was a fight between Tangwena and Nyahuruwa," he nodded demonstratively, "but not between the original chiefs. It was their children; and where there are children, there is always fighting." We shared a knowing laugh as two schoolboys scampered by, one throwing a dried corncob at the other. Robert again emphasized that "the chiefs began living together well. Rekayi Tangwena later came, and he also cooperated with Nyahuruwa." They worked closely together, he stressed: "Tangwena ruled the people and soil and Nyahuruwa brought the rains." Robert stressed an enduring division of labor spanning the political negotiation provoked by Tangwena's initial arrival, the contentious period of colonial evictions from the ranch, and into the postcolonial period.

The path snaking its way up the river valley from Robert's home passed through rain-fed fields, irrigated gardens, and thatched homesteads. Less than a kilometer away, it reached Angela's home. Always already energetic, Angela led me to her paddock situated at the edge of one of her fields. She gave me a milking lesson, laughing joyously at my ineptitude while earnestly tutoring my technique. After the cattle herded home by teenage neighbors were securely enclosed in her kraal, we spoke at length. When I asked her, "What did people do when there was no rain?" I had no idea that the following year would see southern Africa's worst drought in living memory. Angela carried her bucket of milk, perched atop her head, into her cook hut. Stoking her fire, she reflected:

> The older generation used to listen to what the chief explained. They were given laws, and each of them was assigned a duty such as appeasing the ancestral spirits [*kupira vadzimu*]. It is the older people who are instructed to do it. Let's say there is no rain; they will go to the chief or to Nyahuruwa. They will tell people so that they do not plow, and they will go to appease the spirits. They go do it. Then they return. Nobody plows this day, nor do they work, but they eat. When they come from there, the rain will start. People will be told to start plowing. Let's say you have planted and there is no rain. They will go to Nyahuruwa again. They first go to the chief. It is the chief who will go to Nyahuruwa because the chief is under Nyahuruwa. Nyahuruwa has the power over the water and the soil. If he wants anything done, he will tell the people.

Angela inverted Lazarus's hierarchy, placing chief under rainmaker. In contrast to Tewa, Angela conceived Nyahuruwa's dominion to extend over "water and soil" (*mvura nevhu*). When the rainmaker wanted something done, he guided his subjects. These selective sovereignties conceived by Lazarus, Tewa, Angela, and others defied a binary structural opposition between chiefly and rainmaking power. The two modes of rule were integrally entangled, intimately relational, and articulated multiple temporalities and spatialities.

Spirited Powers

While rainmaking and chiefly rule mapped disputed powers to territory and subjects, other idioms of authority, spiritual health, and cultivated conduct linked people and place. Practices of healers (*n'anga*), prophets, spirit mediums (*svikiro*), and the lineage-based propitiation of ancestral spirits animated Kaerezi's landscape, producing sacred sites (*mapiwe*) and targeting the welfare of both living and dead. The universal grid of villagization's "rational" land-use planning denied localized enchantment. Yet practices of place kept alive relations among ancestors, inhabitants, and spirits.

Chekwa was probably the oldest man in Kaerezi. Toothless and difficult to understand, he claimed twelve wives and more than sixty children—even if neighbors quietly questioned the paternity of those born in the past decade. As a powerful *n'anga*, Chekwa used medicinal herbs and spiritual incantations to heal, conjuring ancestral agents to intervene in the fate of the living. Colonial administrators and ethnographers translated *n'anga* as diviner, witch doctor, and traditional healer. Mostly, Chekwa healed, but infrequently he allegedly ensorcelled. Another *n'anga* appeared to handle requests for more dramatic sorcery to intervene in enemies' fates: a snake encountered while they relieved themselves in the bush at night; a lightning bolt dispatched; a magical bundle carried by an owl and dropped into the thatch unbeknownst to the sleeper below. However, Chekwa, who collected a small fee for his services, never figured in accusations of malicious magic.

Lame and blind, in 1991 he sent his wives and children to harvest medicinal herbs. He treated impotency, sexually transmitted diseases, and diarrhea, among other common ailments. Despite the heat, he wore a dark fur cap. A plastic badge pinned to his threadbare jacket proclaimed "ZINATHA," the Zimbabwe National Traditional Healers Association, an official licensing agency ostensibly to weed out charlatans for the masses. I asked Chekwa where his power came from and how he conjured it for afflicted patients. "I mostly ask God because he is the one who created everything for me. Then I ask the ancestral spirits [*vadzimu*] because the ancestral spirits were created by God." Both Christians and *n'anga* called their Creator *Mwari*, the spiritual power from which life flows. They differed markedly, however, in how to handle ancestral spirits.

The "Prophet" was an influential, respected woman whose flock attended services at a thatched, barn-like structure in Nyamutsapa, built in 1990 from offcuts purchased at a nearby sawmill. Born in Tsatse in the early 1940s, she attended mission services at an Anglican church as a girl. But her husband's parents pressured her to stop. After a long illness, her second-born brought her into the church in the mid-1980s. With little formal education, she spoke only a few English words. The Prophet channeled the Holy Spirit, much as spirit mediums channeled ancestral ones. Like a *svikiro*, she was a "pocket" (*homwe*), receiving a spiritual force she enunciated. First, she dreamed of the Holy Spirit suffusing her. Dreams then instructed her to prophesize, and she began having visions, foreseeing potential futures. "In our church," she explained, "a prophet is the 'people's protector' [*muchengeti wevanhu*]" who warns of potential danger and misfortune. Her powers required "fullfilling God's needs" (*zvido zvaMwari*) by aligning human and divine desire. Quarrelling, hitting children, and jealousy could drain her efficacy. Her spiritual powers depended on healthy social relations.

When the rainmaker appeased ancestral spirits to bring the rains in August or September, the Prophet climbed up a high ridge to pray, asking her God for rain. She donned a stark white robe, made from a bedsheet and carefully smoothed with a hot-coal iron. "Why do you climb up the ridge to pray?" I asked. "It's just like the soldiers with their radiophone," she aptly drew on a familiar scene—men in army fatigues walking on ridges with an antenna poking out of a square backpack. Several army camps had emerged in the wake of cross-border MNR attacks, and a small group of soldiers still slept near her home. "We both go to the top of mountains where there is more wind. We go where there is more power [*simba*]." Mountaintops provided both soldier and savior with articulations of *savoir* and *pouvoir*, knowledge and power. For those who appeased ancestral spirits, sacred ridges (*mabinga*) marked privileged places to connect with *vadzimu*, asking for rain, good harvests, and domestic good fortune. Spatial history made places a medley of military and spiritual entities, both visible and invisible. Embodied practices brought radiophones, grain brewed for beer to respect

The Prophet, with arm raised, leads singers in her church, Nyamutsapa, 1991. *Photo by the author.*

vadzimu, and white sheets ironed with care to specific sites. Each sought to protect both territory and population.

Those who prayed (*kunamata*) to a Christian God recognized the Creator *Mwari*'s presence in the landscape, in the vitality of life, and in social relations binding relatives and friends. Yet they directed their prayers upward toward Heaven, an imagined space where divinity dwells beyond the earthly realm infused with the Creator's spirit. The dead, while buried in the ground, if virtuous in life, ascended much like the prayers of those who knelt to offer them. Churches condensed worship while the Prophet climbed mountains to implore *Mwari* to bring the rains. But it was more the *quality* of location—a sheltered meeting place, a high ridge—than a singular place that promoted productive prayer. Few referred to the thatched church as a sacred place, yet prayer and singing exuded from weekly services. On some Sundays, worshippers traveled to celebrate with another congregation a few hours walk away.

Unlike more mobile prayers, propitiation was more site-specific, mapping animism to place. Kaerezians referred to those who "appease ancestral spirits" (*kupira vadzimu*) as "being of the territory" (*vari kunyika*). Animists appeased ancestral spirits with earthly harvests, brewing *rapoko* (millet) beer in respectful offers of thanks. Requests for rain, while they asked for the skies to shower, invoked spirits linked to homesteads and territories. Most offerings emerged from *mapiwe*, propitiation areas designated for family spirits and located in specific groves, rock formations, or other defining features of landscape. Kaerezians referred to both the sites *and* practices as sacred, each defining the other. Unlike a church or the Prophet's preferred ridge, *mapiwe* had prohibitions against visiting except for rituals of appeasement. Adults disciplined children who mistakenly strayed into *mapiwe*, paying fines to their neighbors and amending their children's spatial practices. Appeasement sites could shift when families migrated. To motivate *vadzimu* to migrate to a new homestead required brewing *rapoko* beer as an offering, a situated practice that bound people and place. Like the living, ancestral spirits move across the landscape, becoming reterritorialized and helping to make huts a home. While *mapiwe* were often near homesteads, graves, also honored, usually remained further from dwelling places. The funerals I attended required a short hike from the deceased's home to a burial site, humbly marked after the ceremony with a pile of rocks on a barren ridge or near a lonely tree.

Nyahuruwa's lineage had a privileged relationship to bringing rains and promoting the fertility of land. I rarely heard anyone refer to *mhondoro*, the term for "tribal guardian spirits" associated with spirit mediums elsewhere in Zimbabwe. With the exception of the devout prayerful, most agreed that good rains required the appeasement of Nyahuruwa's family ancestral spirits, *vadzimu* or *midzimu*, whose influence spilled beyond his lineage to include all Kaerezi inhabitants. Residents were expected to contribute grain to his seasonal rainmaking ritual. Most did. Many among those who prayed to a Christian God contributed, but some protested, and I never heard of serious consequences for those who refused. A public discourse distinguished "those who prayed" from "those who appeased," yet some jumped across the divide much as Rekayi had propitiated ancestral spirits while claiming membership in the Anglican Church and appealing to liberal Christians.

"An ancestral spirit [*mudzimu*] is like a married person," the Prophet explained. "It lives at a homestead [*musha*] where an ancestral father died. . . . When I was appeasing spirits [*ndiri kunyika*], I suffered [*ndaitambudzika*]. I lacked clothes, soap, and salt because my husband was a drunkard. Now life in the church has lifted me up." Like many who joined the church, the Prophet spoke of "being troubled" by ancestral spirits before turning to prayer. Giving herself over to God made her no longer subject to the caprice, wrath, or judgment of *vadzimu*. She found a form of freedom through prayer, subjecting her soul to a higher power. She also credited her husband's church-bound flight from drinking and vengeful ancestral spirits as crucial to a healthier turn in her marriage and life. While she mapped *vadzimu* to homesteads where the spirits' embodied origin once lived, she acknowledged their mobility. Spirits animated place yet were not always sedentary.

Mbuya Ngwarai, a grandmother evicted from Gaeresi Ranch in the early 1970s, lived in the forest for four years before fleeing to Mozambique. "No one was struck by snakes," she recalled. "We even lived in sacred places [*nvzimbo dzino-era*]. Nobody died while we were in the forests, but soon after the war, elders began dying. *Midzimu* worked together with God," she insisted, "it's only the people who distinguish them. We have only one God who created everything." Those who envisioned prayer and appeasement as complementary rather than competitive modes of faith stressed their shared subordination to *Mwari*, a supreme Creator and divine power. Despite appeasing *midzimu*, Mbuya Ngwarai shared the Prophet's vision of a marriage joining the living with legacies of the dead: "Your *midzimu* are like your husband," who along with God "see to it that you live well." Her gendered vision of pastoral care metaphorized marriage. Patrilocality meant that most women moved away from sites associated with their ancestors. Thus patriarchs usually controlled the propitiation of patrilineal spirits who also affected affines.

Mbuya Ngwarai's husband propitiated from a clump of rocks near their homestead. Yet she insisted that *midzimu* "accompany you everywhere" like a loyal husband, conjuring a mobile spiritual bond. In this manner, Kaerezians beckoned ancestral spirits to mountain forests after colonial evictions, to Mozambique during wartime flight, and back to new homesteads in postcolonial Zimbabwe. Along the route, many felt guided and protected by traveling ancestral spirits who, like people, yearned to return to a rightful homeland.

The very slipperiness of the term for ancestral spirits defies easy categorization. Shona has twenty-one noun classes. Yet the groupings are a bit like Borges's version of a Chinese encyclopedia, made yet more famous by Foucault's invocation in *The Order of Things*. One noun class groups knives (*mapanga*), horses (*mabhiza*), and riverbanks (*madivi*) in one category; in another, a crocodile (*ngwena*), an angel (*ngirozi*), a fertile woman (*mvana*), a harmful accident (*njodzi*), and an inheritance (*nhaka*) come together; yet a third links school (*chikoro*), bread (*chingwa*), a human finger (*chinwe*), and a metal sign (*chikwangwani*), not to mention a singular environmental resource (*chisikwa*). The last term, in turn, refers back to the crocodile and riverbank, and the whirlpool continues. After all, *njuzu* are mermaidlike water spirits, and they are linguistically akin to accidents and inheritance. Linguists and native speakers perform contortions trying to formulate a semantic logic that might hold together categories beyond "mere" sounds. Noun classes yield semantic clusters with multiple crosscuts and exceptions.

The singular *mudzimu* (ancestral spirit) morphs into two plurals, *vadzimu* and *midzimu*, a linguistic rarity. The first branching charts the pluralization of humans: persons, children, wives and husbands, myriad kinship relations, Europeans, slaves, and owners. The other root is more earthly than human: trees, fields, and medicine (both herbal and pharmaceutical); but also air, breath, and vapor as well as a soul or spirit (all *mweya*) and the firepower of a ramrod musket (*miguguda*). Straddling the spectral and the human, bonding the dead and the living, ancestral spirits cannot be contained in only one noun class. Nor are individual Kaerezians consistent in their usage, a practice I intentionally mimic.

Those who appeased spirits did not agree on gender among *vadzimu*. Elders insisted that women past childbearing age should be the only ones to dry the rapoko to be brewed for spirits. Most claimed that only men should be involved in "the actual appeasing of the ancestors." The failure to follow these gendered rules "nowadays," many lamented, caused spiritual confusion and social misfortune. Several told me that women cannot speak through a medium, though they can be one, channeling the words of the male spirit possessing them. There were no women *midzimu* when Mbuya Ngwarai was a girl, "but nowadays they exist. Things are now going bad," she implied a causal connection. She linked spiritual and political health of more than one *nyika*: "Perhaps it's because of the past war." But she admitted to brewing beer to appease her husband's lineage spirits when he was away as a migrant laborer, asking them to care for her young daughter. But only postmenopausal women *should* do this, she stressed. Others blamed villagization for disturbing *midzimu*, inviting misfortune to the territory and risking the social security of its population.

Rainmaker and Nationalist

Elijah, the eldest Nyahuruwa lineage member, was widely recognized as a powerful rainmaker (*musikamazi* or *munayisi*). He lived in Tsatse, a short walk from Chief Rekayi's home, in a sprawling cluster of huts and a few sun-dried brick buildings with asbestos roofs. We first met while he tended to customers in a

Elijah Nyahuruwa addresses a meeting, Kaerezi Main, 1991. Note the
zanu-pf T-shirt he is wearing beneath overalls. *Photo by the author.*

small brick shop a kilometer from his home, near one of Kaerezi's few grinding
mills. Since most families brought maize weekly to the small, diesel-powered
mill, the shop's location guaranteed a steady flow of people. The lack of local cash
and poorly stocked shelves meant more visitors than customers. Run by a cooperative, it struggled. Elijah Nyahuruwa was then almost seventy, a tall figure clad
in blue overalls and a fashionable cap, giving off an air of graceful dignity
that reminded me of Nelson Mandela, a man we both greatly admired. During
one of our extended conversations in 1991, he greeted me, sold a couple pieces of
candy and a box of matches to schoolchildren returning home, and then took a
break to smoke a hand-rolled cigarette on the shop's cement porch. A gifted
orator, he often chaired local meetings with visiting dignitaries, even when the
chief was present. Nyahuruwa was among Kaerezi's most influential and savvy
political figures.

Born in 1924, the last of seven children, Elijah was the oldest surviving male. His
ancestors, he related, "arrived here long ago, but at first they lived at Nyangani,"
the peak in the neighboring park. Elijah made no literal claim to autochthony—in
the sense of humans who sprung from the soil they inhabit—but rather located
rainmaking territory, Nyahuruwa's sovereignty, and place-affiliated cultural identities in histories of becoming, spatial movement, and power relations. Nya-

huruwa's rights predated Tangwena conquest but were not bound to a sedentarist cultural essence. Tangwena conquest dispossessed the rainmaker's lineage and violated ancestral, but not indigenous, rights. Many Kaerezians referred to the rainmaking range as *Nyahanga*—marking place with the long residence of the rainmaker's totem, *hanga*, or wild pig—pointing to a ridge near Tsatse but sometimes extending it toward Nyafaru. Some still called the Nyafaru area Ditima, the name of Elijah's paternal grandfather who had lived there. The cultural skills of rainmaking, however, while mapped to place, did not exempt members of his lineage from the translocal forces shaping the colonial political economy. Elijah's father, also a powerful rainmaker, labored at a mine in Penhalonga, near Mutare. In 1944, Elijah worked as a waiter in Mutare, before seeking wages in Bulawayo. In that major city in the country's south, he secured a hotel job from 1945 until 1982.

In Bulawayo, when the migrant workers Elijah and his friend and political ally Rekayi Tangwena joined the Nationalist Democratic Party around 1960—and after its banning, its successor, the Zimbabwe African People's Union, in 1963—they found a political organization that helped them organize against the injustices of a white rancher's usurpation of chiefdom and rainmaking territory.[23] Both men's homes lay in Tsatse, the epicenter of resistance to Hanmer's evictions. Militantly particular and highly localized struggles for territory pivoted on translocal articulations: labor tenants' arguments for land rights on the ranch and migrant wage labor opportunities in distant sites; the political alliance between rainmaker and chief forged in the city of Bulawayo, as well as in Kaerezi; and nationalist politics linking rural and urban grievances against Rhodesia's racialized rule.

Nyafaru nationalists and a prominent escape encouraged chief and rainmaker to side in the mid-1970s with Mugabe's ZANU party, which rivaled Nkomo's Bulawayo-based ZAPU. In the early 1990s, Elijah served as the district party chairman for the ruling nationalist party, by then renamed ZANU-PF. Respected as a rainmaker, he commanded "traditional" authority; elected as the area's representative to the nationalist party, he rubbed elbows with prominent district, provincial, and even national politicians. He had long-standing ancestral land claims yet also urban experiences of both wage labor and political organizing. Like the locality that bore his name, his life was thoroughly translocal and transcultural.

I was struck by the details of Elijah's rendering of the area's spatial history, the textures and micropolitics of territory. Like many Kaerezians, Elijah depicted Nyahuruwa's and Tangwena's initial relationship as healthy. As a result, when

Tangwena fled Makombe's wrath in Mozambique, he sought refuge in Nyahuruwa's territory. Elijah elaborated:

Nyahuruwa was in Zimbabwe and Tangwena in Mozambique, so they coordinated their actions. Tangwena was running from war to Mutoko, and Nyahuruwa told him that "when war arrives here, I will make heavy rain so that it will be difficult for them to move." Tangwena was kept at Pangara near the Kaerezi River. After three years, he shifted a **kilometer** toward Nyahuruwa. After a year, he moved another half **kilometer** toward Nyahuruwa again. Tangwena said: "We want to live near each other for easy communication in case war might come." They agreed. Tangwena had seven muskets [*miguguda*]. Nyahuruwa had none. Tangwena had been given them by Makombe. So when Tangwena was invited for beer at Nyahuruwa's home, he looked very carefully to see if Nyahuruwa had muskets and saw that he did not. One day, early in the morning, Tangwena sent his army to collect Nyahuruwa. . . . They took Nyahuruwa and they beat a *shima* as soon as Nyahuruwa entered Tangwena's home.

A *shima* is a distinct drum rhythm associated with a specific chieftainship to be played only by a legitimate ruler. In Elijah's version, Tangwena forcibly seized a potentially competing sovereign's body, uprooting him from home. The refugee also usurped the ruling rhythm of locality. Tangwena's muskets provided mobile force in contrast to Nyahuruwa's territorialized powers to conjure rains. The rainmaker sheltered Tangwena, an ally to whom he offered troops and rain to repel Makombe's potential attacks. That very threat became Tangwena's ruse to move incrementally closer to Nyahuruwa's home. Beer drinking's spatial and social intimacy became Tangwena's opportunity to spy on his host's lack of weaponry and to plot the seizure of Nyahuruwa's territory.

Riveted by the details in his account, I asked Elijah how this history influenced the subsequent powers (*masimba*) claimed, respectively, by Tangwena and Nyahuruwa. Elijah's lineage retained the power to "make rain and control the area's wards [*kutonga matunhu*]." Yet Tangwena's conquest initially sought total usurpation: "Tangwena tried to seize all the power, but there was no rain for five years. When Nyahuruwa's chieftainship [*umambo*] was seized, he took refuge in Rusape because he did not want to be ruled by an outsider [*mutorwa*]." Subjects also refused the new regime of rule, popular unrest exerting pressure: "People started to quarrel with Tangwena, ordering him, 'Kill us with your guns because we cannot live without rain,' and asking why Tangwena had chased Nyahuruwa away." Nyahuruwa sought refuge in Rusape with Chief Madziwa who threatened Tangwena: " 'If you murder Nyahuruwa we will wage war against you because someone who takes refuge in another person's area cannot be followed.' Tangwena agreed," honoring the practice that supported his own refuge from Makombe.

Nyahuruwa moved from Rusape to Dazi, trying unsuccessfully for three years to propitiate territorial spirits from across the Kaerezi River. Exilic appeasement of their ancestral agency was ineffective. Eventually, he returned to Makondo, the area where his father had died in Tangwena territory. Most of those sharing the rainmaker's totem ran away "because they did not want to be ruled by a refugee [*murefugee*]." Tangwena proclaimed that "he will rule only the people [*kutonga vanhu chete*] and Nyahuruwa will rule the area [*kutonga matunhu*]." Yet Nyahuruwa did not listen passively to this decree. He told Tangwena that "this territory [*nyika*] requires special preparation." Moreover, the past rainmaker pronounced, "any chief to be installed other than you, since you were installed in Mozambique, will not live longer than the day of installation." Elijah continued: "They agreed. They lived together, Nyahuruwa appeasing the spirits." He then chronicled the deaths of Tangwena chiefs: "Dzeka later died. Mudima retained the chieftainship and died. He lived longer because he had been installed in *Machena*. Rekayi Tangwena ruled a very short period from the date of installation. Magwendere has not yet been installed, and he is the acting chief." Conquest did not trump the rainmaker's right to "rule territory," he insisted. A chiefly installation within Nyahuruwa's *nyika* would lay claim to sovereignty through forceful dispossession, not rightful rule. *Territorial* spirits would protect against future attempts to usurp *territorial* power, effectively cursing any Tangwena chief installed in Nyahuruwa's reign. In this telling, so potent was the site of chiefly installation that it determined life and death, situating sovereign power in a landscape of usurpation.

In Elijah's rendering of territorial invasion, Tangwena's power over death—his command of firearms and his military strategies—contended with Nyahuruwa's life-sustaining powers of bringing rain. Chiefly assertions of the sovereign power to kill encountered another sovereignty predicated on the power to nurture life. To murder Nyahuruwa would render Tangwena's chiefly subjects at risk, depriving their livelihoods by bringing drought to their homeland. Tangwena's own political survival required Nyahuruwa's ritual practices, the recognition of another sovereignty that necessarily rendered chiefly rule always already less than absolute. Pivotal in these politics was the active agency of subjects whose popular unrest encouraged Tangwena to negotiate the return from exile of the vanquished rainmaker.

For Elijah, this complex precolonial history animated present politics. "Tangwena does not have powers over sacred areas [*mabinga*] because he does not have 'appeasing zones' [*mapiwe*] in this territory. Nyahuruwa has that power," he explained, as an "owner" (*muridzi*) of territory. "If someone does not pay, I do not appease the spirits for rain. So people will have a **boycott** saying they will die of hunger because of that one person who refuses to pay." Elijah cleverly invoked rainmaking's populist precolonial history while poaching from idioms of commodity capitalism. The English term *boycott* connoted political strategies targeting both colonial and postcolonial regimes of rule, as well as unscrupulous retailers who pursued illicit wealth. Dutiful subjects contributed grain through a fusion of consent and coercion, their conduct guided by rainmaker and neighbors' peer pressure alike. Territorial power, in Elijah's rendering, produced political subjection. Commoners mingled their labor with Nyahuruwa's *nyika*, the fruits of their harvests plowed back into beer brewing that beckoned future rain and fomented landscape fertility. Their participation in these practices enlivened rainmaking as a potent postcolonial power.

Reign Clouds

After Rekayi's 1984 death, kraalheads, members of the chiefly lineage, and elite elders met several times to select an acting chief until a permanent successor could be found. In 1985, they chose the fifty-one-year-old eldest son of Rekayi's eldest brother who was also Headman for Tsatse, the area that included Rekayi's homestead.[24] After several more meetings, government officials reported in 1986 that the acting chief Tangwena was chosen from the "4 houses contesting the Tangwena chieftainship." The report outlined the offspring of Tsatse's four wives who comprised four distinct "houses." No single *oikos* modeled government. The "succession custom" involved a sequential rotation of rule among the four houses, appointing as chief the given house's senior male "subject to concurrence of *Madzitete*," the ruling lineage's senior paternal aunts.[25] The earlier choice, Headman Tsatse's son, came undone. Some claimed his shopkeeping and residence beyond the chiefdom along the highlands' major tarred road doomed his candidacy; others claimed he refused the office; still others suggested that he remained the popular choice among elders and headmen. Yet "government," Kaerezians told me, supported another house.

According to the 1986 report, Magwendere, the chosen claimant, was "long overdue for the chieftainship." Before dying, Dzeka "pledged" that his successor would come from Magwendere's house. A competing house's elder was so "shocked" by the news that Magwendere "agreed to let the old man rule." Mudima reigned from 1928 until 1938. At his death, Mudima's son secretly went to Mozambique and "fetched" Kinga, who belonged to Mudima's house, making him a chief "behind Magwendere's back." When Kinga died in 1965, Rekayi "became so influential in leading the Tangwena people in their struggle against the white man" that Magwendere "allowed him to lead." Magwendere's hope was that "at the end of the struggle Rekayi would stand down and hand over the affairs of the tribe." Magwendere allegedly objected when officials allowed Rekayi's reign after independence "for political reasons."[26] In 1983, when the postcolonial state processed the official paperwork for Rekayi's installation the next year, Magwendere was listed as the only other contestant for the chieftainship.[27] After Rekayi's death, officials argued, succession should return to its rightful rotation.

The report is remarkable for illuminating the entanglement of state politics and local tradition. Echoing Holleman's endorsement of "customary law," postcolonial officials invoked rules codified by colonial rulers. In the 1990s, political technologies maintained a chieftainship created with a 1902 government-orchestrated initiation ceremony. The report's rhetoric implied that state recognition and not popular legitimacy defined Rekayi's chiefly status, a ruling tradition that spanned independence. The report struggled, however, to balance orderly principles of rotation with the contentious realpolitik of rule. Headmen came to a consensus on Magwendere, officials reported, and commoners were then "advised of the choice." The "only opposition" recorded was by "Nyahuruwa the rainmaker of the Tangwena tribe." Reportedly, he argued: "I am the owner of this land. Dzeka asked for a place to stay only but now his descendants have established themselves so well and [are] behaving like they own the land. I will not allow these descendants to continue appointing themselves chiefs on my land. I want my land back."[28]

The 1986 report dismissed Elijah Nyahuruwa's claims because he "could not satisfactorily answer why he has remained silent for so long."[29] Seeking to turn the principles of indirect rule into instruments of postcolonial government, officials muted a cacophony of claims and counterclaims that had long held rainmaking and chiefly rule in tension—neither sovereign able to trump the other. In turn, both rainmaking and chiefly rule remained shot through with state administration—traces of colonial books, taxes, labor tenancy, land laws, and postcolonial resettlement. The traction of any specific alignment of sovereignty-government-discipline turned on contingent articulations of cultural politics. Magwendere was not Rekayi, nor was the resettlement scheme a colonial ranch; yet chiefly rule in postcolonial Kaerezi remained haunted by legacies of an anticolonial chief and a nationalist rainmaker.

Elijah Nyahuruwa, a respected member of the ruling nationalist party, invoked his lineage's rainmaking rights, traced to precolonial relations to territory. By recognizing Magwendere as chief, postcolonial officials reinforced Tangwena's conquest, the illegitimate seizure of a rainmaker's territory by a *mutorwa*, an outsider. In both colonial and postcolonial grids of intelligibility, rainmaking— infrequently acknowledged at all—remained structurally subaltern to chiefly rule; official reports referred to Nyahuruwa as "the rainmaker of the Tangwena tribe." Occluded in each official map of power were the traces of pre-conquest spatialities that vied with chiefly rule. When the District Administrator recounted the chiefdom's history at Rekayi's 1983 installation in Tsatse, he traced the chieftainship back to a precolonial era without specifying its territorial claims; Rekayi's predecessors passed their reign from Sakara to Nyamariwodzwa (also Nyamariodzo) to Kubina to Tsatse and finally to Gwindo before, in 1902, colonial officials appointed Rekayi's father, Dzeka, the first Chief Tangwena.[30] Such government practices officially occluded the territorial counterclaims of Kaerezians who deemed rainmaking a form of sovereignty neither derivative of nor subordinate to Tangwena chiefly rule.

"The ancestral spirits have authority over everything," Elijah explained before taking a long drag on his cigarette.[31] In 1992, we met again at his homestead a stone's throw from Mbuya Clarissa's hut that had stopped smelling of DDT months before. Those living in his area should "respect territory," Elijah insisted, thus also honoring his lineage's ancestral spirits.[32] This bond buttressed the rainmaker's "power" (*simba*) over *zvisikwa*, things created—environmental resources such as water, soil, forests, and wildlife. Elijah recalled that during the liberation struggle, "*vadzimu* would say **comrades** should not move because whites [*mabhunu*] are patrolling." Beyond warning guerrillas about the presence of Rhodesian forces, ancestral spirits guided fighters through forests, helped hunters track wildlife, and offered spiritual and material assistance during the war.

In 1991, Nyafaru's secondary school headmaster recounted to me his 1976 arrest along with other members of the multiracial cooperative accused of "aiding terrorists." In the wake of Mugabe's 1975 escape through Nyafaru, Rhodesian authorities targeted the cooperative as a conduit to guerrilla bases in Mozambique. Like Chidumbu, he had returned after release from prison. We spoke in English in his small office, where he sat behind a wooden desk. Months earlier, we had discussed themes in *Macbeth*, which he then assigned for O-level English. Several students confessed their confusion to me, asking for help with linguistic and cultural translation. No teacher ever suggested to them that *Hamlet*, *King Lear*, or *Macbeth* might be read in relation to African idioms of ancestral spirits, specters of vengeance, or epic battles shaped by mortal and ethereal forces. Turning to local heaths, I asked the headmaster if *vadzimu* intervened during the war on behalf of Kaerezians. "We were taken by the army people; they had captured the guerrillas." One "guerrilla was saying he left his ammunition over that hill," he pointed out the window. "We were carrying him up the hill because he was wounded." He named a homestead he knew I frequented to mark the location. He paused for drama, adding animated gestures:

> Suddenly, thunderstorms and heavy rain started to fall, and I have never experi-
> enced such rain until now. We even saw landslides. We did not know where to go.
> We had to come back. We wanted to go to Nyanga, but we did not know where the
> bridge was [implying that it had been washed out or was under water]. So we slept
> here. And the next day we tried to climb that hill again, and there were thun-
> derstorms again. After the war, we collected the ammunition, two years ago. We
> knew where it was. We called the police and went with them.

"Why do you think the *vadzimu* prevented you from going up the hill?" I wondered. "It was going to be worse. They wanted proof that we were helping the guerrillas. We were refusing. . . ." I interrupted, "If they found proof. . . ." He finished my sentence: "Some of us would have been hanged." In his account, abundant rains conjured by ancestral spirits echoed Nyahuruwa's ancestor who promised to protect Dzeka Tangwena from Makombe. In contrast, the colonial state, through military might and legal decree, threatened death. Selective sovereignties again turned on powers of life, countering forces of death. Yet, as SaGumbo's, the Prophet's, and Tewa's narratives underscored, ancestral spirits can avenge as well as protect. They can be as capricious as the weather, visiting plagues on the living. My point is not to counter a life-affirming, romanticized regime of nurturing care over and against the death devices of a unitary state. Rather, I highlight how Kaerezi's practices and understandings of sovereignty were multiple and contested, both imperiling and protecting the welfare of subjects. Far from absolute, selective sovereignties were *situated*, gaining traction on contingent terrain.

Bounding Sovereignties

Which historical eras, what acts of power and violent conquest—of flight and refuge, invasion and opposition—remained consequential for the practices of postcolonial Tangwena territory? Until the late nineteenth century, when competing European empires demarcated two separate colonies, Tangwena rulers had negotiated their territorial influence with subjects, insurgents, and Barwe and Manica sovereigns, as well as with Portuguese officials and imperial strongmen such as Gouveia. In the 1890s, Rhodes's white settlers invaded current-day Zimbabwe, suppressing African uprisings against them. In 1897, actions in Florence affected those along the Kaerezi and Jora Rivers when an Italian arbitrator negotiated British and Portuguese diplomats' approval of the disputed Manica boundary.[33] Portions of both rivers became part of the boundary separating British and Portuguese territory, international law recognizing the signed agreement between two sovereign imperial states. Soon thereafter, Dzeka Tangwena fled Makombe across that border, seeking refuge in Nyahuruwa's rainmaking range inside a new British colony. In the 1970s, Dzeka's son, Rekayi, a Tangwena chief not recognized by white Rhodesians, reversed this route of refuge.

During their exile in the 1970s from Kaerezi, Rekayi and his people lived east of Mount Nyanga and not far from Mount Tangwena—the peak remembered as a landmark near one of Dzeka's nineteenth-century homesteads. In the wake of colonial evictions from Gaeresi Ranch, Rekayi sought refuge in this place linked to Tangwena ancestral claims, negotiating with both Chief Nyauchi and FRELIMO cadres to enable his people to scatter homesteads in land liberated in 1974 from Portuguese colonial rule. After Zimbabwe's own guerrilla war of independence, Tangwena subjects returned to Kaerezi, crossing an international border that now demarcated two sovereign postcolonies. Their transformed Tangwena chiefdom now entangled Gaeresi Ranch's conversion to a state-purchased resettlement scheme. Like Dzeka's migration into a new colonial triad-in-motion, Rekayi and his followers encountered an emergent postcolonial one.

In the 1990s, residents' invocations of "traditional Tangwena territory" carried historical fragments of these shifting sovereignties and rights, expressing widespread consensus on the chiefdom's spatial core, but also revealing diffuse and disputed edges. Few Kaerezians could read maps, and both the names and physical locations of streams and landmarks indicating Tangwena territory, *nyika*, sometimes shifted. All agreed that the area between the Kaerezi and Jora Rivers lay in Tangwena territory, but most elders recognized boundaries that extended beyond the resettlement scheme—south into the national park, east of the Jora into what had once been Crown Land, and south into Holdenby—though they admitted that the neighboring Chief Chikomba in Mutasa District also claimed some of that southern territory.[34] During our walks in the park, months after one young man pointed to the junction of two streams to indicate the boundary, his elder might identify another confluence or rock formation. In differing accounts, the same name might refer to both locations, or the same point might have variant names. A number of elders—whose independent renditions supported one another—traced for me what most who professed detailed on-the-ground knowledge agreed on: the southern boundary ran east from a point where the Tsumba River joined the Kaerezi in the park; in a line connecting two small yet distinctive peaks (big and small Kaomba); to a stone at a recognizable foothill before intersecting the source of the Nyamukombe River; along the Sagure stream to its confluence with the Mucharambeyi stream; and finally running northeast to the Mucharambeyi's source, before again heading east to a known point on the Mozambique border. Yet for many residents, the park's northern border—across which they knew park officials prohibited cattle grazing and regulated firewood harvesting—effectively bounded both Kaerezi and Tangwena territory.

For most, the Kaerezi River marked the western boundary of two *nyikas*, Nyahuruwa's rainmaking range and Tangwena's chiefdom. Most localized Nyahuruwa's reign to the ridges near his Tsatse homestead. A few pushed it south, including Nyafaru, where Elijah's paternal grandfather had lived, or extended it to include parts of the Nyangani range—noting that Nyahuruwa's lineage lived there before migrating to Kaerezi prior to Rhodes's arrival. But they never extended it beyond the Kaerezi River. In contrast, some stretched the chiefdom west to the Nyakamba River and the southeast corner of the Tsanga Valley wheat estate, reaching into Chief Saunyama's land; others insisted that Chief Tangwena once claimed territory extending to Macheke, hours west by bus. Implicitly, such assertions referenced an era when Barwe royalty asserted their influence across a vast expanse before the twentieth century, usually naming a nebulous time of "long ago" (*pasi chigare* or *kare kare*). Many admitted that the chiefdom's boundaries had shifted historically, but many also disagreed on what era or spatial extent should define contemporary articulations of traditional territory. Despite ongoing boundary disputes, eighty years of colonial practices of tax collection, labor extraction, and "tribal" administration had hardened two Tangwena boundaries—the Kaerezi River and the Mozambique border—reinforced, in turn, by postcolonial rule.

However, in Dazi and other areas west of the Kaerezi River yet inside the resettlement scheme, astute subjects could exploit ambivalent borders by bringing disputes—over livestock, fields, or neighbors' conduct—to the *dare*, or court, of either Chief Tangwena, Chief Saunyama, or both.[35] In the 1990s, some as far away as Bende in the Nyangui Forest—where a few Tangwena families remained after their eviction and government resettlement in the late 1960s—brought cases to Magwendere's court. In so doing, they stretched traditional subjection and rule across spaces explicitly created by Rhodesian officials—through legal excision of state forest in 1969—to steer the chiefdom off Gaeresi Ranch. During a couple of visits to Bende, however, I also encountered those who criticized Magwendere for allegedly extorting unjust fees to settle their disputes. Other migrants to Bende denied their subjection to Magwendere, arguing that any Tangwena sovereign only ruled subjects who resided east of the Kaerezi River. I now turn to fractures within that complex geo-body of Kaerezi, focusing on disputes over land allocation, settlement rights, and the authority claimed by headmen.

8 · Spatial Subjection

I left Nyamutsapa one 1992 dawn, my strides lightening to sunrise's warming of the mountain chill as I walked toward Headman's Nyakurita's territory near the Mozambican border. Silhouetted against the morning sky, the ridges of Mount Tangwena in Mozambique beckoned me east, the prominent peak's name betraying historical sediments of a spatiality that spanned borders and eras of conflicting rule. Inside Kaerezi's colonial and postcolonial Tangwena chiefdom, six headmen claimed separate areas, further complicating jurisdiction, subjection, and modes of power. I began my journey in Nyamutsapa, a subsection of Headman Pabwe's territory west of Nyafaru. My walking route to Nyakurita touched Tsatse to the north; returning, I walked through a sliver of Muomba's territory to the south of the Jora River, and then visited homesteads in Goora's area southeast of Nyafaru. That day's journey traversed all of the headmen's areas except that of Madziwanzira, north of Tsatse. The names signified distinct places demarcated by ridges, streams, and other prominent landmarks. They also mapped headmen's family names to jurisdictions referred to as respective "books," *mabhuku*. Headmen were *masabhuku*. *Sabhuku*, a singular headman, was literally a book's custodian. The prefix *sa* performed double duty, signifying at once a responsible authority and also a honorific mode of address.[1]

Bhuku, "the book," referred to territory, population, and rule. The colonial term invoked at once a tax roll and state registry of domicile, a geographical subdivision of a chiefdom, and government legitimacy accorded to an appointed official overseer. For both administrators and rural residents, a "book" proved critical to colonial rule's grid of intelligibility. Integral to indirect rule, the practices associated with books—censuses, tax registers, forced labor, court jurisdiction—contributed to the *production* of both space and subjects. Like tribes, chiefdoms, land, and labor legislation, "books" operated through governing technologies that imbricated subjects and territory. They also spanned the colonial divide. Colonial books subordinated headmen "under" a chief, placing their authority "inside" tribal territory. In postcolonial Kaerezi, how were headmen positioned? Their practices acted on the actions of commoners who subjected themselves to a rainmaker, chief, and his headmen. In open opposition to resettlement policy, all Tangwena headmen claimed to allocate land. However, commoners and governing officials asserted counterclaims that contested *sabhuku* authority while articulating alternative rights and power relations. This chapter explores these tensions.

Headman Nyakurita lived far from roads and transport where steep paths, patches of thick forest, and rugged ridges rolled down to a river at Mozambique's border. Many described his area as "remote," several hours walk to even a small tack shop where matches, salt, or sugar might be found when in stock. Fertilizer and seed purchased from more distant sites required strong bodies to carry fifty-kilogram sacks from a drop-off point on the dirt road to dispersed homesteads. The closest grinding mill was located in Headman Goora's adjacent area. When it broke down, women had two options for daily provisioning. They could grind maize by mortar and pestle the size of a sledgehammer, which made for grueling labor. Or they could balance a heavy sack atop their head, climbing and descending mountain paths to Nyafaru's distant mill, hoping diesel fuel had not run out. Nyafaru was also the closest health clinic for those fit enough to reach it.

In response to MNR raids, a few small army camps dotted strategic sites along the border and near schools. Near one isolated cluster of canvas tents, I once encountered an off-duty soldier reading in the shade. He held a well-worn copy of Walter Rodney's 1972 classic, *How Europe Underdeveloped Africa*. I had left my tattered, underlined copy in another former European colony. A dozen or so soldiers occupied an encampment in Nyakurita's area near Magadzire Primary School, built by state funds in the late 1980s. The closest secondary school at Nyafaru was a difficult daily roundtrip for even the fittest teenagers. Poorer families strained to pay the cost of boarding fees on top of tuition, while at the same time losing valuable family labor, all gambling on the future. Only a few students out of the more than one hundred who annually took the exams passed English O-levels at Nyafaru. Yet the lure of a likely ticket out of a life of manual labor, of an eventual urban economic foothold, remained strong.

"The government has forgotten us," Headman Nyakurita complained bitterly about his impoverished fate. "We have been left behind." He pointed to two barefoot children kicking a dry cob of maize converted to a soccer ball. Unable to afford school fees for all of his children, he lamented the absence of local "development" (*budiriro*), feeling spatially as well as politically peripheral, lagging in the march of modernity's progress.[2] His idiom of being "left behind" conjured an absence of forward movement in history, but also a spatial stasis amid dynamic transformations he imagined in distant sites. Other agents, other places developed by transforming space, economic opportunities, and the production of new kinds of subjects—such as those capable of passing O-level exams. He named clinics, agricultural extension services, infrastructure, and waged work as signs of development from which he felt disconnected. Even the scheme's rarely traveled dirt road was a difficult walk to his home, nestled in thick brush that cascaded down steep slopes on all sides.

While Nyakurita's home lay on Kaerezi's edge, his relationship to histories of place remained central. Active in defying colonial evictions, he had been among Rekayi's most trusted allies who helped shepherd Mugabe to Gonakudzingwa in Mozambique, where displaced squatters mingled with exiled urban nationalists. As Rekayi and Mugabe traveled to meet with FRELIMO and ZANLA cadres, the headman explained, Tangwena refugees selected Nyakurita and Didymus Mutasa, who had comanaged the Nyafaru cooperative, as leaders at Gonakudzingwa. He also credited SaTagadza, another Tangwena elder, for his leadership in exile. Most Kaerezians singled out SaTagadza in the mid-1980s as Gonakudzingwa's "leader." In Nyakurita's words, displaced squatters chose these three exilic leaders "because of our bravery [*ushingi*] during the struggle," noting that Mutasa—who became ZANU-PF's national secretary and the speaker of Parliament—helped "unite us because he was formally educated." In 1991, bitter memories recalled elite nationalists' failure to deliver on promises of liberation from poverty and oppression. "I accompanied Mugabe," Nyakurita's anger almost ached from his body, "and I sustained his survival [*ndichimuponesa*]. But they don't even consider us." His furtive gestures—at once embodied and emplaced—pointed to Mozambique's landscape, then quickly down to ground his current predicament. He scampered to one side of a dilapidated granary, clutched his stomach to mimic hunger, and then walked toward his homestead's edge to point out places he referenced. All the while, one fist smacked his other palm to punctuate key points.

A vocal critic of villagization, Headman Nyakurita described contemporary resettlement policy as "just like the **Land Tenure Act**, only hidden," using the English term for the official 1969 Rhodesian legislative instrument that helped orchestrate colonial evictions from Kaerezi. Not all government interventions, however, were unwanted. Nyakurita emphatically contrasted forms of development that "disturb people's lives" to those that were "constructive." Ancestral spirits (*vadzimu*), he insisted, had welcomed the Rural Service Center in the scheme's north where a small clinic, administrative offices, and a few salaried jobs emerged. "*Vadzimu* did not forbid them to establish it because it helps people," his face grimaced as he hit home the contrast, "not saying 'enter *maline*' because we will be given electricity. The spirit medium [*svikiro*] supports what the people want." Rekayi, who enjoyed strong support from the spirit medium, ancestral spirits, and loyal followers alike, Nyakurita recalled, "made strong laws." Before the war, he argued, "government [*hurumende*] did not smash the laws of the chieftainship and those of headmen."

Since independence, however, elite politicians drew huge salaries while neglecting the rural poor. These new rulers "made mistakes" and "disturbed things." Even the rains had stopped because "people are not respecting the country" (*kukudza nyika*). Nyakurita linked chiefdom to nation-state. Nyafaru's 1970s managers Moven Mahachi and Didymus Mutasa now owned commercial farms, he noted, and Mugabe and Edward Tekere were also rich. "I don't even have a bicycle, and I live in a thatched hut," his cascade of anger flowed into an eddy. "There is no one coming to thank us," he trailed off without invoking the implied suffering for territory. His intimate knowledge of the borderland—river crossings, hunting spots, clandestine paths—had been crucial during Mugabe's 1975 escape. At Gonakudzingwa, Nyakurita and Rekayi had placed their huts to flank Mugabe, he explained, "protecting him with our backs" (*takamudzivirira nemusana*).

Ten years after independence, he felt stabbed in the back, jettisoned by the so-called liberation he helped bring about. Barefoot and humbly attired in a tattered T-shirt, he stroked a grizzled beard while lamenting the unanswered *zvido zve povo*—at once the cries, claims, and needs of the rural poor. His populist use of the Portuguese term *povo*, a FRELIMO staple, invoked traces of anticolonial movements that transgressed colonial borders. Nyakurita's compound bore witness to his claims: mud-and-wattle huts needed rethatching, the granary needed repair, and his three wives and barefoot children all wore torn clothes. By all indications, both cash and male labor were in short supply. At least the colonial government, he argued, "gave *masabhuku* money. Oppression to people was hidden. The present government fails to recognize the importance of *masabhuku*. It doesn't give them money to buy even soap." As if on cue, a young boy

scampered by, caked in dust. Nyakurita took a long sip on his black tea. Too poor
to afford sugar, the headman bitterly tasted his daily poverty.

Colonial indirect rule, Nyakurita recalled, made headmen into salaried civil
servants. They settled disputes, collected taxes, and allocated land. After independence, he complained, headmen's "power was seized by the government." The
postcolonial state, in his view, usurped headmen's authority recognized by colonial rulers. Those powers, he argued, were "traditional," existing long before
white conquest.³ Colonialism brought oppression (*uzhinyiriri*). He cited land
and labor policies, mass detentions and arrests during Smith's heyday, and counterinsurgency operations during the war. Whites seized land by force (*kupamba*),
evictions from Gaeresi Ranch representing the epitome of racial injustice. As
a result of white "oppression," Nyakurita "joined the struggle," shepherding
Mugabe and Tekere to safety in Mozambique's liberated territory. Shared politics,
history, and geography articulated in a common struggle for a *nyika*. But whose
nyika, what *nyika*, and with what rights accorded to those who suffered for it?

Nyakurita's answer was emphatic: "*Masabhuku* should allocate land because
they are the inhabitants of the area. The government should have formed com-
mittees where headmen allocate land, not installing people to whom they give
their laws like the resettlement officer." Headmen, as inhabitants, "know territory" (*kuziva nyika*): the history of settlements, lineage locations, and claimants'
rights; sacred places, prohibited practices, and appropriate appeasement; rightful
relations between people and place—in short, laws *of* the land. In contrast,
salaried civil servants now imposed law *on* the land, enforcing policies out of
place in several senses.

Nyakurita implicitly defended the integration of a salaried *sabhuku* into indirect rule when government utilized localized knowledge that disciplined subjects' settlement. He had no nostalgia for an imagined *Pax Brittanica* or ideologies of Rhodesian benevolent paternalism. Rather, he argued for a particular
practice of government: the *imbrication* of salaried headmen into land allocation.
Postcolonial government, in his vision, should fuse precolonial forms of traditional authority with colonial-era positions. While he wanted "more" development, he wanted *different* practices of government, not more or less of it. The
Rural Service Center's clinic represented wise government; imposed settlement
grids "disturbed" territory and its inhabitants. Like most Kaerezians, Nyakurita
was neither for nor against government. Rather, he sought to shape how subjects
would be governed.

Government (*hurumende*), he argued, should act on Kaerezians' actions, enabling them to improve themselves—through better transport of agricultural inputs and crops to market; by building the infrastructure of modernity, for example, clinics, grinding mills, secondary schools; and with a salary to pay his children's school fees so they could eventually pursue wages in distant urban sites. In his vision, improved spatial integration, notably, with the nation-state, would pull Kaerezi "forward" in history, producing developmental progress. As a colonial ranch tenant, Nyakurita fought for rights to both land in Kaerezi and labor conditions that would allow him to migrate seasonally to seek urban wages. His postcolonial position echoed that earlier one. Translocal connections need not erode local land rights. Amid conditions not of his choosing or making, Nyakurita differentiated between desirable translocal linkages and those he deemed unjust.

For him, across independence, land remained decisive to rights, rule, and freedom. By excluding headmen from control over land, he told me, the postcolonial state did not "rule" (*kutonga*) but rather "forced" (*kumanikidza*) people into settlement patterns against their wishes. He refracted personal victimization—and one shared by his fellow headmen—produced by postcolonial rule through the prism of populism. By not acting on subjects' actions, shaping the conditions under which the *povo* would exercise their own agency, government ceased to govern. By force, it *imposed* its will instead of following the people's. Nyakurita thus suggested that government should support headmen to rule justly, providing an enabling milieu where *masabhuku* and commoners alike would practice the powers of postcolonial freedom.

I asked Nyakurita how his "book" passed through generations. Was it inherited or elected? Some referred to his area as Nyapimbi. Did this mean the book had changed hands? Generations before, I learned, Nyapimbi had migrated to Mozambique. He gave the book to a friend who, in turn, later gave it to Headman Nyakurita's father—married to the friend's daughter. Nyapimbi's friend still lived in Mozambique, where he fled in the 1970s when evicted from Gaeresi Ranch. Nyakurita passed the book onto his son, Driver, who still held the position. A stint steering a cooperative's tractor had earned him the nickname. I asked Driver if Nyapimbi's friend could return to reclaim the book. "Yes, because it is his name which appears in Nyanga at the offices there." Even along Mozambique's remote border—where political allegiances, marriage ties, and colonial evictions shaped the passage of a headman's book—government technologies channeled authority through the traces of indirect rule. Nyakurita vehemently criticized the postcolonial "government" for its disrespect of headmen. Yet he also located the basis for a *sabhuku*'s sanctioned rule in a book deep in the belly of government, securely inscribed in state records. Fusing temporalities, in postcolonial Zimbabwe, he cited colonial rule to buttress claims to authority he traced to precolonial roots.

Many echoed Nyakurita's valorization of headmen's localized knowledge. During a break from planting maize in one of her Tsatse fields, MaiChipo claimed that the local headman should allocate land because "he first lived here. *Sabhuku* knows places that are sacred, but the government doesn't know that." State officials, many argued, were ignorant of ancestral rights, including those enunciated by spirits. For this reason, residents best "knew the territory." This knowledge included *relations* among people, place, and ancestral spirits; among the visible and invisible; between the past and present; and between the local and the translocal, such as rights retained by migrant laborers. Subjecting oneself to those who "knew territory," some argued, promoted just rule. Territorial ignorance could injure the living and the dead, transgressing temporalities of rights and remembrance kept alive through practices often unintelligible to "outsiders."

Sabhuku Bias

In 1991, Angela and her husband feared losing all land rights in Kaerezi. The District Administrator's threatening letter, described in chapter 1, demanded that they demonstrate occupation of their state-allocated Nyamutsapa plot. Yet building there explicitly defied the chiefly edict, strongly supported by his headmen, forbidding any construction in the lines. Angela invoked rights (*kodzero*) to land given to her by government. These, she stressed, trumped the claims of chief and headmen. Hers was a complex case. She lived with her husband on the outskirts of Nyafaru's property. After independence, the cooperative agreed to let five families of shareholders work smallholdings on portions of its estate. Friendly with Rekayi, Angela also hid Mugabe's books from Rhodesian forces during his escape. In the early 1980s, Rekayi endorsed her family's Nyafaru land rights, echoing those of the cooperative's management, giving Angela strong claims on private property located inside a chiefdom. A decade later, with Rekayi dead and the struggling cooperative plagued by management problems, her twin pillars of conditional land rights collapsed. While her elderly husband herded cattle for the cooperative, his declining mobility further eroded their residential rights. The DA's letter arrived amid this convergence, encouraging Angela to seek a more secure place for her family.

Fresh in the wake of the letter's arrival, she dug a large ditch near her resettlement plot. Her two daughters helped her mix mud, clay, and straw with their feet—turning soil and fiber into molded bricks laid to dry in the sun. Angela became a fixture at the new site, clearing grass, leveling ground, and assembling bricks. Initially, less important than establishing a hut was to inscribe her intentions on the landscape, thus following the DA's letter of the law. I never saw her husband James at the plot, though he might have helped clear it. His conspicuous absence appeared tactical. Angela told me of an angry confrontation at their Nyafaru homestead when Headman Mweya's ally visited to complain about their construction in the planned "village." As pointing fingers hardened to fists, the two men almost came to blows. Angela implied that James's absence from the disputed site defused the risk of violence. Much as Angela had joined the front lines of protests against colonial evictions, placing her body between male labor tenants and armed Rhodesian police, her embodied labor insulated her husband from postcolonial threats of physical force.

Mweya, Nyamutsapa's *sabhuku*, became outraged at her direct defiance of the chiefly decree, one he repeatedly echoed at public meetings. Suffering from malaria and severely hobbled with an infected foot, he dispatched his ally to the chief, who called a *dare*, a council or court to deliberate the case. James remained conveniently absent, so Angela provided her own defense. During the war, Angela's savvy performance of gendered subordination to Rhodesian soldiers had concealed Rekayi beneath bales of thatching grass. Tactically, she then played off Rhodesian expectations that women were, in her words, "politically helpless." In 1991, she performed demure respect at the chief's *dare*, apologizing for the affront, agreeing to shift slightly her new homestead. Part of it, she assured the chief, would extend beyond the government's lines. She paid a small fine, convincing the chief's "police" sent to scrutinize her site that she complied with her sovereign. The verb used to chart Angela's case at the chief's court, *kutongwa*, pulls together a sense of "resolution," "decision," and an object of "rule." By all indications, including Angela's own accounts, the "shift" was more gestural than actual, more perspectival than physical. Yet by subordinating her practices to *both* chief and state, Angela effectively secured a stronger foothold.

Angela's politics of location straddled two regimes of rule. Her agency became effective by *subjecting* herself to competing modes of power. If state officials threatened to evict squatters who failed to occupy their assigned plots, her hut demonstrated adherence to a governmental scheme. She could appeal to ignorance or confusion on the plot's precise location or to intimidation by the headman and chief to explain her slight transgression of state-imposed spatiality. Or she could, over time, shift her new homestead, building more huts on her assigned site. At the same time, she convinced the chief that she honored his decree. Her room for maneuver emerged *through*, not outside or between, spatial modes of power. Both chiefly and state rule sought to discipline Kaerezi's space, attempting to arrange bodies in spacing, shaping the conduct of residents who would discipline themselves and each other. Citizens of a nation-state who were also land-hungry settlers lived in a development scheme. Subjects of a chief lived in his *nyika*. "The lines" inscribed both where subjects crafted provisional places to dwell.

Despite the chief's appeasement, Headman Mweya remained angered by Angela's challenge to the laws of the land in *his* area. Not long after her appearance at the chief's court, I encountered her knee-deep in mud and clay one afternoon near her villagization plot. She jumped out of the pit, cheerfully greeting me, and began an unprovoked critique of Mweya. Flecks of mud splattered on me amid her effusive gestures. I barely translated the idiom "Here's mud in your eye" before she launched into a spirited rant. "Long ago," she began with an imagined horizon deep in the past, "*masabhuku* allocated land, but it was seen that they were biased in favor of their relatives. The resettlement officer now has the duty of allocating land, which means he has been given that by the 'eye' of the government." She clarified a historical bias: "*Masabhuku* gave good land to their relatives." Angela challenged those who argued that state officials were blind to complex histories of past land claims, sacred places, and localized forms of esoteric knowledge. The abstract eye of government avoided the nepotism she accused headmen of practicing. Shades of Bentham's panopticon, the device that used visual technologies of surveillance to induce self-discipline among those whose practices it targeted, illuminated her image.[4] Yet her ongoing conflict with Headman Mweya demonstrated his continued involvement in settlement. She used the past rhetorically, arguing implicitly for a regime change that would further marginalize her foe Mweya. She placed good government as the rightful successor to a biased local despot. The pit she dug, the bricks she molded, and the hut she constructed materially and discursively inscribed her political positioning on the landscape.

Angela's *sabhuku* was also her brother-in-law, sharing a father but not a mother with her husband James. There had long been bad blood over Mweya's treatment of Angela's mother-in-law, an elderly widow. In 1987, Mweya accompanied the state officials who pegged fields and residential plots in Nyamutsapa as they recorded the names of settlers allocated parcels of land. Colonial administrators had similarly incorporated "traditional" leaders in their attempts to implement centralization in the 1930s and the Native Land Husbandry Act in the late 1950s. The inclusions of indirect rule, colonial officials hoped, would help secure popular consent and manufacture legitimacy for the exercise. In Kaerezi, postcolonial inclusions of headmen in state-orchestrated allocations confused perceptions of headmen's "official" relationship to land rights. During the demarcation exercises, administrators allegedly allocated James's mother a fine field. Months later, Mweya claimed to reserve the plot for one of his sons, then working for wages far from Kaerezi. Mweya, many claimed, switched the plots that had been recorded on the government registry, leaving the widow a "field of rocks." Poor slope and distance to any water source further impoverished the site. The switch effected both the plot's precise location and its quality.

Angela and James's family cared for his widowed mother. In 1991, she moved from a small, dilapidated hut near her disputed fields to Angela's homestead, more than a kilometer away on Nyafaru property. Since the widow no longer commanded family labor to cultivate much arable land, Angela and her children labored in these fields to reap harvests. I had helped them carry dried maize from the widow's granary over a steep ridge to their Nyafaru home. Angela and James, who provided for the widow's subsistence, would be prime beneficiaries of any new fields she might claim. Mweya's alleged offense not only dishonored an elderly widow; it also thwarted an extended family's access to critical productive resources. While James and Mweya shared a father, their family feud pitted against each other two extended kin groups within the same lineage.

Ignorant of these tensions, I confusedly witnessed James's viscerally angry accusation of his brother's illicit switch of plots at one of the first large gatherings I attended in Nyamutsapa. Leaping to his feet and shaking his fist, James took off his Coke bottle–thick glasses, throwing his cane to the ground. Mweya stood, rolling his sleeves while flexing his arms as if to fight. Several elders and the resettlement officer intervened to prevent a brawl. Angela's generic description of land disputes thus carried more than the usual strain of normative valuation. A headman, she insisted, should discuss with advisors (*makurukota*) how best to resolve a dispute. "Some might say let one person use the land. Others might suggest dividing the land; then they would put boundaries on it. These people will not fight over the boundaries because it was done in the presence of many people." As Angela's experience at the chief's *dare* underscored, *communal hegemony* could emerge through constructed consent.[5] Moreover, a ruling did not necessarily end a dispute, at times leaving open future repositioning. Yet for Angela, a *dare* performed the task of public witnessing, provisionally binding participants to a decision. When she testified at the chief's *dare*, she performed subjection to his rule. Yet her site for hut construction also subjected her practices to a government grid of spatiality. In the cross fire of competing regimes of rule, rights were conditional rather than absolute; social relations, public memory, and situated practices all saturated struggles to assert entitlements.

Without prompting, Angela subordinated headmen to chiefly rule: "*Sabhuku* is a dog to the chief because he watches and tells the chief. If a *sabhuku* fails to resolve a case, the people will go to the chief. Or they will complain to the chief that he is not a good *sabhuku*." In her idealized version, subalterns report to their sovereign to critique a *sabhuku*'s unjust rule. She had little faith in the acting chief's abilities to discipline his subjects. Yet she consistently emphasized the derivative authority of a headman: "Mostly people follow the laws that come from the chief or rainmaker. If the government comes here, they go to Nya-huruwa and the chief. These laws come from the leaders [*vanhu vakuru*]. *Sabhuku* will also be given the laws like the child of the chief. It's like a dog that is sent. If the *sabhuku* imposes his own laws, he will be wronging [*kukanganisa*] the people. We won't live well. . . . *Sabhuku* is the watchdog of the chief. The watchdog must not be the leader." It is difficult not to hear Angela's historical account as a scathing critique of Mweya. Rather than stand as a dictatorial decree, a headman's decisions should be communally conducted. In her vision, the "eyes" of public witnessing promote accountability and good government, conducting conduct. For her, the *sabhuku* should be subject to both chiefly and popular approval. He should receive "laws," but should not impose his own on unwilling subjects.

I was surprised to find that one of Headman Mweya's own sons shared Angela's concerns. David stood to benefit from practices of nepotism. But he was an articulate critic of headmen who abused their authority. While Mweya drank, propitiated ancestral spirits, and was known for his hot temper, David was a teetotaler, worshipped at the Gumbos' church, and stood as a paragon of politeness. His father remained frosty toward Angela and James. In contrast, David's fondness of them was palpable, and he offered them his labor, even to help plow the disputed fields. He lived with his wife and young child at Mweya's homestead, suspended without pay from a hotel job some eighty kilometers from Kaerezi. By most accounts, a supervisor had stolen from the till, while the subordinates suffered. Recently married, David had sought his own homestead and fields in

Kaerezi. He followed the resettlement officer's advice, journeying to the district center offices in search of an application for a plot in the scheme. An official told him that wageworkers were ineligible for resettlement, and David's recent employment placed him in limbo. David left confused and frustrated.

Despite the bureaucratic quagmire, he did not hesitate when I asked who should allocate land in a resettlement scheme: "If the *sabhuku* does it, he will favor [*kufevhera*] his relatives. His relatives will be given good land, while his enemies will be given places with rocks that they will not like." In contrast, he offered without my prompting, "The government just pegs and puts numbers, they do not know who is to occupy the stand—whether it is *sabhuku*, a church leader, or whoever." While rocky fields worked rhetorically to characterize land unfit for cultivation, David's critique of *sabhuku* bias also targeted his father's nepotism. I sensed no jealousy toward his absent elder brother. On good terms with many relatives who had strained relations with his father, the churchgoing David made preachers as well as headmen subject to state law. Angela, but not her husband James, worshipped in David's church. James shared Mweya's practice of ancestral propitiation and his taste for millet beer. What produced and aligned shared interests were affinities forged through relations rather than structural determinations of lineage, kinship, or religion.

David and Angela voiced a perspective shared by many: an impersonal state bureaucracy countered *sabhuku* bias, promoting more equitable land rights. Headman Mweya and other commoners, in contrast, cited state arbitrariness as a problem: allocating land on sacred sites and other prohibited places. Both positions emphasized the *quality* rather than the *quantity* of land, sites imbued with cultural practices rather than the essential natural properties stressed by land-use planners. The process of securing a sustainable settlement site required cultivating social relations as well as crops, negotiating fields of power as well as those of soil and rocks.

Mujuru complained bitterly about resettlement policy: "They are now on the wrong track because it's no longer a local person who allocates the land to his people. It's now government-chosen people who allocate land instead of the 'land's owners' [*varidzi ve nyika*]." Mujuru was a close friend and ally of Headman Mweya. Even critics of Mweya's rule accorded Mujuru tremendous respect, some recalling Rhodesian police setting dogs on him during colonial evictions. He often moderated discussions at public meetings, giving women the opportunity to voice their opinions and politely asking musing elders for nuggets of wisdom to shape a debate. "Now," he complained, "even on a sacred place someone is being settled or plowing the land." One of his age-mates lamented: "The government is now abandoning our African culture [*tsika*] and taking the white one where if you want a field, you go and report; then the field will be pegged." Here, critique pitted white against black, colonial oppression against an authentic African culture, locating that tension in postcolonial time and space. The elder wove racialized oppression into a centralized, top-down system of land allocation. Rather than choosing their own sites, settlers were assigned them. When officials pegged fields, as they did during centralization, the Native Land Husbandry Act, and in the resettlement scheme, they *fixed* Africans to a single holding. Two forms of freedom were denied: settlers' selection of their own site and the cultivation of multiple fields spatially separated. For those favoring headmen's involvement in land allocation, *sabhuku* savoir faire enabled these freedoms.

Emancipation and Equality

In 1988, in the wake of government demarcations, a few Nyamutsapa families began building mud-and-wattle huts in their assigned residential plots within a planned village site. Walter, who worked at a bar in the district tourist hotel, and his young wife, MaiHurudza, felt that the state-allocated plot offered stronger security of tenure than their own homestead. Their friend and neighbor, SaGumbo, also began building a hut in his allocated stand, as did a young couple evicted from Tsanga Valley the previous year. Acting Chief Magwendere fined each of them, ordering Walter and SaGumbo to destroy their unfinished structures and return to their former homesteads. In the early 1990s, ghosts of former intentions haunted the lines. Tall grass grew around half-finished hut frames; weeds covered poles lashed with strips of bark, a roof denied its planned telos atop a new home. The young immigrant couple managed to stay in the lines, paying a fine but continuing construction. Neighbors explained that their youth, poverty, and status as immigrants convinced the acting chief to let them stay in the lines. Unlike the other two families, they had no other huts to call home.

MaiHurudza and her husband were among the "squatters" who received the DA's threatening letter. The rainy season was approaching, and Walter was, as usual, away at his hotel job. I joined a few neighbors who gathered for winter plowing at MaiHurudza's. They yoked oxen mixed from two families' herds; a teenager from yet another family joined us. The plow cut through a fallow field, last planted three years before. Chunks of caked earth emerged in our wake, softer soil coming up where the plow cut deep. With few rocks, a gentle slope, and good soil, this field made for prime land. Nestled below a steep ridge, it received ample water supply from a nearby spring. More than a kilometer's walk away—jumping a stream, scampering up and down a steep ravine, and climbing a long slope—lay the planned resettlement grid.

A few days after winter plowing, MaiHurudza's infectious smile greeted me. During a short break in her endless task of chores, she complained that "*masabhuku* are now taking the law into their hands. They are telling people to plow where they want them to, against the government's laws [*mitemo ye hurumende*]." For MaiHurudza, laws should emanate from a national *nyika*, a postcolonial state. By attempting to allocate land, headmen subverted government, illegitimately exercising powers they seized rather than deserved.

What, I asked, should constitute the basis for land rights? "As I see it," MaiHurudza paused thoughtfully, "the right [*kodzero*] must come from the government. The reason is because the *masadunhu* themselves used to say this area was owned by my sister, so it's my *gura*." She used the term for a fallow field, one where usufruct is often inherited patrilineally. And rather than *masabhuku*, the colonial authority backed by the apparatus of indirect rule, she named *masadunhu*, figures linked to both an indefinite traditional past and to chiefly rather than state rule. By claiming a sister's fallow field, a *sadunhu*'s gendered expropriation also dispossessed another lineage—where a sister might marry. His act represented gendered inequalities, as well as those between lineages.

Women who married commoners excluded from the benefits of headmen's nepotism, as MaiHurudza did, became doubly disenfranchised from land rights. She cited past inequalities, shaped by headmen's injustice, as the reason "some like us were failing to get enough land. When the government came, an area previously owned by one person was now utilized by three people. It's better now because we are all emancipated [*tasunungukirwa*]." MaiHurudza echoed the rhetoric of a national liberation struggle, mapping an emancipated body politic to the embodied cultivation of fields, rights, and political subjects. Struggling to feed four children while her husband worked in a hotel, her relative freedom remained subject to inequalities of wealth, labor burdens, and resource rights. She was well aware of both gender and socioeconomic differences within Kaerezi, and experienced the rough-and-tumble of suffering for territory: witnessing her parents' huts destroyed as a young schoolgirl; living through her kidnap by Rhodesian police; and in 1988, taking heat at the chief's *dare* for building in the lines.

For MaiHurudza, the liberation struggle promised freedom from racialized oppression, but also from the dictates of traditional authorities. "We were told that people are no longer to be controlled by headmen and chiefs," she reflected. "Nowadays, chairpersons and the District Councils are the people who allocate land. So to us, that law is not new because when we were fighting during the war, we were told that fields are going to be pegged. Everything was going to be represented by the right person. What *masabhuku* did is now an old formula. They gained money from cases resolved at the chief's court." Her populist "we" linked anticolonial struggles to postcolonial land rights, nationalist promises of the past becoming state law after independence. Throwing off colonial shackles meant freedom from chiefs' and headmen's authority over land. Elections, rather than tribal tradition, produced rights and political representation. MaiHurudza mapped chiefs and headmen not to a timeless past, but to colonialism's indirect rule. Postcolonial freedom, in her vision, required subjection to government.

Postcolonial headmen, for her, practiced a temporality and spatiality of colonialism, attempting to control land and profit personally. MaiHurudza echoed many who witnessed a time *before* headmen allocated land, a time when people farmed "freely" (*madiro*). Many invoked self-selected land as a foundational freedom independence should restore. MaiHurudza stressed the realpolitik of land hunger in contrast to a past of relative land abundance: "We now have many more people, which means we must all have an equal share. Long ago, people used to go and live on a mountain or on a rocky place. But the government is now settling people on better land. You might fail to have a good harvest, but you will have been settled on good land." She wove together two formative inequalities: racialized land policies that pushed blacks onto overcrowded reserves on marginal lands; and inequitable access to land within African communities. For all its problems, postcolonial resettlement policy, she argued, delivered on both fronts.

Resettlement Rights

Ziko, a Nyafaru schoolteacher born on Gaeresi Ranch in the early 1960s, recalled the 1972 raid when armed police loaded him into a truck bound for Harare. At the time, most of his family lived clandestinely in the nearby mountains, plowing fields on the ranch while sentries watched for the approach of police or troops. Brian, another of the schoolchildren captured, in 1991 described the Rhodesian police handcuffing Ziko nearly two decades before. Large manacles allegedly fell off every time the frightened boy put his skinny arms down. Brian claimed the terrified Ziko implored a Rhodesian soldier not to shoot him: "Please, my wrists are small. I'm not trying to escape." Dumped in a Harare social welfare compound, what they called "a cross between a prison and an orphanage," Ziko and Brian tried to escape, scaling the high wire fence. A thoroughfare with cars and a traffic light, strange new urban technologies, foiled their plan. They asked an older man to point them in the direction of "Tangwena," hundreds of kilometers away. Their desired destination, an anchor for identity, betrayed their forced displacement. The man worked at the welfare compound, and took them back inside their fenced domain. "We just wanted to go home," Ziko told me soberly in 1991.

Since his marriage to another Nyafaru schoolteacher in 1989, Ziko and his wife hoped to be allocated land in the resettlement scheme. He was, after all, a native son, his parents prominent in defiance of colonial evictions and then living in Kaerezi. Ziko, his wife, and their young daughter shared modest stone housing with other teachers at Nyafaru. They cooked outside by open fire, sheltered by windbreaks made of rough planks. One cold night, we huddled close to the fire as the mountain winds whipped through gaps in the boards. Ziko shared his difficulties in acquiring a resettlement plot: "I am working at Nyafaru but wanted to get my own land. You have to be clever nowadays, approaching traditional leaders and the resettlement officer." Yet the process proved a bureaucratic obstacle course:

> First, I went to the resettlement officer, who told me to go see a certain Masuka in the DA's office. So I went to see Masuka. He asked me where I lived and what I was doing. I said I teach at Nyafaru but was born in Bvumbwe, a place close to Nyafaru within the Tangwena area. He said that I was working and therefore could not get land in a resettlement scheme. I protested, saying, "I was born there, I have no land. What do you people in government expect us to do?" He said, "Your father will have to carry you on his back. You can't get land in a resettlement scheme because you are employed. Try to go to a Communal Area and speak with a *sabhuku* and chief. You can get Communal Area land while you have a job. Getting land in a Communal Area is easier."

Masuka, the district official, repeated national resettlement policy. He mapped two different administrative authorities to two distinct, mutually exclusive spaces. Citing Ziko's employment, Masuka denied him resettlement rights, sending him to seek land in a conventional Communal Area. Neither birthright nor land hunger, for Masuka, buttressed Ziko's claim. Yet Masuka's position contradicted the special provisions allowing wageworking Kaerezians to be allocated land in the scheme. The DA, resettlement officer, and provincial DERUDE officials all corroborated the waiving of an unemployment criterion for Kaerezi-born settler selection. Officials reiterated this policy at numerous public meetings in the scheme. While he attended several Kaerezi meetings in the 1980s, Masuka had not been there in years. He was out of this loop, apparently unaware of this exception. During the war, he had spent time in Eastern Europe, training to run what he conceived as Zimbabwe's socialist nation-state. Over beers in the district center, he praised the virtues of centralized state planning and its bureaucratic efficiency. The contingencies that converged when Masuka informed Ziko about his land rights in Kaerezi were thoroughly translocal: the communicative challenges of "government at a distance" that left Masuka out of the loop between district, provincial, and national pronouncements on Kaerezi's exceptional settler-selection criteria; his recent absence from the scheme where those exceptions remained visibly inscribed on the landscape itself; and perhaps his transcontinental experience during the war.

Ziko, the only university graduate I knew living in Kaerezi, had long negotiated bureaucracies. Others might well have taken Masuka's answer as "the law" (*mutemo*), stopping their bid for land. But Ziko met with the resettlement officer who admitted his colleague's mistake and confirmed the policy exception. "He said, 'No problem, here are some papers to fill out.' You need to cover both possibilities," Ziko emphasized, "to talk with traditional leaders and also the resettlement officer—in case resettlement came." For Ziko, resettlement meant villagization, concentrated linear grids. In contrast, "traditional" authorities worked outside state lines. Ziko realized that secure land rights required both channels of recognition. Shortly after Ziko's marriage, his father had helped him survey several spots near the homestead where his parents returned after the war, resettling themselves. Most neighbors shared their lineage. Once they chose a site, several lineage elders helped lobby the *sabhuku* to recognize Ziko's landholding. Only after he had laid this groundwork, did he approach government officials. A number of young married couples pursued similar dual-pronged tactics in the early 1990s.

Born in Nyamutsapa, MaiChipo worked at Nyafaru women's weaving cooperative. A small sheep herd supplied wool, which was spun and knit into rugs and sweaters marketed at the district's tourist hotels and in town. MaiChipo was among the few women I knew who actively negotiated for land with a headman. Captured in the same 1972 raid that seized Ziko, she eventually went to a mission school. She then worked at a cooperative farm outside the district where she married. The young couple moved to Nyafaru shortly after independence. "My husband was not as fortunate as others," she explained. "His father was in Johannesburg, and his mother worked on white farms, so there was no *musha* [home]. We just thought on our own where to go because he had no brothers."

"When did you get your first *musha*?" I wondered aloud, using the term that melded a material homestead and an affective tie. "In 1982, we got our first *musha* in Nyamutsapa. We went to *sabhuku*, telling him that we had seen somewhere to stay, so may we. He agreed." Since I rarely heard of women's involvement in such land negotiations, I asked MaiChipo how she had played a key role. "I am Nyamutsapa born," she explained, "so I said: 'Father, I want somewhere to stay,' and he agreed." This figurative father, Mweya, shared a lineage with her biological father James, Angela's husband. Years later, when government officials pegged plots in Nyamutsapa, they assigned MaiChipo and her husband the same parcel "agreed" to by Headman Mweya. The process of securing land rights might span years and hinged on social relations, the acknowledgment of multiple authorities often at odds with each other, and perseverance.

The resettlement officer complained frequently about headmen's land allocation that defied state legal procedures. In theory, any prospective settler family should apply for resettlement rights by submitting a form to the Ministry of Local Government in the district offices. The elected District Council had legal authority over approving settlers. In practice, the resettlement officer and District Administrator vetted applications. The council's role was principally to ensure that settlers were not double-dipping by retaining rights in the district's Communal Areas. In rare cases, polygamists played this game by establishing their wives on multiple homesteads spread across different land categories. For the scheme's on-site administrator, good government meant ensuring resettlement rights for the landless. He answered to superiors who juggled an entire district.

A 1991 monthly resettlement scheme report noted that "although there are people who are in need of land they prefer to approach the traditional leadership who illegally offer them land, thus avoiding the normal channel whereby people are required to register."[6] In 1992, many spoke of Headman Mweya "threatening" a Kaerezi-born man allocated resettlement rights in Nyamutsapa, dissuading him from farming or establishing a homestead. The man worked and lived at Nyafaru, waiting for a decisive political turn before physically moving his family to the site. State officials openly complained of headmen's "illegal allocations," and of their threats and intimidation of "law-abiding settlers." Whose law of the land would prevail was far from settled.

Self-Settlement

Many referred to Mujuru as the Nyamutsapa *sabhuku*'s vice, using the English word, or as his *mubatsiri* (helper or assistant). They elected him chairman of their Village Development Committee (VIDCO) in 1986. But the paper construct proved ineffectual, the committee not having met in years. Loosely modeled on wartime ZANU-PF grassroots cells, in theory VIDCOS channeled concerns to a ward-level entity and then to the democratically elected District Development Committee in Nyanga Township, where rural representatives met monthly. In practice, the Rekayi Tangwena Ward seat had been vacant for years. Kaerezi's officer explained that because "kraalheads don't want their power taken by VIDCOS," the democratic institutions remained "ineffective." He recalled that during elections in 1986, due to illiteracy and irregularities with hand counts, "nominated candidates stood in front of the group and people would line up behind the candidate of their choice." Not surprisingly, voting surveillance enabled strong headmen to shape the electoral contours of community consent. In those areas where others won elections, "people were threatened by kraalheads" and became "victimized." To further complicate grassroots electoral efforts, VIDCOS cut across headmen's territories, jurisdictions corresponding to planned "villages" that remained empty.

Despite these obstacles, the resettlement officer still introduced Mujuru as the VIDCO chair at public meetings with visiting state officials, giving the phantom institution a performed presence. Kaerezians, in contrast, associated Mujuru with Mweya's rule. Ironically, state promotion of development democracy propped up traditional channels of authority by giving government recognition to a headman's vice. Mujuru's prominence during Gaeresi Ranch skirmishes also accorded him deep respect. I wondered how he perceived land rights long before the era of colonial evictions. When a *mutorwa* (stranger, immigrant) arrived in the area before labor conflicts, I asked, what role did the *sabhuku* play in allocating land? "The *sabhuku* would look and see whether there was a place in his area. Then he would tell the person that he has a plot, and they would go to see it together. If the person likes it, then the *sabhuku* would tell his people that they have a *mutorwa*. If the people agree, the *sabhuku* will go to inform the chief that the name of the person is such-and-such, that she/he comes from such-and-such a place, and that I have allocated them a place to live at this particular spot." For Mujuru, a *sabhuku* served as a middleman between an immigrant, new neighbors, and the chief. Spatially and socially guided to a number of specific sites, a *mutorwa* selects, conditional on neighbors' consent. Significantly, a *sabhuku* legitimated settlement by *remapping* person to place, subject to territory. He told the chief both the location of the *mutorwa*'s former and new home. Knowing where immigrants came from meant having a sense of their conduct in that previous place, their neighborliness, and their reasons for leaving. In turn, as Headman Nyakurita argued, any *sabhuku* knew past and present lineage rights. A headman could discern the difference between fields possessed yet currently fallow and those abandoned by someone who had permanently left the area. And he knew the sacred places to avoid, the boundaries of others' claims. Many echoed Mujuru's formula. If land was ample and unclaimed by others' usufruct, a *sabhuku* was likely to allocate it to a "good" *mutorwa*. No one recalled a *sabhuku* refusing a request for land by despotic decree.

SaGumbo and I were plowing one of his fallow fields, the afternoon winds turning sweat into a chill as twilight approached. The team of four paired two of his oxen with a friend's beasts. Both generously loaned oxen and family labor to MaiHurudza, where I had also recently helped plow new furrows. Practices of neighborliness lingered with shadows as we unyoked the cattle and penned them in SaGumbo's kraal. He carried a harness back to repair by firelight, and we spoke around the smoky glow of the cook hut. SaGumbo explained that when he was young, people chose where to live "freely." "Everyone had their own homestead. There was nothing like 'go and live there.' A person lived where she or he wanted [*munhu aigara paanoda*]." A *sabhuku* might intervene in a land dispute and was informed of where people settled. However, SaGumbo insisted that specific sites were not "allocated," but, rather, were chosen "freely," again repeating the popular idiom of *madiro*. Sites for homesteads and fields were not imposed on residents, but rather identified, investigated, and negotiated with the help of neighbors. The *sabhuku*, in this vision, enabled commoners to exercise agency, helping to smooth the social—the milieu of relations, obligations, and potential conflicts that both enabled and constrained subjects.

Many shared a vision of past self-settlement where chief and headmen legitimated already established land claims. Neighbors remained integral to spatial discipline. But chiefs and headmen, in many accounts, did not initiate land allocation, merely ratifying it. When people approached headmen in the 1940s and 1950s, he recalled, "You mention that you want to live at such-and-such a place near such-and-such a person. You have to go and hear from the neighbor to see if she or he wants to live next to you. Then the person agrees. *Sabhuku* will have accomplished his duty." Settlers initiated the process, selecting their own sites in consultation with a headman. After negotiating with neighbors, they then informed the headman, who bore witness rather than actively allocating rights. Wise residents (*vagari*) commanded localized knowledge of potentially competing land claims and neighbors' compatibility. For SaGumbo, residents rather than headmen best "knew territory" (*kuziva nyika*).

In the middle of the twentieth century, many elders elaborated, a life course of maturation shaped spatial trajectories of increasing self-selection as young couples moved away from a husband's patrilineal home. In 1992, Mbuya Tagadza—the widow of one of Gonakudzingwa's leaders—passed away, her funeral attended by hundreds. We had spoken the year before about the era of her own marriage. She insisted that new couples were "given fields by their parents. People did not go to the *masabhuku*." Like others, she spoke of mothers-in-law "giving" parcels to new couples. Wives effectively managed these fields, usually located within the wider holdings of a lineage patriarch. Both mothers and fathers appeared to bestow land to sons and daughters-in-law, parents informing headmen and chief *after* establishing—through sons—a patrilineage claim to specific sites.

Married in the 1930s, Tendai, born on the rainmaker's range in Tsatse kraal, first lived with his new wife at his parents' *musha*. While he was away much of the time as a migrant laborer, his wife lived close to his mother in a polygamous compound. After their first child, Tendai's father told him that "I must have my own *musha* because now I also have my own family." So he built a hut at his father's *musha*, where he lived for five or six years. "When I saw that it's no longer good to stay with my father," Tendai explained, "I told him, 'I now want my own *musha*.'" His father advised, "'If you see a place that is best for you, then I will allow you to go and stay there.' I told him to go and look at the place so he sees how it looks. He said the law is I have to put a peg as the foundation to show that we have agreed. I started to build." His father's endorsement, relayed to the headman, proved crucial: "Father then said '*sadunhu*, my son is now living there,' so that it did not surprise him tomorrow. That is the law. . . . Your father is your chief and *sabhuku*." Many people charted similar routes to relative autonomy. Adult men and their wives established land rights through maturation: marriage, having children, establishing "one's own family." Lineage patriarchs and their wives encouraged sons to establish their own homesteads. If they approved, fathers informed headmen to recognize this land claim beyond the lineage.

Metaphorizing a father as chief and headman, Tendai echoed Foucault's model of the household as a template for proper rule. Good fathers managed the *oikos* with care for the welfare of each and all, encouraging couples to settle themselves. Yet a Kaerezian *musha* is not a Greek *oikos*, and a provincialized governmentality needs to grapple with the complex cultural idioms assembled through practices that cultivate a *musha*. Senior lineage men, for Tendai, exercised influence over the conduct of their subordinate kinsmen. Patriarchal power worked through subjects' relative freedom. Yet many wives emerged as the effective managers of homesteads and fields, while their husbands pursued migrant wages. These gendered livelihood practices and their distinct spatiality brought women, as wives and mothers, into their sons' and husbands' attempts to secure patrilineal rights to land. Women's agency proved critical, yet became part of patrilineal land rights that excluded women from any independent access to fields of their own. Subjection to patriarchal authority became the condition of possibility for a young couple's relative spatial and social autonomy, phrased as "farming freely" (*kurima madiro*). Practices perceived to thwart freedom were frequently coded as oppression (*uzhinyiriri*). While headmen invoked tradition to legitimate their authority over land allocation, commoners often invoked a populist counter-discourse of relative freedom that emerged from subjection to patriarchal authority within lineage politics.

Despite conditional patriarchal approval, many Kaerezians insisted that fields were not traditionally allocated. On Gaeresi Ranch, SaMuzenda recalled, "*sabhuku* was the one who saw to it that when livestock strayed into a neighbor's field and ate crops, the case was resolved." He admitted that headmen had responsibilities ensuring that people did not cultivate in sacred areas "where farming is not allowed." But as long as territorial spirits were not unsettled, married couples could farm freely and select their own sites. He emphatically insisted that "fields were not allocated [*paisachekwa minda*]." Among the many terms for allocating or distributing land, SaMuzenda deployed the idiom of fields being cut or severed. *Kucheka ukama* is a common expression for severing kin relations, the subject of an Oliver Mtukudzi song on a CD I purchased in Berkeley in 1998.[7] Back in Kaerezi, SaMuzenda's idiom socialized land, linking fields to cultivating subjects. He implied, echoing Tendai, that fields were family matters, best left to lineages and negotiated with neighbors. Headmen who intervened without warrant risked severing the social fabric, as well as farmed fields. A *sabhuku*'s assertion of authority over land could thus be seen as a violation of custom, kinship, and social relations that transgressed tradition.

Chekwa, "to be cut," was also the name of the healer with twelve wives who claimed to recall meeting Cecil Rhodes. He told me of his parents' migrating to Kaerezi from near Mutoko, more than a district away. In the late nineteenth century, Kaerezi was then "Nyahuruwa's land. Tangwena arrived and seized the land. He snatched it from Nyahuruwa. This is not Tangwena's territory [*nyika*]." He described a self-settled landscape envisioned as preceding colonial rule: "People lived scattered randomly. Wherever you wanted to live, you lived. This was before the whites arrived." Early in my research, I probed to get a sense of how land was allocated, not yet having appreciated idioms of farming freely (*kurima madiro*). He politely corrected me: "Land wasn't allocated, but rather where people wanted to farm, they farmed." Again and again, several generations spoke of past practices of self-settlement through conditional freedom, refusing to acknowledge a tradition of authorities allocating land.

Smoking on the porch of his small store one afternoon, Elijah Nyahuruwa surveyed his lineage's ancestral land "seized" by Chief Tangwena. We spoke about repercussions of the DA's threatening letter. Talk turned to Nyahuruwa's farming his father's fields when he first married until his parents "gave" him a site to establish his own homestead. "Did you ask *sabhuku* or *mambo* [the chief]?" I probed. "In the past, we did not do that," he confirmed the perspective of many. "If someone arrived in an area, the chief's advisors would take that person to the chief. The chief would say to the immigrant [*mutorwa*]: 'If you find any place that suits you, you may go and stay there and farm *madiro*. Long back, they changed fields yearly. Where someone stayed, that was the place where her/his field was." Fields and huts shifted across a lightly populated landscape. Even the vanquished rainmaker envisioned past chiefs as defenders of "freedom." For him, immigrants chose, chiefs supported free choice as long as it violated no one else's rights, and people seasonally rotated among spatially scattered fields. Traditional authorities supported self-selection. In this vision, rules only policed against traffic offences. Mobile farmers steered themselves between chosen sites.

Since her husband's passing, Mbuya Clarissa had lived in a hut of her own at Nyahuruwa's homestead. She told me of witnessing Rhodesian police deliver the first eviction orders to her brother Rekayi in the late 1960s. Like Rekayi and Nyahuruwa, she was also born in Tsatse kraal, which became the epicenter of resistance to colonial evictions. While her past made for a delicate topic that warranted my not probing, I learned that her lineage "gave" her to Nyahuruwa's to settle *ngozi*, avenging spirits disturbed by another era's murder. By some accounts, when first entering Nyahuruwa's territory, Dzeka's younger brother Mudima negotiated with Ditima, Elijah's paternal grandfather and a powerful rainmaker. Dzeka remained near Mount Tangwena, but sent a delegation to "seize power" led by his brother Makaza, who murdered Elijah's grandfather. Generations later, Mbuya Clarissa's residence entangled two territories and histories, settling scores that spanned time and the *nyika*s of chiefs, rainmakers, and colonies. She and Elijah demonstrated palpably warm affect and respect toward each other.

After explaining that "long ago" people farmed "where they wanted [*pavanoda*]," Mbuya Clarissa spoke nostalgically about the time when most families lived in large lineage clusters: "We liked it because it demonstrated unity [*kubatana*]." When I asked about the role of chief and headmen in land allocation, she replied emphatically: "It was only a newcomer [*mutatsi*] who was given a field by the *sabhuku*. A resident [*mugari*] chose where he or she wanted [*asarudza paanoda*]." Occasionally, she admitted, "people fought if they both wanted the same place." I could not tell if her tale of homestead sites allegorized the precolonial battle of Tangwena conquest and Nyahuruwa's defeat, her own hut emplacing that epoch's postcolonial restitution. As Headman Mweya, Angela, and her husband James debated another widow's field in Nyamutsapa, they put new twists on an honored Tangwena tradition.

Doubly Derivative Authority

In 1991, I sat in the tall grass with Simba while he took a break from plowing. Born in 1930 and arrested at Nyafaru in 1976 for "aiding terrorists," he shared the Musengezi surname and a lineage with the man most called Headman Mweya. Simba surprised me by remarking that Mweya was "not really a headman." Nyamutsapa was a portion of Pabwe's book, he explained, so the area and its inhabitants were subject to Headman Pabwe. As we spoke, Langston Pabwe, who had inherited his father's position, was in Bulawayo on a stint of wage labor. Simba recalled Langston's grandfather who "controlled the whole area" of a book that included Nyamutsapa as an outpost on its periphery. Only in the late 1980s did Pabwe choose Mweya, the eldest of the Musengezis then living in Nyamutsapa, as his representative (*muriri*).

Two intertwined histories, Simba suggested, animated this postcolonial arrangement: "Pabwe married a Musengezi sister, and so he then trusted Musengezi. Also, Dzeka Tangwena trusted the Musengezis because he slept at their home when he was on his way to and from Nyanga town to be given laws. He was shown good hospitality and so he said 'the Musengezis should control (*kutonga*) Nyamutsapa.'" Simba wove two formative friendships into Nyamutsapa's territoriality of power, positioned in relation to both chief and Headman Pabwe. Note that the salaried civil servant—Chief Dzeka Tangwena—was "given laws" by the colonial state, traveling beyond his territory as obliged by Rhodesian rulers.

For Simba, two scales and jurisdictions encompassed Nyamutsapa, located within Pabwe, and, in turn, within Tangwena territory. Yet Simba did not fix place and power in a single vertical hierarchy of subordination. A past marriage alliance between Pabwe and Musengezi lineages built "trust," the bedrock for delegating authority through political alliance. Away at work in the late 1980s, Pabwe wanted an on-site presence in his territory's hinterlands. Mweya fit the bill: unemployed and farming at home, he was the eldest Musengezi lineage member then living year-round in Nyamutsapa. There, more than fifty years before, Musengezi ancestors had hosted Dzeka's travel to Nyanga town, inserting Nyamutsapa into both translocal practices of colonial government and the contingencies of hospitality. Lineage alliances emerged through marriage and sociality, encouraging headman and chief to delegate territorial "control" to a representative of the predominant lineage then residing in Nyamutsapa.

In contrast to the salaried chief and the headmen's state appointments, the Musengezi political reward for hospitality, however, remained administratively unrecognized. Musengezis, Simba insisted, unlike other Tangwena subjects, still did not contribute finger millet to annual chiefly beer brewing. Rather, they brought maize and a goat to demonstrate their political solidarity. The lineage had its own propitiation ceremony for the area and its inhabitants, marking its relative autonomy. While I pursued an urge for ethnographic precision, seeking full names, relative dates, and concrete events to reveal the smoking gun of social facts, Simba politely confounded my queries by insisting that "Mweya was the first person to be given these powers." Simba's assemblage merged different historical moments—Chief Dzeka's epoch of rule, ending in 1938; a Pabwe-Musengezi marriage in the indefinite past; and Mweya's appointment after independence.

A few months later, Pabwe pushed Simba's story back a generation. Headmen who worked as long-distance migrant laborers, he explained, often appointed assistants to act in their absence. Born in Kaerezi in 1941, Pabwe worked on the ranch in the 1950s before heading south to Honde Valley, joining his brother on a tea plantation from 1958 to 1962. He worked in Johannesburg from 1962 to 1975, returning to find his extended family living as refugees in Mozambique. His mother and elder brother had died during the war, leaving him to care for five nieces and nephews in addition to his own two children. "No matter how much I work, I cannot send them all to school," he lamented.

After having sought wages in Bulawayo the previous year, he returned to Kaerezi in 1991, laboring for cash when he could on a government road construction crew. I ran into the crew several times returning from the dip tank near the Mozambican border. Security concerns along the border helped divert money toward repairing and buttressing a rough dirt road into a surface smooth enough for loaded army trucks. Crews of overall-clad men worked with picks and shovels, digging culverts and smoothing the surface on terrain inaccessible to a bulldozer. Pabwe showed no signs of differentiating himself from the other laborers, all of them local men. Many lauded his egalitarian ethic. And while he had his critics, most applauded his rule and conduct.

Like Headman Nyakurita's, Langston Pabwe's was a poor homestead, but better maintained. Younger than the other headmen, he held a worldly perspective, informed by his work in Bulawayo and Johannesburg. We spoke of international politics and local disputes, national conservation policy and his efforts to promote contour ridging in his book. "Musengezi controls [*anotonga*] Nyamutsapa," he explained, much as Pabwe's own neighbor looked after the territory surrounding his homestead during the headman's extended absences. Pabwe simply honored the agreement his father had made with Mweya's father, recognizing Musengezi authority in a portion of Pabwe territory. Disputes Mweya could not solve, Pabwe suggested, should go to the chief. He cited pragmatism rather than structural hierarchies and ruling principles: the elderly chief rarely traveled, and when he did, it was rarely beyond Honde Valley, where he visited friends and relatives. Pabwe sometimes spent extended periods away from Kaerezi.

As talk turned to past chiefs, Pabwe threw a new twist into local history. When the first Tangwena chief arrived from Mozambique, "my father was the most influential *sadunhu*, along with SaNyahuruwa. This was because they each had 'appeasing areas' [*mapiwe*] here." In Langston's conception, the first Chief Tangwena encountered not one *sadunhu* in Kaerezi, but two. Each had *mapiwe*, marking the landscape with their ancestral claims prior to Tangwena's arrival. Pabwe's people, Langston claimed, received and fed Chief Tangwena. When the new sovereign conquered the rainmaker, Pabwe became one of Tangwena's six *masabhuku*. A woman born in the 1920s recalled that "Pabwe was an influential advisor to Dzeka Tangwena; he was the head of all *masabhuku*." Pabwe had been

Dzeka's "most important *kotsi*," she insisted, using an old ChiManyika term for *sadunhu,* or custodian of a territory. Langston similarly traced his ancestor's passage from *sadunhu* to a Tangwena *sabhuku.* Like Simba's account of the Musengezis, Langston's also stressed relations of hospitality and trust.

Despite my arcane ethnographic efforts to clarify the difference between a *sadunhu* and a *sabhuku,* I never received a stable, fixed definition. In one conversation, the rainmaker Nyahuruwa told me: "Long ago we had *masadunhu,* and a visitor could go to them and then the chief [*mambo*]. An immigrant would first go to *sabhuku,* then the *sadunhu,* and then the *mambo.* The *sadunhu* is responsible for the whole area, and he may have more power than the chief." In the context of our conversation, the rainmaker's invocation of "long ago" conjured precolonial practices. Yet he placed a colonial authority—the custodian of a tax book—in that imagined landscape of power. His tense then pulled a *sadunhu* into the present. Ambivalently placed *between* headman and chief in the chain of authority through which immigrants sought land, a *sadunhu* could also be more powerful than a chief, controlling a vast territory.

In a separate conversation, the rainmaker confused me further, explaining that "a *sadunhu* administers the area he has been given. A *sadunhu* is under the chief. He tries to settle any disputes that arise in the area he administers, but if he cannot resolve the case, it will go to the chief." Now I was beyond confusion. A *sadunhu* could be more powerful than a chief yet was positioned *under* one? My search for a *sadunhu* smoking gun evaporated in ethnographic complexity. But why should there be a fixed hierarchy of power, a structural chain of authority emanating from an apex of singular sovereignty? Selective sovereignties targeted *relations* between subjects and territory. Postcolonial practices of power made recourse to precolonial patterns of authority mediated through colonial histories. Sedimented practices and emergent assertions entangled temporalities and spatialities always already haunted by remembered pasts, experienced presents, and anticipated futures. The triad-in-motion unsettled any stable grid of power that might secure a singular, nested hierarchy of rule.

Arguments for Autonomy

When I heard Kaerezians refer to a *tsungo,* I knew the term signaled a territory, but I could not get a grip on its relation to sovereignty, subjects, and rights. During one 1992 territorial tutorial, Headman Nyakurita explained that "a *tsungo* is a place where people can rule themselves [*kuzvitonga*]." I heard mixed messages on the *tsungo* status of Nyamutsapa. While elders spoke about distinct Kaerezi territories they termed *tsungo*s, most secondary school children were clueless as to the term's meaning or possible geographical location. Those born on the ranch invoked the term much more frequently than did more recent immigrants. Simba, Mweya's lineage brother, one afternoon gestured toward a visible ridge, using his finger to sketch a boundary winding into the river valley. "Musengezi begins there," he pointed toward a small stream, mapping the *tsungo* with his own surname. Then he switched back to the territory's usual referent, its Nyamutsapa place name, locating it "under Pabwe." A *sabhuku*'s territory, most argued, "belonged" to the chief for whom he administered it. The bestowal of a *tsungo*, in contrast, granted relative autonomy. While Kaerezians disputed a *tsungo*'s finer points, most agreed on its formative features: a piece of land with known borders marked by features of the landscape; a chief "gave" the area to a lineage, represented by a senior male whose close relationship, often cemented through marriage, made him a trusted ally. A symbolic payment to the chief sealed the bestowal of territory. Rather than relying on the chief's propitiation of territorial ancestral spirits, members of a lineage entrusted with a *tsungo* secured spiritual and social vitality through their own rituals.

Before her 1992 death, Mbuya Tagadza was among the eldest women in Kaerezi, a widow living in Pabwe's territory on a high ridge far from any dirt road. She claimed her home placed her in Pabwe's *tsungo*, in addition to in his *bhuku* (book). Her father had been headman to Dzeka, the first colonial-installed chief. "A *tsungo*," she explained in 1991, "is an area given to people, usually great advisors to the chief." *Kutsunga* means to persevere, to be determined. A *tsungo*'s recipient, she stressed, having been rewarded for loyalty, "is allowed to rule people living in that particular area." She underscored the autonomy of a *tsungo* by stressing the practices of brewing beer before the rains. Those in a *tsungo* do not contribute to the chief's appeasement of territorial ancestral spirits. They map ritual practices to their own territories, respecting neighbors. On this front, Mbuya Tagadza agreed with Simba, who argued that the Musengezis rather than the Pabwes had been given a *tsungo* by Dzeka Tangwena. Yet another elderly woman, respected for her active role in defying colonial evictions, used this same criterion to argue that Nyamutsapa was *not* a *tsungo*. People living there, she emphasized, contributed maize and finger millet to the chief for his appeasing ceremonies. All this talk of a *tsungo* was foolish, she insisted; any idiot knew that Nyamutsapa was not a *tsungo*. This ethnographic idiot was experiencing some difficulty.

Many elders recognized three *tsungo*s in Kaerezi: Bvumbwe, the area Simba mentioned, belonging to a lineage with long-standing residence; either Pabwe, or Nyamutsapa, the area administered by Mweya inside Headman Pabwe's territory; and Nyahuruwa, the ridge surrounding the home of the rainmaker's lineage. Many spoke of Nyahuruwa's rainmaking territory as predating and extending to the entire Tangwena chiefdom. Yet those who recalled histories of chiefly conquest mapped the rainmaker's *tsungo* solely to the ridge where his lineage had long lived, both before and after colonial evictions. Nyahuruwa's *nyika*, understood as isomorphic with the Tangwena chiefdom, thus contrasted with his *tsungo*, smaller in scale and differently positioned in relation to ruling relations, histories of conquest, and territorial sovereignty.

While most mapped the three *tsungo*s to lineages who still lived there, they were not exclusive to a single lineage. Rather, an immigrant's arrival represented yet another piece of the puzzle. SaMaridzo, born around 1920, explained that a *tsungo* might be given to a chief's son-in-law who would pay a cow as a token of respect. While he never depicted the giving of the tsungo as a "sale" in commoditized terms, and while it remained clearly nontransferable, SaMaridzo described the *mutariri we tsungo*, the area's overseer, as its "owner" (*muridzi*). After arguing that "a *sabhuku* is less powerful than a *mutariri we tsungo*," he elaborated that "a *sabhuku* is under a chief, whereas a *tsungo* is not controlled by a *sabhuku*. A *mutariri we tsungo* is like a chief of that *tsungo*." Like many elders, he marked a *tsungo*'s relative territorial autonomy by emphasizing grain contributions to appeasement ceremonies that conjured seasonal rains.

SaMaridzo similarly emphasized the relative freedom of *tsungo* holders from performing subjection to the chief when receiving newcomers into their territory: "When immigrants arrive, first they go to the chief. The chief will tell them to go to the owner of the *tsungo*, since the chief is not the one who controls it. If there is land available, the owner of the *tsungo* will allocate fields to them." By this time, I had learned to hear *allocation* as an idiom for territorial influence without trumping the possibility of self-settlement. Kaerezians used terms touching on dividing, sharing out, distributing, cutting into parcels, and giving. Families had relative autonomy within a *mutariri we tsungo*'s area of influence, effectively settling themselves. For SaMaridzo, as for Simba, Mbuya Tagadza, and many others, a *tsungo* signified relative rather than absolute autonomy within the chiefdom.

In 1992, I queried Dambudzo, who worked at a district tourist hotel, during his visit to Bvumbwe, his birthplace as well as his lineage's *tsungo*. His father and uncles, also born there, lived outside villagization's grids in homesteads saturated with ancestral claims. Born in 1950, Dambudzo moved to a Communal Area near the hotel on his first marriage. He divorced two wives while a third worked their plot, his hotel wages fueling farming operations. The Communal Area offered better access to roads, markets, and agricultural inputs, as well as housing materials, enabling Dambudzo to invest capital in his rural homestead. But Bvumbwe, he insisted, would always be his *musha* (home). On vacations from work, he visited relatives and friends across Kaerezi, sometimes bringing his third wife. But more often, he left her to tend their homestead beyond Tangwena territory.

Most of the time, Dambudzo lived in a small cement room cramped in a long block of workers' quarters hidden behind the Troutbeck Hotel by carefully planted trees. Few whites, my friends who worked at the hotel often remarked, ever entered the workers' compounds, and fewer still, the rooms themselves. A paraffin-wicked stove boiled water for tea amid the sparseness of a single bed and two handmade wooden chairs. Fumes from the stove and floor polish filled the poorly ventilated room. On the other side of a thick grove of Mexican pine and Australian eucalyptus, European tourists, Afrikaans-speaking families on holiday from South Africa, and Zimbabwe's black bourgeoisie stayed at the hotel, golfed on plush greens, and took in the mountain scenery, breathing clean air.

Dambudzo's large frame spilled out from a wooden folding chair as he recounted his ancestors having long ago "fled war" from Mutoko, to Nyanga's west, into Portuguese territory, probably in the nineteenth century. "In Mozambique, they lived at a place known as the Tree of Mukota, and from there, that's when they came to Bvumbwe during a year of hunger." Despite the famine, Bvumbwe offered a rare type of weed with sweet bulbs bountiful enough to "defeat hunger." Dambudzo's lineage eventually paid a cow to Chief Dzeka Tangwena, who let them settle during difficult times. "As a result, we became respected because of that small territory. Long ago, it was called the place of the Bvumbwes, referring to our **tribe**"; he used the English term. Those who arrived later, from other lineages, were *vatorwa*, foreigners or immigrants. When Dzeka called those in his territory to his homestead to contribute labor to repairs of his huts, Dambudzo's lineage did not go, he suggested, because they had paid a cow. Those without a *tsungo* lived as *varanda*, a term implying subordination to a chief, as well as the absence of kinship ties to a ruler. Lineages with a *tsungo*, while friendly with the chief, lived in his territory but were not *subjected* to him.

Senior men in Dambudzo's lineage propitiated ancestral spirits at their *piwe*, their sacred appeasing area. He described in detail the *kuwi*, or container, formed by an indentation in one of the rocks clustered within this *piwe*. "It can store milk," Dambudzo embedded landscape morphology in history, "because this place was taken through milk from Tangwena." Before the rainy season, Dambudzo's lineage brewed beer, inviting Tangwena's extended family. This, he switched to English for a phrase, "**was a system to control**," changing back to Shona to complete his thought, "pests that ate crops." Postmenopausal women would take milk from specially selected cows and place it in the *kuwi* as an offering to lineage ancestral spirits. Milk and beer flowed, marking communion between the living and the dead. Past childbearing years, an elder woman's body bore the burden of recognizing body politics in territories entangled through patrilineal alliances. Two lineages mingled, mapping dutiful propitiation of ancestral spirits to the protection of the *tsungo*'s inhabitants and crops. Sociality rather than subjection to a sovereign assured relative autonomy, promoting the welfare of territory and population. With no chief and no headman to rule it, Dambudzo suggested, disputes should be handled within the *tsungo* and not be "taken outside."

Government resettlement policy was "outside the law" precisely because it neglected Dambudzo's lineage's rights to rule their *tsungo*'s own affairs. Villagization, for Dambudzo, represented an affront to subjects who struggled for liberation during an anticolonial war. "This is one of the reasons we went to war," he raised his voice angrily. "At first, the white government said 'this place is under the government.' They didn't know that we lived here, that we were living here when they arrived." Referring to whites as "*mabhunu*," he literally called the colonial regime "the government of the Boers." "Boers" referred less to a literal white ethnicity whose members spoke Afrikaans or hailed from South Africa than enunciated a colloquial expression for racist whites. Villagization's governing grids conjured these associations with colonial conquest for Dambudzo because they represented the official eclipse of ancestral land rights.

Next to Dambudzo's red hotel uniform jacket, Rekayi's leather coat hung from a nail hammered into a cracked cement wall. Dambudzo spoke with pride about Rekayi, calling him "our nephew, the son of my grandfather's sister." The jacket was the "inheritance of the nephew given to the grandfather." Gazing at the torn jacket hanging from a rusted nail, Dambudzo mused aloud: "Maybe one day my son will bear a daughter who will be taken to the Tangwena so she can promote the house of our sister." Intermarriage, shared sociality, migration, and the defiance of colonial evictions had long linked those who claimed rights in Bvumbwe with the Tangwena ruling lineage. The anticolonial chief Rekayi—who labored in Bulawayo but refused a white rancher's tenancy contract—passed along a deeply unsettling sense of sovereignty, discipline, and government. Across Tangwena territory, Kaerezians situated their struggles amid this disputed inheritance of modes of power and practices of subjection.

9 · The Traction of Rights and Rule

Many Kaerezians asserted that government should enable the cultivation of subjects and fields positioned in landscapes of postcolonial freedom. Administrators invoked national independence, property purchase, and laws as evidence of state sovereignty in Kaerezi. Opposition to villagization, in turn, gained ground by linking unwanted state imposition to colonial conquest, displacement, and dispossession. Headmen who claimed to practice traditions of land allocation in defiance of state policy also invited commoners' critiques. Rainmaking and chiefly rule further complicated the cross fire. Amid these power relations, what kinds of traction did competing assertions of rights and rule gain in Kaerezi?

In this chapter, I focus on Kaerezians' assertions of land rights as inalienable entitlements earned through their active participation in struggles grounded in Tangwena territory. Such invocations of *nhaka*, or rightful inheritance, raised populist challenges to Magwendere's sovereign pronouncements of his chiefly birthright to rule a *nyika* where he had not historically suffered alongside his subjects. Through voiced arguments and agrarian practices, Kaerezians debated patrilineal birthrights and postcolonial freedoms. Across an uneven geography of power, they mapped specific sites to chiefly conduct, memories of rightful sovereigns, and specters of conquests that spanned Rhodesian rule.

My conceptual metaphor of traction foregrounds the recursive relations between historically sedimented terrain and the microphysics of power exerted in precise times and places. The conditions of possibility for traction depend on both ground and emplaced agency. These provisional points of friction shift across uneven landscapes, historical moments, and the differential abilities of specific subjects to establish footholds that gain ground. My usage of traction thus seeks to convey how the efficacy of situated practices articulates with contingent constellations of geography, history, and environment. Rains render slopes slippery, at times thwarting attempts to climb paths easily ascended during the dry season. In turn, erosion washes away soil and rock while simultaneously redistributing sediments to form potential grip elsewhere. Such transformative processes entangle with the multiple mappings of memory work and the cultural politics of territory to reconfigure the emergent possibilities of place.

Magwendere maneuvered amid these historical sedimentations, connecting claims to rule territory to his predecessor Rekayi, the anticolonial chief and nationalist hero. While this move gained traction against state efforts to impose villagization, Magwendere's assertions also entangled grounded geographies: his own ancestral home in Mandeya, an area in Honde Valley; his 1986 migration to Kaerezi; and his huts' location in Magadzire, the easternmost portion of the chiefdom. Commoners challenged his rule by *positioning* the acting chief beyond popular memories of suffering for territory. They mapped Magwendere outside Kaerezi during colonial evictions, a critical event formative to "Tangwena" identities and interests. In turn, Tsatse, home to Rekayi and Elijah Nyahuruwa, became a privileged place of power in Tangwena territory.

Such struggles situated sovereignties—of state, chief, and rainmaking—amid alternative articulations of inheritance and ownership. At stake in territorial designations—chiefdom, headmen's books, white farms, an administrative annex added to a state scheme, and rainmaking territory—was the relative *traction* afforded to respective rights claims. Grounded geographies mattered in these debates, materially and discursively shaping configurations of sovereignty, discipline, and government.

The Acting Chief Does Not Act as One

Despite Magwendere's chiefly defense of territorial rule, many Kaerezians repeatedly voiced concerns over his conduct, legitimacy, and assertions of power. Elders remembered the rule of Dzeka, installed in 1902, and Mudima, appointed in 1928, much like Rekayi's reign. Some idyllic shades colored memories using terms like *strong*, *just*, and *able* to describe rulers remembered as generous toward and respectful of commoners. Many insisted they had granted considerable autonomy to their subjects while representing local interests to external agents, both private whites and colonial officials. In turn, territorial ancestral spirits (*vadzimu*) sanctioned their rule.[1] In stark contrast, some people openly criticized Kinga, who died in 1965, for compromising local autonomy while acting in pursuit of personal gain. Many branded Magwendere with allegations of cronyism, corruption, and injustice. In 1990, a Nyafaru schoolteacher who was seized as a young boy by Rhodesian police in a 1972 raid, mixed hyperbole and genuine resentment: "Only those directly benefiting from the crumbs of bread falling from the acting chief's table support him." Populists hungered for justice.

Many criticized Magwendere's inability to preside over a *dare*, a court or gathering that rendered binding decisions. "Magwendere is not ruling with all the people," MaiHurudza's husband, Walter, told me. "They are deeply displeased with his way of ruling [*kutonga kwake*]," he reiterated during a rare visit home from his district hotel job. His critique bore the traces of Magwendere's 1988 *dare*, which fined Walter and his wife for building a hut in one of Nyamutsapa's newly demarcated villagization grids. "Rekayi ruled without divisions," Walter insisted, constructing a cohesive *communitas* cultivated through sovereign conduct. While Rekayi consulted advisors, relying on the wisdom of female and male elders and headmen, Magwendere lacked these social relations and localized knowledge. He depended largely on a small clique of male neighbors and rarely appeared to assess popular opinion. Unlike Rekayi, "who acted in accord with the people's will," Walter saw Magwendere as someone who "fails to accomplish" it. Subjection to sovereignty was not without critical evaluation of a ruler's governing wisely or dictating foolishly, acting on or against other's actions.

Angela, summoned to Magwendere's *dare* for building in the lines in 1991, complained that "the 'chief' says if someone is not satisfied by my ruling, then she or he can leave my area. Rekayi did not do that. He would go on with someone until they agreed." Rekayi produced consent, if not always consensus. In Angela's view, Rekayi engendered an understanding among his subjects of their interests being served because he encouraged popular participation in orchestrating justice. She praised his ethical treatment of women, as well as his wisdom to solicit their counsel, rebuking Magwendere for failing to practice either. Without papering over Rekayi's patriarchal practices, many emphasized the same contrast, providing specific examples of his aid to widows, his inclusion of women in crucial decisions, and his respectful rule.

Rekayi, many insisted, acted *in relation* to his subjects' actions, actively encouraging their conduct to inform his own. Yet this populism never eroded his strength and decisiveness as a leader. One of the men arrested in 1976 at Nyafaru for "aiding terrorists" elaborated: "When Rekayi was there, people attended meetings where they were urged to unite, and they united. Nowadays there is no leader. He is in the church. . . . The Tangwena say they chose a chief, but we see him as an acting one. During the war, when Tangwena called for a meeting, everyone attended. Laws were passed and followed. But almost everyone is saying 'I am a chief.' We are now lost." Another of those arrested in the same Rhodesian raid complained: "If you talk to the Tangwena people, they say Magwendere is not a chief. What has he done so far? No development. Do we expect anything constructive from him? Nothing." As a result, "people have lost hope in him. One of his right-hand men was saying he is weak. We cannot be led by such a man." Those arrested and imprisoned during the war felt they had struggled for two *nyika*s—a chief's and nation's. From their perspective, Rekayi, "the Tangwena people," and "the *povo*," the masses of Zimbabwe, all "suffered for territory." That collective social struggle produced a shared interest—articulating anticolonial aspirations of black majority rule, dismantling draconian forms of racial injustice, and pursuing "freedom." Magwendere, many asserted, earned none of these fruits of popular perseverance.

In the mid-1980s, an NGO donated a flatbed truck to "the Tangwena community," hoping to provide transport for people and supplies to a remote area. One of Magwendere's cronies commandeered the truck, seizing it from Nyafaru and driving it near his Magadzire home. The clique offered free passage to loyalists while charging commoners for rides. After seizing this community resource, Magwendere's mafia had the engine seize up on them. The truck sat idle for months, its immobility defying the intentions of many agents—some relatively noble, others nefarious.

Commoners frequently invoked the "Tangwena truck" as a prominent example of how the chief "killed development." Many critiqued such illegitimate seizures, splicing the English term *hijack* into Shona syntax, using translingual traffic to police the chief's transgressions. He had privatized a public good. Kaerezians accused Magwendere of repeatedly trying to "hijack development": trucks, grinding mills, fish ponds, and sheep donated by an NGO. Some claimed he undercut support for women's education that they deemed necessary for "development." Projects failed when Magwendere sought to control (*kutonga*) them, many argued. Critiques of chiefly rule often invoked populist appeals to democratizing development projects.

In 1991, Simba and I climbed a steep Nyamutsapa path winding up from cascading white water. We were returning from a gathering of forty or so who had met to discuss the proposed "protected area" straddling the Kaerezi River. Moments before, we had sat along its shady bank as neighbors evoked idioms of ownership, control, responsible care, and respect for environmental resources. As we climbed deeper into Tangwena territory, a few of Simba's friends walking with us griped about the chief and headmen taking over development projects in the name of "ruling territory." Simba argued that development (*budiriro*) and ruling (*kutonga*) constituted two distinct practices. Magwendere and headmen were welcome to join development projects, but on the same footing with commoners. Otherwise, Simba reflected, the situation turned "oppressive" because they had "double power" (*masimba mairi*).

Like his friends, Simba used a common term for politics, *zvenyika*, literally, "things of territory" or "matters of nation." They understood the contentious cultural politics that shaped development—the siting of projects, the construction of a community of beneficiaries, the distribution of benefits, the unequal sharing of labor burdens, and the differential effects of conditionalities such as prohibitions on resource use. Yet they carved out a discursive distinction between politics and development—*zvenyika* and *budiriro*—through a thoroughly political practice. Across a variety of contexts, they positioned Magwendere as anti-development, against progress, and "trapped in the past." But unlike traditional chiefs such as Dzeka, whose rule they strongly supported, or Rekayi, who crafted hybrid nationalist traditions, the acting chief failed on both traditional and developmental criteria. Rather than pursuing his subjects' interests, they argued, this sovereign sought his own satisfaction.

Installation Anxieties

Initially planned for 1987, a year after his appointment as acting chief, Magwendere's installation ceremony was, according to a Ministry of Local Government report, "postponed indefinitely due to apparent misunderstandings between the current chief and some members of his clan."[2] In 1990, another postponement derailed a second planned installation. Why did the Tangwena chieftainship remain officially vacant years after Rekayi's 1984 death? Senior officials in Harare echoed district officials who spoke of waiting a suitable period to accord respect to a national hero. It also recognized Kaerezi's contentious cultural politics of custom. Deliberations over Magwendere's installation echoed indirect rule's public performance of an orchestrated alliance of chiefly and state authority under the banner of tradition.

Early in his interregnum, Magwendere dragged his feet, writing to the Nyanga

District Administrator in early 1989 to ask for the postponement of his official installation.[3] While government insisted on an orderly rotation among the four Tangwena royal houses, competing understandings of legitimate succession challenged the state sanctioning of a single chiefly sovereignty. According to some elders, Rekayi's brother had hidden the *zvombo zva mambo*, the material instruments of chiefly rule, probably during early deliberations over his successor. Government records listed the "traditional regalia" as a *ngoma* (drum) and a *pfuti* (gun), among the artifacts my sources mentioned.[4] One elder suggested Rekayi's brother planned to "embarrass" Magwendere after the planned state ceremony by bringing out the regalia and staking a counterclaim to rightful rule backed by popular support. Colonial records suggest that a member of Rekayi's extended family had seized possession of the *ngoma* by early 1966, perhaps asserting similar claims, but I never heard this mentioned by Kaerezians.[5]

For his part, the DA repeatedly told me that the "chieftainship dispute is for them to sort out," distancing himself from the quagmire. He continually cited the principles of rotation among royal houses, despite knowing about repeated transgressions of allegedly invariably fixed "rules" of succession. The several times I questioned him about his participation in Magwendere's selection and subsequent appointment, he pointedly steered conversation away from controversy. Another civil servant, however, told me that the DA traveled to Kaerezi in the late 1980s to participate in a ceremony marking the chieftainship's passage between royal houses. Allegedly, he stayed up most of the night, consuming copious quantities of alcohol along with participants in the ceremony. When he awoke in the morning, he was told the ritual he never witnessed had been a success.

In 1991, rumors circulated of a secret meeting among Tangwena elders held to discuss the possibility of choosing a replacement for Magwendere. A chiefly claimant from a competing royal house allegedly arrived with a musket—at once intimidating others and displaying the regalia of his ruling ambitions. A few months later, the resettlement officer told me that Magwendere's son, Panganayi, was among a group that "seized by force" the *zvombo zva mambo* from Rekayi's brother. The administrator presumed that with the chiefly regalia now in his possession, Magwendere would press the Ministry of Local Government to set a firm date for his installation. Yet five more years would pass before the official ceremony.

"Those Tangwena have some superstition," I heard from a township worker in the Ministry of Local Government, "that puts a curse on chiefs when they are installed." His colleagues told similar tales. Yet when I pushed them, I never got anything but a shrug of shoulders, laughter, or a formulaic statement about the "culturally backward" Tangwena. In Harare, a former DERUDE planner recalled to me Rekayi's discomfort during his 1984 nationally televised official installation: "If you watch what Chief Tangwena did with the robe and the helmet when he was throned, I think that said a lot. . . . He was just robed and as quickly as possible he ripped it off again. He had to be robed, and had this hat put on for government as the symbolism of being installed." Initially, I interpreted Rekayi's actions as a refusal to recognize state officials as authorizing chiefly powers he had earned outside the channels of indirect rule. He might not want to submit his sovereignty to *any* government since he forged his populist power by resisting Rhodesian rule. The colonial trappings of an installation ceremony, perhaps, positioned him more as a puppet than a populist rebel. At the time, he angrily objected to rumblings of resettlement policy in Tangwena territory.

In contrast to my interpretation, the DERUDE official attending the ceremony explained Rekayi's actions by recourse to the same "curse" described to me by Elijah Nyahuruwa. Prior to colonial rule, his rainmaking ancestors had refused to recognize Tangwena sovereignty asserted through violent conquest. In the 1990s, Elijah repeated his predecessor's challenge to the hubris of Tangwena chiefs who became installed in his lineage's rainmaking territory. Chiefs Dzeka, Mudima, and Kinga had relatively long official reigns. But the dormant curse resurfaced. Appointed acting chief at his father Kinga's 1965 death, Marijeni died less than a month later. After reigning for nearly two decades, legitimated by popular support, Rekayi died within months of his state-orchestrated installation in Tsatse. So powerful was a vanquished precolonial rainmaker's sovereignty that it cast shadows of death over a postcolonial nationalist hero, keeping alive a legend. Spectral powers influenced Magwendere's foot-dragging.

Ruled by a Refugee?

Magwendere's reluctance was not the only obstacle to his official installation. A 1990 Local Government report observed that "Magwendere does not seem to command the respect of his followers. He has delegated his son, Panganayi to perform all duties involving tradition. Acceptability of this arrangement by the clan is doubtful."[6] The report critiqued his failure to attend a *svitsa* ceremony, a ritual where the Tangwena royal family would bequeath traditional regalia to Rekayi's successor. This official optic greatly mirrored popular perceptions:

Magwendere, a strong member of the Apostolic Faith since birth was not interested in contesting the Chieftainship were it not for the persistence of his sons (especially Panganayi). Magwendere and his sons agreed that after the appointment, Panganayi would take an active part in performing the duties of Chief whilst the father remained in the background and acted as an adviser. After the appointment, Magwendere and Panganayi moved from where they had lived almost the whole of their life (Honde Valley in Mutasa District) and took residence at Magadzire in the Tangwena area. Magwendere then went ahead and operated as originally planned and advised the clan of this mode of operation.[7]

For many Kaerezians, this tag-team rule of an enfeebled puppet and his son who ran the chiefdom's daily affairs rekindled resentments against a colonial tandem. Chief Kinga's son Marijeni had served as acting chief in the last years of his elderly father's life. Their 1965 deaths, months apart, directly preceded Rekayi's reign. Kinga's rule coincided with Hanmer's extension of ranch wattle plantations and a harsher work regime epitomized by the "labor agreement." Hanmer reportedly slaughtered an occasional ox for feasts at Kinga's home and enjoyed what Kaerezians termed "friendly" relations with the chief during the era when the white owner moved to the property and intensified inputs of capital and tenant labor. During Kinga's rule, the Rhodesian Front won white electoral office. Kinga died the year the UDI provoked international sanctions. Kinga's reign—regardless of his intentions—entangled with these local, national, and transnational assemblages to yield deeply resented experiences of labor discipline, diminished African land rights, and increased vulnerability to evictions.

As a result, in the 1990s many Kaerezians sharply contrasted the colonial puppet Kinga with Rekayi's righteous rebellion. Kinga accepted Hanmer's gifts; Rekayi refused what he termed "government bribes." Kinga failed to oppose white alienation of African land and labor; Rekayi defended African property and labor militancy. Some spoke of Kinga as having "sold out Tangwena territory" and having "allowed" Hanmer's unpopular discipline. In this vision, what Marx termed the holy trinity of capital, land, and labor became under Kinga's reign a crucible of coercion fused to fictions of consent. Rekayi challenged these hegemonic articulations, while Kinga, many suggested, enabled them. Critics ranged from those accusing Kinga of complicity in the conversion of the chiefdom into private property to those who saw him as a Rhodesian-imposed injustice lacking popular support. Some Kaerezians felt they paid for Kinga's selling out after his death—through hardship, eviction, and exile.

Opposing geographies of power had mapped contrastive regimes of rule grounded in specific sites. Rekayi had lived in Tsatse where Dzeka, the first officially recognized chief, made his *musha*, a home in the heart of Tangwena territory. Nearby lay the ancestral home of the conquered rainmaker Nyahuruwa. In Tsatse, these two modes of territorial power converged. By the late 1950s, Rekayi Tangwena and Elijah Nyahuruwa were allied in their entangled territories and as urban wageworkers in Bulawayo, where together they encountered African nationalist organizations. As Tsatse became the epicenter of Hanmer's evictions, squatters and landscape became entangled in a *national* liberation struggle. In contrast, Kinga had lived on the chiefdom's eastern edge, along the Mozambican border. Far from epic axes wielded during the chiefly conquest of a precolonial rainmaker, his homestead also remained distant from police batons that menaced squatters during colonial evictions. In turn, spatialities from multiple moments haunted a postcolonial politics of place.

As a squatter defying Gaerezi Ranch's white colonial owner Hanmer, SaGumbo had his name appear on a 1969 Government Proclamation ordering evictions. Almost twenty years later, a government official named Marumahoko recorded SaGumbo's right to a specific residential plot in Kaerezi's official scheme registry. Understandably fearful that his new state landlord might evict him, he reluctantly began to build a hut in his assigned villagization site. The new acting chief Magwendere summoned him to court and fined him cash less than the cost of a single sack of maize meal. SaGumbo stayed at his homestead outside the grids, letting the new hut frame rot. But his conflict with Magwendere endured.

In 1991, SaGumbo deeply resented Magwendere's decree forbidding subjects room to maneuver while Nyamutsapans dwelled in a danger zone targeted for evictions. Magwendere, SaGumbo emphasized, ran no risk of eviction by defying government. The chief received his state salary and lived safely distant from the front line's fray. Magwendere commanded his subjects without suffering alongside them. SaGumbo mediated this contemporary politics of place through colonial memories. Echoing his son Brian's characterization of the 1970s, SaGumbo contrasted ranch tenants' vulnerability with Magwendere's safety: "Our huts were destroyed. All of our cattle were seized. The children were seized from the school. Magwendere was living in Honde resting comfortably. He did not suffer our history."[8]

SaGumbo's history, *nhorohondo*, did more than double duty. At once a narration and the act of accounting, the term contains within itself *hondo*, the word for war. Adding a single consonant would make it *nhoronhondo*, a term infrequently used for "a destitute person without relatives."[9] Whether or not he intended these resonances, SaGumbo fomented their enunciation and linkage, encouraging an effect he may not have noticed. In this way, articulations gained traction without requiring a self-sovereign subject willfully intending an orchestrated outcome. Against Magwendere's intentions, he became peripherally *positioned*. Sedimented spatial struggles that spanned more than a century carved contours that eroded traction for Magwendere's ruling assertions. His conduct, as well as his homestead, *placed* him precariously in relation to the *nyika* of chiefdom, rainmaking territory, and nation.

Magwendere walked into distinct geographies and histories not of his choosing when he migrated to Tangwena territory. So did his son. Recall that Panganayi, not his father, demanded my DA-endorsed document early in my research, stamping "CHIEF TANGWENA" in block letters and misspelling the sovereign's signature. The son also attended a workshop on community-based resource management in the town of Nyanga, angering attendees with his blend of belligerence and seeming indifference to concerns of Kaerezians and administrators. Panganayi repeatedly sought to overstep his position. The program listed him as a "delegate of Chief Tangwena," yet he introduced himself to visitors as "Chief Tangwena." The ruse worked with several white visitors from government ministries and NGOs, but provoked criticism privately voiced to me by Kaerezians attending the workshop. They also critiqued his heavy drinking at the reception following the workshop, where he ran up a tab at the hotel bar. In Kaerezi, many referred to him as a "drunkard," conduct pointedly differentiated from his father, who refused to brew beer from grains harvested in Tangwena territory.

Magwendere was a *Vapostori*, the name for adherents of an apostolic church founded by Johan Marange, marked by men who shaved their heads and wore long beards. While members of Apostolic Faith African Independent churches also prohibited beer drinking and the appeasement of ancestral spirits, they distanced themselves in practice and name from *Vapostori*. Apostolic Faith adherents were "people who pray," *vanonamata*, influenced by missionary Christian churches while advocating faith healing and prophesy. Members encouraged monogamy, spoke of "women's rights," and advocated popular education for all children. Many beyond these churches also coded *Vapostori* practices, including polygamy, as oppressive of women. They cited pronounced gendered hierarchies at worship and home, forced marriages of teenage girls, and the early removal of girls from school. For those who discursively opposed tradition and modernity, *Vapostori* were "backward." Magwendere's lack of formal education further aligned with his often inept oratory and lack of political savvy, despite his agility at the Tsatse meeting.

In the early 1990s, those who appeased ancestral spirits found common cause with Kaerezians who prayed to a Christian God, demanding that the state-salaried Magwendere "throw aside" his *Vapostori* beliefs to brew beer, a chiefly obligation. "He needs to choose between being a *Vapostori* and being a chief," many voiced openly. While framed as an issue of belief—prayer over and against ancestral appeasement—an implicit critique challenged the qualities of *conduct* associated with *Vapostori* as appropriate for rule. A cultivated person of good character *ane tsika*, literally, "has culture" (a respected chief or elder, their personage pluralized, *vane tsika*). Many Vapostori were widely respected outside their own ranks, yet none had been chief. Only a few Vapostori families lived in Nyamutsapa; scores resided in Tsatse, while most lived in or near Magadzire, where Magwendere migrated. These spatial and social links to religious practice further fueled perceptions that he did not represent subjects spread across Tangwena territory.

Several headmen openly objected to Magwendere's rule. One told me angrily that "he is confused, and we don't approve." He specifically criticized Magwendere's efforts at trying to "have his son installed." Another headman spoke of a meeting with all Tangwena headmen in early 1991. They demanded that Magwendere propitiate their territorial ancestral spirits (*kupira vadzimu*). To do that, they pressed, he needed to "cease his praying" as a *Vapostori*. Panganayi tried to intervene, claiming he would brew the beer on behalf of his father. Angrily, the headman rebuked him: "You are a child, get out of here." That stinging salvo brought out a cascade of critique as the headman recalled the incident. Panganayi's pretensions, he elaborated, shamed both father and son. In contrast, while many pulled generational rank, headmen and commoners alike claimed that Rekayi commanded his elders as well as their respect.

Kaerezians frequently invoked Rekayi's heroism to support rightful rule based on laudable leadership and cultivated character, rather than solely on claims of royal inheritance. Yet another headman, Goora, argued that state officials should recognize "the people who are supposed to be chiefs. Those people loved by the people. I do not agree with the inheritance of the chieftainship because some people are weak." I often heard Goora manufacture a vision of authoritarian populism to represent his own interests as those of "the people."[10] Yet he shared with many a common assertion: the position of chief should be an entitlement *earned* through conduct rather than by inherited birthright or state appointment. Ruling, in this vision, required the willing recognition of consenting subjects.

We sat outside Goora's large brick hut, the thatch badly in need of repair, looking toward a Mozambican mountain range marking the eastern horizon. A few chickens and a goat scampered across the large compound. A Shona verse from the Bible was scrawled in charcoal letters on the cook hut's wall. The grouping of huts suggested that generations lived in close proximity, several sons' homesteads emerging on the outer peripheries of a *sabhuku* patriarch. One of his sons, unemployed and newly married, joined us. Goora wore a tattered blazer that looked like an old hotel uniform, repeating the mantra I heard from each headman: government has neglected us; we receive no salary and constantly have our powers challenged. As conversation turned to chiefly rule, he explained that a sovereign's duties entailed "ruling people as well as appeasing [*kupira*] and respecting the land [*kuremekedza nyika*]." Magwendere, he argued, failed at each.

Goora did not know how chiefly powers originated "because when I was born chiefs were already here. But the Bible says there should be chiefs so that everyone will not want to rule." He knew his Bible, citing verses. I awkwardly tried to disentangle Christian and African bases of cultural authority: "I thought the Bible was something written by whites," I repeated what many Kaerezians argued, "yet chiefs are part of your culture. So do the Bible and your culture agree on this point?" The headman admonished the confused ethnographer: "The spirit of the Lord [*mweya ye Mwari*] wrote the Bible. Whites followed this spirit because they were intelligent. The cultures [*tsika*] in the Bible are those of all peoples, all of us. It was not the whites who wrote the Bible." His answer was much more sophisticated than my question. Complementing his argument's strength, I offered a minor clarification: "Well, only *some* whites are intelligent."

For this headman, postcolonial state policy deprived him of the duties and salary colonial rule awarded him. Tradition sought traction through webs of indirect rule and the Bible introduced to him by missionaries. Postcolonial officials ignored Headman Goora's book—the territorialized tax registry that funded his colonial salary—while he invoked biblical legitimization for chiefly rule. Echoing Rekayi's Anglicanism, Goora fused Christian and chiefly conduct, positioning both as righteous critics of Rhodesia's racialized rule. Geography, as well as history, became pivotal in assertions of power. Echoing many of his neighbors, Goora recalled that Magwendere moved to Kaerezi *after* Rekayi's death, having lived in Mandeya, where he was born in 1919, a day's walk south in the Honde Valley. He "did not see the Tangwena war," many told me. As an idiom of rights and identity, "suffering for territory" invoked struggles situated in *space* and *time*. Magwendere's absence from grounded struggles on a colonial ranch weakened his postcolonial claims to rule. Goora repeatedly located the acting chief outside Tangwena territory and history. In sharp contrast, the headman entangled Rekayi's rule in both, linking it to a national struggle for liberation through militantly localized articulations grounded in Tsatse kraal.[11] Amid a tirade against Magwendere's refusal to appease ancestral spirits, Goora mapped the migrant as an imposed outsider:

> We told the Tangwena [extended family] that we don't want the person they gave us. They said all those Tangwena who fought are now dead. [Magwendere] cannot resolve our problems because he was in Mandeya. We do not want a stranger [*muenzi*], a **refugee**. . . . If the chief wants to be a *Vapostori*, then he has to abandon the chieftainship. . . . We are against this old geezer [*mudhara*]. . . . It is time for us also to rule [*tigongewo*] because he is just eating money from the government.

Magwendere's postcolonial paycheck became evidence of several sellouts. First, the compromised chief betrayed "the people" through impotence and incompetence. Crucially, his *conduct*—Magwendere's refusal to brew beer—rendered him unpopular. Goora repeatedly invoked an implicit freedom of religion, but he deemed *Vapostori* practices incommensurable with chiefly obligations. Second, by receiving a civil servant's salary without performing the duties of a chief, Magwendere effectively stole from government, accumulating private wealth from public coffers. Third, the idiom of "eating money" conjured illicit wealth acquired through moral and political transgression. Recall that during the war, those alleged to have betrayed the liberation struggle were deemed sellouts; some were murdered as traitors. By accepting cash without "respecting territory" and subjects, Magwendere "sold out" both. Tangwena's *nyika*, as Rekayi asserted through words and conduct, could not be commoditized.

In Kaerezi's moral topography of power, Goora mapped *sabhuku* rule to governmental recognition of popular will. His colonial salary, he argued, acknowledged popular support for rightful rule. In sharp contrast, his populist postcolonial "we" refused a chief *imposed* on "us" by "government." As Goora later put it, "We are now being ruled by refugees. They are the people disturbing our lives. The people who fought are now being put at the back." Those who suffered for territory now suffered in it, unjustly ruled by a government-appointed outsider.

Others also called Magwendere a refugee, using the English term that interpellated many during their wartime flight to Mozambique. At independence, Rekayi and his Tangwena subjects returned home by crossing the Jora River that did double duty, bounding chiefdom and nation-state on the Mozambican border. From a populist perspective, it was only in exile that those unjustly evicted had become refugees. In postcolonial Kaerezi, Tangwena smallholders claimed rights of belonging to two liberated territories, two *nyika*s for which they suffered. Tangwena critics of Magwendere understood themselves as subjects and citizens with place-specific rather than abstract, ungrounded entitlements; their own wartime experiences informed a discourse of disenfranchisement accorded to refugees as people out of their proper place.

Popular critiques placed Magwendere outside moral economies of kinship and community grounded in specific social relations and places. His royal lineage could not trump his limited knowledge of locality. Again and again, elders of both genders complained: "He doesn't *know* the territory," implying at once a lack of technical mastery and of command over historical detail. I asked a headman whether Magwendere knew the intricacies of which parcels of land were *tsungo*, areas "given" to a particular linage by a previous chief. Practically spitting his words, the headman raised his voice and fist: "Magwendere does not know anything about it. He's blind about whether or not this place is a *tsungo* or what was followed long ago here." In this idiom, knowing territory was necessary to rule it.

Across historical moments, place remained pivotal in constructions of righteous rule. A few men sat in the grass in front of Nyafaru's small store passing around a plastic bucket of thick millet beer. Chidumbu emerged to greet me and soon commented: "There are two chiefs in the Tangwena area: one at Tsatse and one at Magadzire. Magwendere is afraid of MaiElijah." He added an echo of scornful laughter, mapping two *places* of power—the acting chief's home at Magadzire, and Tsatse, where Rekayi's widow, MaiElijah, lived in a government-built cement house along the scheme road.

Chidumbu's naming invoked respect and intimacy. Most addressed mothers as *Mai* of their firstborn or, as years passed, a favored child. Chidumbu was also "father of Chipo," *Baba Chipo*. More commonly used to address women, such naming required relative intimacy in several senses, knowledge of kinship acquired through social relations. Outsiders called MaiElijah either MaiTangwena, "Mrs. Tangwena" or, *Mbuya*, "grandmother." Those who "knew territory" also knew kinship. Another echo, probably unintentional, smuggled in yet more place politics. Another Elijah, the rainmaker, also lived in Tsatse, the area some termed "the heart of the chiefdom." Tsatse's concentrated powers marginalized Magwendere's home in Magadzire.

Prominent in defiance of colonial evictions at Tsatse, MaiElijah endured police beatings and marched to district offices with a contingent of women to protest Rekayi's arrest. She was among a score of women who stripped off their shirts in

Nyanga Township, threw sand at armed police, and scolded them. Such deeds earned her respect for courageous conduct in her own right, in addition to her being Rekayi's widow. The quip about two chiefs in the Tangwena area at once feminized Magwendere's rule and demeaned his character. It implied impotence and fear, hardly chiefly virtues. Many vividly remembered MaiElijah's public performances as a possessed spirit medium. Not all believed her to give authentic voice to ancestral spirits, some denying that she was "a true *svikiro*." Yet Chidumbu's comment implicitly invoked a spirit medium's approval of a new chief.[12] Magwendere's refusal to appease ancestral spirits left him open to such spirited critiques, raising the dead's disapproval while angering the living.

In the early 1990s, many referred to Magwendere as a *muenzi*, a stranger, or a *mutorwa*, an outsider. This last term gendered illegitimate rule, for *mutorwa* is also a common term for a daughter-in-law who moves to her husband's parent's homestead. *Mutorwa*, literally, is "the one taken in" by a groom's patrilineal relatives. In Magwendere's case, many suggested, they did not want a shotgun wedding. Practices at once grounded and gendered further challenged his claims to *nyika* as his patrilineal birthright.[13]

Engendering Inheritance

Resettlement policy officially allocated arable parcels in the scheme to married men, widows, and divorcées, and thus married women only gained legal land rights through their husbands.[14] Names appeared on the scheme's land registry list as "household heads," what Kaerezians termed a *samusha*, literally, "custodian of the homestead." Formal divorce remained relatively rare, while estrangement and separation frequently placed women in vulnerable situations. Younger women whose marriages unraveled usually returned to their parents' home, establishing their own sleeping hut and farming their parents' fields.

While eligible for a resettlement plot, widows and divorcees often lacked the labor, capital for fertilizer and seeds, and cattle to cultivate their own parcels. Widows might be taken in by one of their grown children, or they might move to the homestead of a brother-in-law, a common practice known as *kugarwa nhaka*. Pairing the verb *kugara*—to live, dwell, or settle—with *nhaka*—inheritance—this patrilineal practice wove together gender, spatial settlement, property rights, and personhood. *Kugarwa* indicates a recipient of an active verb, "to be settled" rather than "to settle." While men marry, *kuroora*, women *are* married, *kuroorwa*, gendering the act's agency. When widows become *kugarwa nhaka*, they are "settled inheritance" in several senses: they move to their husband's brother's homestead; and they form part of the dispensation of a man's estate.[15] Viewed from the standpoint of lineage reproduction, the practice of *kugarwa nhaka* wills sexual proprietorship to a brother, who can produce legitimate heirs for his patrilineage. Yet practices covered a wide range of social arrangements, from "forced" (*kumanikidzwa*) arrangements perpetuated against a widow's wishes to those deemed benevolent protection purged of any sexual suggestion. Across this range, however, *nhaka* remained strongly associated with the patrilineal passage of property, land rights, and some positions of authority.[16]

Idioms of inheritance for the chieftainship and for headmen allowed for selection processes among rival lineage mates. In these cases, birth did not guarantee an inherited right, but buttressed cultural assertions to actualize it. Magwendere argued that tradition required his selection as chief by virtue of lineage and birth order. He was the eldest member of the royal house next in line for the title. Elijah Nyahuruwa objected strongly enough to register his claims with the Ministry of Local Government, asserting ruling rights usurped through precolonial Tangwena conquest. Perhaps the postcolonial state might reverse colonial recognition of the wrong rulers. Administrators and Kaerezians alike cited custom to explain Nyahuruwa's exclusion from viable candidacy. Yet all recognized his leadership qualities, political savvy, and popularity. Few perceived Magwendere in such terms.

Most Kaerezians agreed that Rekayi's *nyika* was his *nhaka*, that his chiefly territory was his rightful inheritance. The elderly and frail healer Chekwa was among a few asserting a counterposition, arguing that "there is no inheritance on ruling people. Only a private asset like my *gona* [a packet of medicinal herbs with healing powers] can be inherited." Most, in contrast, recognized inheritance as integral to assertions of rights to rule people *and* territory. Disputes focused on what inheritance implied, its authorization, and the practices that asserted rights. Crucially, challenges to Magwendere's rule *rearticulated* idioms of *nyika* and *nhaka*.

Denying Magwendere's claims to chiefly rule as his birthright, Kaerezi's idioms derived rights from popular participation in the critical event of suffering for territory during colonial evictions. Such sufferings linked Tsatse's epicenter of chiefdom, rainmaking range, and defiance of ranch owner to clandestine mountain lean-tos and subsequent flight to Mozambique. There, Kaerezians cultivated crops and a sense of exilic community amid cooperative fields. Suffering sutured together these distant sites, while it also *engendered* rights grounded in postcolonial Kaerezi. Rural homesteads relied on patrilineal production and reproduction, sons rather than daughters becoming heir to ancestral fields. Yet just as they had done on a colonial ranch, women anchored family fields with their subsistence agriculture while some husbands sought migrant wages in district tourist hotels and distant towns and cities as far away as South Africa.

Women's planting of *tsenza* on mountain slopes, detailed in chapter 3, was among those agrarian micropractices that grounded assertions of political entitlement earned through historical struggle. In an earlier era, women's prominence during defiance of ranch evictions—their spatial and political location on the front lines of struggle—protected men from state violence. After independence, gendered micropractices shifted articulations of rights, rule, and territory as Angela cultivated *tsenza*, mixed mud and clay to bake sun-dried bricks at her villagization site, and spoke defiantly about Magwendere's injustice as she traversed multiple zones of state and chiefly designation. Many women who cultivated *tsenza* similarly grounded their claims on remote hillsides.

Assertions that rights were earned through situated struggles reworked idioms of inheritance in relation to generations as well as gender. Sitting on a hillside overlooking Nyafaru School in 1990, Brian Gumbo traced his finger across his 1972 flight before Rhodesian police captured and trucked him to a Salisbury social welfare compound. A charitable mission school took him in as a boarding student, only to have wartime violence close the school. Many in his generation told me of similar experiences of being bumped by such closures to several schools, increasing their sense of displacement and insecurity. An elder relative eventually smuggled Brian across the Mozambican border to FRELIMO-controlled territory where his parents had fled after more than a year of clinging to mountain hideouts bordering Kaerezi. In general, FRELIMO soldiers discouraged transborder traffic, fearing it would attract Rhodesian attacks. Brian rattled off names of those brutally beaten by armed and aggressive enforcers.

Recalling images of borderland violence during Rhodesia's twilight, Brian pointed out a pivotal place entangled with a critical event: "*There, at that precise spot*, police caught me"; "Old Man Mandipe fled over *that* ridge." Walking through these sites, we traversed a landscape suffused with affect *and* politics. Nyafaru represented both refuge and Rhodesian violation by illegitimate and terrifying force. Repeatedly, Brian spoke of "the Tangwena history of suffering," his body viscerally aching with memories of dispossession. If innocence is a luxuriant weed, as Günter Grass mused, Brian's was violently uprooted at an early age. An earlier hint of moistness turned dry as his angry eyes caught my gaze. "During the armed struggle," his voice became cold and sharp, "the 'chief' was comfortably seated elsewhere, eating yams." Brian mapped Magwendere outside a history of suffering at once locally grounded and integrally woven into national independence. By plotting a pretender to power in the lower-elevation Honde Valley, where yams dotted bogs and stream banks, Brian located Magwendere in a landscape of relative leisure during a moment when Kaerezian women, men, and children all endured evictions. As Simba later told me, conveying the sentiments of many, "Magwendere did not *see* the war."

Positioning Roots

Almost exactly a year later, I helped Brian's father, SaGumbo, plant a few fruit trees in his vegetable garden. Dozens of farmers had long asked me for help and advice in planting fruit, principally apples, and I had for months been trying to connect them to horticulturalists I knew who worked at the Experimental Fruit Station in Nyanga National Park. Few Kaerezians had worked on fruit farms, so most lacked technical knowledge required for tending orchards. They knew the scrawny trees that bore meager yields of poor quality on Nyafaru's cooperative farm, testament to what many termed "poor management." Productive orchards, in contrast, required complex knowledge, timing, and inputs: lime and fertilizer mixtures; pruning and grafting in relation to annual and seasonal cadences of dormancy; pesticides applied precisely. I spent time in experimental plots, in commercial orchards, and sites elsewhere in the district where smallholders with limited capital and only gravity-fed irrigation established healthy orchards. My time in fields, huts, and offices led to meetings, workshops, and a small training program, as well as the donation of grafted trees from a district commercial farm.

Collaborative discussions over the course of months persuaded me to draft a proposal, written in English, figuratively and literally translating cultivating desires as I understood them. Crucially, the proposal positioned fruit orchards at farmers' state-allocated arable sites without diminishing the acreage of other crops. Savvy Kaerezians knew transport would remain difficult, but they wanted fruit marketing opportunities and argued that these came with minimal disadvantageous dependencies. Some feared officials might use the lure of orchards as a wedge to begin mandating fruit. Others worried about implications for villagization. Complex negotiations ensued to minimize perceived threats as we re-

worked visions. Aware of the dangers of unintended and unanticipated outcomes, I turned from deep ambivalence toward more active if cautious advocacy
as increasing numbers of Kaerezians lobbied me. I drafted a document where
literally every line became scrutinized for its potential political implications—in
public meetings and private conversations. Several ministries at the district level
endorsed the proposal.

I did not tell state officials my major motivation that had emerged through
engagements with neighbors: to establish stronger property rights at homesteads
located beyond villagization's assigned residential plots. Governmental approval
for orchards would cut against state claims that Nyamutsapans were squatters by
rooting recognized land rights at scattered homesteads. All knew that fruit trees
took years to mature and produce harvests. Fruits' organic facticity made seedlings a consequential actant in assemblages located in Nyamutsapa's landscape.
By endorsing orchards, officials would implicitly support more temporally enduring land rights. As seedlings rooted and matured, organic processes entangled
earth, plants, and human aspirations for deepening land rights. Nyamutsapans
thus nurtured *nhaka* along with fruit in their small orchards.

Assembled in these humble orchards were months of articulated micropractices: written reports and letters securing ministry approval; lobbying officials in
offices, beer halls, and other social spaces; visits to homesteads, farmers' fields,
and commercial orchards; circuits of capital, knowledge, and labor that included tutorials at the Experimental Fruit Station in the bordering national
park; and distinct constellations of soil, slope, plants, and waterways. In turn,
farmers' embodied agency—located in precise places—*articulated* with these
translocal linkages.

During colonial moments, Alvord's schemes had linked Christian missionary
zeal with colonial conservation, a US education in agriculture with disciplinary
practices in an imperial periphery, and racialized rule with developmental progress. I knew these colonial legacies haunted postcolonial anthropology regardless
of my intentions. My own ethnographic fieldwork was at once a discursive
practice and a labor process. Whatever potential traction it might yield depended
radically on others' agency, articulations far beyond my control, and fields both
metaphorical and material.

Wielding a pick and shovel on a Nyamutsapa hillside in 1992, I lent a modest
hand, hoping grounded labor might nurture an orchard. The trickle of water
from the uphill spring, pruning and tending at crucial times of year, and capital
for fertilizer and to handle pests would be much more consequential than my

small acts. The poorest families could not afford these inputs, nor could they wait years to reap the harvests of this season's labor. While orchards might provide modest improvements in some families' long-term livelihoods, they excluded others, entangling with ongoing rural inequalities. It would be years before I could know how my agency and the much more significant labor of SaGumbo and his family would articulate with politics, agro-ecology, fluctuations in rainfall, and wage remittances sent by sons working afar—the vagaries of "nature" as well as political economy. Many moments, sites, and events shaped our digging of holes and packing of seedling roots into freshly turned earth. Emergence as analytic and harvest takes time, arriving only after uncertainty and appreciating that micropractices matter, shaping the terrain of subsequent struggles.

A Member of Parliament's Map

In early 1991, many described Magwendere as a "puppet" manipulated by a prominent headman who traveled with the chief to the DA's Nyanga office, as resettlement officer Marumahoko told me, "to demand my transfer." That night in a township beer hall, the headman allegedly asked allies if they would look after his family if he were to be arrested. Reporting the hearsay "death threat," Marumahoko filed an official complaint. Police investigated without pressing any charges. Months later, on a drizzly April morning, I sat in a packed Magadzire classroom watching Marumahoko and the implicated headman sitting a few visiting dignitaries apart. Beyond the usual armed police, district party officials, and the DA was the rarely seen face of the area's MP, Masaya, at the time also minister of finance.

Before the meeting, more than a hundred assembled people stared at a golden Mercedes Benz that slowly rumbled up the scheme's newly grated dirt road and parked near cement toilets a short walk from the state-built headmaster's house. Cars were almost never seen on Kaerezi's rough roads, let alone gleaming luxury vehicles. A white woman in high heels stepped gingerly onto wet grass, her floral dress descending from a raincoat. Reading my astonishment, Simba leaned over: "That's Masaya's wife; she's from America." After the meeting, she told me she had met her husband in Indiana, where he had earned his doctorate in statistics. Many complained bitterly that the MP neglected his peripheral constituents, rarely visiting while pursuing a career in the national political spotlight. They recalled a speech where he allegedly proclaimed, "I'm glad to see you people have developed since my last visit. I see many of you are now wearing shoes. Last time I was here, you were all barefoot." Apocryphal or not, such anecdotes abounded. When men used ramrod muskets to drive away pigs that marauded fields by night, Masaya told them they lacked state permits and should use spears instead. One disgruntled elder echoed the sentiments of many: "I'd like to see the MP out there in a field, in the thick of night, throwing *his* spear at a charging pig."

Clad in a Puma logo sweatshirt, Masaya took center stage in front of the classroom, flanked by DA and chief. The MP pumped his fist in the air, shouted nationalist party slogans, and denounced "oppression." All assembled knew the tragedy linking the MP and his wife to Mount Nyangani in nearby Nyanga National Park. Their two children had disappeared without trace on a family outing in the late 1980s. Army troops rushed to join the search, overturning in a truck, further adding to Nyangani's legend as a place of magical power. No bodies were found, and speculations ranged from a treacherous fall to kidnap by MNR bandits. It was a misfortune, a tragic accident (*njodzi*), somber voices whispered as we entered the classroom. In other moments, however, many referred to Masaya as a *tsotsi*, slang for "gangster" that connoted urban sophistication and criminal activity. Unbeknownst to almost all who used it, the term's transnational routes—it derived from refashionings of the US zoot suit in Soweto during the 1940s—also appreciated Masaya's slick casual clothes and the anomaly of Masaya's white American wife.[17]

After formal introductions and formulaic speeches, Magwendere stood to "tell the visiting MP our *zvichemo*," at once problems and pleas. Near Magadzire, a few families lived just across a fireguard from Tangwena territory in the national park. When in 1985 the white owner Igoe sold the parcel of Glen Eagles to state buyers who annexed it to the park estate, he gave permission to a favored labor tenant named Tombo to remain on the property. For years, park officials had tried to evict Tombo and his relatives who settled nearby, defining them as squatters. In 1991, private security guards from Igoe's Honde Valley tea estate allegedly hiked up to deliver eviction notices to the Tombo families now living on state property. Speculations abounded as to whose authority the security guards acted on: theirs, their white boss's, the park's, or some other state entity? Details never came clean, but threats to torch huts rekindled specters of racialized dispossession while politicizing white paternalism. Igoe supposedly granted residence rights in perpetuity to a loyal labor tenant, yet then sold the land. Park officials claimed that they administered a purchased commodity, not a landscape of patronage. If park staff evicted amid popular resistance, they might be perceived as more "white" than Igoe. As a result, years after the land sale, park administrators were perceived by many as having pressured Igoe to evict Tombo.

In Magadzire's packed classroom, Magwendere gave a meandering speech, ending by describing an alleged letter ordering the burning of seven families' huts in the disputed park borderland. "We thought the whites [*mabhunu*] had come again," he said, conjuring colonial evictions. Masaya responded to the crowd: "No one is allowed to burn someone's home without a letter from government [*hurumende*]." If he intended to convey populist outrage, the MP effectively reminded us that state sovereignty, legal ownership, and forceful eviction were of one flammable fabric. Masaya tried to sum up the situation, seemingly as much for himself as for those assembled:

> Igoe sold this land to **Trust**, but the **national park** is doing the administration. He sold it in 1985. We should have a **map** to point out the boundary of the Tangwena area. Government purchased Chimhini's [William Hanmer's] farm, and that's where you are resettled. Nyafaru does not belong to the Tangwena people because it has its own owners. It's a private farm, and they pay taxes to the government each year that you do not pay. You [addressing Magwendere] can rule the people but cannot control that place. So we should have a **map** to see the boundary of Chief Tangwena's area. . . . We can't have a final answer because we do not have a **map**.

To complicate matters, the resettlement officer claimed that the fireguard did not align with property boundaries and "Chief Tangwena's boundary does not correspond with Chimhini's boundary. Chief Tangwena's boundary is the traditional boundary of chiefs." An elder argued that the Tombo families lived in neighboring Chief Chikomba's territory. Masaya took the baton, lecturing the assembly: "Without boundaries, there would only be war. No one should do things outside of the law that rules this area." "Government," he reminded residents, "spent a lot of money to buy this land." As a result, "you should farm productively so government does not waste money on this place." The DA joined in, declaring that "we are following new boundaries, not old ones." Again, the MP addressed Magwendere directly: "You should rule your area, not the *purazi* of other people." *Purazi*, a term for commercial farm, racially coded the disputed park territory, officially state property, as *white*-owned. Masaya and other heavyweight black politicians owned *mapurazi* far away, but the only local commercial farms were remembered as sites of racialized dispossession.

In a tone at once exasperated and scolding, the MP commanded: "First, look at a **map**. Then look at the boundaries." As if to soften his scorn, he added, "The **resettlement officer** will help you." I watched Marumahoko's anxious glance catch the eye of headman who once threatened him. The DA pitched in again: "A chieftainship and a farm are two different things." For good measure, the MP encouraged Kaerezians to send a representative to the deed's office in Harare to find a map defining territorial truth. "A girl from Tangwena" worked there, he recalled, and could help. A "local" would thus welcome them in the capital, guiding them through the bureaucratic labyrinth that mapped property boundaries in turn legitimating ownership, evictions, and state-sanctioned violence.

Months later, a Ministry of Local Government official in Nyanga's district offices confided to me that he had searched fruitlessly for a definitive map of the disputed area. Nor could he find any documentation of land transfers that led to the current configuration of property boundaries. He had seen several maps of the area, but he could not locate the "real boundary" on any one. He asked me to please let him know if I "turned anything up" in my Harare archival research. Inquiries at several ministries produced a converging story: "manpower problems" in the surveyor-general's office had delayed an on-site demarcation and verification of the boundaries. Amid claims of cartographic control, the MP's invocation of a definitive map that grounded truth floated above a landscape where Kaerezians intimately knew territory. I hiked the several hours back to Nyamutsapa from Magadzire with a half dozen neighbors whose footsteps traversed trails that climbed above the grated scheme road, cut through gaps in ridges, and shortened the walk home. Atop a high ridge, SaGumbo stopped and looked back toward the disputed area, musing with a grin: "*Mugano wacho, unopuka-puka*" (That border keeps jumping around).

On a dank Harare day in 1992, an orderly at Harare's National Records Office brought one of dozens of boxes of government documents I had requested by permission slip. Searching for memos about Gaeresi Ranch squatters, I extracted a Ministry of Internal Affairs folder misfiled amid a jumble of dates and topics. Tucked in its flap, a curious hand-sketched map was neatly folded. Laying it flat, I scrutinized its clumsy cartography that resembled my own hand's efforts. Labeled "Gazetted Extent of Chief Tawungwena's Tribal Area," the sketch was dated 1972, the year of helicopter raids and the seizure of Tangwena children from Nyafaru school. Pencil notation referenced Government Notice of 1968 that officially gazetted "Chief Tawungwena's Tribal Areas." Notes scrawled on the bottom acknowledged the extension of African Reserves that cobbled together Crown Land east of Gaeresi Ranch and the northern portion of Holdenby, an estate purchased for state conversion to Tribal Trust Land. The notes omitted the date of land conversions, which other archives reported as 1948. The hand sketch and notes, however, reflected confusion as to whether that transfer effectively extended Tangwena territory into what had been Chief Chikomba's land.[18]

Decades and a liberation war later, the same area now entangled a national park where squatters, an MP, and Magwendere asserted claims. In 1965, one Rhodesian official declared that in Kaerezi the "Chieftainship is no longer functional" and that the "chief no longer has a tribal area."[19] In 1972, another state administrator sketched Tangwena tribal territories, referencing yet other civil servants who gazetted the area in 1968, but not those who named Rekayi Tangwena for eviction in 1969.[20] The 1972 handwritten sketch and notes betrayed no trace of dramatic skirmishes between Tangwena squatters and state evictors that had, for years, made the ranch a battle zone. Kaerezi's cartographic truth remained ambiguously positioned by archives of colonial contradiction complicated by ranch evictions. After independence, the DA and the MP invoked governing laws they located in the fetishistic fiction of a singular property map that would settle territorial disputes. From Tombo's humble huts to Harare high-rises, Kaerezi's multiple spatialities jostled together and tugged against one another.

Through the mid-1990s, Nyanga District administrative reports chronicled "boundary disputes" along Chief Tangwena's southern boundary near the Mozambique border. Magwendere continued to claim land in the national park, as well as within Holdenby Communal Area in Mutasa District. The Assistant District Administrator noted in 1993 that "maps should have increased accuracy" and that "no provision" had been made for producing definitive ones.[21] In 1995, Kaerezi's resettlement officer reported ongoing boundary disputes "spurred" by the 1985 state purchase of Glen Eagles and its subsequent annexation in 1987 to the park estate. Despite the surveyor-general's office's "reaffirming the position of the boundary in question the Tangwena did not and still do not recognize it. They continue sticking to their guns that as far as they are concerned the traditional boundary is the only legitimate boundary and feel that National Parks is on a 'land grabbing spree' that should be curtailed." His 1995 hand-sketched map included a narrative description of the "traditional boundary claimed by Chief Tangwena," but the officer explicitly noted it had not been "physically surveyed (checked)." He warned state officials to "expect some discrepancies" in the differing accounts of the chiefdom's boundary, especially in the "most sensitive area" where the Tombo families remained resident inside the national park. He also recalled the state purchase at independence of Gaeresi Ranch for "the Tangwena people who claimed their rights over the same land . . . belonging to their ancestors."[22] This government administrator—the one whose daily practices in the scheme made him the official with the most detailed knowledge of Kaerezians and Kaerezi—admitted that state boundary beacons, legal property demarcations, and cartographic representations had not politically trumped practices of Tangwena territory grounded in alternative articulations of tradition, rights, and sovereignty.

Precolonial Spoils in a Postcolonial Landscape

Elijah Nyahuruwa smiled outside his Tsatse shop as I greeted him as *Hanga*, respectfully using his lineage totem, a type of bird, to acknowledge our familiarity. A short walk north, past the lumbering diesel grinding mill where women gathered with sacks of grain perched atop their heads, his huts emerged on his lineage's rainmaking ridge bearing his name. In late 1991, Nyahuruwa positioned Magwendere outside yet deeper histories of suffering for territory: "Magwendere's great-grandfather stayed in Mozambique when Dzeka Tangwena came to Zimbabwe and eventually waged war with Nyahuruwa. Tangwena was the one who fought the war. The Tangwena should therefore enjoy the spoils. If you go hunting, you don't share the meat from your kill with someone who has stayed at home resting." Even the vegetarian anthropologist appreciated the allusion. The idiom marked both enduring interweave and tension between those sovereignties situated in patrilineal descent and those actively earned rather than passively received as a birthright.

Descended from generations of defeated rainmakers whose return from exile spliced together chiefly rule and rainmaking, Elijah resented claims to sovereign rights not won through struggle. During Rekayi's reign, Nyahuruwa had formed nationalist and localized alliance with another subversive sovereign *against* colonial rule and white rancher. Those struggles further aligned their ruling interests. On Magwendere's 1986 government appointment papers, officials recorded Elijah Nyahuruwa as the only registered claimant contesting the Tangwena chieftainship.[23] Five years on, as we spoke in Tsatse, Elijah still asserted ancestral entitlements to sovereignty earned through struggles spanning wars, regimes, nation-states, and eras.

Many echoed the alienated rainmaker. A couple in their fifties, speaking in 1991 at their Tsatse homestead, explicitly connected precolonial conquest and post-colonial politics. Nyamubaya supported Elijah's rendering of royal houses, recalling that Magwendere's great-grandfather "remained in Mozambique when Dzeka overthrew Nyahuruwa." After a later war that culminated in Zimbabwe's national independence, "when Magwendere heard that Rekayi was now chief, he came saying that he wants to be the chief. He was told by Rekayi that 'my chieftainship is not for inheritance but for my strong leadership during the war.' Magwendere went back to Honde and returned here after [Rekayi's] death. . . . He is ruling but doing nothing. He did not fight." His wife MaiNhamo broke in, furtive gestures embodying her rhetoric: "People want to burst with anger." A tirade of critique ensued. She paused, pensively, adding: "If a chief is hated by many people, he does not live for a long time." I wondered if her words actualized a wish or conjured Nyahuruwa's curse.

Nyamubaya shared MaiNhamo's anger: "We were simply told at a meeting that Magwendere is now our chief. . . . It was as if we were told that this is our **foreman**." Nyamubaya did not have to connect the dots. Magwendere mimicked a white colonial rancher. Both alienated rightful dwellers, subjecting them to unwanted discipline while claiming "ownership" buttressed by state rule. Popular practices supported alternative sovereignties. Nyamubaya also critiqued a *nyika*'s commoditization, tagging Magwendere's state salary as evidence of "selling out" territory and subjects.

Emplaced Affinities

However, Nyamubaya did mire not in sedentarism, arguing for an essentialized identity rooted to place. Born in Honde Valley, his birthplace was located near Magwendere's Mandeya home. His parents had moved to a Honde tea estate when they were evicted from land near Mount Nyangani, in the heart of Rhodes's estate, now Nyanga National Park. Nyamubaya's father worked first in Bulawayo and then in Cape Town, where he died. His mother, deprived of her husband's urban wages, moved to her parent's home in Honde Valley. She placed her young son with his paternal aunt, the wife of a labor tenant living on Gaeresi Ranch. Born in Mutasa's chiefdom south of Kaerezi, Nyamubaya grew up in Tangwena's.[24] Like his friend SaGumbo, born in Tsatse's kraal to a non-Tangwena father, Nyamubaya lacked a lineage rooted in a tribalized Tangwena ethnicity. Yet their shared struggles became articulated to a Tangwena community of belonging, rather than to pure patrilineages or essentialized bonds to birthplace. As both came of age, they *became* Tangwena, working for a white landowner, becoming subject to a chief, respecting a rainmaker as well as territory, and participating in the rhythms of rural life. Born beyond Tangwena territory, Nyamubaya, like SaGumbo, was proud to suffer for it:

> I moved with Rekayi Tangwena during the war. I went to Harare with him because in this area there were only a few people who were knowledgeable about different places. Also, my identity card [*chitupa*] was written "Mutasa," and those [Tangwena] who received their identity cards during that time had their chief written as "Miscellaneous." So if you were seen with such an identity card, you would be arrested because anyone known to come from the Tangwena area was arrested. Even myself, when I arrived where the police were, I could spy because my identity card was written "Mutasa." Rhodesian officials thought it was an ordinary person moving around. I moved with Chief Rekayi Tangwena.

A political technology that spatially disciplined tribal subjects became the condition of possibility for Nyamubaya's mobility, enabling him to cross police lines that cordoned off a white ranch. Colonial authorities, attempting to manage a racialized population through an ethnic spatial fix, required African bearers to carry identity cards at all times. While an official administrative optic mapped Nyamubaya's "tribal" identity and political loyalty to Honde Valley, his allegiance traveled with his Tangwena chief and their fellow labor tenants. Nyamubaya turned the malleability of a cultural politics of belonging—grounded in a shared sense of struggling for territory—against a security apparatus attempting to fix him in place and to regulate the movement of subversive subjects. Rhodesian refusal to recognize Rekayi's reign became inscribed on identity cards of those born in a chiefdom that lacked a state-sanctioned chief: "Chief Miscellaneous." As one schoolteacher quipped in English, "a most powerful man, that Chief Miscellaneous."

Against intended governmental effect, tribal administration enabled Nyamubaya to mix "Miscellaneous" and "Mutasa" with powerful consequences. He described a tense day during ranch evictions when "huts were being burnt and Rhodesian officials were happy to see me at my home. They wanted to arrest me. I told them I was a visitor passing through, coming from Nyamaropa [to the north] to my home in Zindi [to the south]. They looked at my identity card, and they saw that it was written "Mutasa," so they saw me as someone who had nothing to do with the Tangwena struggle." Governing practices that mapped political loyalties and residence to patrilineal homelands enabled his ruse. Compounding the irony, early colonial administrators had rewarded Chief Umtassa, their inverted spelling of Mutasa, for his political loyalty during major African uprisings in the 1890s. In Rhodesian rule's twilight, Nyamubaya reworked these legacies amid shifting sedimentations. Crucially, he helped give translocal traction to eyewitness accounts of racialized injustice. He dutifully gathered details from Nyafaru's headmaster who "told me that soldiers had come with dogs, guns, and the police. They were burning down huts. I wrote all of this down, and I went with the information. Journalists from around the world came to collect the news. People were surprised the next morning to hear it being broadcast on the radio. They were surprised how the news traveled although Tangwena was in Harare." In his sovereign's absence, Nyamubaya helped enable alliances with distant actors he never met.

Month's after listening to Nyamubaya, I ran across his name in a *Rhodesia Herald* account of Tangwena evictions from the early 1970s. Gaeresi Ranch was then sealed off as a security zone. The Ministry of Internal Affairs forbid reporters access, fearing inflammatory accounts of the state destruction of huts, crops, and possessions, and the flogging of bodies. Publicity on the BBC and other news outlets helped mobilize liberal whites, increasing the flow of blankets, food, and supplies to Nyafaru, then channeled to squatters hiding in mountain forests. Despite their perseverance and significant support, squatters lost traction when increasingly militarized ranch raids forced their flight to Mozambique. Shepherding Mugabe to safety in FRELIMO-controlled territory, they tilled a collective field where exiled chief and nationalist cultivated alongside commoners.

After independence, Kaerezians opposed villagization efforts pursued by officials attempting to impose a spatial discipline that thwarted practices of "farming freely" (*kurima madiro*). Some commoners received support from headmen and rainmaker to challenge sovereignty claimed by state officials, an MP, and the government-appointed chief Magwendere. While headmen claimed traditional rights to allocate land, many commoners remembered landscapes of self-settlement. Populists championed alternative traditions of neighborly negotiation as a more communal and democratic means of governing conduct. Patrilineal practices conditioned but did not guarantee political positions and landholdings. Challenges emerged, inflected but not controlled by those who asserted entitlements at once earned and emplaced through grounded struggles.

Kaerezians' agrarian micropractices—from planting *tsenza* on steep slopes to intercropping maize and beans in household fields embedded in homesteads to building huts—as well as impassioned words—staked site-specific claims. In orchards, family fields, and remote ridges, situated struggles conjured other moments and sites. Social relations in public meetings and private encounters reverberated long after Kaerezians dispersed. Ornery geographies of power grounded in Kaerezi's contentious histories at times thwarted AGRITEX planners who drew the lines of villagization in Harare offices and administrators who tried to implement them. The US-educated MP and DA both referenced property maps they never revealed, deferring verification of ground truth to other times and locations. Resettlement vied with rainmaking and chiefly rule in a territory where Kaerezians remembered ranch evictions, Mugabe's escape, Mozambican exile, and rights asserted amid their redemptive return to ancestral territory at independence. Striated with shifting sediments and practices, Kaerezi's postcolonial landscape remained entangled all the way down.

As *Suffering for Territory* went to press in May 2004, yet another era's cultural politics remapped racialized rights, land ownership, and evictions in a bizarre brawl on the floor of the Zimbabwean Parliament. The 2000 Land Acquisition Act had ushered in new-millennium agrarian politics that gave legislative support to widespread occupations of white farms by black squatters, fusing force to governmental endorsement. That year, so-called war veterans invaded a 7,000-acre Chimanimani estate owned by Roy Bennett who, in 1994, had been one of only three white MPs and a member of the opposition Movement for Democratic Change (MDC). Ongoing violence on his property left workers and MDC members dead amid brutal beatings by ZANU-PF supporters and allegations of police torture. In May 2004, after four High Court rulings in his favor, Bennett learned that his property would remain among the thousands designated for state seizure.

During a legislative session, Patrick Chinamasa, the minister of justice, legal, and parliamentary affairs, coded the dispossession as racial payback: "Mr. Bennett has not forgiven the government for acquiring his farm, but he forgets that his forefathers were thieves and murderers." An enraged Bennett shouted in Shona and assaulted Chinamasa. Didymus Mutasa—ZANU-PF secretary and speaker of Parliament for Zimbabwe's first decade—entered the fray, physically defended his fellow cabinet minister, and in the ensuing scuffle kicked the fallen Bennett. In the early 1970s, Mutasa had comanaged Nyafaru while Gaeresi Ranch's owner Hanmer and state officials inflicted beatings and evictions on Tangwena squatters. More than three decades later, law, race, and violence articulated with radically different effects. ZANU-PF supporters protested in Harare, calling for Bennett's arrest and attacking the MDC headquarters. Also in May 2004, the Supreme Court opened hearings on the constitutionality of a law enacted in 2002 that jailed white farmers who failed to leave their confiscated farms. Courting possible arrest and violence, an unrepentant Bennett proclaimed: "Whatever the consequences, I am ready to die for Zimbabwe. I am a Zimbabwean. I am not a white man; I am not a black man." Trading accusations of racism, Mutasa countered: "We have not forgotten the suffering we went through during the liberation struggle."[1]

Nor did Rekayi Tangwena's widow. In early June 2004, MaiElijah sharply criticized Mutasa—recently appointed minister of anticorruption—alleging that he usurped rights earned by Tangwena territorial suffering. Mutasa became implicated in a shady deal that leased land on Nyafaru, where he remained an absentee shareholder, to an outside timber concession. She demanded in a national newspaper to "see Mugabe and Mutasa," challenging them to "actually tell me that this land no longer belongs to the Tangwena people and that it has been sold." The widow of the anticolonial chief buried in Harare's Heroes' Acre and, for some, a revered spirit medium, told reporters: "My people and I are prepared to die for this land and we will not move away. Let them bring the soldiers as the Rhodesians used to do during the liberation war."[2] MaiElijah implied that Nyafaru's once populist multiracial cooperative, where ZANU-PF elites influenced management, had become a site of postcolonial dispossession.

Encouraging her defiant challenge, in April 2004 a political coalition of Kaerezians spanning generations explicitly responded to Mutasa's actions in a document entitled "The Tangwena Land Struggle"—supported in signature by Chief Magwendere, rainmaker Nyahuruwa, the six Tangwena headmen, and Rekayi's widow, but written in the formally educated English of nameless younger allies who sent it to the *Daily Mirror*, a national newspaper that did not publish it. This text elaborated the entangled histories of the Tangwena chieftaincy and Nyafaru—excised from the surrounding Gaeresi Ranch in the late 1950s—and chronicled numerous meetings with Mutasa at which Kaerezians openly opposed the leasing of Nyafaru land. "To us," the manifesto declared, "Comrade Mutasa represents a re-incarnation of *Chimhini*," Gaeresi Ranch's white owner. Nyafaru "was, and still is, the Tangwena people's ancestral homeland," the authors wrote, accusing Mutasa of "dispossessing people of their birthright and heritage for a few pieces of silver." They sent a related petition to the minister of lands, John Nkomo. In July 2004, police arrested several Tangwena headmen and elders associated with this vocal opposition. A Tangwena friend wrote me a letter describing the jailing of SaGumbo, Simba, and other Kaerezians on trumped-up charges. "Mutasa plays politics," my friend's letter underscored, "when we speak the language of inalienable rights."[3] Supporters raised bail from donations, releasing the detained from bone-chilling cells in Nyanga, where they had been denied blankets for days.

Specters of violent dispossession still haunt Kaerezi as emergent articulations contest legacies of liberation: whose suffering, whose sovereignty, and grounded in whose territory? Ongoing agrarian politics debate these as matters of livelihood, liberty, and rights—in Parliament, in courts, and across landscapes of sedimented struggles. To examine these formations, my analysis drew from a Gramscian emphasis on grounded struggles that entangled translocal political economies. State violence and capitalist discipline imposed coercion, while racialized rule targeted transformations in power relations, agrarian production, and land tenure. I emphasized cultural politics, territory, and labor relations as contested and contingent terrains. My historical and ethnographic elaborations foregrounded a politics "without guarantees" that shaped the precariousness of livelihoods, rights, and vulnerabilities.[4] I also used Foucauldian tools to analyze political technologies of rule that governed conduct and custom in administered spaces, from colonial tribe and ranch to a postcolonial resettlement scheme. Governmentality targeted transformations that enlisted tribal subjects and rural cultivators in projects of self-improvement and developmental progress that were envisioned as contributing to individual, community, and national welfare. I formulated the notion of a triad-in-motion to probe how situated sovereignties, disciplinary practices, and governmental projects shape power relations in Zimbabwe. Such relations, neither reducible to nor determined by "the state," I stress, remain entangled in racialized spaces, subjection, and legacies of violent conquest.

As an analytic of power, governmentality helps provincialize the state yet also needs to be provincialized by the diverse deployments of sovereignty, discipline, and government in colonial and postcolonial contexts. By grounding governmentality in Kaerezi, I counter recent conceptualizations of the term as a singular rationality of rule—a formulation abetted by the twinned tendencies of textualism and ethnographic anemia in governmentality studies. Such visions, I argue, elide the often ornery entanglements of landscape and historically sedimented power relations. In Kaerezi, both Rhodesian indirect rule and postcolonial government have contended with rainmaking and chiefly sovereignty, with headmen's and commoners' claims, and with ancestral spirits and legacies of African and European conquests. The contingencies of memory work, disputed histories, and multiple spatialities in postcolonial Kaerezi unsettle any monolithic conception of power.

Heritage, Foucault wrote around the time of Tangwena evictions, is not an "acquisition, a possession that grows and solidifies; rather it is an unstable assemblage of faults, fissures and heterogeneous layers that threaten the fragile inheritor."[5] Crucial to this genealogical approach, argues Wendy Brown, is an appreciation of "spatial accretion" and an awareness of "power as a field of forces in space."[6] My analytic of entangled landscapes stressed grounded power relations and unstable assemblages. I highlighted how politics pivot on *effective articulations*, gaining traction on this contingent terrain. Foregrounding conditions of possibility, my genealogical perspective rejected historicist teleologies— inevitable outcomes or foretold futures "determined" by the past. Instead, I emphasized how historical *sedimentations* as well as emergent possibilities informed Kaerezi's distinct mixtures of moments, milieus, and micropractices.

Kaerezian livelihoods and identities, I argued, were sedimented but not sedentarist. Since long before white arrival, commoners shifted fields while claiming rights of self-settlement governed by neighborly conduct. Respective lineages of a vanquished rainmaker and a conquering chief disputed sovereignties and territorial powers. Articulated effects moved in multiple directions at once while positioning subjects, discursive fields, social relations, and material inequalities. After an epic precolonial ax murder that exiled Nyahuruwa, Tangwena confronted drought and his subjects' populist pressure to negotiate the rainmaker's return. More than a century later, postcolonial villagization efforts placed commoners in the cross fire between District Administrator and acting chief, both claiming to represent sovereignty, to rule territory, and to discipline subjects.

This book stressed how grounded practices both joined and enunciated disparate moments, places, and events. In 1902, state officials appointed Dzeka Tangwena as chief, entangling him in Rhodesian indirect rule. Generations later, his own son, Rekayi, and Elijah Nyahuruwa, the defeated rainmaker's heir, anchored their ancestral claims to huts and fields in Tsatse kraal. As tenants on Gaeresi Ranch, they sent urban migrant wages to their wives who cultivated subsistence plots. In turn, Tangwena headmen collected state taxes sent home and helped the white landlord secure tenant labor, toiling along with commoners. When, in the late 1950s, Rekayi and Elijah joined an African nationalist party in Bulawayo, urban migrant labor, anticolonial politics, and a colonial ranch became effectively articulated.

By examining Kaerezi's cultural politics of place as locally distinctive and imperially inflected, I elaborated its transcontinental and transnational entanglements. In the late 1920s, Hanmer's imperial connections—his great-grandfather's brother served as governor of New Zealand—helped secure overseas shareholder capital to purchase Gaeresi Ranch. Nyafaru's sale to British investors in the 1950s created an unanticipated anomaly as progressive whites and African nationalists established a multiracial cooperative on land legally declared European. In that era, the Nyafaru cooperative, Gaeresi Ranch, and the Tangwena chiefdom became entangled through property transfers, long-distance shareholders, and political support, and they were linked to black urban elites as well as liberal whites in the UK. In the same moment, Christian humanism, socialist agriculture, a small school, legal advisors, and African nationalists all converged in Tangwena territory.

Similarly, complex entanglements emerged when former political prisoners fled Rhodesian security forces through Kaerezi. In 1975, Kaerezians shepherded Robert Mugabe and Edgar Tekere to Mozambique where commoners and elites cultivated cooperative fields and a shared sense of exilic suffering. Flight to FRELIMO-controlled territory traversed a landscape linked through precolonial regional ruling relations, ongoing Tangwena cross-border connections, and transnational solidarities between Mozambican and Zimbabwean liberation movements. Mugabe met ZANLA guerrillas at Vila Gouveia, an outpost named after the nineteenth-century warlord and colonial administrator from Goa. Gouveia had battled Barwe royalty, the paramount Makombe, whose predations caused Chief Tangwena's flight to territory ruled by Nyahuruwa, a hospitable rainmaker. After years of safe refuge, Tangwena turned against his host, seizing territory through violent conquest. These alternative spatialities haunted Rhodesian attempts to administer a tribal territory and a colony's sovereign space. Specters of selective sovereignties animated entangled geo-bodies that had localized boundaries yet whose contentious histories extended across the temporal and spatial boundaries of colonial rule. When administrators evicted Kaerezians in the 1970s, geographies of power linked to Lisbon, London, and South Asia shaped this landscape of dispossession and exile.

To situate struggles on Kaerezi in these translocal histories of place, I focused on critical events surrounding colonial evictions that articulated chiefdom and nation-state—two *nyika*s entangled through anticolonial politics that opposed injustices of Rhodesia's racialized rule. In the 1970s, Africans on Gaeresi Ranch refused the coercive fiction of a labor "agreement," challenging a white landlord's discipline. Targeted as squatters by governmental proclamations orchestrating their eviction, Kaerezians became dispossessed of land legally designated European. After their attempts to govern African conduct failed, an alliance of white capitalist rancher and state officials fused force and power. Marshaling laws and armed invaders, police torched huts, beat squatters, plowed under crops, and seized cattle, effectively severing livelihoods linked to locale. Amid UDI's excessive unfreedoms, I showed how Kaerezians' refusal to submit to Rhodesian rule exposed the illiberal underbelly of racialized injustice. Even amid displacement, squatters and their supporters laid critical groundwork for subsequent struggles. Tangwena defiance gained translocal traction as newspaper editorials, human rights activists, and African nationalists articulated ancestral territory, challenges to state sovereignty, and appeals to global justice, and antiracist humanism. Kaerezi evictions became evidence of Rhodesia's illegitimate force and inability to *govern* Africans.

Traction lost in one moment and milieu became entangled with ground gained in another. Postcolonial government in Kaerezi struggled with these illiberal colonial legacies while attempting to administer new freedoms. At independence, state purchase converted a white ranch to land redistributed to black smallholders, enabling the nationalist hero Rekayi to rule his chiefdom. Contingent conditions of possibility enabled Mugabe's election as the new country's prime minister and ZANU-PF to become the ruling nationalist party. Tekere turned against his former allies, eventually forming an opposition movement that never gained traction. Similar to Tekere's shifting political alliances, many articulations remained relatively ineffective. Others dormant in one moment emerged in anther. After Rekayi's death in 1984, administrators escalated resettlement efforts, reworking articulations of sovereignty, spatial discipline, and governing conduct.

I focused on villagization to highlight how postcolonial government targeted agrarian micropractices mapped to functionally distinct arable, grazing, and pastoral zones. Colonial technocrats had first sketched this spatial discipline deemed crucial to developmental progress in plans and on rural landscapes through centralization and the Native Land Husbandry Act. Alvord's holy trinity was born again as Harare planners and Nyanga administrators argued that Kaerezians would improve themselves and national welfare by submitting to villagization's governmental grids. Enabled by government, the "free" market would discipline the cultivation of fields and selves as monocrops planted for market would link Kaerezi smallholders to national, regional, and global circuits of capital. However, as I showed, government at a distance also confronted the frictions of alternative articulations, some thwarting state administration.

Government, what Kaerezians termed "*hurumende*," pursued projects that produced unfreedoms and injustices as well as resettlement rights. A widespread refusal to recognize villagization's grids as a legitimately governed space linked *maline* and *kumanikidza*, linear settlement grids and imposed force. While not unitary, Tangwena interests, identities, and entitlements became articulated to "suffering for territory." Both verbal protest and grounded livelihood practices that spatially mixed huts and fields insistently yoked assertions of postcolonial "freedom farming" (*kurima madiro*) to place-based political rights. When the DA or MP invoked ownership and property boundaries to justify state sovereignty, eviction orders, and orchestrated hut burning, their threats rekindled memories of Rhodesian *racialized* violence.

I positioned postcolonial agrarian politics in relation to disputed spatialities, sovereignties, and rights to analyze both administrative attempts to discipline rural subjects and counterclaims staked by Kaerezians. In 1991, Nyanga's DA targeted "squatters" who defied the discipline of their state landlord. On official stationery, in resettlement scheme meetings, and in his Nyanga office, he attempted to map governing distinctions to separate state property purchases, to *disarticulate* Nyamutsapa from the Tangwena chiefdom, *rearticulating* it to an administrative annex. Populists and traditionalists alike argued that Nyamutsapa formed an inalienable portion of the Tangwena chiefdom, not a commoditized transfer defined by title deeds. Eviction threats, conjuring specters of racialized dispossession, produced unintended effects. By imposing villagization by force, officials undermined their claims to govern subjects.

Against this governmental mixture of land, labor, and capital, Kaerezians asserted counterclaims to place. Defiance of villagization's governing grids gained traction not by defending a place sealed off from outside power but rather by *articulating* locality to postcolony through contingent constellations of rights, rule, and legacies of racialized dispossession. In contrast to recent theorists' assertions of a deterritorialized "space of flows" emblematic of globalization's "new spatial logic,"[7] I stressed how Kaerezi's landscape was formed through sediments and striations: from hand-dug irrigation channels, plowed contour ridges, and iron pegs demarcating uninhabited "villages"; to a rainmaking range, chiefly compounds associated with precolonial conquest and colonial sellouts, and a multiracial cooperative; to specific fields and homesteads, *tsenza* plots on distant slopes, and memories mapped to specific sites. Tsatse, as a place of sedimented power relations, entangled precolonial conquest, Dzeka's colonial installation, the ancestral homes of Rekayi Tangwena and Elijah Nyahuruwa, and the epicenter of Hanmer's ranch evictions.

I emphasized agency amid such struggles, but stressed that humans alone did not produce Kaerezi's history and geography. In the 1970s, rains conjured, as many asserted, by ancestral spirits cascaded down steep slopes, thwarting traction for Rhodesian troops who pursued nationalist guerrillas. During colonial evictions, a waterfall hid a subaltern squatter while soldiers converged on smoke seeping through her empty cook hut. That fire, attracting armed evictors in one moment, emerged out of previous sediments. In the 1960s, MaiZiko's labor, at once embodied and emplaced, transformed trees into firewood by carrying bundles home. She mixed mud, clay, and straw bricks, harnessing solar energy to bake them solid. Her husband, home from stints as a migrant wage laborer, erected a roof frame on which he skillfully wove harvested grass. Years before, his African labor, disciplined by a white ranch owner born in Britain, had established plantations of wattle, rooting an Australian tree species in Kaerezi soil. Wattle produced ranch profits, poles for tenants' huts, and fuel for the torching of Kaerezians' homes by colonial police and soldiers.[8]

In my view, a humble hut, as much as colonial evictions and postcolonial villagization, constitutes an articulated *assemblage*: it gathers together nature and culture, labor and landscape, producing material and discursive consequences. I probed such consequential constellations to argue that agency and situated struggles *matter*; both inform, rather than script, landscapes entangled with power relations and geophysical substance. Administrative efforts to shepherd settlers into linear grids encountered the shoals of sedimented livelihoods linked to specific sites and environmental attributes such as springs, slope, and soil quality. For most Kaerezians, a home, or *musha*, mingled fields, huts, and pastoralism in ways that defied state spatial segregation of these zones.

Such micropolitics of place, I argued, underscore that subjects are not self-sovereign agents but rather are subjected to power relations whose outcomes they cannot control. My vision counters renderings of politics as an arena of instrumental actors deploying Machiavellian means to pursue instrumental ends and ensure orchestrated outcomes. Hence I focused on how Magwendere's 1987 appointment by state officials as a new acting chief positioned him, against his intentions, in power relations that challenged his ruling claims. Like postcolonial administrators who represented the property-owning state, Magwendere became an enforced imposition rather than a popular leader.

Kaerezians located the new chief outside geographies and histories of suffering for territory since he had lived outside Tangwena territory during Rekayi's reign. His civil servant salary and Magadzire homestead linked him to Chief Kinga rather than to Rekayi, to idioms of "selling out" that commoditized a chiefdom. Countering Magwendere's claims to a Tangwena *nyika* as his patrilineal birthright, some headmen and commoners refashioned *nhaka*, rightful inheritance, as a political right *earned* through site-specific struggle. Many also argued that Magwendere's *Vapostori* conduct put his subjects' welfare at risk, angering the dead as well as the living. By refusing to brew beer to propitiate territorial ancestral spirits, he failed to rule wisely. Relations between micropractices and milieu, the imbrication of "men and things," and the welfare of population and territory all suffered.

Rainmaker Nyahuruwan, district party chairman of ZANU-PF, countered the salaried Magwendere's claims to rule territory, complicating the postcolonial administration of governed spaces. He dragged precolonial conquest into postcolonial disputes over sovereignties at once selective and situated. Despite Magwendere's defiance of villagization, his leadership remained contested by popular objections, headmen who recalled shepherding Mugabe to safety in 1975, and a rainmaking rival with prominent and personalized connections to ruling party politicos.

Kaerezi's contentious power relations also subjected me to conditions beyond my control. In 1992, a postcolonial army officer and former guerrilla—in that era usually termed an "ex-combatant" rather than a "war veteran"—leveraged his ZANU-PF connections into resettlement rights against the objections of some district and provincial civil servants. Making manifest his military connections, huge army trucks carried the colonel's fencing materials to a Kaerezi site. Rapid infusions of capital hired labor and erected material infrastructure on a prime plot to which he laid claim beyond villagization's grids. The groundwork for orchards emerged inside expensive wire fencing, while disputes raged over his dramatic arrival, his alleged intimidation of a Kaerezian who claimed fields in the site, and who officially authorized his "resettlement right." Heated debates, threats of physical force, and grounded politics positioned my own ethnographic practice amid these disputes.

Ironies abounded where the former freedom fighter established what some called a *purazi*, the term for "commercial farm" and a territorial designation racialized as white. Unanticipated alliances supported the ex-combatant's land claims, while unexpected affinities emerged to challenge his assertions. Official opinion divided in Kaerezi meetings, in offices in Nyanga, Mutare, and Harare, and in more confidential encounters. Some held nationalist party lines, while others openly criticized a "corrupt" process. The savvy colonel, critics noted, intimidated "locals" while circumventing the usual resettlement application process, effectively establishing a commercial farm on state-owned land. They stressed his strategic selection of Kaerezi for political as well as agro-ecological reasons: its soil, climate, and environmental features—with high rainfall and mountain streams to harness for irrigation—were conducive to capital-intensive fruit production.

Some Kaerezians objected to officials over what they perceived as usurpation. Others, fearful of reprisal, waited and watched. Most agreed that the ex-combatant, who had suffered for territory as a guerrilla, deserved land rights. But they disagreed on *where* he was entitled to settle. For some, he was an outsider invading a Tangwena *nyika*, seizing land by force; for others, he represented a powerful patron whose local presence might become a benefit. Some negotiated with transporters hired by this rich entrepreneur to haul home their own fertilizer and building materials or to take their crops to market. Both Kaerezians and state officials enlisted my help in opposing the colonel's initial "invasion"; others lobbied for me to support his land claims. As political terrain shifted, some switched their allegiances, in turn, encouraging me to realign with them. When I left Zimbabwe in 1992 after twenty-six months of fieldwork, contending alliances positioned me in this cross fire while I struggled to position myself amid a volatile politics of place.

When I returned to Kaerezi in 1996 for a couple of months' fieldwork, the commandeered ex-combatant's farm had radically transformed the landscape. Inside hectares of expensive wire fencing, a skillfully engineered cement pond and elaborate networks of gravity-fed irrigation pipes channeled a mountain stream throughout neatly manicured orchard rows tended by an on-site employee hired from elsewhere. I cautiously inquired about perceptions of these emergent entanglements of resettlement rights, legacies of liberation, and territorial cultural politics. "When the colonel arrived," one Kaerezian in his thirties asserted, "he was perceived as a threat . . . as representing the beginning of a process of land grabbing. And that is from one angle." Then this son of a labor tenant evicted from Gaeresi Ranch aptly articulated an alternative political condition of possibility:

> We saw him as sort of a solution to a problem. Because he was going to liberate us, we were no longer going to be pushed into resettlement areas, demarcated areas where there was no water, where there was no access to better soils. So if he succeeded, it means that we could also claim land. So in a way, we saw him as a savior to our problem . . . of enforced villagization. . . . So if [the colonel] succeeded as he has done, then we know that the resettlement people—Marumahoko [the resettlement officer] and his regime—would not come to challenge us. We can claim land at liberty now.

In 1996, not all Kaerezians experienced these agrarian articulations as conducive to their freedoms. A few friends asked me for help in contacting human
rights organizations after they were threatened by ZANU-PF members in the
district center. In Nyanga's administrative offices, I read case files that chronicled
Central Intelligence Organization (CIO) investigations in Kaerezi, suggesting that
the colonel's presence had increased official surveillance in the area. My name
appeared in one of the reports, and neighbors told me of armed visitors who had
made aggressive "inquiries" in Nyamutsapa about my research. Subsequent interviews and fieldwork in 1996 persuaded me to exclude from this book ethnographic details of grounded Kaerezi politics during that period—a decision
reinforced by volatile agrarian struggles since 2000 when self-proclaimed "war
veterans" occupied hundreds of white farms. As Zimbabwe's political violence
continues, my concern for vulnerable Kaerezians shapes my selective silences.
Ethical and political stakes that cannot be corralled by scripted intentions continue to inform my ethnographic positioning.

My 1996 return to Kaerezi engaged ongoing cultural politics surrounding sovereignty, subjection, and territorialized power relations. I missed Magwendere's
official state coronation ceremony by a month; research on agrarian conflicts in
South Africa had delayed my arrival. His leadership remained contested enough
to delay his installation for a decade, yet he was tolerated—his state-salaried rule
produced neither consensus nor consent. At his 1996 installation ceremony, A. O.
Gara, the deputy minister of local government, told the Tangwena people assembled that "the Government of Zimbabwe appreciates the role you played to free
this country." He explicitly acknowledged the history of those "subjected to . . .
tribulation" by colonial evictions from Kaerezi. "Protracted squabbles over the
choice of chief" had delayed Magwendere's official installation, Gara openly admitted in his formal speech, but the new chief had finally "relinquished his
religious commitments" as a *Vapostori*. At the installation, another official who
swore Magwendere into office also recounted the chiefdom's history, congratu-
lating the Tangwena people who "suffered and struggled so that this country
could achieve its independence. I am very proud to be with you today in your
land you fought for in the independent Zimbabwe."[9] Chiefdom and nation-
state, land struggles and liberation, colonial suffering and postcolonial rights
remained entangled in the 1996 government-orchestrated installation ceremony
of a "tribal" chief.

The next month, I took a bus from Harare to Nyanga Township where I
grabbed a ride to Kaerezi in the back of Nyafaru's truck, jumping out on a

Nyamutsapa ridgeline. Below me the Kaerezi's sparkling headwaters bounded Tangwena territory. Across the river, Dazi's lines of state discipline still stood straight. In Nyamutsapa, where a *tsungo* entangled Tangwena and Nyahuruwa territory, scattered homesteads dotted the landscape, defying governmental grids still marked by rusted stakes that demarcated uninhabited "villages." A few more permanent structures made from brick, gathered stones, or cement blocks suggested that some felt more secure in their land rights outside the lines. Yet only a few could afford houses rather than huts, a sign of urban wages sent home by husbands and grown children.

Angela's son's remittances from a Bulawayo job had purchased building materials for a modest brick house—built on the spot where, in the early 1990s, she had straddled the lines of state power and chiefly decree. The Gumbos and MaiHurudza, with less capital and more mouths to feed, struggled to make ends meet. Villagization's fate remained uncertain, if unlikely due to the shortage of government funds, staff, and political will in the face of sustained popular opposition. While most spoke of the colonel's commercial farm operations as a positive influence, opinion remained divided concerning its political implications. Some worried that if an absentee "outsider" could establish effective land claims, political caprice could evict those who lacked political patrons. But they also recognized that a new DA preferred carrots to sticks. The Syracuse-trained molecular biologist had moved on; the new official had a development studies degree from Birmingham. In that British city, Didymus Mutasa attended university in the 1950s and, in a later moment, Stuart Hall taught and wrote work that deeply informs this book.

While villagization's success appeared much less viable than in the early 1990s, debates still raged over spatiality, sovereignty, and freedom farming. Women continued to cultivate steep mountain slopes far from arable sites designated by state administrators or household patriarchs. Agrarian micropractices and impassioned speeches still asserted land rights as earned entitlement in tension with the scheme's plotted patrilineal inheritance. Settlement remained governed by a judicious mix of neighborly conduct, social relations, and ancestral claims that vied with state administration and Chief Magwendere's rulings. Triads-in-motion still spun.[10]

As I sat in the Gumbos' smoky cook hut, affect flowed as warmly as the tea. MaiHurudza arrived, ululating through a cupped hand, rough and strong, turning scat-sung shouts into a sonic rhythm at once embodied and ensouled. News of friends and family, Mandela and Mbeki, marriages, funerals, and births produced smiles and sadness. Tales of hardship darted across the flickering fire, along with news of drought, the AIDS epidemic, and struggles to make a living during Zimbabwe's economic crises. Assembled around that fire, we appreciated suffering, for it reminded us that we are not self-sovereign subjects. We did not control the powerful practices articulated through suffering that engendered our affinities, helped produce interests that provisionally allied some of us, and positioned us differently in radical asymmetries of race, class, and other constructed cultural differences. Laughter also emerged, accompanying tales of educational triumphs and friends' children landing a coveted urban job. As I bit into a chunk of freshly dug *tsenza*, its skin scraped off by a piece of kindling also harvested by MaiNyasha, I knew from the moist root's texture that Nyahuruwa, the rainmaker, had dutifully performed his work. Powerful assemblages of ancestral spirits and pious prayers, located labor and cultivated landscapes, historical sediments and emergent ambitions had produced a sustaining harvest. So, too, each remains entangled in suffering for territory.

Notes

Preface

1 Martin and Johnson 1981, 35–36. This episode echoed Britain's imperial dimensions of racialized exclusion brilliantly chronicled by Gilroy [1987] 1991.

2 Televised address by president Robert Mugabe on the occasion of Zimbabwe's twentieth anniversary, Pockets Hill, Harare, April 18, 2000, available at www.gta.gov.zw.Presidential%20Speeches/televised.address.html.

3 Televised address by president Robert Mugabe on the occasion of Zimbabwe's twentieth anniversary, Pockets Hill, Harare, April 18, 2000, available at www.gta.gov.zw.Presidential%20Speeches/televised.address.html.

4 Amnesty International chronicled more than 1,000 reported cases of torture in 2002 alone and "at least 58 politically motivated deaths." See "Zimbabwe Rights under Siege," May 2, 2003, available at web.amnesty.org/library/Index/ENGAFR460122003. Government officials have also seized a discourse of human rights. In March 2003, the minister of justice Patrick Chinamasa complained to the United Nations Commission on Human Rights in Geneva about "the arrogance of the developed countries and their insensitivity to the gross human rights violations and crimes against humanity that they, as former colonial powers and slave-trading and slave-owning societies, had committed against the majority of peoples of developing countries." See Mthulisi Mathuthu, "As Chinamasa Fails to Sell Land Reform, Government Rapped for Human Rights Violations," *Zimbabwe Independent*, March 21, 2003, available at www.theindependent.co.zw/news/2003/March/Friday21/1529.html.

5 See Rutherford 2003 for an elaboration of the plight of farmworkers.

6 ZANU-PF took 4 billion Zimbabwean dollars from the country's coffers to pay 50,000 dollars compensation to each of the 55,000 war veterans. See "State Gives War Vets Extra $1 Billion," *Zimbabwe Standard*, July 29, 2001.

7 See Hammar, Raftopoulos, and Jensen 2003 and Worby 2001 for superb overviews

of this transformation. Figures for the total number of farms in the large-scale commercial farm sector vary from 4,000 to 4,500.

8 Michael Hartnack, "Share Cropping," zwnews, August 13, 2003, reporting figures announced at the Commercial Farmer's Union annual congress.

9 Michael Hartnack, "Share Cropping," zwnews, August 13, 2003, quoting the minister of agriculture Joseph Made.

10 Before the 2000 land occupations, approximately 4,500 large-scale commercial farms, by most accounts more than 90 percent of them owned by whites, extended over 11.2 million hectares of Zimbabwe's total estimated 32.4 million hectares of arable land. A million families occupied 16 million hectares of Communal Areas, smallholder plots in former Native Reserves owned by the state. Approximately 70,000 black resettlement families carved furrows on 3.5 million hectares, while state farms and mainly black small-scale commercial farms combined for less than 2 million hectares of Zimbabwe's total geographical extent of 39 million hectares. See Hammar, Raftopoulos, and Jensen 2003. Moyo 2000 emphasized that of the approximately 1,500 farms targeted for acquisition in 2000, around 250 were black-owned. Multiple ownership of farms, a subject of continued controversy, makes reliable figures extremely difficult.

11 Robert Mugabe, qtd. in "Mugabe Vows Land Seizures to Go Ahead, Calms Whites." *New York Times*, June 26, 2002.

Introduction

1 I use pseudonyms for all Kaerezians except the chief, rainmaker, and six Tangwena headmen whose views on state policy are documented in government reports.

2 This and all subsequent translations from ChiManyika, a dialect of ChiShona, are my own. In Nyanga district, so-called Standard Shona and ChiManyika are often mixed. Boldface designates English words embedded in ChiShona syntax.

3 As I elaborate, an emplaced idiom of suffering for territory drew historically from transnational human rights discourses as well as Christian humanism. Yet I wish to foreground its geographical, historical, and cultural distinctiveness. Elsewhere in Zimbabwe, scholars have explored postcolonial memories animated by idioms of enduring violence. See especially Alexander, McGregor, and Ranger 2000; Bhebe and Ranger 1995; Werbner 1991; and Worby 1998. For a related yet distinct literature on "social suffering," see Bourdieu et al. 1999 and Kleinman, Das, and Lock 1997.

4 Goldberg and Quayson (2002), Hall (1996), and Young (2001) provide generative reflections on the analytical and political stakes surrounding the use of the term *postcolonialism*, emphasizing themes of sovereignty, power relations, and multiple histories.

5 Foucault, few note, did not *coin* the term *governmentality* (*gouvernementalité*), but

his work has crucially informed its distinct deployments. For an earlier elaboration, see Barthes [1957] 1984, 130.

6   Among the most influential perspectives on structure and agency were those of Bourdieu [1972] 1977, Giddens 1979, and Sahlins 1981. In addition to Foucault's generative work, strands of poststructuralism and feminism elaborated how power relations produced subjects who were not self-sovereign actors. This shift also tended to unyoke agency from consciousness and intentionality. See Butler 1993 for an influential elaboration of these stakes.

7   Rose 1999.

8   Foucault (1983, 210) encouraged empirical analysis of "specific rationalities," rather than the "dangerous" abstract formulation of "rationalization." Contributions to Burchell, Gordon, and Miller (1991), the journal *Economy and Society*, and scholars associated with the History of the Present group in Britain have greatly shaped subsequent scholarship. See Barry, Osborne, and Rose 1996 and Dean and Hindess 1998 for interventions that focus on governmentality, liberalism, and neoliberalism. Dean (1999) and Rose (1999) offered helpful overviews of governmentality studies. While much of this literature is richly *empirical*, it is rarely *ethnographic*. Ethnographic perspectives are even less evident in recent elaborations of relations between culture and governmentality (e.g., Barnett 1998; and Bratich, Packer, and McCarthy 2003).

9   In so doing, I also build on a rich ethnographic literature on state practices (Gupta 1998; Hale 1994; Herzfeld 1987; and Verdery 1996). Governmentality oriented some contributions to Hansen and Stepputat (2001), as well as the ethnographic projects of Hansen (2001), Li (1998), and Ong (2003). Yet ethnographic attention to micropractices grounded in distinctive cultural politics and specific localities remains rare.

10   Foucault 1983, 221.

11   Foucault [1997] 2003, 28.

12   Lefebvre [1974] 1991, 191. Bourdieu famously proposed that "to think in terms of field is to *think relationally*" (in Bourdieu and Wacquant 1992, 96). He also stressed that the "notion of *space* contains, in itself, the principle of a *relational* understanding of the social world" ([1994] 1998, 31). Yet my analysis departs from his emphasis on cognitive and other structures, the "logic of fields," and his insistence on defining fields through "objective relations between positions" that are, in turn, also "objectively defined" (in Bourdieu and Wacquant 1992, 97). In contrast to Bourdieu, I thus share Lefebvre's (2003, 63) emphasis on the "relations of force" constitutive of political history that involve struggles shaped by "*conjunctures*, which are not reducible to *structures*."

13   "L'exercice du pouvoir," for Foucault (1994, 237), is "un ensemble d'actions sur des actions possibles." I translate his "exercise of power" as "an ensemble of actions on other possible actions." My point is to highlight the ambivalent *spatial* and *temporal* implications of acting on other actions. Contingent conditions of possibility embed alternatives in multiple histories, including ongoing debates over the meanings and materialities of

past, present, and future. Thus acting on a landscape of sedimented practices may also act on potential futures.

14 Many simply *equate* governmentality with state administration (e.g., Lomnitz 2001, 198).

15 It includes the emergence of sciences and technologies that generate fields of expertise rendering the economy amenable to management—statistics, censuses, taxonomies of improvement. So-called nongovernmental organizations (NGOs) are more accurately nonstate entities (NSOs) that are frequently engaged in projects of government.

16 The "subject" implies both subjection to power and a subject of action. Agency, in this vision, is always already entangled in power relations, never outside or beyond them.

17 Foucault [1975] 1979, 11; my emphasis. When Foucault writes of the "art of government" bearing on "the complex unit constituted by men and things," I hear an echo of Gramsci's (1971 [1985], 213) elaboration of "the art of command" in relation to "ordering 'men and things' into an organic whole."

18 Braun 2000. See Hannah 2000 for a related perspective.

19 In his reading of *The Prince*, Foucault (1979, 11) suggested that Machiavelli simply echoed a juridical principle that, since the Middle Ages, had asserted that "sovereignty is not exercised on things, but above all on a territory and consequently on the subjects who inhabit them." According to Kantorowicz ([1957] 1997, 247), thirteenth-century French jurists invoked notions of sovereignty derived from Rome that hinged on "the loyalty to the new limited territorial *patria*, the common fatherland of all subjects of the Crown."

20 Foucault 1979, 19.

21 See Rabinow 1989 and Scott 1995 for influential formulations of colonial governmentality, and Pels 1997 for a critical overview.

22 Mitchell [1988] 1991, ix. Mitchell further argued that the "precise specification of space and function," as well as their hierarchical coordination, contribute to the disciplinary effects of power (xii).

23 Quotes are taken from Prakash (1999, 7), Rose (1999, 28), and Scott (1995, 201), respectively.

24 Hardt and Negri 2000, xii.

25 For a notable exception to this tendency, see Mitchell 2002.

26 Geertz (1973, 452) famously argued that "the culture of a people is an ensemble of texts, themselves ensembles, which the anthropologist strains to read over the shoulders of those to whom they properly belong." See Moore 1998 for a critique of metaphors of culture as a text within influential formulations of power and resistance.

27 Ironically, this tendency smuggles structural functionalism's key concept, society, into a singular systemic logic regulated by rules and principles. Projects of government, in this vision, become channeled by power's functional needs.

28 For insightful analyses of archival sources that cut against the grain of textualism that I critique, see Dirks's (2001) elaboration of the "ethnographic state" in British colonial India and Stoler's (2002, 7) analysis of the "microphysics of colonial rule."

29 Scott 1995, 215. He similarly suggested that colonial projects were "concerned above all with disabling old forms of life by systematically breaking down their conditions, and with constructing in their place new conditions," obliging, rather than simply enabling, distinctive modes of conduct (1995, 193). Despite our relative differences, I find Scott (1999) to offer among the most analytically rigorous anthropological elaborations of governmentality.

30 Rose 1996, 331.

31 Foucault 1983, 220–21.

32 Foucault [1979] 2000, 324. Gramsci ([1971] 1985, 360) mused: "Possibility means 'freedom.' The measure of freedom enters into the concept of man."

33 Foucault himself suggested that Gramsci was an "author more often cited than actually understood": C'est un auteur plus souvent cité que réellement connu (qtd. in Buttigieg 1992, xix).

34 Gramsci [1971] 1985, 55 n. 5.

35 Gramsci [1971] 1985, 151. Poulantzas ([1978] 1980, 68) contrasted Marxist and Foucauldian perspectives on "the economic," relating them to "the institutional materiality of modern power" (see also 148–51). For Foucault, he argued, "the techniques of power absorb not only the question of physical violence but also that of consent" (79).

36 Gramsci [1971] 1985, 258.

37 Gramsci [1971] 1985, 360.

38 Gramsci (1995, 357) credited Lenin with this break from economism in Marxist theory and the elaboration of the doctrine of hegemony.

39 On governing, Gramsci [1977] 1990, 169; on culture, Gramsci 1985, 41.

40 Hall 1981, 233.

41 For elaborations, see Crehan 2002, Hall 1986a, and Williams [1977] 1985.

42 Gramsci [1971] 1985, 161.

43 As Hall ([1988] 1990, 167) suggested, "Gramsci is one of the first modern Marxists to recognize that interests are not given but always have to be politically and ideologically constructed." Discursively produced interests, Hall stressed, can be both contradictory and unstable. In their reflections on governmentality, Miller and Rose (1990, 10) draw on Callon and Latour's notion of "'*intéressement*'—the construction of allied interests through persuasion, intrigue, calculation or rhetoric."

44 Gramsci ([1973] 1989, 213) conceived of individuals as belonging to multiple "social worlds . . . composed of heterogeneous fragments of fossilized cultures."

45 Cooper and Stoler 1997, 18, 27.

46 My phrasing also invokes Du Bois's (1945, 85) brilliant critique of the "provincialism" that linked US imperialism, racism, and the constitutive exclusions waged in the name of liberalism both domestically and abroad.

47 Chakrabarty 2000.

48 See in particular Gilroy 2004, Goldberg 2002, and Hesse 2004.

49 For related formulations, see Gregory 1998, Keith 1993, and Pred 2000.

50 Officials sought to govern Africans through what Chatterjee (1993, 10) termed the racialized "rule of colonial difference." I am not arguing that a unitary racial formation linked forms of colonial rule in India and Africa. Rather, both forms of rule relied on foundational fictions of essential cultural difference, an evolutionary understanding of Britain's moral and political authority, and thus a legitimation for imperial government.

51 Lugard 1926, 66, 68.

52 Fabian 1983.

53 Foucault [1997] 2003, 103. While Foucault's original French did not use the term *boomerang*, he may have been implicitly invoking Sartre's ([1961] 2002, 28) "*le moment du boomerang*" that returned racialized violence from colony to Europe. Césaire ([1955] 1972, 20) similarly elaborated the "boomerang effect of colonization" that dehumanized those who brutalized as well as those targeted by colonial violence, explicitly linking transcontinental spaces. Such acts injected "poison" into the "veins of Europe" as "the continent proceeds to savagery" (13). Spivak (1988, 290) explicitly critiqued Foucault's neglect—despite his being a "brilliant thinker of power-in-spacing"—of the "means of territorial imperialism crucial to his representation of sovereignty."

54 Gramsci 1994, 143.

55 Foucault [1997] 2003, 69, 70. Foucault ([1976] 1980, 143) conceived "bio-power to designate what brought life and its mechanisms into the realm of explicit calculations and made knowledge-power an agent of transformation of human life."

56 For a range of positions debating deployments of Foucauldian analytics in African contexts, see Ferguson 1994, Mbembe 2001, and Vaughan 1991.

57 Mamdani 1996, 24.

58 Malkki 1992.

59 See Li (1998) for a related perspective, and Lemke (2002) and Thomas (1994, 105) for elaborations of the notion of "project" in relation to governmentality.

60 Mandela also chronicled the history of "depredations of generations of European land-sharks, achieved by force and by cunning" ([1965] 1987, 79).

61 See Hart 2002, Ramphele 1993, and Robinson 1996.

62 On the constitutive exclusions of liberalism, see Hesse 2004 and Mehta 1999.

63 On "ethnic absolutism," see Gilroy [1987] 1991; on "ecologies of belonging" and the "raciology of statecraft," see Gilroy 2000.

64 For elaborations of race critical theory, see Essed and Goldberg 2002. For racism and modernity, see Eze 2001 and Hall 1992. The quotation is drawn from Stoler 1995, 9.

65 See Hesse 2004 for a brilliant analysis of these tensions.

66 Fanon [1964] 1967, 32. For related perspectives, see Appiah 1992, de la Cadena 2000, and Moore, Kosek, and Pandian 2003.

67 Enlightenment discourses cast long shadows on the "Dark Continent." Contemporary deployments of nativism in Africa, Mbembe (2002, 256) has asserted, echo Hegel by linking cultural identity to the presumed "quasi-equivalence" of geography and race (see also Livingstone 1992).

68 See Soyinka 1998.

69 Césaire 1983, 77; my emphasis.

70 The name pluralizes *nhamo*—problems, adversities, or calamities—and maps them to a country, territory, or nation (*nyika*). Meredith (2002, 34) provided helpful historical details of Nhamodzenyika's birth and death, yet appeared unaware of his Shona name's semantic resonances.

71 Smith and Simpson 1981, 22. Among Mugabe's inspirations was the US-educated Kwame Nkrumah, who enunciated a nationalist vision of Pan-Africanism.

72 Meredith 2002, 34.

73 Martin and Johnson 1981, 206.

74 Moyana 1987, 42.

75 Mugabe would later become president in 1987.

76 In Massey's (1994, 154) conception, places are "articulated moments in networks of social relations and understandings," constellations "meeting and weaving together at a particular locus." Thus, places' " 'identities' are constructed through the specificity of their interaction with other places rather than by counterposition to them" (121). In Lefebvre's terms, places are "intercalated, combined, superimposed" with social, political, and economic relations; they are "traversed" and "intertwined," subject to multiple scales, sites of "interpenetration" ([1974] 1991, 88, 86). Much like Massey and Lefebvre, Foucault emphasized comingling spatialities in "a heterogeneous space" (1986, 23).

77 Certeau [1975] 1988, 69.

78 For perspectives on the salience of translocal routes in relation to articulations of cultural identity, see Clifford 1997 and Gilroy 2000. Some essentialisms are translocal while some anti-essentialisms are extremely localized; *local* and *essence* are thus not necessary twins.

79 See Ortiz [1940] 1947 and Kenyatta [1938] 1989. Interestingly, Malinowski introduced both books. See Richards 1939 for an important countercurrent.

80 See Appadurai 1998.

81 Gupta and Ferguson 1997, Hall 1996.

82 On multisited ethnography, see Marcus 1998; on multilocal social spaces, see Rouse 1991; on the "global-in-the-local," see Donham 1999, xvi.

83 See, for example, Feld and Basso 1996, Hirsch and O'Hanlon 1995, and Stewart 1996.

84 The only nonanthropologist to contribute to Feld and Basso's 1996 influential

Senses of Place was the philosopher Edward Casey. Humanist subjects, in Casey's 1997 vision, were the agents whose "gatherings" of meaning make place over and against space.

85 Basso 1995.

86 Escobar (2001) productively proposed a processual understanding of place as a project. While he invoked Massey, his argument cuts against her formulations, conceiving "a reassertion of place, noncapitalism, and local culture against the dominance of space, capital, and modernity" (194).

87 See Baviskar 1995, Li 2003, and Povinelli 2002.

88 See Hart 2002 for a compelling critique of "impact" models of globalization. Malinowski ([1945] 1961, 15) envisioned "culture contact" as the action of one billiard ball on another, and he spoke of a directional flow: the "impact of a higher, active culture upon a simpler, more passive one."

89 Foucault [1982] 1984, 252. For perspectives on the geographical implications of Foucault's work, see especially Allen 2003 and Philo 1992.

90 Lefebvre ([1974] 1991, 21) critiqued Hegel's influence on the "fetishization of space in the service of the state." Lefebvre conceived of a "conceptual triad" of what he termed spatial practice, representations of space, and representational spaces (33, 38–39). He also explicitly linked sovereignty, violence, and space (280).

91 Lefebvre [1974] 1991, 62. Metaphors of landscape as a text (Cosgrove and Daniels 1989) similarly run the risk of purging process, practice, and power from unstable assemblages.

92 Lefebvre [1974] 1991, 109.

93 Lefebvre 2003, 63. Brenner's 1997 insightful elaborations of Lefebvre are weakened, in my reading, by an implied economistic structural determinism.

94 Harvey 2001.

95 Weber 1946, 78.

96 Scott 1998, 5.

97 Thongchai's (1994, 16) history of Siam proposed the term *geo-body* to describe the "technology of territoriality which created nationhood spatially."

98 Rather than conceiving place as a bounded, hermetically sealed site, critical human geographers and a growing number of anthropologists have promoted visions of place as nodal points embedded in translocal power relations. I build on the insights of ethnographies of place making (Gregory 1998; Myers 2000; and Raffles 2002), as well as of the cultural politics of spatiality and power (Caldeira 2000; Gupta and Ferguson 1997; Moore [1986] 1996; and Watts 2000).

99 Breaking from more Euclidian understandings, Baker (1984, 3) sought metaphors for a matrix in the blues that I find richly resonant with my mappings: a "matrix is a point of ceaseless input and output, a web of intersecting, crisscrossing impulses always in productive transit."

100 See Massey 1995, 321 for astute reflections on the potential misreadings of geological process into metaphors of spatial sedimentation.

101 While Deleuze and Guattari popularized the conceptual vocabulary of "striated space," I also invoke a much deeper agrarian entanglement to the term's rhizomatic roots. Furrowed fields are striated, suggesting both the assemblage of embodied labor, material implements, and environmental landscape. Furrows both require work and bear its traces. Sedimented soil, while part of the landscape, can also be unearthed and turned through toil to produce new alignments.

102 Lefebvre 1996, 118. See also Lefebvre [1974] 1991, 188.

103 Much of this work remains indebted to Appadurai 1996.

104 Berger 1972. Developing this notion, Cosgrove ([1984] 1998) traced the emergence of an ideology of landscape to the early fifteenth century in Italy and Flanders, linking the cultural production of a spectator's view of scenery to class relations and landed property.

105 In older English and other Germanic languages, *Landschaft* signified both geographical territory and polity, both place and political community. In Renaissance Denmark, Olwig (2002, 10, 17) has argued, "Custom and culture defined a *Land*, not physical geographical characteristics. . . . The identification between the meaning of *Land* as a political community and *Land* as dry land, terra firma, was strengthened by the fact that *Land* was often translated into Latin as *terra* or *territorium.*" Rerouting unsettled etymologies, Bhabha (1994, 99–100) found scenes of recognition in practices of colonial signification where " 'territory' derives from both *terra* (earth) and *terrere* (to frighten) whence *territorium*, a place from which people are frightened off."

106 Mitchell 1994, 2. In a related vein, Matless (1998, 14) elaborated the "processes of subjectification effected through landscape." Such interpellation of a subject, I underscore, is a contingent *process*, not a structural guarantee.

107 See Carter 1987 and Pratt 1992.

108 Gramsci [1971] 1985, 178.

109 In Said's (2000, 465) view, Gramsci produced a "critical consciousness" that was "geographical and spatial in its fundamental coordinates." I echo Said's (466) emphasis on Gramsci's "*situated*" analysis.

110 Foucault ([1976] 1980, 95) underscored: "Where there is power, there is resistance, and yet, or rather consequently, this resistance is never in a position of exteriority in relation to power."

111 Hall 1997, 35.

112 See, in particular, Carney and Watts 1990 and Peters 1994. For generative perspectives on African landscape, see Cohen and Odhiambo 1989; Fairhead and Leach 1996; Kalipeni and Zeleza 1999; and Luig and Von Oppen 1997. For Zimbabwe, see Alexander, McGregor, and Ranger 2000; Mandondo 2001; and Schmidt 1996.

113 For reflections on the "merely cultural," see Butler 1998. The "politics of custom" have shaped debates over cultural understandings of authority, tradition, and entitlement, as well as access to—and distribution of—material resources (Berry 1993; and Chanock [1985] 1998). On the cadences and textures of peasant micropolitics—extending from fields to homesteads, from debates over access to land and labor to the multiple identities mediating resource access—see Fairhead and Leach 1996; Mackenzie 1996; and Moore and Vaughan 1994.

114   Deleuze and Parnet ([1977] 1987, 132) explicitly conceived that "an assemblage is, precisely, a multiplicity." The very English term *assemblage* is an impoverished rendering of Deleuze's French *agencement*, suggesting ordered orchestration, an arranged layout, and harmonized modulation. The English also evicts resonances of *agence* and *agent*, specters of effective and affective action that unsettle a humanist subject. In English translation, Deleuze ([1986] 1988, 42) and Deleuze and Guattari ([1980] 1987) have consistently used the term *assemblage*. Rose ([1996] 1998, 171) has elaborated this analytic in relation to governmentality and the techniques of the self. Barry (2001, 10–11, 218) translated *agencement* as "arrangement," contrasting the term with Foucault's *dispositif* (often translated as "apparatus"), as has Deleuze (1990, 119). For Barry (2001, 218 n.38), Deleuze's concept of "arrangement has the virtue of suggesting an entity which is always in process; an ordering rather than a completed order in which agency is emergent." My thanks to Jocelyne Guilbault for extended discussions of this translingual traffic.

115   Deleuze and Guattari [1980] 1987, 337; see also 406.

116   Deleuze and Guattari [1980] 1987, 88. Significantly, their notion of "territorial assemblage" contained within it impulses of deterritorialization and reterritorialization, lines of flight away from locality and rootedness, as well as emplaced reconfigurations of arrangements within specific sites (see 336).

117   In Latour's (1999, 186) formulation, objects, organisms, and animals, like humans, are "actants" assembled together in "articulations." He explicitly endorsed the notion of articulation as a counter to terms that "imply an all-powerful human agent imposing his will on shapeless matter." For him, "nonhumans also act, displace goals, and contribute to their definition"; see 194 for his elaboration of "actants."

118   The two analytics are not mutually exclusive. I write against widespread *tendencies* while acknowledging exceptions. Rabinow (1999, 10), for instance, wove "power relations" into his elaboration of assemblage. In such a vision, Foucault's reflection on the soul as an "element in which are *articulated* the effects of a certain type of power" becomes formative (Foucault, qtd. in Rabinow 1999, 10; my emphasis). In my reading, Foucault provides a critical bridge between articulation and assemblage, emphasizing their conjoined consequentiality.

119   Hall 1980. Hall's Gramscian vision broke from this rigid structural determinism and class reductionism, as well as from the state-centric account of subject formation and interpellation formulated by Althusser [1960] 1971. Laclau (1977, 70) elaborated a notion of articulation to counter the twinned evils of Althusserianism: taxonomy and

formalism. For an alternative genealogy and deployment of the term, see Derrida [1967] 1976. For influential discussions of articulation in relation to hegemony and Gramsci's critique of economism, see Mouffe 1979 and Laclau and Mouffe 1985.

120 James 1963.

121 Haraway 1989, 193. She stressed the "heterogeneous multiplicities" that position any knowing subject, emphasizing that "positioning implies responsibility for our enabling practices." Her perspective also shared affinities with Foucault's (1977, 156) elaboration of "effective history" as the "affirmation of knowledge as perspective."

122 Fabian 2001, 4–5. Rosaldo (1989) offered an influential formulation of the relationship between anthropological knowledge and the "positioned subject."

123 As Stuart Hall aptly argued, identity is a tension between positioning and being positioned in fields of power and knowledge (Hall 1990).

1 Lines of Dissent

1 See CONEX, May 1981. The report classified 1,570 hectares (11 percent of the area) as arable land, with each family to receive a 2.8-hectare net holding, a 0.25-hectare housing site, and a minimum grazing right for five livestock units. The balance of arable land was accounted for by village sites, access roads, and "inaccessible" arable areas. Two alternative proposals mentioned in the report were for each of 170 families to receive 5-hectare holdings with twenty livestock units granted, and a plan for 343 settler families, each one receiving 2.5 hectares of land with grazing rights of ten livestock units.

2 Nyanga DA Files, Kaerezi Resettlement Scheme, April 14, 1986, "Re: Remainder of Lot Z of Nyanga Downs of Nyanga Block (Nyamutsapa Area)."

3 For elaborations of these implications for gender and resettlement nationally, see Jacobs 1992 and Gaidzanwa 1988.

4 By the end of 1983, 62 percent of resettlement farmers had originated in Communal Areas and 15 percent were former farm laborers. Only 1 percent comprised returning refugees from neighboring countries, the category composing the majority of Kaerezi residents in the early 1980s. For national figures, see Geza 1986, 35.

5 CONEX, May 1981.

6 Moyo 1991, 58. Zimbabwe's five so-called Natural Regions are differentiated by agro-ecological criteria. Region 1, where rainfall exceeds a thousand millimeters, comprises approximately 2 percent of national territory and is limited to the highest elevations of the Eastern Highlands.

7 Some used MNR's Portuguese acronym, RENAMO. See Vines 1991 for its history.

8 See comments by minister of state for national security, Sekeramayi, in POZ 1991.

9 Nyanga DA Files, Kaerezi Resettlement Scheme, June 26, 1990. RSO to Nyanga DA, "Administration Problems in the Kaerezi Scheme."

10 The director of DERUDE took pains to distinguish postcolonial resettlement policy from protected villages (Geza 1986). In 1991, the minister of state for national security Sydney Sekeramayi expressed concern that in several MNR-affected areas far from Nyanga, villagization had been imposed "grudgingly as some people compared it with the 'Protected Villages' of the Rhodesian era. . . . where the villagers' every move was monitored and freedom curtailed" (POZ 1991, 8).

11 While many Kaerezians recalled the hardships of their wartime Mozambican experiences, few explicitly discussed popular opposition to FRELIMO's villagization policies (see Vines 1991).

12 Total allocations per family were 3.5 hectares, consisting of a three-hectare "arable" site and a half-hectare "residential" site, designed to include a small vegetable garden and woodlot, within the consolidated linear grids.

13 See Hannan [1959] 1987, 230; and Chimhundu 1996, 197.

14 Bayart 1993, 252.

15 See Mitchell 1999 for an eloquent elaboration of this position.

16 Shona uses pluralizing verbs for singular subjects of respect, trumping grammatical agreement. For example, "Rekayi, they walked," instead of "Rekayi, he walked."

17 *Matemba* were harvested from Lake Kariba, created in the late 1950s by the colonial damming of the Zambezi River. That government project evicted Tonga people, who were then moved into a state-administered resettlement scheme (Colson 1971b).

18 Nyanga DA Files, Kaerezi Resettlement Scheme, June 26, 1990, RSO to Nyanga DA, "Administration Problems in the Kaerezi Scheme."

2 Disciplining Development

1 Fanon [1961] 1982 233.

2 Fanon [1964] 1967, 43. See Senghor [1961] 1964, 12; and Kenyatta 1968, 233 for resonant formulations of African nationalism.

3 Gramsci [1977] 1990, 25. The quotation is from a secondary school essay, probably penned in 1911.

4 Gramsci [1971] 1985, 229.

5 Gramsci ([1926] 1995) famously analyzed Italy's "Southern Question," reflecting on histories that positioned the agrarian south in relation to urban interests, unions, and alliances. The politics and analytics of articulation, at once spatial and political, remained pivotal to subsequent reworkings of such southern questions in other territories.

6 See the First Declaration of the Lacandon Jungle of January 2, 1994, attributed to the General Command of the EZLN, the Zapatista Army of National Liberation, and authored by Subcomandante Marcos (2000, 13–16).

7   Marcos 2000, 86.

8   Marx [1894] 1991, 969. Marx's couplet is notably gendered, as is his implied historical agency.

9   See Coronil 1997 for a related argument and an elaboration of the salience of Marx's holy trinity for reconfiguring analyses of the politics of nature in the global South.

10   Moyana 1984; Ranger 1985b.

11   Palmer 1977a, 227. See Tshuma 1997 for a history of the legal instruments of dispossession.

12   N. H. Wilson, Native Affairs Department, 1944, qtd. in Sudbeck 1989, 63.

13   For elaborations of these patterns, see Moyo 1995; Palmer 1977b; and Riddell 1978.

14   Roth and Bruce 1994, 13.

15   Machingaidze 1991, 558.

16   See Brown 1959.

17   The wording is in the act; see Riddell 1978 for an elaboration.

18   See Herbst 1990 and Sylvester 1991 for analyses.

19   Astrow (1983, 112) termed the Internal Settlement a "white blocking mechanism." For Thatcher's announcement, see 134.

20   Astrow 1983, 115.

21   Mugabe 1983, 102.

22   Mugabe in a 1978 ZANU party publication, qtd. in Astrow 1983, 140.

23   Mugabe in 1979, qtd. in Astrow 1983, 140. For a sense of discourses of land, rights, and freedom in other nationalist speeches, see Nyagoni and Nyandoro 1979. For resonances of this rhetoric in land debates during the early 2000s, see David Moore 2003 and Sithole et al. 2003.

24   The US Congress voted 75–19 in favor of the Muzorewa government in 1979, advising president Jimmy Carter to lift sanctions (Astrow 1983, 134).

25   Roth and Bruce 1994, 21.

26   Kinsey 1999; Moyo 2000.

27   For figures on the white exodus during the war, see Astrow 1983, 150; and Kriger 1992.

28   See DERUDE 1991, 2.

29   Roth and Bruce 1994, 18.

30   Palmer 1990, 169. Rutherford (2003, 194) estimated that in early 2000, "perhaps 800 or so of the approximately 4,600 commercial farms have been owned and operated by black Zimbabweans." Most commentary, as he noted, "presumes" white owners of these estates.

31   Some estimates suggest that the actual number of resettled farmers is less than half of what government claimed. For a discussion of competing estimates, and an elaboration of post-2000 land politics, see Hammar, Raftopoulos, and Jensen 2003; Masiiwa

2004; and Worby 2001. For the regional contexts of these conflicts, see Cousins 2003 and Peters 2004. For incisive perspectives on Zimbabwe's land reform initiatives in the 1990s, see Bowyer-Bower and Stoneman 2000.

32 Model A accelerated schemes made up slightly more than 4 percent; Model B cooperative schemes made for approximately 6 percent; Model C, a designated hybrid model, constituted less than 0.5 percent of resettlement land, while Model D, a massive pilot scheme in Matabeleland where grazing areas rotated, constituted 10 percent of resettlement land. See DERUDE 1991, 3.

33 See Cusworth 1990.

34 For elaborations of AGRITEX's technocratic approach, see Drinkwater 1991.

35 Bassett 1993, 8.

36 Leach and Mearns 1996.

37 Latour 1987, 68.

38 Haraway 1991, 189.

39 See Crary 1990 on relations between modernity and visual technologies of observation.

40 Berger 1972.

41 Smith ([1984] 1990) offered incisive elaborations of these themes.

42 Lefebvre [1974] 1991, 50.

43 Deutsche 1996, 52.

44 Mitchell [1988] 1991, 44.

45 DERUDE 1985, 22–23.

46 Nyanga DA Files, LAN 30/2, Resettlement Schemes, July 30, 1991, DERUDE circular no. 4 of 1991, signed by M. Paraiwa.

47 Fraser 1989, 164.

48 Rose 1996, 121.

49 Rose [1989] 1999, 5, 6.

50 Roth and Bruce 1994, 51.

51 ZNA, File ZBJ 3/1/1, 1944, Alvord's testimony to the 1944 Native Production and Trade Commission, 3054.

52 Alvord 1929, 11.

53 See Bassett and Crummey 1993; and Beinart 1984.

54 Alvord 1929, 11.

55 ZNA, File S 1563, 1940, Southern Rhodesia, Annual Reports of District Native Commissioners for 1940, Inyanga NC Annual Report 1940. Note the presumed gender of farmers.

56 See Alvord 1958.

57 Alvord 1929, 9.

58 For an exploration of this text, see Sudbeck 1989.

59 Comaroff and Comaroff 1997. Bond (1948, 6) celebrated centralization's making possible "a more settled and civilized life."

60 Drayton 2000, xv.

61 See Sudbeck 1989, 60.

62 ZNA, File ZBJ 1/1/4, 1944, Trade (Godlonton), 1944 Production and Trade Commission. See Alvord's testimony, esp. 3049.

63 Robinson 1996.

64 Qtd. in Slater 1980, 157.

65 Atkins 1993, 47.

66 Bundy 1979, 78.

67 See Beinart 1984; Cliffe 1988; De Wet 1995; and Grove 1995.

68 Ranger 1985b, 72–73, 75.

69 ZNA, File S 1051, 1943, Southern Rhodesia, Native Commissioners' Annual Reports, 1943, Inyanga NC Annual Report 1943.

70 Robinson 1960, 29, quoting the 1951 Natural Resource Board annual report.

71 Government of Southern Rhodesia 1955. See also Machingaidze 1991, 557.

72 Brown 1959.

73 See Munro 1998 and Wilson 1989.

74 See Ranger 1985b, 154–55. In Inyanga District, a 1961 report chronicled open hostility: "Land Development Officers and Demonstrators have had an almost impossible task during the year trying to carry out their work in the face of political agitators preaching non-co-operation, and hostility to the agricultural staff. At one stage in Holdenby and Manga the Demonstrators were almost too afraid to move out of their house, and all work and progress was virtually at a standstill." ZNA, File S 2728/2/2/8, vol. 2, 1961, Internal Affairs, Annual District Reports, 1961, Inyanga NC Annual Report 1961.

75 See Robinson 1953 and Werbner 1991.

76 ZNA, File S 1051 1946–1948, vol. 3, Internal Affairs, Annual District Reports, 1951–1952, Manicaland, Inyanga NC Annual Report 1948; ZNA, File S 2827/2/2/2, vol. 5, Internal Affairs, Annual District Reports, 1952, Manicaland, Inyanga NC Annual Report 1952.

77 ZNA, File S 2827/2/2/2, vol. 5, Internal Affairs, Annual District Reports, 1952, Manicaland, Inyanga NC Annual Report 1952. ZNA, File S 2728/2/2/8, vol. 2, 1961, Internal Affairs, Annual District Reports, 1961, Inyanga NC Annual Report 1961.

78 ZNA, File S 2728/2/2/8, vol. 2, 1961, Internal Affairs, Annual District Reports 1961, Inyanga NC Annual Report 1961.

79 Machingaidze 1991, 557–58.

80 Moyo 1991.

81 ZNA, File S 1051 1946–1948, vol. 3, Internal Affairs, Annual District Reports, 1951–52, Manicaland, Inyanga NC Annual Report 1948. ZNA, File S 2827/2/2/2, vol. 5, Internal Affairs, Annual District Reports, 1952, Manicaland, Inyanga NC Annual Report 1952.

82 ZNA, File S 2827/2/2/2/4, vol. 2, 1956, Internal Affairs, Annual District Reports 1956, Inyanga NC 1956 Annual Report.

83 Qtd. in Sylvester 1991, 42.

84 For analyses of these events, see Astrow 1983 and White 2003.

85 ZNA, File S 2827/2/2/6, vol. 3, 1958, Annual District Reports 1958, Inyanga NC 1958 Annual Report.

86 ZNA, File S 2728/2/2/8, vol. 2, 1961, Internal Affairs, Annual District Reports, 1961, Inyanga NC Annual Report 1961.

87 See Bulman 1970, 16; and Machingaidze 1991, 583.

88 1962 Chief Native Commissioner annual report, qtd. in Machingaidze 1991, 587.

89 CONEX May 1981. A revised plan followed in October.

90 Some Kaerezians pointed out that the name also referred to a notorious Rhodesian prison in Midlands Province.

91 While the DA here used the male gender exclusively, land was allocated to married men, widows, and divorcees.

92 The May 1981 CONEX plan "suggested that . . . settlers be confirmed on their individual present lands provided this is sound conservation. Only where conservation is not sound would attempts be made to resite arable holdings."

93 Nyanga DA Files, LAN 16/1, vol. 1, Resettlement: Removal of Squatters from Exchange Block, 13/2/84 to 11/3/87, September 16, 1986, J. H. Bannerman, Regional Rural Development Officer to Director, DERUDE, Harare, "Resettlement Nyanga Downs Lot Z" appended as "Lot Z of Nyanga Downs Expansion of Summer Wheat Production and Movement of Squatters of Tenants from the Land Concerned."

94 Nyanga DA Files, LAN 16/1, vol. 1, Resettlement: Removal of Squatters from Exchange Block: 13/2/84 to 11/3/87, April 14, 1986, "Re: Remainder of Lot Z of Nyanga Downs of Nyanga Block (Nyamutsapa Area)."

3 Landscapes of Livelihood

1 On biopower and biohistory, see Foucault [1976] 1980, 143.

2 Certeau 1984, xix.

3 Scholars have debated the relative dating, uses, and archaeological implications of Nyanga's stone forts and pits. See Garlake 1966 and Soper 2002. Summers (1958) conducted excavations in Kaerezi and elsewhere in Nyanga.

4 See Baviskar 1995, 147–48; Fairhead and Leach 1996; and Marx [1867] 1990, 899.

5 See Schroeder 1999 and Carney and Watts 1990.

6 While widows and divorcees received resettlement rights to arable and residential plots, they did so by virtue of once having been married.

7 Marx 1975, 232, 234.

8 Among the most helpful elaborations of the boundary work accomplished by the discursive demarcations of "nature" and "culture," see Haraway 1989; Orlove 2002; and Strathern 1988.

9 Hall [1988] 1990, 170. He underscored Gramsci's germinal recognition that "interests are not given but always have to be politically and ideologically constructed" (167).

10 Fairhead and Leach (1996) provide a brilliant ethnographic elaboration that critiques essentialized assertions of indigenous ecological knowledge and practice.

11 By the mid-1990s, all the US state departments in Africa received a faxed copy of Robert Kaplan's influential 1994 article, "The Coming Anarchy," which flagged environmental politics as *the* national security issue for the new millennium. Reading like a B-movie of African environmental degradation scripted by Malthus and Hobbes, his account drew heavily from violence-torn Sierra Leone, where diamond wars mined the social and natural landscape. See Kaplan 1994, and Richards 1996 for an incisive critique.

12 See World Commission on Environment and Development 1987.

4 Racialized Dispossession

1 Palmer 1977a, 225–26.

2 Petheram 1974.

3 Rhodes's letter to his mother, September 11, 1870, qtd. in Rotberg 1988, 40. I draw these details of Rhodes's life from Rotberg.

4 Rhodes's letter to his mother, June 7, 1871, qtd. in Rotberg 1988, 51.

5 See Rotberg 1988, 339.

6 Rhodes's 1896 letter to McDonald, qtd. in Garlake 1966, 29.

7 Rhodes purchased twelve different farms totaling 38,743 hectares and even considered purchasing the vast Inyanga Downs area, including Kaerezi. The estate acquired Warrandale in 1925 and the Pungwe Falls in 1938. See Petheram 1987 and ZNRO, File LAN/16, Squatters and Resettlement Schemes GU-LE, 1963–1968, Internal Affairs, box 100839, April 5, 1962, Secretary of Lands letter.

8 Petherman 1974, 16.

9 ZNA, File NUC 2/1/1, August 28, 1902, Inyanga NC Hulley, "Improvement of Farms Standing in the Name of the Late Mr. Rhodes." At that time, Rhodes's estate had apple orchards, sheep, and cattle ranging across his property (Petheram 1974, 14).

10 Palmer 1977b, 259.

11 ZNA, File S 1563, Inyanga District NC Annual Report 1934. Some lived in Umtali, while others "managed" properties from as far away as Johannesburg (Petheram 1987, 44).

12 In 1902, the first year Nyanga became a distinct district, the newly installed Native Commissioner estimated three occupants per hut, generating an African population of 20,400 from the 6,800 huts he counted. ZNA, File NUC 2/1/1, October 7, 1902, Hulley, NC Inyanga, Half Year Report.

13 ZNA, File N9/4/1, NC Monthly Reports 1898, January 7, 1899, Gray, Inyanga Acting NC, to NC, Umtali. For reports of chickens, see Clutton-Brock 1969, 8.

14 ZNA, File N9/1/3, NC Annual Report, Umtali, 1897, Umtali Annual Report, March 1897.

15 ZNA, File No/1/4, NC Annual Reports 1898, Umtali Annual Report 1898.

16 Foucault 1979, 11.

17 ZNA, File NUC 2/1/2, May 11, 1907, NCI Inyanga to Acting CNC, Sals. no. 168.

18 See ZNA, File NUC 2/3/1, Inyanga District Report for the Year of 1906; and ZNA, File NUC 2/3/1, Inyanga District Annual Report 1905.

19 ZNA, File NUC 2/1/3, November 8, 1909, D. H. Moodie, NC Inyanga, Report on First 9 Months of 1909.

20 Between 1903 and 1906, the NC Inyanga reported 101 huts under Chief Tangwena crossing the international border. In 1908, the chief stayed and paid rent on Inyanga Block. "All Tangwena's people," however, reportedly moved to Portuguese territory. See ZNA, File NUC 2/1/3, January 31, 1908, D. H. Moodie, NC Inyanga to CNC, Salisbury; ZNA, File NUC 2/3/1, Inyanga District Reports for the Years of 1905 and 1906; ZNA, File NUC 2/3/1, Inyanga District Report for Month of July 1906; and ZNA, File NUC 1/4/1, May 5, 1908, D. H. Moodie, NC Inyanga to Superintendent of Natives, Umtali.

21 ZNA, File L2/2/2/6/8, August 29, 1906, D. H. Moodie, NC Inyanga, to CNC, "Minutes Relating to Memo from Sawerthal, Barue Boundary Commission, to the Surveyor General, Salisbury, Ruera-Pungwe Camp, August 20, 1906." A couple of years before, Africans near the Gaeresi River had moved across the border into Portuguese territory "in consequence of the warning that they would have either to pay rent to the company on whose land they were living, or move." ZNA, File NUC 2/3/1, Laing, NC Inyanga, Inyanga District Report for the Month of November 1904.

22 ZNA, File NUC 2/1/2, March 26, 1907, NC Inyanga to CNC Salisbury.

23 ZNA, File NUC 2/3/1, March 31, 1905, W. T. Laing, NC Inyanga, Inyanga District Report for the Year Ended the 31st March, 1905.

24 ZNA, File NUC 2/3/1, October 18, 1906, D. H. Moodie, NC Inyanga, letter to Taberer.

25 ZNA, File NUC 2/1/1, April 12, 1904, Inyanga NC Laing to CNC, Salisbury.

26 At that point, the NC noted 465 adult males and 398 adult females who crossed into Portuguese territory. ZNA, File NUC 2/3/1, January 1905, W. T. Laing, NC Inyanga, Inyanga Monthly Report.

27 ZNA, File NUC 2/3/1, January 1906, NC Inyanga, no. 447. For comments on seniors seizing juniors' earnings, see March 13, 1906, memo, NC Inyanga to CNC.

28 ZNA, File NUC 2/3/3, August 31, 1922, NC Inyanga, "Native Reserves: Inyanga District."

29 See ZNA, File S 1563 1940, Southern Rhodesia, Annual Reports of District NCs for 1940, Inyanga District NC Annual Report 1940; ZNA, File S 1051/1946–1948, Annual NC Reports, Inyanga District NC Report 1948.

30 ZNA, File S 2827/2/2/1-v.3, 1951, NC Inyanga Annual Report.

31 ZNA, File S 2588/1977, Land Inyanga, May 15, 1950, Inyanga NC Memo to Umtali, May 19, 1950, Manicaland Provincial Commissioner letter to Chief Native Commis-

sioner. At the time, two hundred Africans lived under labor agreements on the Rhodes Inyanga Estate.

32 ZNA, File S 2728/2/2/8, vol. 2, 1961, 1961 NC Inyanga Annual Report.

33 See Schmidt 1992.

34 ZNA, File S 603/1929, December 10, 1929, Agent to Liquidator, Anglo French Matabeleland Company Ltd. to NC Inyanga, Rhodesia, "Native Rentals."

35 ZNA, File S 604/1926, November 13, 1925, NC Inyanga to District Veterinary Officer, Umtali.

36 Hanmer recalled the first visit to the property as 1929 or 1930. See ZNA, File MS 335/10/6, Rekayi Tangwena's Court Cases, April 22, 1967, Court Statement by William Francis Busby Hanmer.

37 Petheram 1987, 47–48.

38 Deed of Grant 6151.

39 The Native Commissioner counted 214 natives in 1925 and 191 the following year. See ZNA, File S 604/1930, Native Commissioner Inyanga, Outletters, March 25, 1929, Acting NC Inyanga to Agent to the Liquidator, Anglo-French Matabeleland Company, Johannesburg, "Private Location Fees: Inyanga Block."

40 Petheram 1987, 48–49.

41 ZNA, File S 604/1930, Native Commissioner Inyanga, Outletters, December 29, 1930, NC Inyanga to CNC Salisbury.

42 According to a 1970 government report, in 1930 the Hanmers entered into a labor agreement with the "26 Tangwena people resident on the estate." ZNRO, File LAN 16/16/3, Gaeresi Ranch Squatters, Press, Internal Affairs, box 116598, location 8.14.3 R., March 27, 1969, Ministry of Internal Affairs, "The Tangwena Issue at Gairezi."

43 Most accounts place six headmen under Chief Tangwena. Presumably, the seventh would have been in Saunyama's territory, which overlaps Dazi.

44 Qtd. in Clutton-Brock 1969, 8.

45 See ZNA, File MS 335/10/6, Rekayi Tangwena's Court Cases, April 22, 1967, Court Statement by William Francis Busby Hanmer. In a 1992 interview, Gilmour recalled bringing three hundred cattle up from Melsetter to Gaeresi Ranch.

46 He was one of only 3 students who received a passing grade on the O-level English exam among the more than 120 students who, in 1990, took the test at Nyafaru.

47 ZNA, File S 2588/1977, Land Inyanga, January 29, 1948, Charles G. Hanmer to the Hon. E. C. F. Whitehead, MP.

48 ZNA, File S 2588/1977, Land Inyanga, January 29, 1948, Charles G. Hanmer to the Hon. E. C. F. Whitehead, MP.

49 ZNA, File S 2588/1977, Land Inyanga, July 28, 1948, Charles G. Hanmer, Inyanga Downs, to Chief Native Commissioner, Salisbury.

50 ZNA, File S 2588/1977, Land Inyanga, February 9, 1948, CNC, Salisbury to Secretary to the Prime Minister (Native Affairs), "INYANGA DOWNS: C. G. HANMER."

51 ZNA, File S 2588/1977, Land Inyanga, August 23, 1948, L. V. Jowett, Provincial NC, Umtali to CNC, Salisbury, "LABOUR AGREEMENT: INYANGA DOWNS."

52 ZNA, File S 2588/1977, Land Inyanga, March 22, 1951, Charles G. Hanmer, Managing Director, Pulpwood Co. of Rhodesia, Inyanga Downs, P. B. Rusape to Chief NC, Salisbury.

53 Marx [1867] 1976, 699.

54 See Bourdieu [1972] 1977, 191, for an analysis of euphemization.

55 Van Onselen 1976, 99.

56 See Hannan ([1959] 1987, 59) for an elaboration of *chibharo*'s semantic range.

57 Isaacman 1976, 156–57. In contrast to these colonial Mozambican memories, Kaerezians emphasized *chibharo*'s focus on adult men.

58 The 1899 Portuguese Native Labor Code informed policy until 1961. On *chibalo*'s usage, see Isaacman and Isaacman 1983, 34; and Harries 1994.

59 Atkins (1993, 134) cited Dohne's 1857 *The Zulu-Kaffir Dictionary*. Harries (1994) noted the term's usage in Natal as early as 1876. On forced recruitment, see also Van Onselen 1976.

60 Phimister 1977, 258.

61 Marx [1867] 1990, 878.

62 Marx [1867] 1990, 881.

63 Marx [1867] 1990, 895.

64 Marx [1867] 1990, 915. "Force," he mused, "is the midwife of every old society pregnant with a new one. It is itself an economic power" (916).

65 Marx [1867] 1990, 885, my emphasis.

66 Foucault 1979, 6.

67 Foucault 1979, 8.

68 Foucault 1979, 20, 21.

69 Foucault [1997] 2003, 27.

70 Marx [1894] 1991, 953. The posthumously published text, edited by Engels, appeared after the 1890 white settler invasion of Zimbabwe and before the 1896 *Chimurenga* (uprising).

71 Lefebvre [1974] 1991, 325.

72 Locke [1690] 1999, 394. He elaborated his foundational freedoms: "Every Man is born with a double Right: First, a *Right of Freedom to his Person*, which no other Man has a Power over, but the free Disposal of it lies in himself. *Secondly, A Right*, before any other man, to *inherit*, with his Brethren, his Father's Goods" (394–95).

73 Locke [1690] 1999, 397.

74 Locke [1690] 1999, 395.

75 Locke [1690] 1999, 394.

76 See Pongweni 1982, 55.

77 See Asad 1992 for astute elaborations of colonized subjects as "conscripts of western civilization."

5 *The Ethnic Spatial Fix*

1 See Duffy (1959, 221–24) for the imperial context of the boundary disputes.

2 ZNA, File N9/4/2, J. W. Gray, Acting NC Inyanga, Inyanga Monthly Report, January 1899. Administrative reports used several variant spellings, most commonly Tawungwena.

3 Foucault [1976] 1980, 68. Zeleza and Kalipeni 1999 and Mbembe 2001 offer recent discussions of sovereignty and territory in Africa.

4 Foucault [1975] 1979, 219.

5 Fanon [1964] 1967, 34. Elsewhere, Fanon ([1952] 1967, 109, 116) famously glossed the white inscription of his black body as "the glances of the other fixed me there. . . . I am *fixed*."

6 See Nelson 1999. I am cautious of the theoretical work linguistic affinities may be enlisted to perform, especially across multiple translations, but stress three glosses on the English term *fix* that figure throughout this chapter. The first describes anchoring, stabilizing, and siting in a precise location. The second means repairing, restoring, and returning to a previous state after an injury in the social fabric. Third is the sense of a hostile act of reprimand, vengeance, or discipline. Thus "putting people in their place" can fix them in several senses. *Fix* can also imply acute or obsessive focus, as in "to fixate."

7 Carter 1987, xvi, xxii.

8 See Gregory 1994 for an elaboration within the wider context of geographical imaginations.

9 Thongchai 1994, 16.

10 ZNA, File N9/1/4, NC Annual Reports 1898, T. B. Hulley, Umtali NC, Umtali Annual Report 1898.

11 ZNA, File NC Annual Reports, 1902 Inyanga NC Annual Report. Bhila (1982, 231) provides details on Umtassa not participating in the 1896–97 rebellions. See Schmidt 1996 for an astute history of the Mutasa (Umtassa) chieftaincy.

12 ZNA, File N9/1/3, NC Annual Report, Umtali, 1897, T. B. Hulley, Umtali NC, Umtali Annual Report 1897. The paramount Umtassa in question was Tendai Mutasa. Colonial spellings differed from Shona terms and, especially with names, had multiple variations. When referencing archival sources, I retain their spellings. In my elaborations of Kaerezians' discussions of historical figures, places, and events, I use spellings in accord with local conventions.

13 For accounts of Barwe territorial influence, see Beach 1980 and Newitt 1995.

14 See Bhila 1982, 3, 124; and Newitt 1995, 93–94. Variant spellings of Makombe include Macombe and Makombi. When the Portuguese arrived at the Indian Ocean port of Sofala in 1505, their geography of desire oriented toward gold mines believed to lie in the Zambesi region. A massive military defeat in the 1570s put the Portuguese on the

defensive, while slave raiding and the ivory trade forged transcontinental links through imperial circuits.

15 ZNA, File N9/4/12, NC Monthly Reports, 1902, T. B. Hulley, NC Inyanga, July 1902.

16 ZNA, File NUC 2/3/3, March 8, 1918, NC Inyanga, "Border Intelligence Scouts."

17 See Comaroff and Comaroff 1991 for a discussion of this "civilizing mission."

18 Guha 1997 used the phrase to analyze power relations in British colonial India.

19 Qtd. in Low (1973, 22).

20 Agamben ([1995] 1998, 6) proposed that "*the production of a biopolitical body is the original activity of a sovereign power.*"

21 ZNA, File NUC 1/1/1, October 6, 1905, Native Commissioner, Inyanga to CNC, Salisbury, "Telegram to Scouts, Nyanga."

22 ZNA, File NUC 1/1/1, January 18, 1908, W. Laing, Inyanga Acting Commissioner, to Acting CNC.

23 ZNA, File N9/4/5, NC Monthly Reports, 1899. T. B. Hulley, Umtali NC, Umtali Monthly Report, November 1899.

24 Massey 1999.

25 Foucault 1986, 25.

26 Gilroy 2000, 59.

27 Mbembe 2000, 17.

28 Lugard 1926, 66, 68.

29 ZNA, File ZBJ 2/2/2, 1944, W. M. Munro, writing on behalf of the Godlonton Commission, Report on Native Production and Trade Commission, Salisbury, Southern Rhodesia. See Moore 1999 and Worby 2000 for a contextualization of disciplinary power and development regimes in colonial Rhodesia.

30 Hegel [1831] 1956, 80.

31 Hegel [1831] 1956, 99. He stressed that Africa's "isolated character," its fundamental difference from Europe as a place without History, resided "essentially in its geographical condition" (91).

32 Kopytoff 1987, 4.

33 Renan [1882] 1990, 10. Renan had contradictory positions on race and ethnicity. Césaire ([1955] 1972) famously blasted Renan's racism, comparing him to Hitler. Yet Renan, also uncannily anticipating the ethnic cleansing of twentieth-century Europe, wrote: "Be on your guard, for this ethnographic politics is in no way a stable thing and, if today you use it against others, tomorrow you may see it turned against yourselves" (15–16).

34 Maine 1861.

35 Morgan [1878] 1985, 7. Marx ([1867] 1990, 471) similarly wrote of a "natural" social evolutionary trend based on a sexual division of labor grounded in biology. "Within a family and, after further development, within a tribe, there springs up naturally a division of labour caused by differences of sex and age, and therefore based on a purely

physiological foundation." Engels's ([1884] 1972, 229) social evolutionary reflections, subtitled "In Light of the Research of Henry Lewis Morgan," also argued that "the state is distinguished firstly by the grouping of its members *on a territorial basis.*" Durkheim ([1893] 1984, iv) implied a contrary evolutionary perspective, taking pains to emphasize "how, as history unfolds, . . . organisation based on territorial groupings (village, town, district or province, etc.) becomes progressively weaker."

36 ZNA, File N 9/1/1–4, NC Umtali, Hulley, Native Commissioner's Yearly Report 1898.

37 Radcliffe-Brown 1940, xiv.

38 Fortes and Evans-Pritchard [1940] 1963, 5.

39 Fortes and Evans-Pritchard [1940] 1963, 10.

40 Lucy Mair (1965, 12) stated boldly that "there is no agreement at all about what a *tribe* is." Contributors to Colson and Gluckman 1951, including Holleman, stressed the organizational principles of tribal social structure and political authority. However, Bullock's 1928 elaboration of tribal customs among the "Mashona" emphasized that "tribal appellations . . . are not static, nor can the tribes themselves be said to be distinct." He noted the "fusion and confusion" of tribal groupings ([1928] 1970, 13).

41 Malinowski, qtd. in Schapera 1956, 3. Elsewhere Malinowski distinguished between "the tribe, in the cultural sense of the word, and the tribe as a politically organized unit" (1944, 164–65). Territoriality remained crucial to both, while central authority and administration became defining features of what Malinowski coined a "tribe-nation" (165). Malinowski's evolutionary assumptions were cautious yet telling: the "tribe as a cultural unit probably existed long before the political tribe became organized on the principle of force" (61).

42 Schapera 1956, 5.

43 Mafeje 1971, 256. See also Magubane 2000.

44 Mamdani 1996, 51.

45 See Mamdani 2001 for elaborations of his analytical separation of culture and politics.

46 Feierman (1990, 136) asserted that "Tanganyika's government needed to find 'tribal' groups with clear boundaries for administrative purposes; the functionalist anthropologists tended to study bounded tribes." Iliffe (1979, 324) argued that colonial officials in Tanganyika "erected indirect rule by 'taking the *tribal* unit.' They had the power and they created the political geography." Wilmsen (1989, 25) suggested that ethnographers' practices of systematic codification buttressed administrative ideologies holding that the "colonial world was manageable by certifying that it was divisible." For critical analyses of anthropology's imbrication with indirect rule in Africa, see especially Apter 1999 and Moore 1994. Ranger 1985a and Vail 1989 reflect explicitly on relations between constructed tradition and the politics of tribalism in southern Africa.

47 Berry 1993, 31.

48 Berry 2001, 50.

49 See Berry 1993 and Chanock [1985] 1998.

50 Berry 1993, 29.

51 ZNA, File ZBJ 1/1/4, 1944 Trade (Godlonton), "Native Production and Trade Commission 1944," 3079.

52 ZNA, File ZBJ 1/2/3 1942–1944, vol. 2, Native Production and Trade Commission, 1944, "Native Production and Trade Commission 1944," 277

53 Around the time of Stead's testimony, Malinowski ([1945] 1961, 150) wrote: "While we can appreciate the fact that the administrator is not an anthropologist, . . . many mistakes have been unnecessary. . . . The real problem of contact, which the anthropologist is bound to assess, depends then largely on how to strengthen financially, politically, and legally the present-day chief under present-day conditions."

54 ZNA, File ZBJ 1/2/3 1942–1944, vol. 2, Native Production and Trade Commission, 1944, "Native Production and Trade Commission 1944," 277.

55 ZNA, File ZBJ 1/1/4, 1944 Trade (Godlonton), "Native Production and Trade Commission 1944," 3080.

56 Mamdani 1996.

57 ZNA, File ZBJ 1/1/4, 1944 Trade (Godlonton), "Native Production and Trade Commission 1944," 3090.

58 ZNA, File ZBJ 1/1/4, 1944 Trade (Godlonton), "Native Production and Trade Commission 1944," 3090.

59 ZNA, File ZBJ 1/1/4, 1944 Trade (Godlonton), "Native Production and Trade Commission 1944," 3096.

60 ZNA, File ZBJ 1/1/4, 1944 Trade (Godlonton), "Native Production and Trade Commission 1944," 3090.

61 ZNA, File ZBJ 3/1/1, 1944 Trade (Godlonton), "Report of Native Production and Trade Commission 1944," 2.

62 ZNA, File ZBJ 3/1/1, 1944 Trade (Godlonton), "Report of Native Production and Trade Commission 1944," 2.

63 Lugard 1893, 628, 630.

64 Lugard 1893, 630.

65 Bullock [1928] 1970, 69, 67–68.

66 Guha [1981] 1996, 3–4.

67 Dirks 2001, 123.

68 Colson 1971a, 197. See Murombedzi 1990 for an insightful analysis of the enduring legacies of so-called communal land tenure in Zimbabwe.

69 Bohannan and Bohannan 1968, 78–79. They quote Malinowski on 87.

70 Lefebvre [1974] 1991, 21.

71 ZNA, File ZBJ 3/1/1, "Report of Native Production and Trade Commission, 1944," 2.

72 Chanock 1991.

73 Cousins 1993.

74 Cheater 1990, 190.

75 Ranger 1993, 356, 357.

76 For details on Holleman's personal and professional history, I draw from Schumaker 2001 and Holleman's obituary available at *www.leidenuniv.nl/mare/2001/04/ memoriamholleman.html.*

77 Mangwende Commission Report, 1961, qtd. in Munro 1998, 117.

78 For critical genealogies of *adat* in relation to the politics of customary rights in Indonesia, see Li 2003 and Zerner 1994.

79 See Schumaker (2001, 44) for an excellent elaboration of volkekunde, its influence on Holleman, and his fieldwork techniques.

80 Schmidt 1992, 107.

81 Holleman [1951] 1968, 364–65.

82 Fallers 1956.

83 Fernando Ortiz ([1940] 1947) coined the term *transculturation* in a classic introduced by Malinowski, while Pratt 1992 has elaborated on imperial discourses of cultural encounter amid radically asymmetrical power relations.

84 His name has been rendered de Souza, de Sousa, Gouveya, and Gouveia. Bhila (1982, 225) argued that at the advent of company rule, "Mutasa, Saunyama, Katerere, Chisewere, Dore, Rupire and Gurupira were already paying tribute to" him.

85 For Newitt (1995, 339), Gouveia's ambitions included expanding "his domain from Barwe and Gorongosa on the highveldt, absorbing the Shona chieftaincies of Rupire and Mtoko and making himself master of the Mazoe goldfields." In the 1890s, his lands reportedly stretched from the Zambesi to the Pungue (Pungwe), the latter river a day's walk south of Kaerezi.

86 Newitt 1995, 289, 369.

87 Newitt 1995, 288.

88 Governor of Manica J. J. Fereira, December 1890 report, qtd. in Newitt 1995, 339. Newitt (350) suggested that the new Portuguese administrative district of Manica, founded in 1884, was "little more than a front for the personal ambitions" of Gouveia.

89 Bhila 1982, 225; Isaacman 1976, 50.

90 For quotations, see Isaacman 1976, 188.

91 See Newitt 1995, 315. Isaacman (1976, 28) situated Gouveia's influence in relation to widespread patterns of descendants of Afro-Goans who ruled secondary states in the late nineteenth century.

92 Clutton-Brock 1969, 7.

93 Gouveia waged war against the "Shona chieftaincies" of Rupire and Mtoko, establishing garrisons deep within Mashonaland along the Mazoe River (Newitt 1995, 340). A force of more than 5,000 allegedly countered his attacks (Bhila 1982, 28). Rhodes appears

to have been well rewarded for encouraging revolt since his agents operated within "the unpacified enclave of Barue" up until his death in 1902. "Up till 1902," Newitt argued, "Barue remained independent, the last African chieftaincy south of the Zambesi to do so" (1995, 360, 371). See Isaacman 1976 for Barue's "tradition of resistance" to Portuguese and British rule.

94 Isaacman (1976, 128) dated Gouveia's death in 1891, while Newitt (1995, 370) has him killed in 1892 during a Barue revolt.

95 Massey 1994.

96 Qtd. in Low (1982, 22).

97 See Summers 1958, 263, 266.

98 Beach 1994, 110. Bhila (1972, 12) conceived Manyika as a "virtually independent polity" from the sixteenth to the early nineteenth centuries.

99 Garlake 1966 identified four distinct Iron Age cultures in the district—the Ziwa from the fourth to eleventh century; Zimbabwe, seventeenth century; Inyanga Uplands, sixteenth to seventeenth centuries; and Inyanga Lowlands, seventeenth to eighteenth centuries. Yet archaeological interpretations have been far from conclusive. Bhila (1982, 8) described the fortresses, pits, and water terraces associated with Nyanga "culture" that spanned 1700–1800, yet he describes their fate or potential migration as a "matter of conjecture." Beach (1994, 126) characterized "the Nyanga Culture" as "an important culture about which practically nothing is known."

100 See Garlake (1966, 6) for a critical review and Randall-MacIver [1906] 1969 for a notable exception.

101 Summers 1958, 313.

102 ZNA, File N9/4/12, NC Monthly Reports, 1902, T. B. Hulley, NC Inyanga, Inyanga District Monthly Report, September 1902.

103 ZNA, File NUC 2/3/3, November 9, 1923, H. M. Smith, NC Inyanga, Chiefs and Headmen, Inyanga District. In 1905, for instance, Private Bandi of the BSA Native Police reported spending a night at Nyapimbi's in Tangwena's kraal. See ZNA, File NUC 2/4/1, undated Laing, NC Inyanga, to NCO, BSA Police, Inyanga, no. 118.

104 The phrase is taken from Cooper and Stoler 1997.

105 ZNA, File S 604/1926, November 13, 1925, NC Inyanga to District Veterinary Officer, Umtali.

106 Berry 1993.

107 ZNA, File S 603/1930, August 29, 1930, NC Inyanga to CNC Salisbury, "Boundary between Inyanga Block and Nyamaropa Reserve."

108 ZNA, File NUC 2/3/2, January 17, 1912, Moodie, NC Inyanga to CNC, Salisbury, Classification of Chiefs.

109 In 1912, Tangwena brought in a tenth of the tax revenue of Saunyama and a fourth that of Katerere. All three paramounts trailed far behind the income of Shiovu, the representative of the loyalist Chief Umtassa. ZNA, File NUC 2/3/2, January 17, 1912, Moodie, NC Inyanga to CNC, Salisbury, classification of chiefs. In 1923, Katerere, "Taw-

unguena," and Sawunyama all received an annual subsidy of twelve pounds. By the 1950s, Tangwena's salary remained the same, while the next lowest salary of the district's four chiefs rose to eighty-four pounds. ZNA, File S 2583 542, NC, Chiefs, General Correspondence, vol. 2, 1950–1951, Chiefs' Subsidies for 1953.

110 ZNA, File S 604/1926, January 8, 1926, Inyanga District Amendments to Military Intelligence Supplied under Police.

111 See Worby 1994 for an astute analysis of ethnic mapping elsewhere in Zimbabwe.

112 ZNA, File NUC 2/3/2, January 17, 1912, Moodie, NC Inyanga to CNC, Salisbury, classification of chiefs.

113 A 1913 report describes "Tangwena's people who fled from the Portuguese and settled in the Gaeresi Valley—*mtupo Inewa*, the leopard." ZNA, File NUC 2/4/2, January 13, 1913, D. H. Moodie, NC Inyanga, "Inyanga District: General Characteristics," no. 372.

114 ZNA, File NUC 2/3/2, January 17, 1912, Moodie, NC Inyanga to CNC, Salisbury, classification of chiefs.

115 ZNA, File NUC 2/4/2, January 13, 1913, D. H. Moodie, NC Inyanga, "Inyanga District: General Characteristics," no. 372.

116 ZNA, File NUC 2/3/3, October 12, 1923, Smith, NC Inyanga, "Ethnographical Map." Administrators sometimes dropped the prefix *wa*, meaning people, in their ethnic appellations.

117 ZNA, File S 1561/10, vol. 6, 1923–1924, Chiefs and Headmen Files, January 23, 1925, "Meeting held between Chief Native Commissioner and the Chiefs, Headmen, and Followers of the Inyanga District."

118 Nyanga DA Office, CHK/Tangwena-Chief Tangwena File, February 28, 1950, ref. no. 18, Assistant Native Commissioner Inyanga to Provincial NC, Umtali, "Native Chiefs: Resolution by the Native Affairs Advisory Board on the Abolition of Redundant Chieftainships."

119 ZNA, File NUC 2/3/3, October 12, 1923, Smith, NC Inyanga, "Ethnographical Map."

120 ZNRO, File PER 5/TAWUNGWENA FILE, Inyanga District, March 1948 to March 1960, Internal Affairs, box 116598, location 8.14.3R, 19/3/48 NC Inyanga, no. 60 of 1948.

121 ZNA, File S 2588/1977 Land Inyanga, January 24, 1949, Provincial NC, Umtali to CNC, Salisbury, "Cumberland Block: Inyanga District."

122 ZNA, File S 2588/1977 Land Inyanga, March 24, 1948, memo from J. Armstrong, for Secretary to the Treasurer, Salisbury, to the Auditor General.

123 ZNA, File S 2588/1977 Land Inyanga, April 12, 1948, Inyanga NC to Provincial NC, Umtali, "Removal of Natives from Crown and Alienated Land and from Overpopulated Reserves: Inyanga."

124 ZNRO, File Internal Affairs, box 116598, location 8.14.3R, March 25, 1948, Provincial NC, Umtali to CNC, Salisbury, "Rex vs. Chief Tangwena of the Inyanga District: Contravention of Section 24 (b) of Native Affairs Act, Chapter 72."

125 Nyanga DA Office, CHK/Tangwena-Chief Tangwena File, February 28, 1950, ref.

no. 18, Assistant Native Commissioner Inyanga to Provincial NC, Umtali, "Native Chiefs: Resolution by the Native Affairs Advisory Board on the Abolition of Redundant Chieftainships." This might be the administrators' mistranscription or confusion of *ngwena*; Tangwena's totem, a crocodile, was usually invoked as *gwara*. This disjunction at once challenges the archive's fetish of facticity while highlighting administrative attempts to map tribal roots through chiefly totems. The report's use of *Wanyanga* implies a territorial referent—probably Mount Nyanga—for the Tangwena ethnicity.

126 Nyanga DA Office, CHK/Tangwena-Chief Tangwena, April 23, 1948, NC Inyanga, "Family Tree: Tawungwena Chieftainship."

127 Nyanga DA Office, CHK/Tangwena-Chief Tangwena, June 20, 1950, Acting NC Inyanga to PNC Umtali, ref. no. 18/50.

128 In 1951, the chief NC in Salisbury included "Tawungwena" on the official schedule for chiefs and headmen in Inyanga District. See ZNA, File S 2583 542, vol. 2, 1950–1951, August 3, 1951, L. Powys-Jones, Chief NC, Salisbury, "New Establishment of Chiefs and Headmen," schedule B. The acting DC Inyanga, writing to the Provincial Commissioner of Manicaland in 1972, mentioned two letters from 1950 recommending that "the Tawungwena Chieftainship be abolished on Kinga's death." He then went on to state, "There are no replies to these on my files." Nyanga DA Office, CHK/Tangwena-Chief Tangwena File, June 1, 1972, A. P. Rudolph, Acting DC Inyanga, to Provincial Commissioner Manicaland, "Tawungwena Chieftainship: Inyanga District." That same year, administrators searched both Salisbury's Internal Affairs files and the National Archives, yielding no record of a reply. Such disjunctions disturb any unproblematic flow of power and knowledge through the capillary networks of colonial administration.

129 Bhabha 1987, 120.

130 Under a section of the report with the heading "Boundaries," one finds a terse explanation: "The Chief no longer has a tribal area." ZNA, File S 2929/1/3, 1965 September–1965 October, Inyanga District: Delineation Report (Internal Affairs), "Report on Tawungwena Chieftainship, Holdenby Tribal Trust Land: Inyanga District."

131 ZNA, File S 2929/1/3, 1965 September–1965 October, Inyanga District: Delineation Report (Internal Affairs), "Report on Tawungwena Chieftainship, Holdenby Tribal Trust Land: Inyanga District." Noting a list of villages that "comprise the community," the report listed 282 taxpayers under five of Tangwena's headmen on Inyanga Downs (Gaeresi Ranch) and 89 taxpayers under Tawungwena in Holdenby Tribal Trust Land.

6 Enduring Evictions

1 For Nyafaru's history, see Clutton-Brock and Clutton-Brock 1972 and 1987; and International Defence and Aid Fund 1972.

2 Das 1995.

3 Benjamin 1978, 16.

4 See Butler 2003, 468.

5 Nora [1992] 1996, 15.

6 Boyarin 1994, 2.

7 Davis and Starn 1989.

8 On memory work, see Cole 2001; Rofel 1999; and Yoneyama 1999. Starn's 1999 eloquent ethnography explicitly links the politics of memory to livelihood struggles.

9 Comaroff 1985.

10 ZNRO, File LAN/16, Squatters and Resettlement Schemes GU-LE, 1963–1968, Internal Affairs, box 100839, location 25.10.6R, May 31, 1962, NC Inyanga to Provincial NC Manicaland, "Resettlement: S.N.A. 'B' (St. Swithins) and Sawunyama Highlands."

11 ZNRO, File LAN 16/16, Gaeresi Ranch Squatters, Correspondence, Internal Affairs, box 116598, location 8.14.3R, n.d., C. M. Hayes, Senior Inspector, to W. F. B. Hanmer, Managing Director, Gaeresi Ranch; January 1, 1973, Ministry of Internal Affairs, "The Tangwena: Background Information."

12 ZNRO, File LAN 16/16/3, Gaeresi Ranch Squatters, Press, Internal Affairs, box 116598, location 8.14.3R, March 27, 1969, Ministry of Internal Affairs, "The Tangwena Issue at Gairezi."

13 ZNRO, File LAN/16, Squatters and Resettlement Schemes GU-LE, 1963–1968, Internal Affairs, box 100839, location 25.10.6R, September 18, 1963, DC Inyanga to PC Manicaland.

14 Rekayi Tangwena, letter to the *Guardian*, July 29, 1966. ZNA, catalogued under "Tangwena" in Historical Manuscripts Catalog. ZNA, File MS 308/42/3 LAND 1980.

15 It is unclear, however, whether this figure included the seventy-six alleged families evicted in 1965. Most likely, this is a preeviction figure for the year. See ZNRO, File LAN/16/16/3, Gaeresi Ranch Squatters, Press, Internal Affairs, box 116598, location 8.14.3R, March 27, 1969, Ministry of Internal Affairs, "The Tangwena Issue at Gairezi."

16 ZNRO, File 16/16/2, Gaeresi Ranch Squatters, Correspondence, box 116598, location 8.14.3R, Internal Affairs, LAN/9/1-LAN 16/16/7, October 31, 1966, letter from Nicolle, Secretary of Internal Affairs to PC, Matabeleland North, "Eviction of Tangwena Africans: Gaeresi Ranch: Inyanga."

17 A 1971 government report, retrospectively reflecting on that period, described "two kraals (not Tangwena) which between them have 198 taxpayers. These people have indicated a willingness to move, voluntarily." ZNRO, File LAN 16/16, Gaeresi Ranch Squatters, Correspondence, Internal Affairs, box 116598, location 8.14.3R, May 25, 1971, I. H. C. Moffit, DC Inyanga to PC, Manicaland. A 1966 figure cited 152 Tangwena families on the ranch. ZNRO, File LAN 16/16/2, Gaeresi Ranch Squatters, Correspondence, Internal Affairs, box 116598, location 8.14.3R, August 5, 1966, Stanley Keeble to Minister of Internal Affairs.

18 ZNRO, File LAN 16/16/2, Gaeresi Ranch Squatters, Correspondence, Internal Af-

fairs, box 116598, location 8.14.3R, August 5, 1966, Stanley Keeble to Minister of Internal Affairs; and Nyanga DA Files, CHK/Tangwena-Chief Tangwena File, July 13, 1966, for J. L. Fowle, DC Inyanga to PC, Manicaland, "Re: Tawengwena Chieftainship: Land: Removal of Squatters: Gaeresi Ranch."

19 Nyanga DA Files, CHK/Tangwena-Chief Tangwena File, July 13, 1966, for J. L. Fowle, DC Inyanga to PC, Manicaland.

20 ZNRO, File LAN 16/16/2, Gaeresi Ranch Squatters, Correspondence, Internal Affairs, box 116598, location, 8.14.3R, January 8, 1969, Senior Information Officer, Internal Affairs to D. G. Lewis, Greendale.

21 ZNRO, File LAN 16/16, Gaeresi Ranch Squatters, Correspondence, Internal Affairs, box 116598, location 8.14.3R, September 22, 1965, C. K. Latham, "1965 Report on Tawungwena Chieftainship. Holdenby TTL: Inyanga District." By 1970, Lance Smith, the minister of Internal Affairs, would declare in Parliament that "this land was never a traditional African area." See "Rekayi 'Not a Chief,'" *Rhodesia Herald*, June 6, 1970.

22 Nyanga DA Files, CHK/Tangwena-Chief Tangwena File, June 14, 1966, memorandum from J. L. Fowle, DC, Inyanga to PC, Manicaland, "Tawungwena Chieftainship: Inyanga."

23 Nyanga DA Files, CHK/Tangwena-Chief Tangwena File, August 5, 1966, J. B. W. Anderson for Secretary for IA to DC, Inyanga, Appointment of Marjeni, X 2701 Inyanga as Acting Chief Tawungwena, Inyanga District (19/11–7/12/65).

24 Nyanga DA Files, CHK/Tangwena-Chief Tangwena File. Undated handwritten note stating, "All came in again on 2/3/66 with chief."

25 Nyanga DA Files, CHK/Tangwena-Chief Tangwena File, March 2, 1966, handwritten note with illegible signature, date-stamped DC Inyanga.

26 ZNRO, File ACC 8, Internal Affairs, Annual Reports, 1966, box 86732, location 8.17.5F, "Report of the District Commissioner, Inyanga for the Year Ended 31 December, 1966."

27 Nyanga DC Files, CHK/Tangwena-Chief Tangwena File, April 4, 1966, memo from B. P. Kascula for Secretary for Internal Affairs to DC, Inyanga, "Death of Acting Chief Tawungwena"; see also undated handwritten note referring to a March 2, 1966, meeting in Inyanga "with chief."

28 ZNRO, File PER 5/Tawungwena–Chief Tawungwena, Inyanga District, March 1948 to March 1960. Internal Affairs, box 116598, location 8.14.3R, June 1, 1972, Acting DC, Inyanga to PC, Manicaland. Some records exceed dates of the file's label.

29 ZNRO, File PER 5/Tawungwena–Chief Tawungwena, Inyanga District, March 1948 to March 1960. Internal Affairs, box 116598, location 8.14.3R, June 7, 1972, PC Umtali to Secretary Internal Affairs.

30 Braun 2000 and Rose 1999 have deployed Latour's 1987 notions of "action at a distance" and "centers of calculation" in their elaborations of governmenality.

31 See Martin and Johnson 1981, 10; Kriger 1992, 88.

32 Martin and Johnson 1981, 11.

33 ZNRO, File LAN 16/16/2, Gaeresi Ranch Squatters, Correspondence, Internal Affairs, box 116598, location 8.14.3R, October 28, year unknown, W. H. H. Nicolle, Secretary of Internal Affairs to Archdeacon Lewis.

34 ZNRO, File LAN 16/16/2, Gaeresi Ranch Squatters, Correspondence, Internal Affairs, box 116598, location 8.14.3R, September 8, 1966, M. E. Hayes, PC, Manicaland to Secretary IA, Gaeresi Squatters.

35 ZNRO, File LAN 16/16, Gaeresi Ranch Squatters, Correspondence, Internal Affairs, box 116598, location 8.14.3R, September 26, 1969, W. F. B. Hanmer's Power of Attorney to R. Wyatt, Inyanga DC.

36 See Moyana 1984, 160. For an incisive history of squatting in Zimbabwe, see Nyambara 2000.

37 Qtd. in Moyana 1984, 161.

38 "Tangwena 'Chief' Is Fined as Squatter," *Rhodesian Herald*, June 3, 1967.

39 "Inyanga 'Chief' Bases Defence on Land Act," *Rhodesia Herald*, November 4, 1967.

40 See Moyana 1987, 17.

41 "Gaeresi Kraal Told to Move to Nearby Site," *Rhodesia Herald*, January 21, 1969.

42 ZNRO, File LAN 16/16, Gaeresi Ranch Squatters, Correspondence, Internal Affairs, box 116598, location 8.14.3R, February 12, 1968, Nicolle, Secretary of Internal Affairs, to Provincial Administrator, Umtali.

43 Rekayi Tangwena, qtd. in " 'They Can Kill Me' Says Tangwena," *Sunday Mail* (Rhodesia), September 28, 1969.

44 See Rekayi's accounts in Clutton-Brock 1969, 5.

45 *Chena* is the Shona term for "white."

46 Qtd. in Clutton-Brock 1969, 18.

47 See "Would the Queen Agree to Move to Italy?" *Sunday Mail* (Rhodesia), November 21, 1971. In an uncanny entanglement of imperial sovereignty, territory, and national politics, that same month the US Department of State published a study of the boundary between Mozambique and Southern Rhodesia, mentioning cement pillars and other demarcation points along the Gaeresi (Kaerezi) and Jora Rivers in Tangwena territory. The report noted that in the 1890s, Portuguese and British colonial officials negotiated for years over "the Manica boundary" that separated their respective territories, and it included a section running along Kaerezi's eastern edge. In 1897, representatives of both nations signed the formal demarcation in Florence, finalizing the international border only after arbitration by an Italian diplomat (United States Department of State 1971).

48 "Tangwena Wants Queen to Know," *Rhodesia Herald*, February 21, 1972.

49 Rekayi Tangwena, qtd. in *Rhodesia Herald*, May 7, 1971.

50 See "Tangwena 'Chief' Fined $75 for Subversion," *Rhodesia Herald*, July 3, 1971.

51 See "Tribesman Sues Two Ministers for $1318," *Rhodesia Herald*, July 17, 1971.

52 ZNRO, File LAN 16/16, Gaeresi Ranch Squatters, Correspondence, Internal Affairs, box 116598, location 8.14.3R, June 25, 1970, B. H. Lucas for DC Inyanga to PC, Manicaland.

53 ZNRO, File LAN 16/16, Gaeresi Ranch Squatters, Correspondence, Internal Affairs, box 116598, location 8.14.3R, September 2, 1971, B. H. Lucas for DA Inyanga to PC, Manicaland, "Land Tenure Act: The State vs. Naboth, Herbert Goora, and Others."

54 ZNRO, File LAN 16/16, Gaeresi Ranch Squatters, Correspondence, Internal Affairs, box 116598, location 8.14.3R, November 25, 1970, R. Wyatt, DC Inyanga to PC Manicaland.

55 ZNRO, File LAN 16/16, Gaeresi Ranch Squatters, Correspondence, Internal Affairs, box 116598, location 8.14.3R, December 1, 1970, Noel Hunt, PC Manicaland to Secretary Internal Affairs, "Tangwena Situation Report."

56 ZNRO, File LAN 16/16/4, Gaeresi Ranch Squatters, Legal Opinions, Internal Affairs, box 116598, location 8.14.3R, June 26, 1972, G. R. Broderick to Mr. Hagelthorn, "Gaeresi Squatters: Nyanga District: Legal Sit-Rep as at 23 June, 1972."

57 See ZNRO, File LAN 16/16, Gaeresi Ranch Squatters, Correspondence, Internal Affairs, box 116598, location 8.14.3R, October 26, 1970, Ministry of Internal Affairs report, "The Tangwena Issue at Gaeresi."

58 ZNRO, File LAN 16/16, Gaeresi Ranch Squatters, Correspondence, Internal Affairs, box 116598, location 8.14.3R, November 2, 1970, R. Wyatt, Inyanga DC to PC, Manicaland, "Operation Rawhide: Tangwena Cattle"; ZNRO, File LAN 16/16, Gaeresi Ranch Squatters, Correspondence, Internal Affairs, box 116598, location 8.14.3R, November 23, 1970, memorandum from Noel Hunt, PC Manicaland to Secretary Internal Affairs, Salisbury.

59 "Tangwena Cattle to Be Sold Today," *Rhodesia Herald*, December 18, 1970.

60 "Tangwena's Tribesmen Take to Hills," *Rhodesia Herald*, November 3, 1970.

61 "Rain Lashes Fugitive Tangwena People," *Rhodesia Herald*, November 23, 1970.

62 "Twenty of Tangwena Huts Razed: 'I Will Build Again' Says Tribesman," *Rhodesia Herald*, November 25, 1970.

63 "Tangwena Rebuilding at Gaeresi Ranch," *Rhodesia Herald*, December 20, 1971.

64 See "Copter Police at Tangwena," *Rhodesia Herald*, July 26, 1972.

65 See "Criticism of Police Dogs," *Rhodesia Herald*, August 14, 1972.

66 "Gaeresi Children at Harari," *Rhodesia Herald*, July 29, 1972.

67 See "Director Charged under Land Tenure Act," *Rhodesia Herald*, September 11, 1971.

68 "Failures of Anticipation," editorial, *Rhodesia Herald*, August 28, 1969.

69 "It Began as a Private Dispute," *Rhodesia Herald*, October 11, 1969.

70 "Inyanga 'Chief' Bases Defence on Land Act," *Rhodesia Herald*, November 4, 1967.

71 "Verdict Reserved in 'Chief' Appeal," *Rhodesia Herald*, May 15, 1968.

72 " 'They Can Kill Me' Says Tangwena," *Sunday Mail* (Rhodesia) September 9, 1969.

73 Rekayi Tangwena, letter to the *Guardian*, July 29, 1966.

74 ZNRO, File 16/16/3, Gaeresi Ranch Squatters, Press, Internal Affairs, box 116598, location 8.14.3R, copy of letter attributed to Rekayi Tangwena that appeared in the *Times* of London, December 14, 1966, appended to memorandum from N. J. Brendom, Undersecretary for Information to Secretary, Internal Affairs.

75 See ZNRO, File LAN/16/16/3, Gaeresi Ranch Squatters, Press, Internal Affairs, box 116598, location 8.14.3R, August 11, 1966, memorandum, W. H. H. Nicolle, Secretary of Internal Affairs to Secretary to the Prime Minister, "Land Apportionment Act: Chief Tangwena."

76 For press coverage, see ZNRO, File LAN/16/16/3, Gaeresi Ranch Squatters, Press, Internal Affairs, box 116598, location, 8.14.3R; for correspondence, see ZNRO, File LAN/16/16/2 and ZNRO, File LAN 16/16, both entitled "Gaeresi Ranch Squatters, Correspondence," Internal Affairs, box 116598, location 8.14.3R.

77 See "Hut Burning Filmed by U.K. Team," *Sunday Mail* (Rhodesia), May 9, 1971.

78 Statements made in Britain's House of Commons referred to "the Tangwena tribe, who have been illegally dispossessed by the Southern Rhodesia regime" and stated that "the position of the Tangwena tribe gives cause for concern." See "Talks May Include Tangwena," *Rhodesia Herald*, February 20, 1971. Rekayi Tangwena's direct appeal to the British foreign secretary, however, yielded "concern," but no direct intervention.

79 ZNRO, File 16/16/2, Gaeresi Ranch Squatters, Correspondence, Internal Affairs, box 116598, location 8.14.3R, LAN/9/1-LAN 16/16/7, October 31, 1966, Nicolle, Secretary of Internal Affairs to PC, Matabeleland North, "Eviction of Tangwena Africans: Gaeresi Ranch: Inyanga."

80 ZNRO, File 16/16/3, Gaeresi Ranch Squatters, Press, Internal Affairs, box 116598, location 8.14.3R, August 11, 1966, memorandum from W. H. H. Nicolle, Secretary for Internal Affairs to Secretary to the Prime Minister, "Land Apportionment Act: Chief Tangwena."

81 "Subversion Claim: 'Communists and Fellow Travellers' Blamed,'" *Rhodesia Herald*, August 27, 1969. The 1969 position, presented in Parliament by the minister of Internal Affairs, echoed a 1966 memorandum by the secretary of Internal Affairs who complained that "the Gaeresi matter merely reflects an attempt to make political capital out of the Land Apportionment Act and in my view, has been raised at this juncture in an endeavour to embarrass Government." ZNRO, File 16/16/2, Gaeresi Ranch Squatters, Correspondence, Internal Affairs, box 116598, location 8.14.3R, LAN/9/1-LAN 16/16/7, September 19, 1966, letter from Nicolle, Secretary for Internal Affairs to D. Tyndale Biscoe, Unvukwes.

82 Stanley Keeble, "Ranch Shareholders Sympathetic," letter to the editor, *Rhodesia Herald*, August 4, 1969.

83 I draw these details from Mutasa [1974] 1983 and contributors to Clutton-Brock and Clutton-Brock 1987.

84 "Clutton-Brock Tries 'to Live by the Gospels,'" *Rhodesia Herald*, September 7, 1969.

85 Nyerere 1987, 130.

86 Mugabe 1987, 132.

87 Interview with Guy Clutton-Brock at Cold Comfort Farm, qtd. in "Clutton-Brock Issues Challenge to Minister," *Rhodesia Herald*, August 28, 1969. Clutton-Brock invoked the discourse of citizenship in his introduction to a 1969 booklet defending Tangwena land rights. In 1970, Smith's regime banned the Cold Comfort Society, the organization managing Cold Comfort Farm.

88 Hall and Held [1989] 1990, 174.

89 Guy Clutton-Brock, "No Good Reason Has Been Given for Moving Tangwena and His People," letter to the editor, *Rhodesia Herald*, July 14, 1969.

90 Didymus Mutasa, "Clutton Brock Acts Not Inspired by Communism," letter to the editor, *Rhodesia Herald*, September 4, 1969.

91 Qtd. in International Defence and Aid Fund 1972, 27.

92 Qtd. in Mutasa [1974] 1983, 8–11.

93 See International Defence and Aid Fund 1972, 18, 22. A representative statement of Rekayi's was: "We don't wish to fight. . . . We don't want to throw stones at anyone." "Tangwena 'Chief' Gives Evidence," *Rhodesia Herald*, May 7, 1971.

94 "Organized Terrorism," letter to the editor, *Rhodesia Herald*, November 30, 1970.

95 "Rekayi Meets Bishop," *Rhodesia Herald*, October 7, 1969. When the archdeacon of Inyanga denied Rekayi's membership in the church in a letter to the editor, Rekayi replied: "I am now turning to the Apostolic Faith, because no one from the Anglican Church is prepared to come and preach to my people." ("Rekayi Tangwena's Case Not Strengthened by His Claim to Be an Anglican," *Rhodesia Herald*, October 13, 1969.)

96 ZNRO, File LAN 16/16/2, Gaeresi Ranch Squatters, Correspondence, Internal Affairs, box 116598, location 8.14.3R, August 8, 1966, Christian Movement of Peace to William Hanmer.

97 *Moto* editorial, qtd. in "'We Will Return,' Says Rekayi," *Rhodesia Herald*, August 31, 1969.

98 See Catholic Mission for Justice and Peace in Rhodesia 1975; and International Defence and Aid Fund 1972.

99 "What Is Best for the Tangwena?" *Rhodesia Herald*, October 1, 1969.

100 "Still Time to Think Again," editorial, *Rhodesia Herald*, September 19, 1969.

101 "Petition of Support from UCR," *Rhodesia Herald*, August 27, 1969.

102 *Moto* editorial, qtd. in "'We Will Return,' Says Rekayi," *Rhodesia Herald*, August 31, 1969.

103 Garfield Todd, "Tangwena Plight Angers Africans," letter to the editor, *Rhodesia Herald*, December 3, 1970.

104 "Tangwena Did Not Seem Angry," *Rhodesia Herald*, December 11, 1970.

105 See "Tangwena Move Not Settled," *Rhodesia Herald*, June 11, 1970. The minister of Internal Affairs told Parliament that "squatters" from several areas would be moved by government. A total of 47,000 acres in Que Que and Gokwe had been reserved for African resettlement.

106 Headman Madziwanzira, qtd. in International Defence and Aid Fund 1972, 21.

107 ZNRO, File LAN 16/16, Gaeresi Ranch Squatters, Correspondence, Internal Affairs, box 116598, location 8.14.3R, February 11, 1971, Nicolle, Secretary of Internal Affairs to the Minister.

108 International Defence and Aid Fund 1972, 27.

109 ZNRO, File LAN 16/16, Gaeresi Ranch Squatters, Correspondence, Internal Affairs, box 116598, location 8.14.3R, February 11, 1971, Nicolle, Secretary of Internal Affairs to the Minister, "Gaeresi Ranch and the Tangwena"; Lance Smith, qtd. in "No Tribesmen Remain on Gaeresi," *Rhodesia Herald*, March 20, 1971.

110 "Tangwena at Gaeresi Ranch," *Rhodesia Herald*, December 20, 1971.

111 ZNRO, File LAN 16/16, Gaeresi Ranch Squatters, Correspondence, Internal Affairs, box 116598, location 8.14.3R, January 23, 1973, Ministry of Internal Affairs, "The Tangwena: Background Information."

112 ZNRO, File LAN 16/16, Gaeresi Ranch Squatters, Correspondence, Internal Affairs, box 116598, location 8.14.3R, June 4, 1971, Noel Hunt, PC Manicaland to Secretary of Internal Affairs.

113 In 1969, Rekayi responded to the Bende offer: "The government has tried to bribe me. They say that if I move to this place, Bende, I will be paid 25 pounds a month and will be officially recognized as chief." " 'We Prefer Death to Losing Land,' " *Sunday Mail* (Rhodesia), August 11 or 17, 1969.

114 Qtd. in International Defence and Aid Fund 1972, 31.

115 ZNA, File Historical Manuscripts, MS 335/10/2, Interdict Cases, 1969–1970, August 18, 1970, "Conversation between Rekayi Tangwena and Nyanga District Commissioner."

116 ZNRO, File 16/16, Gaeresi Ranch Squatters, Correspondence, Internal Affairs, box 116598, location 8.14.3R, July 22, 1971, DC Inyanga to PC Manicaland.

117 ZNA, File Historical Manuscripts, MS 335/10/6, Rekayi Tangwena's Court Cases, April 22, 1967, court statement by William Francis Busby Hanmer.

118 ZNA, File Historical Manuscripts, MS 335/10/6, Rekayi Tangwena's Court Cases, April 4, 1968, court testimony of Rekayi Tangwena at Inyanga.

119 ZNRO, File LAN/16/16/1, Gaeresi Ranch Squatters, Correspondence, Internal Affairs, box 116598, location 8.14.32R, July 21, 1966, memorandum from J. B. W. Anderson for Secretary, Internal Affairs to Portuguese Curator of Africans, Salisbury, "Proposed Movement of Kraals into Mozambique."

120 ZNRO, File LAN/16/16/1, Gaeresi Ranch Squatters, Correspondence, Internal Affairs, box 116598, location 8.14.32R, July 2, 1966, handwritten and unsigned note.

121   ZNRO, File LAN/16/16/1, Gaeresi Ranch Squatters, Correspondence, Internal Affairs, box 116598, location 8.14.32R, July 13, 1966, J. L. Fowle, Inyanga DC to PC Manicaland, "Tawungwena Chieftainship: Removal of Squatters from Gaeresi Ranch."

122   Rekayi's testimony, as reported by Clutton-Brock 1969, 10–11.

123   ZNRO, File PER 5/Tawungwena, Chief Tawungwena, Inyanga District, March 1948 to March 1960, Internal Affairs, box 116598, location 8.14.3R, handwritten sketch and notes, May 2, 1972, signed by G. R. Broderick, "Gazetted Extent of Chief Tawungwena's Tribal Areas," Government Notice 519/68. Some records exceed the catalogue dates.

124   Qtd. in Clutton-Brock 1969, 23.

125   ZNRO, File LAN 16/16/2, Gaeresi Ranch Squatters, Correspondence, Internal Affairs, box 116598, location 8.14.3R, November 10, 1966, letter attributed to Rekayi Tangwena, to Father Lewis, Archdeacon.

126   Qtd. in International Defence and Aid Fund 1972, 31.

127   Qtd. in "New Tangwena Eviction Move Expected Soon," *Rhodesia Herald*, May 28, 1970.

128   ZNRO, File LAN 16/16, Gaeresi Ranch Squatters, Correspondence, Internal Affairs, box 116598, location 8.14.3R, October 26 1970, Ministry of Internal Affairs memo, "The Tangwena Issue at Gaeresi."

129   See Blair 2003; and Smith and Simpson 1981.

7 Selective Sovereignties

1   See Williams [1977] 1985, 115–18.

2   Asad 2003, 179.

3   Mbembe 2000, 263.

4   Bartelson 1995, 29. Bartelson (2001, 171) echoed Foucault by encouraging analysts to "ask questions about how sovereignty has in fact been exercised."

5   Agnew and Corbridge 1995; Taylor 2003.

6   Goldberg 2002, 154.

7   Comaroff [1995] 1997, 217.

8   On graduated sovereignty, see Ong 1999; on shadows, see Nordstrom 2004. For attempts to unhinge sovereignty from the state, see Appadurai 2002; Luke 1996; and Hansen 2001.

9   Appadurai 1996, 161.

10   Sassen 1996, 29; my emphasis.

11   Roitman 2001. Mbembe 2001 has termed similar patterns in postcolonial Africa a mode of "Private Indirect Government."

12   On "governable spaces," see Watts 2003; on ethnicized violence, see Watts 2000.

13 See Ferme 2001; Reno 1998; and Nordstrom 2004. Ferguson 1997 provided a probing critique of how normative anthropological notions of sovereignty, culture, and nation-state have depoliticized analyses of poverty.

14 Bourdillon (1987, 105) noted that "defeated autochthons often become the centre of the most important rain-making cults." Lan's (1985, 226) study of spirit mediums and *mhondoro* (royal ancestors) in Dande, Zimbabwe, suggested that the "lineage that has lived within a territory the longest is considered its owner and, as its owner, it or its ancestors can ensure its fertility." Eschewing essentialism, he astutely elaborated *autochthons* as a term fusing mythical, historical, and attitudinal references (14). See Geschiere and Nyamnjoh 2000 for a superb analysis of the contemporary cultural politics of autochthony in an African context.

15 See Guyer and Belinga's 1995 excellent analysis of Africanist deployments of "wealth-in-people"; and Yudelman's (1964, 10) study of land use in Southern Rhodesia, where, he argued, power and status did "not depend on control over material wealth but rather on the claims that are held against persons."

16 Feierman 1990. Contributors to Schoffeleers 1978 offered historical studies on "territorial cults and ecological religions" in Zambia, Malawi, and Zimbabwe.

17 *Upenyu* can be glossed as both "health" and "life."

18 Both practices of rule sought to govern what Foucault (1979, 11) termed the "imbrication of men and things" by producing an effective articulation among natural, spiritual, and political forces within a specific territory. In this assemblage of power, rain and cultivated crops are consequential actants, whereas Nyahuruwa, Tangwena, and their human subjects constitute political agents. For Kaerezians, the ability to rule productively the imbrication of humans and things in their territory entailed an orchestration of the powers of nature and culture.

19 *Vanatete* can also refer to older sisters.

20 *Mugadziri* derives from the verb *kugadzira*, to repair, make, or restore; a guardian or custodian thus carried the responsibility of ensuring the health of a territory. *Mutanha* can be either territory or the plateau of highlands. In this case, the two semantic spaces overlapped.

21 See, for example, Hannan [1959] 1987, 139–40.

22 Robert both echoes and complicates conventional ethnographic wisdom in Zimbabwe. Lan (1985, 26) argues that "the lineage that has lived within a territory the longest is considered its owner and, as its owner, it or its ancestors can ensure its fertility." It is also from the title of Lan's influential account of spirit mediumship in the context of Zimbabwe's liberation struggle that I take part of the title for this subchapter, "Guns and Rain."

23 Elijah told me that he joined the NDP in 1959. That organization was founded in 1960 to succeed the banned SRANC, which Elijah may have first joined.

24 Nyanga DA Files, CHK/Tangwena-Chief Tangwena File, September 24, 1985, minutes of meeting at DA's office with "Tangwena delegation."

25 Nyanga DA Files, CHK/Tangwena-Chief Tangwena File, July 3, 1986, J. S. N. Makoni for Nyanga DA, to PA, Manicaland, "RE: Appointment: Nyabinde Tickey Mangwendere."

26 Nyanga DA Files, CHK/Tangwena-Chief Tangwena File, July 3, 1986, J. S. N. Makoni for Nyanga DA, to PA, Manicaland, "Re: Appointment: Nyabinde Tickey Mangwendere." Both Magwendere and Mangwendere appear in reports, referring to one of the four royal houses descended from Tsatse's four wives.

27 Nyanga DA Files, CHK/Tangwena-Chief Tangwena File, July 29, 1983, J. S. N. Makoni for DA, Nyanga to Mr. Takawira, the Undersecretary (Development), Manicaland, "Appointment of Rekanyi as Chief Tawangwena: Nyanga District." This spelling of the chief's name suggests that the document's author lacked localized knowledge of Kaerezi.

28 Nyanga DA Files, CHK/Tangwena-Chief Tangwena File, July 3, 1986, J. S. N. Makoni for Nyanga DA, to PA, Manicaland, "RE: Appointment: Nyabinde Tickey Mangwendere."

29 Nyanga DA Files, CHK/Tangwena-Chief Tangwena File, July 3, 1986, J. S. N. Makoni for Nyanga DA, to PA, Manicaland, "RE: Appointment: Nyabinde Tickey Mangwendere."

30 Nyanga DA Files, CHK/Tangwena-Chief Tangwena File, June 25, 1983, District Administrator Chingosho, "Installation of the Ninth Chief Tawangwena at the Guta on June 25th 1983." Moyana's 1987 booklet, produced as a Zimbabwean school text, echoed the same genealogy but used variant spellings. While he emphasized the role of spirit mediums, he excluded rainmaking from the politics of Kaerezi territory and sovereignty.

31 Throughout his narrative of the importance of ancestral spirits in Kaerezi, Elijah Nyahuruwa continually referred to them as *vadzimu* or sometimes *midzimu*, two plural variations of a "spirit elder of family" or "the soul of a dead relative" (Hannan [1959] 1987, 372). Ethnographic literature on *vadzimu*, while recognizing that the term applies to a range of spirits, has often distinguished "guardian spirits" of particular families from *mhondoro*, or "tribal spirits" of specific territories deemed critical in rainmaking ceremonies (see, for example, Gelfand 1959, 5, 37).

32 He used both *kuremekedza nyika* and *kukudza nyika*.

33 See United States Department of State 1971.

34 Elder males were the ones most likely to specify Tangwena territory precisely, while some women who had lived in the chiefdom all their lives claimed ignorance of exact boundaries but pointed to places they "knew" to be inside or outside the chiefdom. While concentrated among elder males, this esoteric knowledge was neither exclusive to any gender or generation nor uniform among those who professed it.

35 They could also press formal charges in the district magistrate court if these avenues for a ruling (*kutonga*) failed. Legally, chiefs could only preside over civil cases and small claims, rather than conduct criminal proceedings.

8 Spatial Subjection

1 Hence *samusha*, transforms *musha*, home, into "head of household," while Sa-Makomba would be akin to "Mr. Makomba," yet imbued with more respect than the English term implies.

2 For thoughtful reflections on modernity in relation to desires discursively articulated to visions of "progress," see Ferguson 1999 and Rofel 1999.

3 He made repeated reference to *tsika ye chinyakare*, culture of the distant past.

4 Foucault [1975] 1979 famously elaborates this technology of surveillance.

5 See Mallon 1995 for an elaboration of communal hegemony.

6 Nyanga DA Files, Kaerezi Resettlement Scheme, March 1991, Kaerezi Main Resettlement Report.

7 See and hear "*Cheka ukama*" on Mtukudzi 1998.

9 The Traction of Rights and Rule

1 While Rekayi claimed membership in the Anglican Church, and invoked his Christianity to lobby liberal white support in the 1960s and 1970s, this never precluded his propitiations.

2 Nyanga DA Files, CHK/Tangwena-Chief Tangwena File, August 1, 1990, E. T. Siyamachira for Secretary for Local Government, Rural and Urban Development to Provincial Administrator, Manicaland, "Installation of Chief Tangwena: Nyanga District."

3 Nyanga DA Files, CHK/Tangwena-Chief Tangwena File, April 23, 1989, letter from Chief Tangwena to DA, Nyanga.

4 Nyanga DA Files, CHK/Tangwena-Chief Tangwena File, July 3, 1986, J. S. N. Makoni for Nyanga DA, to PA, Manicaland, "RE: Appointment: Nyabinde Tickey Mangwendere."

5 A handwritten note with the District Commissioner date stamp of May, 9, 1966, mentions "*Nhumbi* [possessions] of Tawungwena," recording "*Ngoma*'s [drum] only with Tsatsi K. H. [kraalhead]." According to the report, his source of information was Maicho, then the eldest son of Kinga. It was unclear whether Maicho was attempting to assert a claim to the chieftainship. See Nyanga DA Files, CHK/Tangwena-Chief Tangwena File, May 9, 1966, unsigned note.

6 Nyanga DA Files, CHK/Tangwena-Chief Tangwena File, October 2, 1990, Local Government report, "Postponement of the Official Installation of Nyabinde Magwendere as Chief Tangwena."

7 Nyanga DA Files, CHK/Tangwena-Chief Tangwena File, October 2, 1990, Local Government report, "Postponement of the Official Installation of Nyabinde Magwendere as Chief Tangwena."

8   SaGumbo used the verb *kutambudzika*, which in this context also connoted being troubled.

9   Hannan ([1959] 1987, 467) suggests *nhoronhondo* as a Zezuru derivative, further marking it as linguistically outside the more localized forms of spoken ChiManyika.

10   On authoritarian populism, see Hall [1988] 1990.

11   What Raymond Williams (1989, 242) termed "militant particularism" suggests a cultural politics of place that *articulates* localized struggles and particular demands with claims that travel translocally.

12   A 1986 government report described the "spiritual influence" of the chieftainship as "dormant at this stage." See Nyanga DA Files, CHK/Tangwena-Chief Tangwena File, July 3, 1986, J. S. N. Makoni for Nyanga DA, to PA, Manicaland, "RE: Appointment: Nyabinde Tickey Mangwendere."

13   Chidumbu's criticisms and their widespread popular resonances echoed Weta's depiction, in chapter 7, of Tangwena's conquest of Nyahuruwa as representing a *mutorwa*'s inappropriate cultural conduct in the home of a generous and sheltering host.

14   These gendered patterns of land access have been well chronicled in Zimbabwe. See Batezat and Mwalo 1989; Gaidzanwa 1989; Jacobs 1992; and Schmidt 1992.

15   Holleman 1952 outlined a women's "matri-estate" consisting of cooking utensils, personal effects, and sometimes livestock claimed by her lineage after her death.

16   Elders remembered an era when mothers-in-law "gave" small parcels of their family holdings to newly married daughters-in-law. Mothers and mothers-in-law also "gave" young women yam fields. Yet I never heard this spoken of through idioms of *nhaka*, "inheritance."

17   Nixon (1994, 33) conceived *tsotsi* as having entered South African parlance in the 1940s "as a corruption of the American idiom, 'zoot suit.'" He stressed the multiracial spaces of shebeens and underground clubs as crucial to *tsotsi* style. Nixon, in turn, credits Trevor Huddleston with this origin story. See Coplan 1985, 270 for an elaboration.

18   ZNRO, File LAN 16/16, Internal Affairs, box 116598, location 8.14.3R, handwritten sketch and note, signed by G. R. Broderick, dated May 5, 1972, "Gazetted Extent of Chief Tawungwena's Tribal Areas, Government Notice 519/68." For Holdenby's purchase, see ZNA, File S 2588/1977, Land Inyanga, March 24, 1948, J. Armstrong for Secretary to the Treasurer, Salisbury to the Auditor General, "Holdenby Estate: Purchase of Land for Native Occupation."

19   ZNRO, File LAN 16/16, Internal Affairs, box 116598, location 8.14.3R, September 22, 1965, C. K. Latham, "1965 Report on Tawungwena Chieftainship: Holdenby Tribal Trust Land: Inyanga District."

20   In turn, two years later in 1974, Internal Affairs published figures listing 403 followers under the "Barwe Tribe" of "Chief Tawungwena" in Inyanga District. This was eight years after district officials first refused Rekayi's claims to the chieftainship, five years after the Government Proclamation mandated his eviction from Gaeresi Ranch, and during a period when no census could possibly count his followers who were hiding in ranges surrounding Mount Nyangani or had fled to Mozambique. Almost a decade after one administrator declared the chieftainship dysfunctional, a governmental archive perpetuated stealth followers for an evicted chief who officials refused to recognize. See Internal Affairs 1974; Tawungwena is listed as chief number 80.

21 Nyanga DA Files, October 13, 1993, J. S. N. Makoni for DA to PA, "Demarcation of Each Chief and Headman's Area of Jurisdiction."

22 Nyanga DA Files, Kaerezi Resettlement Scheme, November 14, 1995, Kaerezi Resettlement Office to DA, "Tangwena and National Parks Boundary (Traditional/Administrative).

23 Initiated by Nyanga officials in 1986, the appointment received official presidential approval in 1987.

24 When I asked Nyamubaya which chief he was born "under," he replied "Zindi, but he was Mutasa's vice. It is written Mutasa on our identity cards." Mutasa was recognized, by colonial officials and many Africans, as a paramount chief whose territory was divided into smaller portions overseen by lesser chiefs such as Zindi.

Epilogue: Effective Articulations

1 See "Committee to Prove MP over Assault Appointed," *Herald*, online edition, May 20, 2004, available at www.herald.co.zw/index.php?id=32105&pubdate=2004-05-20, and the transcript of a *Voice of America* radio interview from the same date. For a differing account, see "MP in Punch-Up with Ministers in Zimbabwe's Parliament," an unsigned May 19, 2004, posting on NewZimbabwe.com.

2 "Chief Tangwena's Widow Invades Farm in Bizarre Conflict," *Zimbabwe Standard*, online edition, May 24, 2004, available at www.zimbabwesituation.com/may24_2004.html; see also Michael Hartnick, "Generations Later, Tangwena Still Fight for Land Rights," *Herald*, online edition, June 8, 2004, available at www.epherald.co.za/herald/2004/06/08/news/n26_08062004.htm.

3 In 2004, the rainmaker Nyahuruwa's contingent support of Tangwena claims to Nyafaru, where his paternal grandfather Ditima lived before being murdered by a conquering Tangwena chief, has, I presume, not occluded his own assertions of inalienable rights.

4 Hall 1986b elaborated this phrase in relation to Gramscian cultural politics. For reflections on the formation's generative influence, see Gilroy, Grossberg, and McRobbie 2000.

5 Foucault [1977] 1984, 146. For his reflections on genealogy in relation to the "micro-physics" through which "are *articulated* the effects of a certain type of power," see Foucault [1975] 1979, 29; my emphasis. My emphasis on "effective articulations" also invokes his "effective history."

6 Brown 2001, 105.

7 Castells 1996, 378. As a corollary, he conceived place as a "locale whose form, function and meaning are self-contained within the boundaries of physical contiguity" (423), a position I counter analytically and ethnographically.

8 Neither Rhodesian owner nor armed invaders "knew territory" well enough to recognize the hut's location in a *tsungo* named Bvumbwe.

9 Nyanga DA Files, CHK/Tangwena-Chief Tangwena File, June 7, 1996, "Official Installation of Nyabinde Magwendere as Substantive Chief Tangwena at Magadzire Primary School," text of speech by A. O. Gara; and Nyanga DA File, CHK/Tangwena-Chief Tangwena File, uncredited text, "Official Installation of Nyabinde Magwendere Tangwena as the Tenth Chief Tangwena."

10 Triads-in-motion are still spinning. Magwendere's July 2004 death—news of which arrived after I completed the book—will likely rekindle future contestations over chiefly succession, sovereignty, and relations among traditional and governmental powers in Kaerezi.

References

Agamben, Giorgio. [1995] 1998. *Homo Sacer: Sovereign Power and Bare Life*. Stanford, CA: Stanford University Press.

Agnew, James, and Stuart Corbridge. 1995. *Mastering Space: Hegemony, Territory, and International Political Economy*. New York: Routledge.

Alexander, Jocelyn, JoAnn McGregor, and Terence Ranger. 2000. *Violence and Memory: One Hundred Years in the 'Dark Forests' of Matabeleland*. Portsmouth, NH: Heinemann.

Allen, John. 2003. *Lost Geographies of Power*. Oxford: Blackwell.

Althusser, Louis. [1960] 1971. *"Lenin and Philosophy" and Other Essays*. Trans. Ben Brewster. New York: Monthly Review Press.

Alvord, E. D. 1929. "Agricultural Life of the Rhodesian Natives." NADA, no. 6:35–43.

———. 1958. *Development of Native Agriculture and Land Tenure in Southern Rhodesia*. Salisbury: Waddilove.

Anderson, Benedict. 1983. *Imagined Communities: Reflections on the Origin and Spread of Nationalism*. London: Verso.

Appadurai, Arjun. 1988. "Putting Hierarchy in Its Place." *Cultural Anthropology* 3 (1): 36–49.

———. 1996. *Modernity at Large: Cultural Dimensions of Globalization*. Minneapolis: University of Minnesota Press.

———. 2002. "Deep Democracy: Urban Governmentality and the Horizon of Politics." *Public Culture* 14 (1): 21–47.

Appiah, Kwame Anthony. 1992. *In My Father's House: Africa in the Philosophy of Culture*. New York: Oxford University Press.

Apter, Andrew. 1999. "Africa, Empire, and Anthropology." *Annual Review of Anthropology*, no. 28:577–98.

Arendt, Hannah. [1951] 1968. *Imperialism: Part Two of the Origins of Totalitarianism*. New York: Harcourt Brace Jovanovich.

Asad, Talal. 1992. "Conscripts of Western Civilization." In *Civilization in Crisis: Anthropological Perspectives*, ed. Christine Ward Gailey. Gainesville: University of Florida Press, 333–51.

———. 1993. *Genealogies of Religion: Discipline and Reasons of Power in Christianity and Islam*. Baltimore, MD: Johns Hopkins University Press.

———. 2003. *Formations of the Secular: Christianity, Islam, Modernity*. Stanford, CA: Stanford University Press.

Astrow, André. 1983. *Zimbabwe: A Revolution That Lost Its Way?* London: Zed.

Atkins, Keletso. 1993. *The Moon Is Dead! Give Us Your Money! The Cultural Origins of an African Work Ethic, Natal, South Africa, 1843–1900*. Portsmouth, NH: Heinemann.

Baker, Houston A., Jr. 1984. *Blues, Ideology, and Afro-American Literature*. Chicago: University of Chicago Press.

Barnett, Clive. 1998. "Culture, Geography, and the Arts of Government." *Environment and Planning D: Society and Space* 19 (1): 7–24.

Barry, Andrew. 2001. *Political Machines: Governing a Technological Society*. London: Athlone.

Barry, Andrew, Thomas Osborne, and Nikolas Rose, eds. 1996. *Foucault and Political Reason: Liberalism, Neoliberalism, and Rationalities of Government*. Chicago: University of Chicago Press.

Bartelson, Jens. 1995. *A Genealogy of Sovereignty*. Cambridge: Cambridge University Press.

———. 2001. *The Critique of the State*. Cambridge: Cambridge University Press.

Barthes, Roland. [1957] 1984. *Mythologies*. Trans. Annette Lavers. New York: Hill and Wang.

Bassett, Thomas. 1993. "Cartography, Ideology, and Power: The World Bank in Northern Cote d'Ivoire." *Passages*, no. 5:8–9.

Bassett, Thomas, and Donald Crummey, eds. 1993. *Land in African Agrarian Systems*. Madison: University of Wisconsin Press.

Basso, Keith. 1995. *Wisdom Sits in Places: Landscape and Language among the Western Apache*. Albuquerque: University of New Mexico Press.

Batezat, Elinor, and Margaret Mwato. 1989. *Women in Zimbabwe*. Harare: Southern African Political Economy Series Trust.

Baviskar, Amita. 1995. *In the Belly of the River: Tribal Conflicts over Development in the Narmada Valley*. Delhi: Oxford University Press.

Bayart, Jean-François. 1993. *The State in Africa: The Politics of the Belly*. Trans. Mary Harper, Christopher Harrison, and Elizabeth Harrison. London: Longman.

Beach, D. N. 1980. *The Shona and Zimbabwe, 900–1850*. Gweru, Zimbabwe: Mambo.

———. 1994. *A Zimbabwean Past*. Gweru, Zimbabwe: Mambo.

Beinart, William. 1984. "Soil Erosion, Conservationism and Ideas about Development: A Southern African Exploration." *Journal of Southern African Studies* 11 (1): 52–83.

Benjamin, Walter. 1968. *Illuminations*. Trans. Harry Zohn. Ed. Hannah Arendt. New York: Schocken.

——. 1978. *Reflections*. Trans. Edmund Jephcott. New York: Schocken.

Berger, John. 1972. *Ways of Seeing*. London: Penguin.

Berry, Sara. 1993. *No Condition Is Permanent: The Social Dynamics of Agrarian Change in Sub-Saharan Africa*. Madison: University of Wisconsin Press.

——. 2001. *Chiefs Know Their Boundaries: Essays on Property, Power, and the Past in Asante, 1896–1996*. Portsmouth, NH: Heinemann.

Bhabha, Homi K. 1987. " 'What does the Black Man Want?' " *New Formations*, no. 1:118–30.

——. 1994. *The Location of Culture*. London: Routledge.

Bhebhe, Ngwabe, and Terence Ranger, eds. 1995. *Society in Zimbabwe's Liberation War*. Harare: University of Zimbabwe Publications.

Bhila, H. H. K. 1982. *Trade and Politics in a Shona Kingdom: The Manyika and Their African and Portuguese Neighbors*. Harlow, UK: Longman.

Blair, David. 2002. *Degrees in Violence: Robert Mugabe and the Struggle for Power in Zimbabwe*. London: Continuum.

Bohannan, Paul, and Laura Bohannan. 1968. *Tiv Economy*. Evanston, IL: Northwestern University Press.

Bond, W. E. 1948. "Soil Conservation and Land Use Planning in Native Reserves in Southern Rhodesia." *Tropical Agriculture* 25 (1): 4–13.

Bourdieu, Pierre. [1972] 1977. *Outline of a Theory of Practice*. Trans. Richard Nice. Cambridge: Cambridge University Press.

——. [1991] 1999. *Language and Symbolic Power*. Trans. Gino Raymond and Matthew Adamson. Cambridge, MA: Harvard University Press.

——. [1994] 1998. *Practical Reason: On the Theory of Action*. Trans. Gisele Sapiro et al. Stanford, CA: Stanford University Press.

Bourdieu, Pierre, et al. 1999. *The Weight of the World: Social Suffering in Contemporary Society*. Trans. Priscilla Parkhurst Ferguson et al. Stanford, CA: Stanford University Press.

Bourdieu, Pierre, and Loïc J. D. Wacquant. 1992. "The Logic of Fields." In *An Invitation to Reflexive Sociology*. Chicago: University of Chicago Press, 94–114.

Bourdillon, Michael. 1987. *The Shona People*. Gweru, Zimbabwe: Mambo.

Bowyer-Bower, Tanya, and Colin Stoneman, eds. 2000. *Land Reform in Zimbabwe: Constraints and Prospects*. Aldershot, UK: Ashgate.

Boyarin, Jonathan, ed. 1994. *Remapping Memory: The Politics of TimeSpace*. Minneapolis: University of Minnesota Press.

Bratich, Jack Z., Jeremy Packer, and Cameron McCarthy, eds. 2003. *Foucault, Cultural Studies, and Governmentality*. Albany: State University of New York Press.

Braun, Bruce. 2000. "Producing Vertical Territory: Geology and Governmentality in Late-Victorian Canada." *Ecumene* 7 (1): 7–46.

Brenner, Neil. 1997. "Global, Fragmented, Hierarchical: Henri Lefebvre's Geographies of Globalization." *Public Culture* 10 (1): 135–67.

Brown, Ken. 1959. *Land in Southern Rhodesia*. London: Africa Bureau.

Brown, Wendy. 1995. *States of Injury: Power and Freedom in Late Modernity*. Princeton, NJ: Princeton University Press.

———. 2001. *Politics Out of History*. Princeton, NJ: Princeton University Press.

Bullock, Charles. [1928] 1970. *The Mashona: The Indigenous Natives of S. Rhodesia*. Westport, CT: Negro University Press.

Bulman, Mary. 1970. "The Native Land Husbandry Act of Southern Rhodesia." D.Phil. diss., University of London.

Bundy, Colin. 1979. *The Rise and Fall of the South African Peasantry*. Berkeley: University of California Press.

Burchell, Graham, Colin Gordon, and Peter Miller, eds. 1991. *The Foucault Effect: Studies in Governmentality*. Chicago: University of Chicago Press.

Butler, Judith. 1993. Bodies that Matter: On the Discursive Limits of "Sex." New York: Routledge.

———. 1998. "Merely Cultural." *New Left Review*, no. 227:33–44.

———. 2003. "Afterword: After Loss, What Then?" In *Loss: The Politics of Mourning*, ed. David L. Eng and David Kazanjian. Berkeley: University of California Press, 467–73.

Buttigieg, Joseph. 1992. Preface to *Antonio Gramsci's Prison Notebooks*. Trans. and ed. Joseph Buttigieg. New York: Columbia University Press, 1:ix–xix.

Caldeira, Teresa P. R. 2000. *City of Walls: Crime, Segregation, and Citizenship in São Paolo*. Berkeley: University of California Press.

Carney, Judith, and Michael Watts. 1990. "Manufacturing Dissent: Work, Gender, and the Politics of Meaning in a Peasant Society." *Africa* 60 (2): 207–41.

Carter, Paul. 1987. *The Road to Botany Bay: An Exploration of Landscape and History*. Chicago: University of Chicago Press.

Casey, Edward S. 1997. *The Fate of Place: A Philosophical History*. Berkeley: University of California Press.

Castells, Manuel. 1996. *The Rise of the Network Society*. Oxford: Blackwell.

Catholic Mission for Justice and Peace in Rhodesia. 1975. *The Man in the Middle*. Salisbury: Catholic Commission for Justice and Peace in Rhodesia.

Certeau, Michel de. 1984. *The Practice of Everyday Life*. Trans. Steven Rendell. Berkeley: University of California Press.

———. [1975] 1988. *The Writing of History*. Trans. Tom Conley. New York: Columbia University Press.

Césaire, Aimé. [1955] 1972. *Discourse on Colonialism*. Trans. Joan Pinkham. New York: Monthly Review Press.

———. 1983. *Aimé Césaire: The Collected Poetry*. Trans. Clayton Eshleman and Annette Smith. Berkeley: University of California Press.

Chakrabarty, Dipesh. 2000. *Provincializing Europe: Postcolonial Thought and Historical Difference*. Princeton, NJ: Princeton University Press.

Chanock, Martin. 1991. "A Peculiar Sharpness: An Essay on Property in the History of Customary Law in Colonial Africa." *Journal of African History* 32 (1): 65–88.

——. [1985] 1998. *Law, Custom, and Social Order: The Colonial Experience in Malawi and Zambia*. Portsmouth, NH: Heinemann.

Chatterjee, Partha. 1986. *Nationalist Thought and the Colonial World: A Derivative Discourse?* London: Zed.

——. 1993. *The Nation and Its Fragments: Colonial and Postcolonial Histories*. Princeton, NJ: Princeton University Press.

Cheater, Angela. 1990. "The Ideology of 'Communal' Land Tenure in Zimbabwe: Mythogenesis Enacted?" *Africa* 60 (2): 188–206.

Chimhundu, Herbert. 1996. *Duramazwi rechiShona*. Harare: College Press.

Cliffe, Lionel. 1988. "The Conservation Issue in Zimbabwe." *Review of African Political Economy*, no. 42:48–58.

Clifford, James. 1988. *The Predicament of Culture*. Cambridge, MA: Harvard University Press.

——. 1997. *Routes: Travel and Translation in the Late Twentieth Century*. Cambridge, MA: Harvard University Press.

Clutton-Brock, Guy. 1969. *Rekayi Tangwena: Let Tangwena Be*. Salisbury: Cold Comfort Farm Society.

Clutton-Brock, Guy, and Molly Clutton-Brock. 1972. *Cold Comfort Confronted*. London: Mowbray.

——, eds. 1987. *Guy and Molly Clutton-Brock: Reminiscenses by Their Family and Friends*. Harare: Longman.

Cohen, David William, and E. S. Atieno Odhiambo. 1989. *Siaya: The Historical Anthropology of an African Landscape*. London: J. Currey.

Cole, Jennifer. 2001. *Forget Colonialism? Sacrifice and the Art of Memory in Madagascar*. Berkeley: University of California Press.

Colson, Elizabeth. 1971a. "The Impact of the Colonial Period on the Definition of Land Rights." In *Colonialism in Africa, 1870–1960*, vol. 3, *Profiles of Change: African Society and Colonial Rule*, ed. Victor Turner. Cambridge: Cambridge University Press, 193–215.

——. 1971b. *The Social Consequences of Resettlement: The Impact of the Kariba Resettlement upon the Gwembe Tonga*. Manchester: Manchester University Press.

Colson, Elizabeth, and Max Gluckman, eds. 1951. *Seven Tribes of British Central Africa*. London: Oxford University Press.

Comaroff, Jean. 1985. *Body of Power, Spirit of Resistance: The Culture and History of a South African People*. Chicago: University of Chicago Press.

Comaroff, Jean, and John L. Comaroff. 1991. *Of Revelation and Revolution*. Vol. 1,

Christianity, Colonialism, and Consciousness in South Africa. Chicago: University of Chicago Press.

Comaroff, John L. [1995] 1997. "The Discourse of Rights in Colonial South Africa: Subjectivity, Sovereignty, Modernity." In *Identities, Politics, and Rights*, ed. Austin Sarat and Thomas R. Kearns. Ann Arbor: University of Michigan Press, 193–238.

Comaroff, John L., and Jean Comaroff. 1997. *Of Revelation and Revolution.* Vol. 2, *The Dialectics of Modernity on a South African Frontier.* Chicago: University of Chicago Press.

CONEX (Department of Conservation and Extension). 1981. "Preliminary Report: Gaeresi Intensive Resettlement Area," Inyanga Intensive Conservation Area, Manicaland Province, May 1981. Reference 131/28/FA. Salisbury: Planning Branch, CONEX.

Cooper, Frederick, and Ann Laura Stoler, eds. 1997. *Tensions of Empire: Colonial Cultures in a Bourgeois World.* Berkeley: University of California Press.

Coplan, David. 1985. *In Township Tonight! South African's Black City Music and Theatre.* London: Longman.

Coronil, Fernando. 1997. *The Magical State: Nature, Money, and Modernity in Venezuela.* Chicago: University of Chicago Press.

Cosgrove, Denis E. [1984] 1998. *Social Formation and Symbolic Landscape.* Madison: University of Wisconsin Press.

Cosgrove, Denis E., and Stephen Daniels, eds. 1989. *The Iconography of Landscape.* Cambridge: Cambridge University Press.

Cousins, Ben. 1993. "Debating Communal Tenure in Zimbabwe." *Journal of Contemporary African Studies* 12 (1): 29–39.

——. 2003. "The Zimbabwe Crisis in Its Wider Context: The Politics of Land, Democracy, and Development in Southern Africa." In *Zimbabwe's Unfinished Business: Rethinking Land, State, and Nation in the Context of Crisis*, ed. Amanda Hammar, Brian Raftopoulos, and Stig Jensen. Harare: Weaver, 263–316.

Crary, Jonathan. 1990. *Techniques of the Observer: On Vision and Modernity in the Nineteenth Century.* Cambridge, MA: MIT Press.

Crehan, Kate. 2002. *Gramsci, Culture and Anthropology.* Berkeley: University of California Press.

Cusworth, John. 1990. "Land Resettlement Issues." The World Bank Background Paper for Zimbabwe Agriculture Sector Memorandum. Washington, DC: World Bank.

Das, Veena. 1995. *Critical Events: An Anthropological Perspective on Contemporary India.* Delhi: Oxford University Press.

Davis, Natalie Zemon, and Randolph Starn. 1989. Introduction to "Memory and Counter-memory." Special issue, *Representations*, no. 26:1–6.

Dean, Mitchell. 1999. *Governmentality: Power and Rule in Modern Society.* London: Sage.

Dean, Mitchell, and Barry Hindess, eds. 1998. *Governing Australia: Studies in Contemporary Rationalities of Government.* Cambridge: Cambridge University Press.

De la Cadena, Marisol. 2000. *Indigenous Mestizos: The Politics of Race and Culture in Cuzco, 1919–1991.* Durham, NC: Duke University Press.

Deleuze, Gilles. [1986] 1988. *Foucault.* Trans. and ed. Sean Hand. Minneapolis: University of Minnesota Press.

——. 1990. *Pourparlers, 1972–1990.* Paris : Éditions de Minuit.

——. [1990] 1995. *Negotiations, 1972–1990.* Trans. Martin Joughin. New York: Columbia University Press.

Deleuze, Gilles, and Félix Guattari. [1980] 1987. *A Thousand Plateaus: Capitalism and Schizophrenia.* Trans. Brian Massumi. Minneapolis: University of Minnesota Press.

Deleuze, Gilles, and Claire Parnet. [1977] 1987. *Dialogues.* Trans. Hugh Tomlinson and Barbara Habberjam. New York: Columbia University Press.

Derrida, Jacques. [1967] 1976. *Of Grammatology.* Trans. Gayatri Chakravorty Spivak. Baltimore, MD: Johns Hopkins University Press.

DERUDE (Department of Rural Development). 1985. *Intensive Resettlement Policies and Procedures.* Harare: Ministry of Lands, Resettlement, and Rural Development.

——. 1991. *Resettlement Progress Report: 1991.* Harare: Ministry of Lands, Resettlement, and Rural Development.

Deutsche, Rosalyn. 1996. *Evictions: Art and Spatial Politics.* Cambridge, MA: MIT Press.

De Wet, C. J. 1995. *Moving Together, Drifting Apart: Betterment Planning and Villagisation in a South African Homeland.* Johannesburg: Witwatersrand University Press.

Dirks, Nicholas. 2001. *Castes of Mind: Colonialism and the Making of Modern India.* Princeton, NJ: Princeton University Press.

Donham, Donald. 1999. *Marxist Modern: An Ethnographic History of the Ethiopian Revolution.* Berkeley: University of California Press.

Drayton, Richard. 2000. *Nature's Government: Science, Imperial Britain, and the "Improvement" of the World.* New Haven, CT: Yale University Press.

Drinkwater, Michael. 1991. *The State and Agrarian Change in Zimbabwe's Communal Areas.* London: Macmillan.

Du Bois, W. E. B. 1945. *Color and Democracy: Colonies and Peace.* New York: Harcourt, Brace.

Duffy, James. 1959. *Portuguese Africa.* Cambridge, MA: Harvard University Press.

Durkheim, Emile. [1893] 1984. *The Division of Labor in Society.* Trans. W. D. Halls. New York: Free Press.

Engels, Frederick. [1884] 1972. *The Origin of the Family, Private Property, and the State.* Ed. Eleanor Burke Leacock. New York: International Publishers.

Escobar, Arturo. 2001. "Culture Sits in Places: Reflections on Globalism and Subaltern Strategies of Localization." *Political Geography* 20 (2): 139–174.

Essed, Philomena, and David Theo Goldberg, eds. 2002. *Race Critical Theories*. Oxford: Blackwell.

Eze, Emmanuel Chukwudi. 2001. *Achieving Our Humanity: The Idea of the Postracial Future*. New York: Routledge.

Fabian, Johannes. 1983. *Time and the Other: How Anthropology Makes Its Object*. New York: Columbia University Press.

———. 2001. *Anthropology with an Attitude: Critical Essays*. Stanford, CA: Stanford University Press.

Fairhead, James, and Melissa Leach. 1996. *Misreading the African Landscape: Society and Ecology in the Forest-Savanna Mosaic*. Cambridge: Cambridge University Press.

Fallers, Lloyd. 1956. *Bantu Bureaucracy: A Century of Political Evolution Among the Basoga of Uganda*. Chicago: University of Chicago Press.

Fanon, Frantz. [1952] 1967. *Black Skin, White Masks*. Trans. Charles Markmann. New York: Grove.

———. [1964] 1967. *Toward the African Revolution*. Trans. Haakon Chevalier. New York: Grove.

———. [1961] 1982. *The Wretched of the Earth*. Trans. Constance Farrington. New York: Grove.

Feierman, Steven. 1990. *Peasant Intellectuals: Anthropology and History in Tanzania*. Madison: University of Wisconsin Press.

Feld, Steven, and Keith Basso, eds. 1996. *Senses of Place*. Santa Fe, NM: School of American Research Press.

Ferguson, James. [1990] 1994. *The Anti-politics Machine: "Development," Depoliticization, and Bureaucratic Power in Lesotho*. Minneapolis: University of Minnesota Press.

———. 1997. "Paradoxes of Sovereignty and Independence: 'Real' and 'Pseudo' Nation-States and the Depoliticization of Poverty." In *Siting Culture: The Shifting Anthropological Object*, ed. Karen Fog Olwig and Kirsten Hastrup. London: Routledge, 123–41.

———. 1999. *Expectations of Modernity: Myths and Meanings of Urban Life on the Zambian Copperbelt*. Berkeley: University of California Press.

Ferme, Mariane. 2001. *The Underneath of Things: Violence, History, and the Everyday in Sierra Leone*. Berkeley: University of California Press.

Fortes, Myer, and Edward Evans-Pritchard, eds. [1940] 1963. *African Political Systems*. London: Oxford University Press.

Foucault, Michel. [1975] 1979. *Discipline and Punish: The Birth of the Prison*. Trans. Alan Sheridan. New York: Vintage.

———. 1979. "On Governmentality." *Ideology and Consciousness*, no. 5:5–22.

———. [1976] 1980. *The History of Sexuality*. Vol. 1, *An Introduction*. Trans. Robert Hurley. New York: Vintage.

———. 1983. "Afterword: The Subject and Power." In *Michel Foucault: Beyond Structuralism and Hermeneutics*, Hubert Dreyfus and Paul Rabinow. Chicago: University of Chicago Press, 208–39.

———. [1977] 1984. *Language, Counter-Memory, Practice.* Ed. Donald Bouchard. Trans. Bouchard and Sherry Simon. Ithaca, NY: Cornell University Press.

———. [1982] 1984. "Space, Knowledge, and Power." In *The Foucault Reader*, ed. Paul Rabinow. New York: Pantheon, 239–56.

———. 1986. "Of Other Spaces." Trans. Jay Miskowiec. *Diacritics*, no. 16:22–27.

———. 1994. *Dits et écrits.* Vol. 4. Paris: Éditions Gallimard.

———. 1997. *"Il faut défendre la société": Cours au Collège de France, 1976.* Paris: Éditions Gallimard.

———. [1979] 2000. " '*Omnes et Singulatim*': Toward a Critique of Political Reason." In *Power*, ed. James D. Faubion and trans. Robert Hurley et al. New York: New Press, 298–325.

———. [1997] 2003. *"Society Must Be Defended": Lectures at the Collège de France, 1975–1976.* Trans. David Macey. New York: Picador.

Fraser, Nancy. 1989. *Unruly Practices: Power, Discourse, and Gender in Contemporary Social Theory.* Minneapolis: University of Minnesota Press.

Gaidzanwa, Rudo. 1988. *Women's Land Rights in Zimbabwe.* Harare: Rural and Urban Planning, University of Zimbabwe.

Garlake, Peter. 1966. *A Guide to the Antiquities of Inyanga.* Salisbury: Historical Monuments Commission.

Gelfand, Michael. 1959. *Shona Ritual.* Cape Town: Juta.

Geschiere, Peter, and Frances Nyamnjoh. 2000. "Capitalism and Autochthony: The Seesaw of Mobility and Belonging." *Public Culture* 12 (2): 423–52.

Geza, Sam. 1986. "The Role of Resettlement in Social Development in Zimbabwe." *Journal of Social Development in Africa*, no. 1:35–42.

Giddens, Anthony. 1979. *Central Problems in Social Theory.* Berkeley: University of California Press.

Gilroy, Paul [1987] 1991. *"There Ain't No Black in the Union Jack": The Cultural Politics of Race and Nation.* Chicago: University of Chicago Press.

———. 2000. *Between Camps: Nations, Cultures and the Allure of Race.* London: Allen Lane.

———. 2004. *After Empire: Melancholia or Convivial Culture?* London: Routledge.

Gilroy, Paul, Lawrence Grossberg, and Angela McRobbie, eds. 2000. *Without Guarantees: In Honour of Stuart Hall.* London: Verso.

Goldberg, David Theo. 2002. *The Racial State.* Oxford: Blackwell.

Goldberg, David Theo, and Ato Quayson, eds. 2002. *Relocating Postcolonialism.* Oxford: Blackwell.

Government of Southern Rhodesia. 1955. *What the Native Land Husbandry Act Means* to the Rural African and to Southern Rhodesia: A Five Year Plan That Will Revolutionize African Agriculture. Salisbury: Government Printers.

Gramsci, Antonio. [1971] 1985. *Selections from the Prison Notebooks.* Ed. and trans. Quintin Hoare and Geoffrey Nowell Smith. New York: International Publishers.

———. 1985. *Selections from Cultural Writings.* Ed. David Forgacs and Geoffrey Nowell Smith. Trans. William Boelhower. Cambridge, MA: Harvard University Press.

———. [1973] 1989. *Letters from Prison.* Ed. and trans. Lynne Lawner. New York: Noonday.

———. [1977] 1990. *Selections from Political Writings, 1910–1920.* Ed. and trans. Quintin Hoare. Minneapolis: University of Minnesota Press.

———. 1994. *Pre-prison Writings.* Ed. Richard Bellamy. Trans. Virgina Cox. Cambridge: Cambridge University Press.

———. [1926] 1995. *The Southern Question.* Trans. Pasquale Verdicchio. West Lafayette, IN: Bordighera.

———. 1995. *Further Selections from the Prison Notebooks.* Ed. and trans. Derek Boothman. Minneapolis: University of Minnesota Press.

Gregory, Derek. 1994. *Geographical Imaginations.* Oxford: Blackwell.

Gregory, Steven. 1998. *Black Corona: Race and the Politics of Place in an Urban Community.* Princeton, NJ: Princeton University Press.

Grove, Richard. 1995. *Green Imperialism: Colonial Expansion, Tropical Island Edens, and the Origins of Environmentalism, 1600–1860.* Cambridge: Cambridge University Press.

Guha, Ranajit. [1981] 1996. *A Rule of Property for Bengal: An Essay on the Idea of Permanent Settlement.* Durham, NC: Duke University Press.

———. 1997. *Dominance without Hegemony.* Cambridge, MA: Harvard University Press.

Gupta, Akhil. 1998. *Postcolonial Developments: Agriculture in the Making of Modern India.* Durham, NC: Duke University Press.

Gupta, Akhil, and James Ferguson, eds. 1997. *Culture, Power, Place: Explorations in Critical Anthropology.* Durham, NC: Duke University Press.

Guyer, Jane, and S. M. Eno Belinga. 1995. "Wealth in People as Wealth in Knowledge: Accumulation and Composition in Equatorial Africa." *Journal of African History* 36 (1): 91–120.

Hale, Charles R. 1994. *Resistance and Contradiction: Miskitu Indians and the Nicaraguan State, 1894–1987.* Stanford, CA: Stanford University Press.

Hall, Stuart. 1980. "Race, Articulation, and Societies Structured in Dominance." In *Sociological Theories: Race and Colonialism.* Paris: UNESCO, 305–45.

———. 1981. "Notes on Deconstructing 'the Popular.'" In *People's History and Socialist Theory,* ed. Raphael Samuel. London: Routledge and Kegan Paul, 227–41.

———. 1986a. "Gramsci's Relevance for the Study of Race and Ethnicity." *Journal of Communication Inquiry* 10 (2): 5–27.

———. 1986b. "The Problem of Ideology—Marxism without Guarantees." *Journal of Communication Inquiry* 10 (2): 28–43.

——— [1988] 1990. *The Hard Road to Renewal: Thatcherism and the Crisis of the Left*. London: Verso.

———. 1990. "Cultural Identity and Diaspora." In *Identity: Community, Culture, Difference*, ed. Jonathan Rutherford. London: Lawrence and Wishart, 222–37.

———.1992. "The West and the Rest." In *Formations of Modernity*, ed. Hall and Bram Gieben. Cambridge: Polity, 275–320.

———. 1996. "When Was the 'Post-colonial'?" In *Thinking at the Limit: The Post-colonial Question*, ed. Ian Chambers and Lidia Curti. London: Routledge, 242–60.

———. 1997. "Culture and Power." *Radical Philosophy*, no. 86:24–41.

Hall, Stuart, and David Held. [1989] 1990. "Citizens and Citizenship." In *New Times: The Changing Face of Politics in the 1990s*, ed. Hall and Martin Jacques. London: Verso, 173–88.

Hammar, Amanda, Brian Raftopoulos, and Stig Jensen, eds. 2003. *Zimbabwe's Unfinished Business: Rethinking Land, State, and Nation in the Context of Crisis*. Harare: Weaver.

Hannah, Matthew G. 2000. *Governmentality and the Mastery of Territory in Nineteenth-century America*. Cambridge: Cambridge University Press.

Hannan, M. [1959] 1987. *Standard Shona Dictionary*. Harare: College Press.

Hansen, Thomas Blom. 2001. *Wages of Violence: Naming and Identity in Postcolonial Bombay*. Princeton, NJ: Princeton University Press.

Hansen, Thomas Blom, and Finn Stepputat, eds. 2001. *States of Imagination: Ethnographic Explorations of the Postcolonial State*. Durham, NC: Duke University Press.

Haraway, Donna. 1989. *Primate Visions: Gender, Race, and Nature in the World of Modern Science*. New York: Routledge.

———. 1991. "Situated Knowledges: The Science Question in Feminism and the Privilege of Partial Perspective." In *Simians, Cyborgs, and Women: The Reinvention of Nature*. New York: Routledge, 183–202.

Hardt, Michael, and Antonio Negri. 2000. *Empire*. Cambridge, MA: Harvard University Press.

Harries, Patrick. 1994. *Work, Culture, and Identity: Migrant Laborers in Mozambique and South Africa, c. 1860–1910*. Portsmouth, NH: Heinemann.

Hart, Gillian. 2002. *Disabling Globalization: Places of Power in Post-Apartheid South Africa*. Berkeley: University of California Press.

Harvey, David. 2001. *Spaces of Capital: Towards a Critical Geography*. New York: Routledge.

Hegel, Georg Wilhelm Friedrich. [1831] 1956. *The Philosophy of History*. Trans. J. Sibree. New York: Dover.

Herbst, Jeffrey. 1990. *State Politics in Zimbabwe*. Harare: University of Zimbabwe Publications.

Herder, Johann Gottfried. 1997. *On World History*. New York: M. E. Sharpe.

Herzfeld, Michael. 1987. *Cultural Intimacy: Social Poetics in the Nation-State*. New York: Routledge.

Hesse, Barnor. 2004. "Im/plausible Deniability: Racism's Conceptual Double Bind." *Social Identities* 10 (1): 9–29.

Hirsch, Eric, and Michael O'Hanlon, eds. 1995. *The Anthropology of Landscape*. Oxford: Clarendon.

Holleman, J. F. 1952. *Shona Customary Law*. London: Oxford University Press.

——. [1951] 1968. "Some 'Shona' Tribes of Southern Rhodesia." In *Seven Tribes of Central Africa*, ed. Elizabeth Colson and Max Gluckman. Manchester: Manchester University Press, 354–95.

——. 1969. *Chief, Council, and Commissioner: Some Problems of Government in Rhodesia*. Netherlands: Royal Van Gorcum.

Iliffe, John. 1979. *A Modern History of Tanganyika*. Cambridge: Cambridge University Press.

Internal Affairs, Rhodesia. 1974. *Tribe, Language, Relationship of Chiefs and Headmen*. Vol. 1. Salisbury: Government Printers.

International Defence and Aid Fund. 1972. *Rhodesia: The Ousting of the Tangwena*. London: Christian Action Publications.

Isaacman, Allen. 1976. *The Tradition of Resistance in Mozambique: Anti-colonial Activity in the Zambesi Valley, 1850–1921*. Berkeley: University of California Press.

Isaacman, Allen, and Barbara Isaacman. 1983. *Mozambique: From Colonialism to Revolution*. Boulder, CO: Westview.

Jacobs, Susie. 1992. "Gender and Land Reform: Zimbabwe and Some Comparisons." *International Sociology* 7 (1): 5–35.

James, C. L. R. 1963. *The Black Jacobins: Toussaint L'Ouverture and the San Domingo Revolution*. 2d rev. ed. New York: Vintage.

Kalipeni, Ezekiel and Paul Zeleza, eds. 1999. *Sacred Spaces and Public Quarrels: African Cultural and Economic Landscapes*. Trenton, NJ: Africa World Press.

Kantorowicz, Ernst. [1957] 1997. *The King's Two Bodies: A Study in Mediaeval Theology*. Princeton, NJ: Princeton University Press.

Kaplan, Robert. 1994. "The Coming Anarchy." *Atlantic Monthly*, February, 44–76.

Keith, Michael. 1993. *Race, Riots, and Policing: Lore and Disorder in a Multi-racist Society*. London: University College London Press.

Kenyatta, Jomo. 1968. *Suffering without Bitterness: The Founding of the Kenyan Nation*. Nairobi: East African Publishing House.

——. [1938] 1989. *Facing Mount Kenya: The Traditional Life of the Gikuyu*. Nairobi: Heinemann.

Kinsey, Bill. 1999. "Land Reform, Growth, and Equity: Emerging Evidence from Zimbabwe's Resettlement Programme." *Journal of Southern African Studies* 25 (2): 173–96.

Kleinman, Arthur, Veena Das, and Margaret Lock, eds. 1997. *Social Suffering*. Berkeley: University of California Press.

Kopytoff, Igor, ed. 1987. *The African Frontier: The Reproduction of Traditional African Societies*. Bloomington: Indiana University Press.

Kriger, Norma. 1992. *Zimbabwe's Guerrilla War: Peasant Voices*. Cambridge: Cambridge University Press.

Laclau, Ernesto. 1977. *Politics and Ideology in Marxist Theory: Capitalism, Fascism, Populism*. London: New Left Books.

Laclau, Ernesto, and Chantal Mouffe. 1985. *Hegemony and Socialist Strategy*. London: Verso.

Lan, David. 1985. *Guns and Rain: Guerrillas and Spirit Mediums in Zimbabwe*. Berkeley: University of California Press.

Latour, Bruno. 1987. *Science in Action: How to Follow Scientists and Engineers through Society*. Cambridge, MA: Harvard University Press.

——. 1999. *Pandora's Hope*. Cambridge, MA: Harvard University Press.

Leach, Melissa, and Robin Mearns, eds. 1996. *The Lie of the Land: Challenging Received Wisdom on the African Environment*. London: J. Currey.

Lefebvre, Henri. [1974] 1991. *The Production of Space*. Trans. Donald Nicholson-Smith. Oxford: Blackwell.

——. 1996. *Writings on Cities*. Ed. and trans. Eleonore Kofman and Elizabeth Lebas. Oxford: Blackwell.

——. 2003. *Key Writings*. Ed. Stuart Elden, Elizabeth Lebas, and Eleonore Kofman. New York: Continuum.

Lemke, Thomas. 2002. "Foucault, Governmentality, and Critique." *Rethinking Marxism* 14 (3): 49–64.

Li, Tania Murray. 1998. "Compromising Power: Development, Culture, and Rule in Indonesia." *Cultural Anthropology* 14 (3): 295–322.

——. 2003. "*Masyarakat Adat*, Difference, and the Limits of Recognition in Indonesia's Forest Zone." In *Race, Nature, and the Politics of Difference*, ed. Donald S. Moore, Jake Kosek, and Anand Pandian. Durham, NC: Duke University Press, 323–55.

Livingstone, David. 1992. "Race, Geography, and Empire." In *The Geographical Tradition*. Oxford: Blackwell, 216–59.

Locke, John. [1690] 1999. *Two Treatises of Government*. Cambridge: Cambridge University Press.

Lomnitz, Claudio. 2001. *Deep Mexico, Silent Mexico: An Anthropology of Nationalism*. Minneapolis: University of Minnesota Press.

Low, D. A. 1973. *Lion Rampant: Essays in the Study of British Imperialism*. London: Cass.

Lugard, Frederick. 1893. *The Rise of Our East African Empire*. Vol. 2. London: Blackwood.

——. 1926. "The White Man's Task in Tropical Africa." *Foreign Affairs* 5 (1): 57–68.

——. [1922] 1965. *The Dual Mandate in British Tropical Africa*. New York: Anchor.

Luig, Ute, and Achim Von Oppen, eds. 1997. Introduction to "Landscape in Africa: Process and Vision." Special Issue, *Paideuma* no. 43: 7–45.

Luke, Timothy. 1996. "Governmentality and Contragovernmentality: Rethinking Sovereignty and Territoriality after the Cold War." *Political Geography* 11 (6/7): 491–507.

Machingaidze, Victor. 1991. "Agrarian Change from Above: The Southern Rhodesia Native Land Husbandry Act and African Response." *International Journal of African Historical Studies* 24 (3): 557–89.

Mackenzie, Fiona. 1996. *Land, Ecology, and Resistance in Kenya, 1880–1952*. Portsmouth, NH: Heinemann.

Mafeje, Archie. 1971. "The Ideology of 'Tribalism.' " *Journal of Modern African Studies* 9 (2): 253–61.

Magubane, Bernard. 2000. *African Sociology: Towards a Critical Perspective*. Trenton, NJ: Africa World Press.

Maine, Henry. 1861. *Ancient Law*. New York: Scribner.

Mair, Lucy. 1965. *An Introduction to Social Anthropology*. Oxford: Clarendon.

Malinowski, Bronislaw. 1944. *A Scientific Theory of Culture, and Other Essays*. Chapel Hill: University of North Carolina Press.

———. [1945] 1961. *The Dynamics of Culture Change: An Inquiry into Race Relations in Africa*. New Haven, CT: Yale University Press.

Malkki, Liisa. 1992. "National Geographic: The Rooting of Peoples and the Territorialization of National Identity among Scholars and Refugees." *Cultural Anthropology* 7 (1): 24–44.

Mallon, Florencia E. 1995. *Peasant and Nation: The Making of Postcolonial Mexico and Peru*. Berkeley: University of California Press.

Mamdani, Mahmood. 1996. *Citizen and Subject: Contemporary Africa and the Legacy of Late Colonialism*. Princeton, NJ: Princeton University Press.

———. 2001. *When Victims Become Killers: Colonialism, Nativism, and the Genocide in Rwanda*. Princeton, NJ: Princeton University Press.

Mandela, Nelson. [1965] 1987. "Verwoerd's Tribalism." In *No Easy Walk to Freedom*. London: Heinemann, 67–79.

Mandondo, Alois. 2001. "Situating Zimbabwe's Natural Resource Governance Systems in History." Occasional Paper 32, Centre for International Forestry Research, Bogor, Indonesia.

Mapfumo, Thomas. 1989. *The Chimurenga Singles, 1976–1980*. Newton, NJ: Shanachie.

Marcos, Subcomandante. 2000. *Our Word is Our Weapon*. Ed. Juana Ponce de León. Trans. Juana Ponce de León et al. New York: Seven Stories.

Marcus, George. 1998. *Ethnography through Thick and Thin*. Princeton, NJ: Princeton University Press.

Martin, David, and Phyllis Johnson. 1981. *The Struggle for Zimbabwe*. New York: Monthly Review Press.

Marx, Karl. [1867] 1990. *Capital*. Vol. 1. Trans. Ben Fowkes. New York: Penguin.

———. [1894] 1991. *Capital*. Vol. 3. Trans. David Fernbach. New York: Penguin.

———. 1975. "Debates on the Law on Thefts of Wood." In *Collected Works*, by Marx and Friedrich Engels. New York: International Publishers, 1:224–63.

Masiiwa, Medicine. 2004. "Land Reform Programme in Zimbabwe: Disparity between Policy Design and Implementation." Working paper, Institute of Development Studies, University of Zimbabwe, Harare.

Massey, Doreen. 1994. *Space, Place, and Gender*. Minneapolis: University of Minnesota Press.

———. 1995. *Spatial Divisions of Labour: Social Structures and the Geography of Production*. 2d ed. New York: Routledge.

———. 1999. *Power-Geometries and the Politics of Space-Time*. Hettner-Lecture 1998, Department of Geography, University of Heidelberg, Germany.

Matless, David. 1998. *Landscape and Englishness*. London: Reaktion.

Mbembe, Achille. 2000. "At the Edge of the World: Boundaries, Territoriality, and Sovereignty in Africa." *Public Culture* 12 (1): 259–84.

———. 2001. *On the Postcolony*. Berkeley: University of California Press.

———. 2002. "African Modes of Self-Writing." *Public Culture* 14 (1): 239–73.

McClure, Kirstie. [1995] 1997. "Taking Liberties in Foucault's Triangle: Sovereignty, Discipline, Governmentality, and the Subject of Rights." In *Identities, Politics, and Rights*, ed. Austin Sarat and Thomas R. Kearns. Ann Arbor: University of Michigan Press, 149–92.

Mehta, Uday. 1999. *Liberalism and Empire: A Study in Nineteenth-Century British Liberal Thought*. Chicago: University of Chicago Press.

Meredith, Martin. 2002. *Our Votes, Our Guns: Robert Mugabe and the Tragedy of Zimbabwe*. New York: Public Affairs.

Miller, Peter, and Nikolas Rose. 1990. "Governing Economic Life." *Economy and Society* 19 (1): 1–31.

Mitchell, Timothy. [1988] 1991. *Colonising Egypt*. Berkeley: University of California Press.

———. 1999. "Society, Economy, and the State Effect." In *State/Culture: State Formation after the Cultural Turn*, ed. George Steinmetz. Ithaca, NY: Cornell University Press, 76–97.

———. 2002. *Rule of Experts: Egypt, Techno-politics, Modernity*. Berkeley: University of California Press.

Mitchell, W. J. T., ed. 1994. *Landscape and Power*. Chicago: University of Chicago Press.

Moore, David. 2003. "Zimbabwe's Triple Crisis: Primitive Accumulation, Nation-State Formation and Democratisation in the Age of Neo-Liberal Globalisation." *African Studies Quarterly* 7 (2/3). Available at: http://web.africa.ufl.edu/asq/v7/v7i2a2.htm.

Moore, Donald S. 1998. "Subaltern Struggles and the Politics of Place: Remapping Resistance in Zimbabwe's Eastern Highlands." *Cultural Anthropology* 13 (3): 344–81.

Moore, Donald S. 1999. "The Crucible of Cultural Politics: Reworking 'Development' in Zimbabwe's Eastern Highlands." *American Ethnologist* 26 (3): 654–89.

Moore, Donald S., Jake Kosek, and Anand Pandian, eds. 2003. *Race, Nature, and the Politics of Difference*. Durham, NC: Duke University Press.

Moore, Henrietta. [1986] 1996. *Space, Text, and Gender: An Anthropological Study of the Marakwet of Kenya*. New York: Guilford.

Moore, Henrietta, and Megan Vaughan. 1994. *Cutting Down Trees: Gender, Nutrition, and Agricultural Change in the Northern Province of Zambia, 1891–1990*. Portsmouth, NH: Heinemann.

Moore, Sally Falk. 1994. *Anthropology and Africa*. Charlottesville: University Press of Virginia.

Morgan, Lewis Henry. [1878] 1985. *Ancient Society*. Tucson: University of Arizona Press.

Mouffe, Chantal, ed. 1979. *Gramsci and Marxist Theory*. London: Routledge and Kegan Paul.

Moyana, Henry. 1984. *The Political Economy of Land in Zimbabwe*. Gweru, Zimbabwe: Mambo.

——. 1987. *The Victory of Chief Tangwena*. Harare: Longman.

Moyo, Sam. 1995. *The Land Question in Zimbabwe*. Harare: SAPES.

——. 2000. "The Political Economy of Land Acquisition and Redistribution in Zimbabwe, 1990–1999." *Journal of Southern African Studies* 26 (1): 5–28.

——, ed. 1991. *Zimbabwe's Environmental Dilemma: Balancing Resource Inequities*. Harare: Zimbabwe Environmental Research Organization.

Mtukudzi, Oliver. 1998. *Ndega zvangu*. Harare: Shava Musik.

Mugabe, Robert Gabriel. 1983. *Our War of Liberation: Speeches, Articles, Interviews, 1976–1979*. Gweru, Zimbabwe: Mambo.

——. 1987. "An Inspiration for Reconciliation." In *Guy and Molly Clutton-Brock: Reminiscences by their Family and Friends*, ed. Guy Clutton-Brock and Molly Clutton-Brock. Harare: Longman, 131–32.

Munro, William A. 1998. *The Moral Economy of the State: Conservation, Community Development, and State Making in Zimbabwe*. Athens: Ohio University Center for International Studies.

Murombedzi, James. 1990. "Communal Land Tenure and Common Property Resource Management: An Evaluation of the Potential for Sustainable Common Property Resource Management in Zimbabwe's Communal Areas." Working Paper, Centre for Applied Social Sciences, University of Zimbabwe, Harare.

Mutasa, Didymus. [1974] 1983. *Black behind Bars: Rhodesia, 1959–1974*. Harare: Longman.

——. 1987. "St. Faith's and Cold Comfort Farm." In *Guy and Molly Clutton-Brock: Reminiscences by their Family and Friends*, ed. Guy Clutton-Brock and Molly Clutton-Brock. Harare: Longman, 106–9.

Myers, Fred. 2000. "Ways of Placemaking." In *Culture, Landscape, and the Environment:*

The Linacre Lectures, ed. Kate Flint and Howard Morphy. Oxford: Oxford University Press, 72–110.

Nelson, Diane. 1999. *A Finger in the Wound: Body Politics in Quincentennial Guatemala.* Berkeley: University of California Press.

Newitt, Malyn. 1995. *A History of Mozambique.* Bloomington: Indiana University Press.

Nixon, Rob. 1994. *Homelands, Harlem, and Hollywood: South African Culture and the World Beyond.* New York: Routledge.

Nora, Pierre, ed. [1992] 1996. *Realms of Memory.* Vol. 1, *Conflicts and Divisions.* Trans. Arthur Goldhammer. New York: Columbia University Press.

Nordstrom, Carolyn. 2004. *Shadows of War: Violence, Power, and International Profiteering in the Twenty-first Century.* Berkeley: University of California Press.

Nyagoni, Christopher, and Gideon Nyandoro, eds. 1979. *Zimbabwe Independence Movements: Select Documents.* New York: Harper and Row.

Nyambara, Pius. 2001. "The Closing Frontier: Agrarian Change, Immigrants and the 'Squatter Menace' in Gokwe, 1980–1990s." *Journal of Agrarian Change* 1 (4): 534–549.

Nyerere, Julius. 1987. "Fighter for Peace." In *Guy and Molly Clutton-Brock: Reminiscences by their Family and Friends*, ed. Guy Clutton-Brock and Molly Clutton-Brock. Harare: Longman, 127–30.

Olwig, Kenneth R. 2002. *Landscape, Nature, and the Body Politic: From Britain's Renaissance to America's New World.* Madison: University of Wisconsin Press.

Ong, Aihwa. 1999. *Flexible Citizenship: The Cultural Logics of Transnationality.* Durham, NC: Duke University Press.

———. 2003. *Buddha Is Hiding: Refugees, Citizenship, the New America.* Berkeley: University of California Press.

Orlove, Ben. 2002. *Lines in the Water: Nature and Culture at Lake Titicaca.* Berkeley: University of California Press.

Ortiz, Fernando. [1940] 1947. *Cuban Counterpoint: Tobacco and Sugar.* Trans. Harriet de Onís. New York: Knopf.

Palmer, Robin. 1977a. "The Agricultural History of Rhodesia." In *The Roots of Rural Poverty in Central and Southern Africa*, ed. Palmer and Neil Parson. Berkeley: University of California Press, 221–54.

———. 1977b. *Land and Racial Domination in Zimbabwe.* Berkeley: University of California Press.

———. "1990. Land Reform in Zimbabwe, 1980–1990." *African Affairs* 89 (335): 163–81.

Pels, Peter. 1997. "The Anthropology of Colonialism: Culture, History, and the Emergence of Western Governmentality." *Annual Review of Anthropology*, no. 27:163–83.

Peters, Pauline. 1994. *Dividing the Commons: Politics, Policy, and Culture in Botswana.* Charlottesville: University Press of Virginia.

Peters, Pauline. 2004. "Inequality and Social Conflict Over Land in Africa." *Journal of Agrarian Change* 4 (3): 269–314.

Petheram, R. W. 1974. *Inyanga, with Special Reference to Rhodes Inyanga Estate*. Salisbury: National Trust of Rhodesia.

———. 1987. "Nyanga History: A Miscellany." *Heritage of Zimbabwe*, no. 7:40–55.

Philo, Chris. 1992. "Foucault's Geography." *Environment and Planning D: Society and Space* 10 (2): 137–61.

Phimister, Ian. 1977. "Peasant Production and Underdevelopment in Southern Rhodesia, 1890–1914, with Particular Reference to the Victoria District." In *The Roots of Rural Poverty in Central and Southern Africa*, ed. Robin Palmer and Neil Parsons. Berkeley: University of California Press, 255–68.

Pongweni, Alec J. C. 1982. *Songs that Won the Liberation War*. Harare: College Press.

Poulantzas, Nicos. [1978] 1980. *State, Power, Socialism*. Trans. Patrick Camiller. London: Verso.

Povinelli, Elizabeth. 2002. *The Cunning of Recognition: Indigenous Alterities and the Making of Australian Multiculturalism*. Durham, NC: Duke University Press.

POZ (Parliament of Zimbabwe). 1991. *Protocol of Proceedings for Workshop on Current Issues in Regional Development, Land-Use, Planning, and Villagization in MNR Affected Areas of Zimbabwe. 28–30 May, 1991*. Harare: Parliament of Zimbabwe.

Prakash, Gyan. 1999. *Another Reason: Science and the Imagination of Modern India*. Princeton: Princeton University Press.

Pratt, Mary Louise. 1992. *Imperial Eyes: Travel Writing and Transculturation*. New York: Routledge.

Pred, Allan. 2000. *Even in Sweden: Racisms, Racialized Spaces, and the Popular Geographical Imagination*. Berkeley: University of California Press.

Rabinow, Paul. 1989. *French Modern: Norms and Forms of the Social Environment*. Chicago: University of Chicago Press.

———. 1999. *French DNA: Trouble in Purgatory*. Chicago: University of Chicago Press.

Radcliffe-Brown, A. R. 1940. Preface to *African Political Systems*, ed. Myer Fortes and E. E. Evans-Pritchard. London: Oxford University Press, xi–xxiii.

Raffles, Hugh. 2002. *In Amazonia: A Natural History*. Princeton, NJ: Princeton University Press.

Ramphele, Mamphela. 1993. *A Bed Called Home: Life in the Migrant Labour Hostels of Cape Town*. Cape Town: David Philip.

Randall-MacIver, David. [1906] 1969. *Mediaeval Rhodesia*. New York: Negro Universities Press.

Ranger, Terence. 1985a. *The Invention of Tradition in Zimbabwe*. Gweru, Zimbabwe: Mambo.

———. 1985b. *Peasant Consciousness and Guerrilla War in Zimbabwe*. Harare: Zimbabwe Publishing House.

———. 1993. "The Communal Areas of Zimbabwe." In *African Agrarian Systems*, ed. Thomas Bassett and Donald Crummey. Madison: University of Wisconsin Press, 354–88.

Renan, Ernest. [1882] 1990. "What Is a Nation?" Trans. Martin Thom. In *Nation and Narration*, ed. Homi K. Bhabha. New York: Routledge, 8–22.

Reno, William. 1998. *Warlord Politics and African States*. Boulder, CO: Lynne Rienner.

Richards, Audrey. 1939. *Land, Labour, and Diet in Northern Rhodesia: An Economic Study of the Bemba Tribe*. London: Oxford University Press.

Richards, Paul. 1996. *Fighting for the Rain Forest: War, Youth, and Resources in Sierra Leone*. Oxford: J. Currey.

Riddell, Roger. 1978. *The Land Question*. Gwelo, Zimbabwe: Mambo.

Robinson, D. A. 1953. "Land Use Planning in Native Reserves in Southern Rhodesia." *Rhodesian Agriculture Journal Bulletin* 50 (4): 327–33.

———. 1960. "Soil Conservation and Implications of the Land Husbandry Act." NADA, no. 37.

Robinson, Jennifer. 1996. *The Power of Apartheid: State, Power, and Space in South African Cities*. Oxford: Butterworth-Heinemann.

Rofel, Lisa. 1999. *Other Modernities: Gendered Yearnings in China after Socialism*. Berkeley: University of California Press.

Roitman, Janet. 2001. "New Sovereigns? Regulatory Authority in the Chad Basin." In *Intervention and Transnationalism in Africa: Global-Local Networks of Power*, ed. Thomas Callaghy, Ronald Kassimir, and Robert Latham. Cambridge: Cambridge University Press, 240–66.

Rosaldo, Renato. 1989. *Culture and Truth: The Remaking of Social Analysis*. Boston: Beacon.

Rose, Nikolas. 1996. "The Death of the Social? Re-figuring the Territory of Government." *Economy and Society* 25 (3): 327–56.

———. [1996] 1998. *Inventing Our Selves: Psychology, Power, and Personhood*. Cambridge: Cambridge University Press.

———. [1989] 1999. *Governing the Soul: The Shaping of the Private Self*. London: Free Association Books.

———. 1999. *Powers of Freedom: Reframing Political Thought*. Cambridge: Cambridge University Press.

Rotberg, Robert. 1988. *The Founder: Cecil Rhodes and the Pursuit of Power*. New York: Oxford University Press.

Roth, Michael, and John Bruce. 1994. *Land Tenure, Agrarian Structure, and Comparative Land Use Efficiency in Zimbabwe*. Research Paper 117. Madison, WI: Land Tenure Center.

Rouse, Roger. 1991. "Mexican Migration and the Social Space of Postmodernism." *Diaspora* 1 (1): 8–23.

Rutherford, Blair. 2003. "Belonging to the Farm(er): Farm Workers, Farmers, and the Shifting Politics of Citizenship." In *Zimbabwe's Unfinished Business: Rethinking Land, State, and Nation in the Context of Crisis*, ed. Amanda Hammar, Brian Raftopoulos, and Stig Jensen. Harare: Weaver, 191–216.

Sahlins, Marshall. 1981. *Historical Myths and Metaphorical Realities: Structure in the Early History of the Sandwich Island Kingdoms*. Ann Arbor: University of Michigan Press.

Said, Edward. 2000. "History, Literature, and Geography." In *Reflections on Exile and Other Essays*. Cambridge, MA: Harvard University Press, 453–73.

Sartre, Jean-Paul. [1961] 2002. Preface to *Les damnés de la terre*, by Frantz Fanon. Paris: La Découverte.

Sassen, Saskia. 1996. *Losing Control? Sovereignty in an Age of Globalization*. New York: Columbia University Press.

——. 2001. "Spatialities and Temporalities of the Global: Elements for a Theorization." In *Globalization*, ed. Arjun Appadurai. Durham, NC: Duke University Press, 260–78.

Schapera, Isaac. 1956. *Government and Politics in Tribal Societies*. London: Watts.

Schmidt, Elizabeth. 1992. *Peasants, Traders, and Wives: Shona Women in the History of Zimbabwe, 1870–1939*. Portsmouth, NH: Heinemann.

Schmidt, Heike. 1996. "The Social and Economic Impact of Political Violence in Zimbabwe, 1890–1990: A Case Study of the Honde Valley." D.Phil. diss., Oxford University.

Schoffeleers, J. M., ed. 1978. *Guardians of the Land: Essays on Central African Territorial Cults*. Gweru, Zimbabwe: Mambo.

Schroeder, Richard. 1999. *Shady Practice: Agroforestry and Gender Politics in the Gambia*. Berkeley: University of California Press.

Schumaker, Lyn. 2001. *Africanizing Anthropology: Fieldwork, Networks, and the Making of Cultural Knowledge in Central Africa*. Durham, NC: Duke University Press.

Scott, James C. 1998. *Seeing Like a State: How Certain Schemes to Improve the Human Condition Have Failed*. New Haven, CT: Yale University Press.

Scott, David. 1995. "Colonial Governmentality." *Social Text*, no. 43:191–220.

——. 1999. *Refashioning Futures: Criticism after Postcoloniality*. Princeton, NJ: Princeton University Press.

Scott-Heron, Gil. 2000. *Now and Then: The Poems of Gil Scott-Heron*. Edinburgh: Payback.

Senghor, Léopold Sédar. [1961] 1964. *On African Socialism*. Trans. Mercer Cook. London: Praeger.

Sithole, Bevlyne, Bruce Campbell, Dale Doré, and Witness Kozanayi. 2003. "Narratives On Land: State-Peasant Relations Over Fast Track Land Reform In Zimbabwe." *African Studies Quarterly* 7 (2/3). Available at: http://web.africa.ufl.edu/asq/v7/v7i2a4.htm.

Slater, Henry. 1980. "The Changing Pattern of Economic Relationships in Rural Natal, 1838–1914." In *Economy and Society in Pre-industrial South Africa*, ed. Shula Marks and Anthony Atmore. London: Longman, 148–70.

Smith, David, and Colin Simpson. 1981. *Mugabe*. Salisbury: Pioneer Head.

Smith, Neil. [1984] 1990. *Uneven Development: Nature, Capital, and the Production of Space*. Oxford: Blackwell.

Soper, Robert. 2002. *Nyanga: Ancient Fields, Settlements, and Agricultural History in Zimbabwe*. Oxford: Oxbow.

Soyinka, Wole. 1998. *The Open Sore of a Continent: A Personal Narrative of the Nigerian Crisis*. New York: Oxford University Press.

Spivak, Gayatri Chakravorty. 1988. "Can the Subaltern Speak?" In *Marxism and the Interpretation of Culture*, ed. Cary Nelson and Lawrence Grossberg. Urbana: University of Illinois Press, 271–313.

Starn, Orin. 1999. *Nightwatch: The Politics of Protest in the Andes*. Durham, NC: Duke University Press.

Stewart, Kathleen. 1996. *A Space on the Side of the Road: Cultural Poetics in an "Other" America*. Princeton, NJ: Princeton University Press.

Stoler, Ann Laura. 1995. *Race and the Education of Desire: Foucault's "History of Sexuality" and the Colonial Order of Things*. Durham, NC: Duke University Press.

——. 2002. *Carnal Knowledge and Imperial Power: Race and the Intimate in Colonial Rule*. Berkeley: University of California Press.

Strathern, Marilyn. 1988. *The Gender of the Gift: Problems with Women and Problems with Society in Melanesia*. Berkeley: University of California Press.

Sudbeck, Hans-Ulrich. 1989. "African Peasants, Colonial Bureaucrats, and Conservation in Colonial Zimbabwe." Hannover, Germany: Historishes Seminar der Universitat Hannover.

Summers, Roger. 1958. *Inyanga: Prehistoric Settlements in Southern Rhodesia*. Cambridge: Cambridge University Press.

Sylvester, Christine. 1991. *Zimbabwe: The Terrain of Contradictory Development*. Boulder, CO: Westview.

Taylor, Peter. 2003. "The State as Container: Territoriality in the Modern World-System." In *State/Space: A Reader*, ed. Neil Brenner et al. Oxford: Blackwell, 101–14.

Thomas, Nicholas. 1994. *Colonialism's Culture: Anthropology, Travel, and Government*. Princeton, NJ: Princeton University Press.

Thongchai Winichakul. 1994. *Siam Mapped: A History of the Geo-body of a Nation*. Honolulu: University of Hawai'i Press.

Tshuma, Lawrence. 1997. *A Matter of (In)Justice: Law, State and the Agrarian Question in Zimbabwe*. Harare: SAPES.

United States, Department of State. 1971. *International Boundary Study No. 118 (November 1, 1971): Mozambique-Southern Rhodesia Boundary*. Washington, D.C.: Office of the Geographer, Bureau of Intelligence and Research.

Vail, Leroy, ed. 1989. *The Creation of Tribalism in Southern Africa*. Berkeley: University of California Press.

Van Onselen, Charles. 1976. *Chibaro: African Mine Labour in Southern Rhodesia, 1900–1933*. London: Pluto.

Vaughan, Megan. 1991. *Curing Their Ills: Colonial Power and African Illness*. Stanford, CA: Stanford University Press.

Verdery, Katherine. 1996. *What Was Socialism and What Comes Next?* Princeton, NJ: Princeton University Press.

Vines, Alex. 1991. RENAMO: *Terrorism in Mozambique.* London: J. Currey.

Watts, Michael. 2000. *Struggles over Geography: Violence, Freedom, and Development at the Millennium.* Hettner-Lecture 1999, Department of Geography, University of Heidelberg, Germany.

———. 2003. "Development and Governmentality." *Singapore Journal of Tropical Geography* 24 (1): 6–34.

Weber, Max. 1946. *From Max Weber.* Ed. and trans. H. H. Gerth and C. Wright Mills. New York: Oxford University Press.

Werbner, Richard. 1991. *Tears of the Dead: The Social Biography of an African Family.* Harare: Baobab Books.

White, Luise. 2003. *The Assassination of Herbert Chitepo: Texts and Politics in Zimbabwe.* Bloomington: Indiana University Press.

Williams, Raymond. [1977] 1985. *Marxism and Literature.* Oxford: Oxford University Press.

———. 1989. *Resources of Hope: Culture, Democracy, Socialism.* London: Verso.

Wilmsen, Edwin. 1989. *Land Filled with Flies: A Political Economy of the Kalahari.* Chicago: University of Chicago Press.

Wilson, Ken. 1989. "Trees in Fields in Southern Zimbabwe." *Journal of Southern African Studies* 15 (2): 369–83.

Worby, Eric. 1994. "Maps, Names, and Ethnic Games: The Epistemology and Iconography of Colonial Power in Northwestern Zimbabwe." *Journal of Southern African Studies* 20 (3): 371–92.

———. 1998. "Tyranny, Parody, and Ethnic Polarity: Ritual Engagements with the State in Northwestern Zimbabwe." *Journal of Southern African Studies* 24 (3): 561–78.

———, ed. 2001. "The New Agrarian Politics in Zimbabwe." Special Issue, *Journal of Agrarian Change* 1 (4).

World Commission on Environment and Development. 1987. *Our Common Future.* New York: Oxford University Press.

Yudelman, Montague. 1964. *Africans on the Land: Economic Problems of African Agricultural Development in Southern, Central, and East Africa, with Special Reference to Southern Rhodesia.* Harvard: Cambridge University Press.

Yoneyama, Lisa. 1999. *Hiroshima Traces: Time, Space, and the Dialectics of Memory.* Berkeley: University of California Press.

Young, Robert J. C. 2001. *Postcolonialism: An Historical Introduction.* Oxford: Blackwell.

Zeleza, Paul Tiyambe. 2003. *Rethinking Africa's Globalization.* Trenton, NJ: Africa World Press.

Zerner, Charles. 1994. "Through a Green Lens: The Construction of Customary Environmental Law and Community in Indonesia's Maluku Islands." *Law and Society Review* 28 (5): 1079–122.

Index

African Development Trust, 201
African National People's Union, 202
Agency: academic debates about, 5; gender and, 210–13, 257–58; nonhuman, 25, 245–48, 316–17; power relations, subjection and, 3, 6, 9, 42, 242–43, 257–58. *See also* Hegemony; Nature; Subject; Suffering for territory; Tactics
Agrarian micropolitics. *See* Livelihood practices
Agricultural and Rural Development Authority (ARDA), 37
Agricultural and Technical Extension (AGRITEX), 75, 78, 94–95, 115
Alvord, E. D., 80–83, 105, 117, 125–26, 144, 173, 200, 299, 315
American Friends Service Committee, 185
Ancestral spirits. See *Vadzimu* (ancestral spirits)
Anthropology: engaging with governmentality, 3, 5, 8; engaging with sovereignty, 359 n.13; engaging with spatiality, 12, 22, 221; ethnographic emergence as fieldwork and, xi, 2, 4, 25–30, 45–48, 186–87, 276, 298–300, 312, 318; ethnographic positioning and, 25–26, 48, 318, 320; imperial legacies of, 29, 31, 160–73, 176–77, 222, 299

Apartheid, 14, 19, 71, 169, 171
Apostolic Faith African Independent (church), 290
Articulated assemblage, 23–25, 317. *See also* Nature; *Tsika* (culture)
Atkins, Keletso, 82, 144
Authority. *See* Chiefs and headmen; *Simba* (power); *Kutonga* (rule)

Bantustans. *See* Apartheid
Bartelson, Jens, 221, 222
Bende (proposed resettlement site), 204
Benjamin, Walter, 184, 186
Bennett, Roy (white land owner and MDC MP), 310–11
Berry, Sara, 162, 178
Biopower: as nonstate entities targeting welfare, 221, 231, 234–37, 242, 245–46, 271, 318; as political technologies targeting welfare, 5–7, 42, 65–66, 92–95, 99, 103–5, 131–32, 219–20, 312, 315; as producing particular subjects, 77–80, 125–26; racializing spaces and spatializing races, 12–14, 80–83, 163–64. *See also* Governmentality
Border: migration and, 85; as moral, political contagion, 155–58; refugees and, 44, 180–81, 293–94, securing of,

DONALD S. MOORE is an Assistant Professor
of Anthropology at the University of
California, Berkeley.

Library of Congress Cataloging-in-Publication Data
Suffering for territory : race, place, and power in Zimbabwe / Donald S. Moore.
p. cm.
Includes bibliographical references and index.
ISBN 0-8223-3582-4 (cloth : acid-free paper)
ISBN 0-8223-3570-0 (pbk. : acid-free paper)
1. Land use—Government policy—Zimbabwe. 2. Land settlement—Zimbabwe.
3. Land settlement—Government policy—Zimbabwe. 4. Land tenure—Zimbabwe.
5. Zimbabwe—Race relations. I. Title.
HD992.Z63M665 2005
333.3'16891—dc22
2005004618